THE MACHINERY OF TALK

Cultural Memory
in
the
Present

Mieke Bal and Hent de Vries, Editors

THE MACHINERY OF TALK

Charles Peirce and the Sign Hypothesis

Anne Freadman

STANFORD UNIVERSITY PRESS

STANFORD, CALIFORNIA

2004

Stanford University Press,
Stanford, California

Printed in the United States of America
on acid-free, archival-quality paper

Library of Congress Cataloging-in-Publication Data

Freadman, Anne, 1944–
    The machinery of talk : Charles Peirce and
the sign hypothesis / Anne Freadman.
        p.   cm. — (Cultural memory in the present)
    Includes bibliographical references and index.
    ISBN 0-8047-4739-3 (alk. paper) —
    ISBN 0-8047-4740-7 (pbk. : alk. paper)
    1. Peirce, Charles S. (Charles Sanders),
1839–1914.   2. Semiotics.   I. Title.   II. Series.
B945.P44 F69 2004
121'.68'092—DC22

                            2003014879

Original Printing 2004

Last figure below indicates year of this printing:
13   12   11   10   09   08   07   06   05   04

For Ross Chambers

Contents

Preface   *xi*

Acknowledgments   *xvii*

List of Works by Charles Sanders Peirce   *xix*

Introduction   *xxi*

PART ONE: THOUGHT AND ITS INSTRUMENTS

1   1867–1885   5

2   A Vagabond Sign   32

PART TWO: THINGS AND EVENTS

3   Around 1903   65

4   Traveler, Stay Awhile   105

PART THREE: "MY WHOLE THEORY"

5   1904–1909   137

6   The Ways of Semiosis   170

    Conclusion: The Machinery of Talk   215

    Epilogue   247

    Notes   *275*

    Index   *305*

[Let us] agree to apply the word "talk" to all ways of expressing sensations, actions, and ideas in signs of any kinds, and also to all ways of interpreting signs, and [let us] apply this word "sign" to everything recognizable whether to our outward senses or to our inward feeling or imagination, provided only it calls up some feeling, effort, or thought. (MS 678, p. 23 bis.)

Nothing does speak for itself, strictly nothing, speaking strictly. One cannot bid his neighbor good morning, really, effectually, unless that neighbor supplies the needed commentary on the syntax. If he does not, I might as well shake a rattle. (MS 427, p. 146)

Preface

    The present book is offered as a contribution to semiotics, but the reader should not seek in it a formalization of some set of theoretical postulates. It focuses on a question that semiotics often takes for granted: what is the sign hypothesis good for? And it seeks its answer modestly, within the scope of an authorial oeuvre. What was it good for, for Peirce? I accept William James' dictum, that theories are instruments, not answers to questions, and I seek an account of the kind of instrument semiotic is in the Peircean enterprise. I do not ask whether Peirce was right or wrong; rather, I ask what tasks semiotic was designed to do, and how well it does them. Only by understanding its pragmatic function can we make informed decisions about its usefulness for our tasks.

    What I mean by the sign hypothesis is simply that "the sign" is an indispensable presupposition of (descriptions of) what it is for a sentient being to be in the world and to interact with its fellows, taking "interacting with its fellows" as integral to the project of "being in the world," as well as the reverse. It will be clear that this formulation allows for continuity across what is commonly called the animal kingdom and possibly beyond, but while I acknowledge that it is a proper part of semiotics to study the sign-making competence of the full range of species, that is not the scope of this book. Nor is it my business to indulge in the opposite temptation, which is to make a case for some definition of human culture that would mark it off from the interactional habits of all other species taken together as constituting "nature." Claude Lévi-Strauss taught us years ago that "nature" was nothing but a self-confirming and self-defining postulate of culture, that such gestures of marking-off are unrevealing about their objects, that they teach us only about the culture that makes them. Accordingly, I simply acknowledge that the study of signs is one of the sites where the marking-off of the human, or cultural, from the animal, or natural, has been most insistently pursued and likewise, most vigorously contested. This is the topos from which semiotics as a field of topics emerges. I take Peirce as reflecting upon this topos, not as entering its debates. Beyond these preliminary remarks, nor shall I.

Broadly, debates concerning the nature/culture divide rest on grounds such as the following: (1) that "man" is distinctively human, in some special sense, because he speaks, that human language possesses special properties that mark it off from systems of communication characteristic of all other species; or the denial of this proposition; this might include (2) that human symbolic systems are distinctively self-reflexive, a property that is said to give rise to the full range of creativity but that is easily shown not to be exclusively human; (3) that "man" is not only subject *to* evolution but is subject *of* history, in the special sense this term has come to acquire from the technical practices of historiography; or the denial of some part, or all of this proposition: for example, history is nothing but speeded-up evolution, or, the claim that man is the subject of his history is a humanist delusion; (4) that "man" is the narrative animal, in that it is by telling stories that he teaches his young, and that these stories constitute a fund of collective transgenerational memory without parallel in other species; or the obvious objection that we simply do not know what the whales are singing; (5) that "man" is distinctively rational in some special sense that excludes instinctive behaviors, a characterization that encounters the objection that this excludes so much about what it is to be human, including femininity, that it is self-defeating; and so on.

Peirce considers that the distinction between "man" and "the animals" is based on a belief unworthy of modern science. Thus the following manuscript passage, which is by no means an isolated example:

Some seventy years ago, my beloved and accomplished school-ma'am taught me that humankind, being formed in the image of a Maker, were [*sic*] endowed with the power of Reasoning, while "the animals," lacking that power (which might have made them dissatisfied), received, each kind, certain "instincts" to do what was generally necessary for their lives. At least, so I understood her. But when I subsequently came to observe the behaviours of several big dogs and little birds, and two parrots, I gradually came to think quite otherwise. For . . . I gradually amassed a body of experiences which convinced me that many animals, perhaps all the higher ones, do reason. (MS 672, pp. 1–2)

Nevertheless, it is the case that Peirce sometimes claims that there is a difference between humans and "the brutes" and that it resides in the fact that the latter rarely know that they use signs: this corresponds to (2) above, but we should note that he writes "rarely," which undermines the binary opposition. He deems this binary—in any of its forms—to arise from pre-Darwinian assumptions. This means that his work is only with difficulty assimilable to the project of the "human" or "social" sciences whose rise is contemporary with his work, but it does not mean that it is premodern. On the contrary, it leads one to reflect that in their very defensiveness in relation to the physical and the biological sciences, the human sciences have held to conceptions of the human that are now thoroughly out of date. Peirce's work is mercifully free of these assumptions and is interesting to contemporary work precisely because it helps to free the sign hypothesis from the problems they entrain. This freedom allows for a remarkable move affecting a familiar assumption of traditional sign theory that derives from the nature/culture divide. Where his philosophical predecessors had relied on the distinction between the "motivated" or natural signs and the arbitrary and conventional ones, Peirce comes to include them all within the grasp of the same hypothesis. This move is not made for ideological reasons, but for practical ones; it emerges from Peirce's application of sign theory to the logic of science. The so-called natural signs are seen to be the outcome of special technical apparatuses, with the result that Science is no longer explicable by the postulate of Reason; rather, the work of reason itself demands explanation. In Peirce's practice, this amounts to analysis of the machinery of semiosis. Thus, Reason fails even to explain a special class of signs (the symbol) and can no longer provide the rule for the field of signs in general. This is a story that demands to be told; its consequences are radical and far-reaching.

I am a product of my age and training, and both my competence and my interest are restricted to human cultural practices. It is the case that I have some sympathy with some parts of some of the propositions above because they give me reasons, or excuses, for studying the things that I do. I am interested in the self-reflexive properties of human semiotic systems and the second-order manipulation of signs that this permits, and I am also interested in the stories we tell, taking that in a broad enough sense to cover the writing of books about Charles Peirce. I am simply agnostic about whether these constitute grounds for a definition of the human, but I have no difficulty with the assertion, say, that semiotics is something that only humans do, and likewise for the objects that I select for semiotic description: philosophy, cinema, photography, poetry, and so on. In other words, making the characteristic move of a pragmatism inspired by Peirce, I do not ask what the human is, I ask what human beings do. The answer is a list that does not consist of generalizations that attempt to capture some exclusive universal property expressible in pithy Latin—*homo loquens, homo ridens, homo ludens*, and the like. I take it that for every item on my list, it must necessarily be true that not all humans do everything that only humans do—write, paint, invent musical notations, and so on. Culture is an open set of specifiable practices; it is not an essential property of some species. Small groups of humans write philosophy or found religious orders, and while the traditions thus instituted are recognized widely among their fellows who may enter into a variety of active relationships with them, they are not practiced universally.

I am interested in this untidy articulation of groups, which involves meeting with strangers or with neighbors, of whom Peirce writes that we sometimes feel inclined to class them within our world, and sometimes without (CP 7.438). I am particularly interested in one such untidy articulation, found in the writings of Peirce himself. This is the neighborhood in which philosophy, mathematics, logic, and semiotic sometimes converse and sometimes jostle for position. Conversation with neighbors is a practice of the fence. We recognize, and can learn, or learn about, practices that are not "ours." What constitutes "we" changes as a result. Practices are conversations that confer membership of particular groups and distinguish those groups from others, but they are not exclusive, and no human individual engages in only one kind of conversation. Of this I am absolutely certain: what matters about our humanity resides somehow in the fact that we can learn other languages, enter into intelligently self-interested symbiotic relationships with animals, both domestic and in the wild, adapt to customs not our own, and question the habits of behavior and understanding that may for a time have stood as unexamined assumptions.

I believe I learned this from Peirce, as I have learned slowly and with great difficulty to read his work from a set of assumptions that did not readily accommodate it. It is close to fifteen years now since I embarked on this reading, and this book registers the provisional culmination of a process which started by marking what was recalcitrant in his text to me, and what was recalcitrant in me to his text.[1] I was trained in the structuralist tradition, and I thought then, as I continue to do, that the principle of difference allied with the relational theory of value was, as the French say, *incontournable*. Yet a sign defined exclusively upon this basis is a poor thing, and I went looking for something with descriptive purchase. So I began to talk across the fence with a crusty, demanding, uncompromising, but amazingly interesting old philosopher. This book records what I heard him say; it also puts the questions to him that I think we must put.

I was frequently surprised, as Peirce would put it, and frequently dazzled; there is great brilliance here. But I also find that Peirce's work on signs is acutely contradictory at some points. If I have something to say to semiotics, it has to do with these contradictions, with why they matter, and with what it is for sign theory to return to them as a way of understanding its own questions. For one thing that is indubitable about semiotics is surely this: that it is generated by the self-reflexive properties of human sign systems; as such, it behooves us from time to time to reflect upon it.

In a touching draft for the introduction of one of his unwritten books, Peirce writes that an introduction seeks a reader for the book to follow, like the description given by a householder who wants to let his house out to rent (MS 678, alt. p. 14). Readers seldom buy, and rarely take long leases; they beg or borrow, staying just a while, sometimes stopping long enough to make a case for a certain interpretation, but inevitably moving on to swap their stories with others on the road. There is something of the tramp in us all. This is a vagabond book, addressed to other vagabonds. It deals in lists, not in systems, in examples, not in definitions, in stories, not in doctrines. Like Peirce's exemplary tramps, it leaves its mark on fences until the next rain.

Acknowledgments

Thanks are due to those people and organizations who have supported the project for this book during the long years in which it developed from fictional status to its emergence in the real: to André Gallois, who made me the inestimable gift of his copy of the *Collected Papers of Charles Sanders Peirce*; to Spencer Routh, at that time collections librarian at the University of Queensland, for his decision to purchase some expensive primary materials that only I, at that time, was likely to use; to the then French Department and my colleagues of the past, for moral and intellectual, as well as financial support; and, for generous scholarly hospitality in various forms, to the Centre for Semiotic Research at the University of Aarhus, to the University of Michigan Ann Arbor, the Centre for Advanced Study at Indiana University Bloomington, the Peirce Edition Project, and the University of San Marino.

My thanks to some more distant colleagues whose interest in, and discussions of, earlier versions of some of this work have been invaluable: Vincent Colapietro, Carl Hausman, André de Tienne, Paolo Fabbri. I wish also to acknowledge the work of the unnamed readers of the book in manuscript. One of them suggested that I take more seriously "New Elements"; he may not be grateful for the way I have taken his advice, but I thank him for it. Several of my students have had a particular interest in "the Peirce work" and some have acted in the capacity of research assistants. My thanks to you all for your contributions. I am particularly grateful for Siobhan Brownlie's painstaking and impeccable work on the final draft, and for Carmen McNaught's preparation of the manuscript. Helen Tartar of Stanford University Press was enthusiastic, encouraging, and patient. I am boundlessly in her debt.

To my friends over all these years whose patience I have tried and who, in some instances, have tested my resolve to persist and found me defiant, I offer the book—because I had to do it—with love and in some trepidation. I want especially to mention the following people. Some of them have read or listened to endless drafts of parts of this book. It was a lot to ask, and I am grateful for their forbearance and suggestions: Peter Cryle, Waddick Doyle, John Frow, Deirdre Gilfedder, Roger Lamb, John Macarthur, Amanda Macdonald, Jeffrey Minson, Lesley Stern, James Wheatley. Meaghan Morris was unstinting with her time and practical support. My thanks to you all, and to all those friends who have supported me with my project-incubus along the way. I cannot name you all. Dr. John Slaughter (no relation, as far as I know, to the Dr. John Slaughter who waited in vain to publish Peirce's last *summa*) has accompanied the project from its inception to its completion: *sine qua non*.

Ross Chambers, reader extraordinaire, teacher, friend: your gifts to me in—of— the intellectual life are uncountable. Would that the book could thank you as I wish to do.

Early versions of material in some chapters have been previously published; I thank the editors of the named publications for permission to reuse this material: part of Chapter 1 in *Southern Review*, 26, no. 2 (1993); parts of Chapters 1 and 3 in *The Peirce Digital Encyclopedia*; parts of Chapter 3 in *Peirce's Doctrine of Signs: Theory, Applications, and Connections*, ed. Vincent Colapietro and Thomas M. Olshewsky (New York: Mouton de Gruyter, 1996); part of Chapter 2 in *Mattoid* 52/53 (1998); part of Chapter 6 in *History of the Human Sciences*, 4, no. 1 (February 1991).

I acknowledge permission to quote extensively from the manuscripts of the Peirce papers, granted by the Department of Philosophy at Harvard University.

Publication of the book has been supported by generous grants from the Australian Academy of the Humanities and the Faculty of Arts at the University of Queensland.

List of Works by Charles Sanders Peirce
(with abbreviations used)

Collected Papers of Charles Sanders Peirce. 8 vols. Edited by Charles Hartshorne and Paul Weiss. Cambridge, Mass.: Harvard University Press, 1931–58. (CP)

The Charles S. Peirce Papers [microform]. Houghton Library, Harvard University. Cambridge, Mass.: Harvard University Photographic Department, Widener Library, 1966. Manuscript sources. (MS)

Semiotic and Significs: The Correspondence Between Charles S. Peirce and Victoria Lady Welby. Edited by Charles S. Hardwick. Bloomington: Indiana University Press, 1977. (PW or WP)

Writings of Charles S. Peirce: A Chronological Edition. 6 vols. Edited by Max H. Fisch. Bloomington: Indiana University Press, 1982–. (W)

The Essential Peirce: Selected Philosophical Writings. 2 vols. Edited by Nathan Houser and Christian Kloesel. Bloomington: Indiana University Press, 1992–98. (EP)

Pragmatism as a Principle and Method of Right Thinking: The 1903 Harvard Lectures on Pragmatism. Edited by Patricia Turrisi. New York: State University of New York Press, 1997.

Reasoning and the Logic of Things: The Cambridge Conferences—Lectures of 1898. Edited by Kenneth Laine Ketner and Hilary Putnam. Cambridge, Mass.: Harvard University Press, 1992.

Note on usage: The term *semiotic,* used as a noun, cites Peirce's own usage; otherwise, *semiotics* is the standard contemporary usage.

Introduction

He finished almost nothing, but he began almost everything.
—Ian Hacking, *Representing and Intervening*

One of the works that moves me most deeply in the canon of western sculpture is the series of unfinished "Slaves" by Michelangelo. We see the human figures barely emerging from their rock: matter and idea, matter and form, they struggle against, but also with, the stone that both holds and releases them. It is the struggle for freedom that we watch, and the allegory of this struggle, art appearing from its raw materials but always dependent on them, as the body is on the earth, and spirit on the body. Never released, forever locked in its matter, this is something like the paradox Peirce discerns in the conditions of semiosis when he seeks to explain that thought is powerless without what western philosophy has traditionally conceived as the opposite of thought. As there is no sculpture without stone or chisel, Peirce wrote that there is no thought without signs, and much of his work is about their fashioning.

The "Slaves" have accompanied my reading of this work, and I invoke them here as an emblem of Peirce's own struggle to give form to the sign hypothesis out of materials derived from this very same tradition of western philosophy. At every point that tradition resists his efforts, the emergence of his account of signhood is impeded by the very materials of which it is made. This book is about that struggle, about those impediments, for there is much to learn from them, as well as about its breakthroughs. There are two stories to tell: Peirce sought to replace the spatial

premisses of the philosophy of representation—where that which can val-
idate what arises "in" the mind is deemed to lie "outside" it—with a temporal premiss—where truth is a finding arising from an experimental series—but the language of the philosophical tradition threatened always to
undermine that replacement. Equally, Peirce brought to bear on the metaphysical problematic of "signs" or "representation"—that is, of cognition—insights arising from the crafting of a logical notation, the "signs" of
which have no cognitive content. It is to the story of these two struggles
that I devote the pages to come.

   And because it sets out to tell a story or two, this is not a book about
a body of ideas called "Peirce" with, in, or about which to pursue the conversation of the philosophers. It does not participate in that conversation,
although it must heed it. And from that conversation we learn a first lesson
concerning the problematic nature of the materials with which we must
work. Peirce scholarship has its habits, and on these grounds is a genre; one
of its commonplaces—always to be found near the beginning, in the preface or the introduction—is the claim—accusation, or lament—that
Peirce's thinking is either fragmentary or self-contradictory, and in any
case, difficult to interpret synthetically.[1] This genre accepts by and large
that there is no pure Peirce. As Christopher Hookway writes, Peirce himself "never produced a unified and coherent presentation of the system,"[2]
but as this very formulation implies, the temptation remains to go on supposing that such a system is to be found in some way and to write it in his
place. However, "it is difficult to produce a unified treatment of a philosopher who seems to incorporate the anti-metaphysical prejudices of a critical philosopher of language, with a predisposition to speculative metaphysics derived from Hegel and the German idealists" (p. 2). Surveying the
range of (then extant) attempts to do so, Hookway provides a loose classification: some, such as Goudge, have been "forced to acknowledge two
Peirces"; others have studied the evolution of his work; still others have
given up on the attempt to provide a systematic account. Hookway himself insists that Peirce "was the most systematic of philosophers" (p. 2), and,
with Rorty, that he was, by and large, a traditional philosopher:

The interest of Peirce's work lies in the ways in which, within a traditional conception of the task of philosophy, he transformed how the problems arose and
used his new logic and claims about meaning to resolve them. He tried to undermine a host of mistaken beliefs about reality—he called them "nominalism"—
which had disfigured the discussions of earlier philosophers. For some of the

thinkers that Rorty admires, the traditional problems and aspirations of philosophy vanish when these errors are exposed; for Peirce, they remained but became tractable. (p. 3)

This provides the framework for Hookway's own attempt to write a coherent account of Peirce, but "Peirce's views changed" (p. 11), and Hookway acknowledges that the synthetic account must be inflected by a history of these changes. Accordingly, a "bifurcation into 'early and late' Peirce" is proposed as "the most important chronological division for the understanding of his thought" (p. 3).[3]

No less than for any other topic, Peirce's reflections on the sign hypothesis display modifications over time that correspond to the changes in direction and emphasis he brought to his overall project. I shall accept the convention, inspired by Murphey's classic study, of using the manuscript sources where appropriate and reading Peirce's work as a sequence of dated writings,[4] but the highly nuanced chronology that Murphy argues for is less useful for my purposes than the broader division into "early" and "later." Manley Thompson was the first to argue for this division, on grounds derived from Peirce's own revisions and assessments of his early work in view of a collection of his essays. He was working on this collection, the "Search for a Method," in 1898, and Thompson shows that this date effectively distinguishes the published papers and lecture series before it from those following.[5] This broad division is helpful, but particular dates will be right for particular topics and not for others. Even within the semiotic, we need to distinguish between topics: while a clear chronology, broadly conforming to Thompson's, can be established for the classifications of signs, the first major change to be introduced to the topic of semiotic is the concept of semiosis. Its explicit introduction occurs very early, in the figure of "conversation"; it remains constant thereafter.

The first formulation of the sign hypothesis occurs as part of the argument of Peirce's first published paper, "On a New List of Categories" (1867). It is an account of "representation" couched in fairly standard terms, where "representation" is posited as the solution to the problem of universals. As Joseph Ransdell puts it, what is meant by a "sign" for the early Peirce is the idea of "manifestation," or "appearance": a sign is "that through which the world manifests itself."[6] But how, exactly, does the world manifest itself? In Peirce's philosophic universe, there were two, and only two, answers to this question, nominalism and realism, and his first published papers engaged in debates with his colleagues over which was the more satisfactory position. Thus, Max Fisch argues, his first answer was nominalistic, against the Hegelians, and his second inaugurated his lifelong search for a pragmatic realism that would take due account of the work of practical science and yet acknowledge the reference to metaphysical reality of (some, eventual) general synthetic judgments.[7]

The "New List" is nominalistic. The sign there is the medium through which the world manifests itself to the cognizing mind, and the task of the cognizing mind is to bring it to unity by means of the proposition. So far, so orthodox: the sign here is a binary relation of world and mind. However, as Fisch shows, Peirce finds the nominalistic account of representation unsatisfactory, and he replaces this structure by a three-term relation that is, moreover, dynamic. The third term is the "interpretant." The issue turns on the status accorded to any particular act of cognition, which for Peirce is not the nub of the problem. He objects to the "individualism" of modern philosophy since Descartes and turns to a collective account. It is not that any particular judgment, made at any particular point of time, is "true," but that truth is arrived at over time, by people working together. A number of influences came together for Peirce as he formulated this idea, but perhaps the clinching one was his own experience of international teamwork in astronomical research (W 2, p. xxxi ff.) and his engagement in the very precise work that corrected for error the measurements arrived at by previous "pendulum swingers" (W 1; introduction, passim). Reality is something essentially involving the notion of "community" (W 2, p. xxviii); true statements about it are arrived at gradually, in "conversation." Following the explicit formulation of this move, the semiotic solution to the nominalism–realism dispute is this: that Peirce identifies nominalism with the "backward reference" of the term *reality*, and realism, with its "forward reference." The former focuses on the relation with the object and the latter on the relation with the interpretant.[8] This latter is always provisional, always awaiting completion or modification.

The figure of "conversation" first makes its appearance in public in Peirce's so-called cognition series of 1867–68, that is, the series of papers that immediately followed publication of the "New List." While the concept of the interpretant is introduced in the first paper, its implications are not elaborated until the cognition series. These papers are also known as the "anti-Cartesian" papers. As for Descartes, it is the question of where to begin that is at issue: "We cannot begin with complete doubt. We must begin with all the prejudices which we actually have when we enter upon the study of philosophy"; complete doubt is a form of self-delusion, possible only in the absolute solitude of the "individual consciousness" (W 2:22, p. 212), and since no consciousness is absolutely singular but is always divided by its condition in time and in history (W 2:22, pp. 212, 238), the postulate of the solitary and absolutely autonomous mind, able to clean the slate and start *ab origo*, is itself a delusion. This Cartesian delusion displaced the assumptions of medieval logic, and Peirce intends to rehabilitate some crucial features of scholastic practice: "the multiform argumentation of the middle ages is replaced [in 'modern philosophy'] by a single thread of inference depending often upon inconspicuous premisses" (W 2:22, p. 212). Against the single thread of inference, "philosophy ought to imitate the successful sciences in its methods, so far as to proceed only from tangible premises which can be subjected to careful scrutiny, and to trust rather to the multitude and variety of its arguments than to the conclusiveness of any one. Its reasoning should not form a chain which is no stronger than its weakest link, but a cable whose fibers may be ever so slender, provided they are sufficiently numerous and intimately connected" (W 2:22, p. 213).[9] For "to make single individuals absolute judges of truth is most pernicious"; in science, "men come to agreement," and they do so in conversation, in solitary debate with themselves over current alternative opinions (MS 610, pp. 6–10) as well as with one another. Conversation takes place over time. Against the figure of solitary meditation, Peirce launches the philosopher who works in a community of like-minded searchers; doubt and certainty arise in the daily business of advocating and objecting to findings, and the conversation of men involved in this business is just as much the conversation of their sciences and their methods as it is of the practitioners themselves.

The anti-Cartesian papers inaugurate Peirce's formulation of pragmatism, which investigates truth-searching as the business of scientific practices; these take place among people unable to transcend the historical conditions of their disciplines. Doubt arises in the "community of philosophers," among the "candid and disciplined minds" engaged in the careful examination of a theory (MS 610, pp. 6–10). And if conversation is how it is done, then pragmatism requires a theory of conversation. Hence the sign hypothesis, which is the device that Peirce selects to replace the construal of "thought" under the Cartesian model of disembodied mental processes, with the model of the practices of knowing in conversation, for "all thought is in signs" (W 2:21, p. 208).[10] Rather than being the form of the manifestation of the world to the mind, the "sign" thereafter is Peirce's attempt to formalize the pertinent event unit of conversation. Signs matter in practice because signs are the matter of practice. Semiosis is the name of the process whereby, in practice, signs displace one another and are transformed. They do so through the interpretant, the point of mediation that orients them toward their consequences, entailing their upshot with their uptake. In principle, this process is infinite. "The interpretant is nothing but another representation to which the torch of truth is handed along; and as representation, it has its interpretant again. Lo, another infinite series" (CP 1.339).

Semiosis is the feature of Peirce's work on signs that remains effectively unchallenged throughout his writings. However, in the strongly argued opinion of some senior Peirce scholars, the "mature pragmatism" is thought to challenge its "infinity." Semiosis must be finite, it is argued, for if it is not, then Peirce's theory of inquiry and his account of truth as the "final opinion" are self-contradictory. I shall discuss this reading at some length in Chapter 6. For now, it is enough to point out that if these scholars are right, then it signals a highly significant change to have occurred in Peirce's work. In their view, it must be dated at around 1903–6. While something important did indeed happen to the theory of signs during this period, I shall argue that this event does not imply the reduction of "infinite semiosis" to "finite semiosis."[11] I shall do so on two grounds. First, this view is based on the premiss that the three terms—semiosis, conversation, and inquiry—are coextensive. I shall argue that this premiss is false. Second, I shall show that the modifications that are brought to "semiosis" arise as a direct result of the changes in the classifications of signs. These changes have as their practical outcome an account of the concrete mechanisms of semiosis. It is not consistent with that account that semiosis should, or even could, come to an end.

It is part of the argument of this book that Peirce's classification of signs changes radically in 1903, some time between the Harvard Lectures on Pragmatism of March of that year (EP 2:10–16 [CP 5.14–212]) and the Lowell Lectures delivered in Cambridge in October of the same year.[12] This change can be documented with some precision and is evident in the shift from the familiar division of signs into three kinds to the more elaborate classification into three trichotomies and ten classes (cf. EP 2:21, pp. 289–96 [CP 2.233–64]).[13] This change does not come out of the blue. Peirce had by and large abandoned his work in the algebraic paradigm by the mid-1890s, and his long review of Schröder's *Vorlesungen* of 1895 (CP 3.425–55) marks the end of his active work in the kind of logic that it surveys. Shortly afterward, in 1898, William James called on Peirce to assume the mantle of pragmatism.[14] Peirce responded to this call both as a mission and as a provocation, and his debate with James is well known.[15] The period from 1898 to 1906 saw him engaged in a philosophical enterprise of considerable importance: he sought to define and to "prove" pragmatism[16] and to explore the difference it would make to philosophical problems if one were to follow its implications. Peirce returned to the theory of signs during this period for reasons germane to this project, and his work on it and on the problems associated with it was more intense and more productive than at any other time.

The year 1903, the date at which the classification changes, is also the date of a serendipitous event in Peirce's life: his correspondence with Victoria Lady Welby, containing important expositions of the theory of signs as it came to be, dates from this year. We cannot attribute to this correspondence the renewal of Peirce's interest in signs, since this was already well in place, but we can speculate that his sudden elaboration of certain features of the hypothesis was in some way fostered by this conversation with a sympathetic interlocutor. Peirce all but says so himself. Conversations are struck up among friends and companions in the community of scholars among whom interests are held, and problems or lines of inquiry are pursued in common. "I wanted to write to you about signs," writes Peirce to Welby, "which in your opinion and mine are matters of so much concern" (PW, October 12, 1904, p. 23).

Peirce usually writes of the "conversations of men," but this was a conversation with a woman. As Susan Haack remarks, Peirce was no feminist, and he had opened his review of Welby's *What Is Meaning?* with the concession that some readers might find it a trifle feminine.[17] Masculine minds might find it weak, and Peirce recommends to his male readers a particular strategy for reading the book that will help them discover its substance. One of the reasons for which he finds this "little" book "feminine" is that it is not a treatise; another is that it considers the problem of meaning from the point of view of "contemporary writing" and the views of modern ethnology. Yet for all that, the book is "logic," in his view; it treats of matters of "universal and ubiquitous concern." Hence, though the review couples *What is Meaning?* with Russell's *Principles of Mathematics*, Peirce spends scarcely a paragraph on this latter (presumably, the exemplar of the "masculine" side of the contrast), and takes it as his special mission to tell his fellow logicians why they must take Welby's question seriously.

It is tempting to read this gendering of logic—of styles of logic, of questions presupposed by, and central to, logic—as having more than anecdotal significance in forming the conversation that Peirce was to have with Welby. For one thing, there is the question of the proper genre—a "treatise" or a "little" book—in which to write about these matters. Peirce's attempt to systematize his work on the sign hypothesis dates from the Lowell Lectures of October of the same year, the very month in which his review of Welby's book appeared; yet his most systematic exposition is in a personal correspondence. No more than Welby does Peirce write a "treatise." For another, it is also from this time that his repertoire of exemplary signs displays far greater heterogeneity than hitherto. Welby had certainly raised issues for him that philosophy, in the conversations of men, was unlikely to notice, and she had raised them from sources—literature and ethnology—that were to become the domain par excellence of twentieth-century semiotics. But the very systematization that characterizes this period of Peirce's work on signs, designed to bring order to the wealth of scattered reflections that had characterized his work on this topic until then, seems also to be an act of disciplining, a supplying of appropriately scientific gravitas to a topic propounded in a "little volume . . . not what one would understand by a scientific book" (by contrast with Russell's, "which can hardly be called literature"). In one of the drafts for the book Peirce hoped to write, on which topic he reported frequently to Welby during their correspondence, he genders his readership: the book is not for women, whose "genius" may "lie in a different quarter"; "it is only men's way of finding out the truth, the method of reason,—strong but slow,—too slow, apparently, for most women" that the book will discuss (MS 678, 1910). Yet he describes this book as a "small book" (PW, April 17, 1911), and Welby became the chosen interlocutor for Peirce's developed reflections on the sign hypothesis: two of his letters will be the subject of Chapter 5, and the Epilogue will reflect on the correspondence as a whole.

Biographical narrative is fun, and part of its pleasure consists in the way it provides a reassuring anchoring for our interpretations of the man and his work. But alas, there is a great deal that it cannot explain. Neither the move toward an elaboration of his pragmatism, in the 1890s, nor the encounter with Welby, can account for the fact that, in 1885, Peirce deployed a version of the sign hypothesis that is significantly different from the one he had first set down in 1867. Nor do such facts explain why Peirce's work on signs seems restive and experimental, why it changes in apparently random ways, why the practical implications of his hypotheses are so often not followed; or why, the more elaborate his later classifications of signs became, the less he used them. Above all, the biography has nothing to say about the particular structures and functions of the sign hypothesis as it is deployed in different pieces of writing.

The difference between the sign hypothesis as it is formulated in "On a New List of Categories" (1867) and as it is formulated in "On the Algebra of Logic" (1885) cannot be attributed to an evolution in Peirce's thought, but to a difference between the topical environments in which it appears. This is a difference of genre.[18] In the earlier paper, the sign hypothesis is deduced through a derivation process and counts in that argument as the presupposition, the transcendental condition of possibility, of predication and hence of cognition. In the later paper, the sign hypothesis is the apparatus designed for the metasemiotic description of an algebraic notation. Later, when Peirce abandons the algebraic notation he had helped to develop and designs a topological notation, this too receives a metasemiotic description. This capacity of the sign hypothesis to travel across generic boundaries, doing different jobs depending on the project germane to each genre, is displayed in the late work in the most remarkable way: he uses semiotic both to describe the representational content of the sentence-objects of the notation and to describe the properties that fit the notation to represent them. These two kinds of description require different means. The two uses are brought into the same project but remain distinct. I shall argue that some of Peirce's most productive work—as well as some of his most problematic—arises from attempts to synthesize into a "theory" the results of these two quite different uses of the hypothesis.

It is this situation in Peirce—the fact that the sign hypothesis is two quite distinct instruments at work on two different tasks—that I shall take as my working assumption and the proposition that I shall seek to demonstrate and to explore. The Lowell Lectures of 1903 are Peirce's first sustained attempt to bring them together, and thereafter, their synthesis, in the form of the elaborate classifications, is the issue. I shall argue that these proposed syntheses display frictions and leakages at those very points where the projects of formal logic and metaphysics require different properties of their instrumental concepts—or in other words, that the emergent "genre" of semiotics is a boundary formation, and always, like Janus, inclined to look in two directions at once.

Allow me to tell a story. In 1990 I spent part of my research leave at the Centre for Semiotic Studies at Aarhus University, Denmark. My visit happened to coincide with that of the late and much lamented Jean-François Lyotard, with whom I shared hours of good fare and stimulating conversation. I recall with gratitude the generosity of his interest in my work on Peirce. Give me more, he would say, miming the gestures of feeding; or he would potter into my room with a question. I was emboldened enough to tell him that my other work was on genre. I was interested, I explained to the author of *The Differend,* in the way Peirce's theory of signs worked differently in different genres, and I was intent on providing an account of genre that would allow me to explain these differences. His response was one of utter scorn: if there's one thing I don't need, he said, it's a semiology of genre.[19]

One can see why. A "general theory," or a semiology, of genre is exactly what is precluded on ethical grounds by the argument against metalanguage elaborated in *The Differend.* Instead of theorizing genre, the Philosopher bears witness to the differends that arise at the encounter of genres, which is to say, at their limits. Arguing in this respect directly against Habermas, Lyotard's point is that conversation does not transcend such limits but is conditioned by them; conversations take place within genres, not across the abysses that separate them. There is no language in which they could take place, no genre, however abstract, however theoretical, however universal its pretensions, that would do the trick. There is no temple on the hill, to use William James' metaphor for a certain style of philosophy, where we could avoid what Quintilian calls "the heat and dust of the forum."

Lyotard's interest in Peirce had been sparked not by me, of course, but by Deleuze. At the time I knew him, he was working on his study of Kant's *Third Critique,* and I understood his questions to me to be motivated by a historical query: what happened to the Kantian project at the hands of an American pragmatist? But the answer to this question is what Lyotard spent most of his energies writing against: what happened to the Kantian project in the hands of Peirce was the project for a general theory of "the sign." As Lyotard writes in one of his more provocative pronouncements, there is no such thing as language, except as the object of a special theory. Whether in the form of a general linguistics, a semiotics, or indeed of a rhetoric of genre, the problem remains the same. There can be no theory of the sign outside the local conditions of the genre within which it is posited and whose purposes it serves. Equally, however, there can be no general theory of genre. Indeed, the very postulate of genre is subject to what I think of as the first axiom of semiotics, the principle of difference; for "genre" is a meaningless concept outside the uncontainable—and *unsystematizable*—plurality of genres whose competences are conditioned by the play of relational contrasts among them.[20]

This study of Peirce takes its place within the terms of this paradox, but it does not attempt to solve it. The sign is a postulate without which we can do no work; but that is what it must remain. A theory of signs is thus imperative, but it is also imperatively impossible. *Mutatis mutandis*, the same paradox holds in the case of genre. This paradox represents the structure of the discursive conditions within which Peirce worked. The study demonstrates the very complexity of Peirce's struggle with these conditions.

It does not explain why it is that many people are defeated by the complexity of the demands of *reading* Peirce, or why Peirce has become a battleground in the contemporary humanities academy. My hunch is this, that the major differend besetting scholarship at present is what came to be known as the "two cultures." Peirce developed the sign hypothesis for the purposes of accounting for the production and modification of knowledge in scientific practice, but many of the preoccupations of his work have more in common with those of the interpretive humanities than with those of the natural sciences. Accordingly, literary scholars have been inclined to plunder his writings for a philosophical rationale of "undecidability," at the same time setting aside the central problem of his work, which is that of reference. Contrariwise, for many philosophers, the theory of the sign is a side issue in relation with questions that already have an assigned place in philosophical debate. In my reading, Peirce's work is a semiotics of reference; in this, it is difficult to read it with the presuppositions of a semiotics informed by the Saussurean tradition. Equally, however, it *is* a semiotics, and is therefore difficult to read in terms of the standard problematics of reference.[21]

One of the tasks I undertake in this book is to trace the development of Peirce's semiotic under the influence of the changing paradigm of formal logic and of his changing involvement with it. The crucial issues for this undertaking are not the technical problems of logical research itself, but the facts associated with these for the kind of writing—the genre—that logic became. I shall trace the changes by referring to the work of three crucial periods, 1867–85, 1903, and 1904–8. In 1885, when Peirce first uses semiotic to describe a formal notation, he discovers the need to include icons and indices with symbols as germane to the business of logic. This is in marked contrast with the position he takes in 1867, where he considers these two classes of signs only to set them aside from the work of logic proper. In 1903, we find the three classes integrated both in an account of logical notations and in the philosophy, but with this, Peirce is forced to consider again the "pure mathematics" of notational systems. The outcome of this move is what I have called elsewhere the "second classification" of signs; it inaugurates the proliferating divisions of signs that Peirce propounds in his last sustained writings on the topic, his letters to Welby and his *Monist* series of 1905. However, a remarkable fact about the work of this last period is that Peirce sometimes reverts to the earliest form of the three-way classification, as if the questions raised by the experiments in classification left untouched the philosophical questions from which he had started out.

The chapters are arranged in pairs: Chapters 1, 3, and 5 study key texts in which Peirce expounds sign theory; these chapters are arranged chronologically, in such a way that the changes that emerge in Peirce's reflections on signs can be traced genealogically. Chapters 2, 4, and 6 study examples of the sign in general, or of a class of sign, showing how these examples operate either to disturb, or to explore, the logic of those expositions. It is in his practice of exemplification that Peirce comes closest, I believe, to submitting his "formal, necessary"—that is, speculative—theorizing to the requirement of empirical, descriptive adequacy. Examples are not interchangeable. Much has been made in recent years of the paradox of exemplarity, and a study of Peirce's examples demonstrates it anew. Insofar as an example is adduced for its peculiarly telling properties, it is unique; as such, it compromises the posited generality of the class. But it is precisely at this point that Peirce's practice is revealing: he works with his examples—in particular, with his troublesome examples—in the mode of an empirical scientist. This is his laboratory, this is where his theory is tested, this is where it is modified. And this is where my writing has indulged in "the small pleasures of 'fugue.'"[22]

Chapter 1 tells a story in which the sign hypothesis is adapted from an explanatory role in Peirce's account of cognition to a descriptive role in his account of the functional logic of a notational system. This story takes us from 1867 to 1885, covering the period during which the bulk of Peirce's most creative work was in formal logic; this work drives the changes which have, notwithstanding the formal paradigm in which they emerge, some important implications for the philosophical uses of semiotic. By the end of the century, Peirce had returned to his philosophical preoccupations and had all but given up his work in algebraic logic; during the decade of the 1890s, he turned to the project of a topological notation designed to include the issues of philosophy that the algebra had precluded. Chapter 2, "A Vagabond Sign," traces the ramified implications of an example from work of this period.

Chapter 3 focuses on 1903, an exceedingly productive year, in which again we can pair a text from "philosophy" and one from "formal logic" to demonstrate their exchanges. The story to be told here concerns the progressive pragmatization of sign theory itself. Far from the sign's being simply an instrument *of* Pragmatism,[23] the theory of the sign itself must conform with the requirements of the pragmatic maxim: a sign is not only a law, but must on occasion be a "thing" and an "event." The key issue here is Peirce's distinction between a "type" and its "tokens." This allows Peirce to outline the formal conditions for answering a crucial question: how do signs act? And it is also this that results in what is known as the 1903 classification. Following this, Chapter 4 reflects upon examples of the index. The significance of the index in Peirce's work cannot be overstated, since it is given the task of effecting reference, but the range of examples that he adduces to constitute the class threatens to defeat its classhood. Under what set of presuppositions can something as content laden as a historical monument be classed along with pronouns and prepositions to form this class? I use a particular example, also dating from 1903, to provide the framework for an analysis of this problem.

Chapter 5 discusses the period following the work of 1903, where Peirce attempts to synthesize his findings from forty years of labor across the generic range delimited by philosophy and logic. This synthesis takes the form of frequent attempts to systematize the classifications, which purport to organize into a single conceptual space an extraordinary heterogeneity of material. They can be taken to represent iconically the desire of theory for unity and wholeness. Under scrutiny, however, they reveal the problems associated with that enterprise: homogeneity is bought at the considerable price of reductiveness. Chapter 6 asks the question, "how infinite is infinite semiosis?", answering it by investigating the logic of a range of examples and analogies used by Peirce throughout his writings.

These studies focus on changes in the scope of the sign hypothesis resulting from modifications to it and especially from modifications to the classifications. Let us include under the term *sign*, writes Peirce late in his career, "every picture, diagram, natural cry, pointing finger, wink, knot in one's handkerchief, memory, dream, fancy, concept, indication, token, symptom, letter, numeral, word, sentence, chapter, book, library, and in short whatever, be it in the physical universe, be it in the world of thought . . . causes something else, its interpreting sign, to be determined to a corresponding relation to the same idea, existing thing, or law" (EP 2:23, p. 326). Pervading them is a crucial issue: whether the material form of the sign itself has semiotic status. The two answers to this question correlate with the two genres of Peirce's writing on signs. The question first arises as a necessary implication of Peirce's adaptation of his theory for the purposes of describing a notation: the signs themselves are what matter here, for the logician is designing the instruments of his work and scrutinizing them for their properties (Chapter 1). It is in the very logic of this adaptation that he should develop the type/token distinction, which goes through two stages: the material thinghood and eventhood of the sign first emerges as an explicit issue in the "replica," which both has a place in the theory and is marginalized as having no significant status. Then Peirce develops the first trichotomy and shows how it is intricated in the work of all signs (Chapter 3). Nowhere is this intrication more evident than in the case of the index (Chapter 4). However, in parallel with this finding, Peirce continues to assert in relation with the symbol that the essence of the sign lies in the abstract form of its representational content. This contradiction is explored in Chapter 2, where I find that the material thinghood of the sign is at times an ungraspable object, and again in Chapter 5, where I assess Peirce's repeated attempts to synthesize his findings from both sources following 1904. A major debate in Peirce studies, concerning whether semiosis is or is not infinite, turns on this issue (Chapter 6).

To conclude, I review the topic of conversation in the light of the findings of the previous chapters. This review engages with a debate in recent Peirce studies concerning the relation between Peircean pragmatism and the requirements of certain arguments in social philosophy for an account of intersubjectivity. The topic of conversation is a key to this issue, where the opposing positions can be characterized by their view of whether conversation accounts for semiosis, or whether, on the contrary, semiosis accounts for conversation.[24] I take the latter view. In the course of this discussion, I scrutinize the symbol, *primus inter pares* of the kinds of signs, yet the one least subject to theoretical revision in the course of the career. As a result, it crystallizes the nature of the difficulties that beset the whole enterprise of semiotic.

I have written that "there is no pure Peirce": for this reason, the complexities and modifications in his views cannot and should not be reduced in a single synthetic account. This is true for the classifications of signs as it is for the relation between logic and metaphysics: it seems clear that Peirce did not achieve a final version of his classifications, and it is not within the scope of my argument to adjudicate on the success with which he managed to bring logic and metaphysics together in his pragmatism. That he attempted to do so is not in doubt, and if nothing else, the persistence of his effort to do so—to reach the telos of a unified philosophy—bears witness to their effective separation in the business of their writing. When Peirce writes prose that argues the ultimate unity of philosophy, he is writing metaphysics, not formal logic. I insist on this point: my premiss depends upon it.

If I am asked, therefore, on what theory of genre I rely to distinguish logic from metaphysics, I answer, with Aristotle (or with Plato), that it is a question of mimesis: what is the object represented, and what are the means of its representation? Hence: what does logic talk about, and how does it do so?[25] And: what are the representational claims of metaphysics, how does it identify its objects, what does it do with them? Peirce clarified the distinction for his purposes when he formulated his phenomenological foundation for philosophy: the signs with which philosophy does business are content laden; they represent the real things of ordinary experience because that is what requires investigation by philosophy. By contrast, the signs of logic mime certain abstract properties of sentences; they purport only to display their own formal properties. For this reason, the means of philosophy are primarily those provided by ordinary language, whereas those of formal logic are notational—algebraic or topological. It is true nonetheless that philosophy can—indeed, must—use the instruments devised by logic to investigate the formal properties of its propositions, and it is equally true that no logic is devised in the absence of philosophical assumptions. But they *use each other* for purposes that are their own. I answer also, therefore, with Wittgenstein (or with Quintilian), that genres, like language games (but I think these are the same) differ crucially in terms of what they *do* (with words, or other signs), and that this depends upon how they are taken up—used, interpreted—that is, the consequences they can have in the contexts in which they are deployed. What we do with the findings of formal logic or with its devices is quite different from what we do with the conclusions and techniques of metaphysics. The combination of these two answers—the mimesis of a genre and its mode of action, its address—delineates the same range as that to which Peirce insists we attend in construing "representation": portraits, flags, and words, certainly, and alongside them, representatives such as vicars, deputies, and diplomats. Peirce's talk about signs helps to capture something important about the working of genre.

Genre is a rhetorical topic, and one in poetics; we take it for granted that it is a question legitimately asked of film or literature, of sculpture and of television, of painting and of journalism. To deploy it as I do in investigating the writing of philosophy—"scientific writing"[26]—is deliberately provocative, although readers of Peirce will know (and my epigraphs remind them) how deeply the difference between logic and metaphysics reaches in his search for a solution to the problems he raised. This provocation is not gratuitous, nor is it part of the recent attempts at imperialism by literary studies over the humanities. This book is an intervention into semiotics. Given that genre is a major category and a central heuristic technique in my enterprise, and given that I take intellectual disciplines to be something like genres, it is of no interest to me to override disciplinary categories in favor of categories such as "text," "discourse," or "writing." Hence, my project does not entail a flattening out of all generic categories into the norms of "literature." I have attempted at all times to take seriously the fact that these are technical writings, philosophical and logical, but at no time have I attempted to write philosophy (or logic). This is a reading: it *reads* the generic determinations of its object texts, but it does not respond "in genre" to their propositions.

My premise is instrumental both in my argument concerning Peirce's writings on signs and in the wider argument I derive from it. There is no pure Peirce, and this is not a pure book. It is not purely "about" Peirce: the interest I take in the standard philosophical and logical topics plays servant, not master, to my interest in Peirce's engagement with the topic of signs. To that extent only, it is a book about Peirce: it is a book about the machinery of talk insofar as this question is raised by his work. Peirce's writings on signs—these writings being "talk" in the intended sense—provide the case study through which I investigate the adequacy of a theory of signs to account for the way talk works. Peirce's semiotic does not account for Peirce's talk about signs.

Pervasively, however, Peirce's talk about signs implies and sometimes makes explicit the rhetorical conditions under which a sign counts as a sign. These rhetorical conditions are (at least) generic. When Peirce erects a notice on the front boundary of his house announcing its offer for sale, this notice elicits a certain kind of conversation that is unlikely to occur under other circumstances. This genre is used opportunistically, moreover, by a passing stranger who needs hospitality and, being destitute, cannot seriously take on the role of purchaser. But he and the householder enter into a conversation nonetheless, of a different kind entirely from the one each had expected. That conversation bears directly on "the machinery of talk" insofar as the visitor had been an instrument maker and the householder a philosopher of science whose attention has always focused on the place of instruments in the production of scientific truths. Their conversation lends itself to allegorical exploitation in the Epilogue, which discusses the transformation of genres into one another to achieve particular local purposes. This is semiosis at work. The example is intended to reflect upon the much more complex example that I scrutinize throughout the book. Peirce's writings on signs display a similar process: semiotic is opportunistic in relation with the standard topics both of formal logic and of metaphysics. Both are transformed by its peculiar needs, and it in turn is transformed by talking under the conditions they provide.

I might argue, then, with and against Lyotard, that Peirce sought an idiom to speak the relation of logic with metaphysics; he devised its vocabulary and some elements of its syntax, and the extent to which he was successful is the extent to which he was able to make them do business together, at least to the extent of colluding in its creation. I would like to think, too, that in my adoption of the techniques of exegesis and my deliberate eschewal of the techniques of philosophical argument, in my adaptation of the habits of literary and cultural analysis to a text that, naming itself philosophy, resists them, I too have contested the dire forebodings of the differend: there is more to do than navigate around the borders of genres, though the mapping that that entails cannot be done without. I would like to think that in my work, rhetoric and philosophy have done a little business together, for in both, signs are an indispensable topic—the saying and what is said, address and mimesis, representation. I trust that one neither colonizes nor disempowers the other, but that their encounter creates the occasion for an interpretant, and an interpretant for that occasion. This is not a pure book, but what act of mediation could be?

Peirce is the author of a highly elaborate theory of signs, complex and difficult of access and interpretation. Into my reading of that corpus of writing, I have introduced genre in order to argue (1) that the transformation of materials from one genre in and by the objectives of the other can be held to account for the modifications in sign theory observable through the course of Peirce's career; (2) that the points at which some materials deriving from one genre are unassimilable by the other can likewise be accounted for in terms of the resistances of those genres to each other's means and purposes; and (3) that generic variety accounts for the astonishingly heterogeneous range of examples that Peirce adduces; things work as signs, and as certain classes of signs, only under specifiable generic conditions. Hence, (4) any semiotic theory of interpretation requires to mobilize both "sign" and "genre." Peirce himself is interpretable only on that condition, and Peirce's theory is unable to sustain its own argument without that gloss. More importantly, without that gloss, it cannot lend itself to the description of talk and its machinery by other semioticians in other times for the purposes that impel their work.

A man, tramping along a weary and solitary road, meets an individual of strange mien. (PW, appx. G)

The mathematician and the logician meet upon a common highway. But they face in contrary directions. (MS 459, p. 8)

One is facing one way while the other is facing just the other way. Each of them, it is true, finds it interesting to turn around occasionally and take a glance in the opposite direction. (MS 465, pp. 6–7)

A mathematical reasoning may be defined as a reasoning in which the following of the conclusion does not depend on whether the premisses represent experience, or represent the state of the real universe, or upon what universe it may be that they apply to. This erects, as we shall see, a definite party-wall between the reasoning of mathematics and much of the reasoning of all the positive sciences, including philosophy. (MS 459, p. 9)

It is not really contradictory . . . to say that a boundary is both within and without what it bounds. (CP 2,420)

PART ONE

THOUGHT AND ITS INSTRUMENTS

1

1867–1885

The Space of Thought

Peirce's first published paper on signs, "On a New List of Categories" (W 2:4), is an argument in which Peirce reinterprets Kant in such a way as to transform the "critique of reason" into a "critique of representation." To this end, he reconstrues the vocation of logic: beyond its familiar scope as the critique of arguments, logic takes on for Peirce, as it had for the scholastics, the responsibility of providing an account of representation itself.

In the long term, this was to have radical consequences. Yet the project he delineates in this paper is determined by a topos of the most classically conceived metaphysics. This is the knowledge of knowledge, the reason of reason. If reason is the human capacity to know things truly, what are the transcendental conditions of true knowledge, and how do we know when we know them truly (and so on, regressively)? If the *empirical* nature of knowledge is generalized as "representation," what are the formal, necessary conditions of representation? Peirce's answer to this question will be his analysis of "the sign." It is not a foregone conclusion that this reformulation of the question should lead where it did. Peirce will pursue the path thus opened by asking something else: it is one thing for "the sign" to be the general form of any knowledge, the constitutive structure of any experience, but quite another, so to say, to bump into a sign: what is it, to know "signs"—that is, to represent them—as themselves the objects of experience? This question has an effect *on* the topos of its own emergence. Peirce works toward a phenomenal account of signs as objects, as well as devices, of experience.[1] Semiotic will occupy the place of metaphysics, but live there, one might say, like a cuckoo.

I take metaphysics to be a genre. This genre can be characterized in several ways: it is the genre that denies its own generic specificity; it is the genre that seeks its own foundations; it is the genre that stands outside experience in order to account for the conditions of possibility of all knowledge, knowledge of things, as well as knowledge of knowledge; it is the exercise of reason, directed to a transcendental account of reason; it is the knowledge of the essentially human, and so on. Here is Kant's opening to the preface to the first edition of the *Critique of Pure Reason*: "Human reason has this peculiar fate that in *one species of its knowledge* it is burdened by questions which, as prescribed by the very nature of reason itself, it is not able to ignore, but which, as transcending all its powers, it is also not able to answer."[2] The paradox lies not only in the founding dilemma of metaphysics, but in the relation of a "species" of reason's knowledge to "the very nature of reason itself." It is in the interstices of this paradox that the decision to describe metaphysics as a genre is made.

I shall not seek to characterize metaphysics as a genre, either exhaustively or indicatively, by listing its topoi or by studying its lexis.[3] Nor shall I seek to prove that Peirce's "New List" is metaphysics in this sense, by matching its features with those of an ideal description. Rather, I shall accept that "we"—defined by a certain intellectual tradition—know when we are, and when we are not, "reading" or "writing" metaphysics; we know when something that claims not to be metaphysics stumbles into metaphysics, or seeks to dissociate from it, and we also know—"we" here defined both as readers of Peirce and as those who refuse to read Peirce on these grounds—that much of Peirce's oeuvre—including and especially his critique of metaphysics—is uncontentiously metaphysics, both in its problems and in its methods of proceeding. Instead of bothering with the positive description of the genre taken as genre, I shall accept with John Frow that a genre operates as it does through its presuppositions, through what it takes for granted, through what, in particular, it does not make available for debate, what is not, in that genre, open to contention.[4] Hence what I shall do in my study of the "New List" is to demonstrate that the boundary drawn around the topic of representation is drawn on the assumption of the presuppositions of metaphysics. Thus, the boundary serves to draw attention to these presuppositions, but it is drawn in such a way as to open them to question.

K.-O. Apel argues that the "New List" proposes an "answer to Kant's problematic," an "interpretation, rather than a refutation of Kant"[5]; this is the substitution of the "critique of meaning" for the "critique of knowledge."[6] It proposes a list of categories that, like those of both Aristotle and Kant, is a general speculative theory of the conditions of true synthetic propositions. Apel argues that this theory finds a "third way," alternative to Hume's skepticism and Kant's claim to provide a transcendental account of the conditions of true synthetic propositions by adopting a fallibilist epistemology and by "proving in a transcendental deduction the necessary validity of the *inferential procedure* through which science's synthetic propositions are attained." This is the place of the transcendental, but in this place, Peirce attends to the very nature of propositions themselves. The analysis of the proposition into its "subject" and "predicate" is not, Peirce argues, the significant issue (this may count as his first move against formalism); what is fundamental to an account of the proposition is its function as a representation. This is presupposed in logic, but the focus of interest only for the scholastic logicians, and is lost from philosophical attention with the oblivion of medieval philosophy that followed the Cartesian break with its tradition. That propositions rest on "representation" is given; "the three fundamental categories *[are derived] from* the function of sign representation as the unity of all forms of synthesizing sense data for a consciousness."[7] The crucial move is here: the categories are derived from the postulate of representation; representation does not rest on them as its transcendental ground.

Let us follow more closely this interpretation of Kant: "This paper is based upon the theory already established, that the function of conceptions is to reduce the manifold of sensuous impressions to unity" (W 2:4, p. 49).[8] The categories will be derived from a formalization of the presuppositions of this synthesis. Pure attention is distinguished from predication:

That universal conception which is nearest to sense is that of *the present, in general.* . . . But . . . the act of *attention* has no connotation at all, but is the pure denotative power of the mind, that is to say, the power which directs the mind to an object, in contradistinction to the power of thinking any predicate of that object. . . . Before any comparison or discrimination can be made between what is present, what is present must have been recognized as such, as *it.* (W 2:4, p. 49)

However, the unity of apprehension is given neither by predication nor by attention taken apart. The understanding reduces the manifold of experience to the unity of their work together:

The unity to which the understanding reduces impressions is the unity of a proposition. (W 2:4, p. 49)

A proposition always has, besides a term to express the substance, another to express the quality of that substance. (W 2:4, p. 52)

Unity is then analyzed as the effect of "comparison":

Empirical psychology has established the fact that we can know a quality only by its contrast with or similarity to another. By contrast and agreement a thing is referred to a correlate. (W 2:4, p. 53)

The occasion of reference to a correlate is obviously by comparison. (W 2:4, p. 53)

Peirce discovers that there are three grounds of "comparison": one is the concurrence of some quality, the second is "opposition," and the third is the "imputation" of some character. The distinctions among these three grounds will become the basis for the division of signs. However, in a move that we will find to be characteristic, Peirce desists from the temptation to provide a general definition before he has gathered some facts. These facts are examples:

The occasion of reference to a correlate is obviously by comparison. This act has not been sufficiently studied by the psychologists, and it will, therefore, be necessary to adduce some examples to show in what it consists. (W 2:4, p. 53)

The comparison of *b* with *p*, the complementarity of the murderer with the murdered person, the imputation of a shared character of the word *homme* with the word *man*, will become, respectively, as the technical deduction proceeds, the icon (here termed the likeness), the index, and the symbol (W 2:4, pp. 55–56).

These are examples of "comparison," and there follows a further list of examples of "representation." They are parallel, and this parallelism achieves a translation from the terms provided by psychology to those Peirce is intending to establish, the transcendental account of Representation through the account of empirical representations. This spells out what Peirce has adumbrated as the matter of logic:

Logic is said to treat of second intentions as applied to first. It would lead me too far away from the matter in hand to discuss the truth of this statement; I shall simply adopt it as one which seems to me to afford a good definition of the sub-ject-genus of this science. Now, second intentions are the objects of the under-standing considered as representations, and the first intentions to which they ap-ply are the objects of those representations. (W 2:4, p. 56)

This translation—from "comparison" to "representation," from psy-chology to logic—has further implications. The act of pure attention oc-curs *prior* to "any *comparison or discrimination*" (W 2:4, p. 49).

This is the apprehension that there is something. The postulate of *presence* is a presupposition of *representation*, but the act of attention that posits presence appears to be presemiotic. At this point, Peirce's argument rests on a dualism that distinguishes what is there from our coming to know it, attention from comparison, presence from representation. Max Fisch has argued persuasively that the "New List" is fundamentally nomi-nalistic on these grounds, and that it is not until the so-called anti-Carte-sian (or cognition) series of 1868–69, and the Berkeley review of the same period, that Peirce moves to a realist metaphysics.[9] In order to achieve this, he will have to address a technical difficulty in sign theory: he will have to find a way for the act of pure attention to count as a sign. This will become the definition of the index, and the solution will be achieved by the logical work of the 1880s.

However, our scrutiny of the translation throws up an equivocation in the argument of the "New List": what exactly can be meant by a "first intention"? Is it the object of the pure act of attention? Or is it, on the con-trary, the object of a representation? Peirce argues explicitly for the latter interpretation. The nominalism of the argument has comparison start, or stop, at "qualities"—that is, at predicates—and appears to have no bearing on the discernment of subjects, which are "substance." Yet this does not answer the question—the semiotic question par excellence—how "the present, in general" yields the subjects of propositions. How, in other words, does a representation *refer*? The answer is suggested in the phe-nomenological terminology that Peirce has adopted from Hegel. The "it" is not an object until and unless it *represents*. There is no originary singu-lar, it is always already two. Peirce writes "Before any *comparison or dis-crimination* can be made between what is present, what is present must have been recognized as such, as *it* (W 2:4, p. 49). Note "*re*-cognized," then note that the sentence is structured by an apparent solecism. The preposition "between" normally requires a complement constructed of *two* substantives; here there is only one. The difficulty is clarified by an insight due to Gilles Deleuze: repetition presupposes difference.[10] Peirce's sentence shows that "what is present" is subject to internal splitting. This is the structure and the dynamics of re-presentation. Subjects are produced by difference, and difference is the condition of re-cognition and hence of comparison.

It follows that the first intentions of all signs, even of indexical signs, are always already re-presentations. This will become hereafter an unshakable premise in Peirce's work on signs: the "object" of a sign—its "first intention"—has the same structure as, and therefore is, a sign. Only then, when he can establish this as a metaphysical postulate, will he be able to claim that "the whole universe is perfused with signs."

Insofar as there is tension between the nominalistic and the realistic implications of this argument, it will be resolved very simply in Peirce's later work: he will drop the reference to "substance" and "being"; and he will give up the reference to "empirical psychology," which presumes some metaphysical stuff—say, the mind—required to account for the mediation of the world with human knowledge. The outcome will be a list of categories that is through and through derived from Representation.

This brings us back to the classes of sign. There are three grounds of comparison, of representation; or, mediation happens in three ways; or, there are three kinds of signs. It is usual to consider the inclusion of the three classes as delineating the scope of semiotic, and to consider this scope as firmly established from the beginning, that is, from this move in the "New List." But Peirce's gesture is more ambiguous than this, because almost immediately, icons and indices are relegated outside the scope of philosophy.

The objects of the understanding, considered as representations, are *symbols*, that is, signs which are at least potentially general. But the rules of logic hold good of any symbols, of those which are written or spoken as well as those which are thought. They have no immediate application to likeness or indices, because no arguments can be constructed of these alone, but do apply to all symbols. (W 2:4, p. 56)

This move is a frequent feature of Peirce's semiotic: Peirce delineates a domain far larger than the one he thinks he needs for his purposes, then delimits a pertinent and useful class of objects within that domain. The pattern can be described as being the opposite of a certain deductive use of examples, usually called "illustration" in the manuals. Illustration starts from a definition, then uses that definition to determine the selection of examples. Here, by contrast, Peirce starts from the ordinary use of language, then asks a specifying question that will establish the technical stipulation: these things seem to be what we mean by "comparison," so what are the special features of the subclass of "comparison" to which "the rules of logic" pertain?

In order to answer this question, and hence to restrict "representations" to those signs that constitute arguments—this being the effective definition of the "symbol" in this paper—"Peirce defines logic, not as a descriptive or normative theory of human inferences, but as part of a general study of representations such as propositions and arguments."[11] Accordingly, this restriction applies to the symbol and excludes from the scope of logic the icon and the index.

What is it about the icons and the indices that puts them, so to say, beyond the pale? In some very significant respects, all three kinds of comparison are alike: all three depend on a "mediating representation"

which represents the relate to be a representation—

—note this moment, because it is this that takes the sign as sign, or as "second intention"—

—to be a representation of the same correlate which this mediating representation itself represents. (W 2:4, p. 53)

Mediation; taking the sign as sign; taking it as sign of something; taking the two signs as referring to the same object. Note, then, that "comparison" does not refer to a perceptual act on the unmediated data of the real; in particular, it does not refer to a Lockean account of the building up of inductive generalizations from the sense impressions made by individuals. "Comparison" is what occurs when we interpret a sign, and to do so, produce another sign of the same object. Take the example of the bilingual dictionary, which is crucial in this regard:

Suppose we look out the word *homme* in a French dictionary; we shall find opposite to it the word *man*, which, so placed, represents *homme* as representing the same two-legged creature which *man* itself represents. (W 2:4, p. 53)

This example is exemplary of the claim that signhood depends on there being two signs of the same object; but note that the sameness of that object is established by the conventions of dictionaries—"we shall find opposite it the word *man*, which, so placed." A bilingual dictionary—I note this in passing—is a genre, an instrument, a contrivance or device, its typography and its layout designed to provide the premises for an inference of this sort.

The "mediating representation" is the interpretant; the mechanism described thus far does not make the difference between icons and indices on the one hand, and symbols on the other. All are representations, and hence, all are of the "third" category. Peirce moves, therefore, to make distinctions within this category. The distinction he makes is this: those representations "whose relation to their objects is a mere community in some quality" are termed likenesses (=icons); those "whose relation to their objects consists in a correspondence in fact" are termed indices; but those "the ground of whose relation to their objects is an imputed character" are called symbols (W 2:4, p. 56). The three classes are distinguished by the *grounds* of their claim to be representations, and to be representations of what they represent. Only one ground is of relevance to logic: it is "imputation," that is, *thought*. This harks back to a very old philosophical tradition. Icons and indices are "natural" signs; only symbols are human and intellectual. It is as if, though all signs arise from "comparison," though all signs by definition are "second intentions," though all signs by definition arise from the work of a mediating interpretant, only some signs are "pure thought."

I digress briefly to note the function of the "ground," which has given rise to some contention in Peirce scholarship.[12] A cursory look at the passage suggests, contrary to all Peirce's formal definitions, that the sign relation is constituted by *four* terms:

By a further accumulation of instances, it would be found that every comparison requires, besides the related thing, the ground, and the correlate, also a *mediating representation which represents the relate to be a representation of the same correlate which this mediating representation itself represents*. Such a mediating representation may be termed an *interpretant* (W 2:4, p. 53)

I offer two complementary accounts of this apparent discrepancy. One is Hegelian. The "ground" of the first intention is sublated in the second intention, or the ground of the comparison is sublated in the interpretant.[13] It is likely that some such dynamic is at work.[14] The other is based on a necessary feature of any branching taxonomy. The general structure of representation is indeed a three-term relation. But in any classificatory system, subclasses are formed by features *additional* to those required for the class as a whole. In the divisions of signs, the extra feature is required to account for how each class of sign sustains its special claim to represent its object in the way that it does. This is its ground, which I take to mean the formal properties of the representations themselves: a sign may share sensory qualities with its object (the icon); it may relate with it in fact (the index); or its ground may be a product of thought (the symbol) (W 2:4, p. 56). This second reading is consistent with Peirce's account of the first category, quality, and the use of the term *ground* in that account; it is also consistent with the fact that the lower categories are presupposed in the higher ones. Furthermore, it allows signs themselves to have qualities and to be facts of the real, an implication that Peirce will require and that he will spend some energy on elaborating.[15] It accords with Short's view, that the ground is the *interpretability* of the sign; this is what Peirce will later specify as the "immediate interpretant."

I return to the boundary drawn between symbols on the one hand, and icons and indices on the other. Icons (likenesses) and indices are *signs*, yet in the "New List," Peirce sets them aside, as if they were not sufficiently signlike for philosophy to have any truck with them. Let us consider their defects. The relation of an icon to its object is "a *mere* community in some quality," as if this kind of sign were not sufficiently disentangled from its object, or perhaps, as if the shared qualities between sign and object meant that the sign was in some way qualitatively objectlike, not thoughtlike. The issue here is that pure thought is not counted as having sensory qualities, yet icons, which are representations, function as such because of their sensory qualities. It will be exactly this feature that Peirce will seize on in his later work, when he gives to iconicity a crucial role in logic. I shall return to this point below. At this point, it is enough to refer to Robert Innis' insight: if Peirce needs a theory of signs to account for perception, then that theory must account for the perception of signs.[16] A different point is at issue in the case of the index: its relation with its object "consists in a correspondence in fact"; its *differentia specifica* makes it more factlike than signlike, and indeed, Peirce will often say that an index would continue to be an index whether or not it was interpreted as a sign—or, in other words, it would have the same properties whether it functioned as a first or as a second intention. I conclude as follows: while the distinction between first and second intentions is a formal and a functional distinction, not a difference of properties, the distinction between symbols and the other two kinds of signs is a metaphysical distinction, holding between thought and its others, and grounded in ontological assumptions. I also suggest that the operative boundary is the boundary *of* metaphysics, because that ontological distinction, between thought and its others, is the very ground of its constitutive problematic. Peirce will come to be highly critical of any philosophy that allows untheorized metaphysical presuppositions to underpin its logic and its account of representation. Metaphysics must be subject to the protocols of a theory of representation and must be subjected to rigorous logical analysis to this end. But this is Peirce's first published paper, and this very problem is to become the stuff of his whole philosophical enterprise. He spent his life trying to establish assumptions that would *undo* the assumption of the problem that here, in the "New List," preempts his semiotic.

Notwithstanding their exclusion from the scope of logic in the "New List," Peirce nevertheless provides examples of both the icon and the index. His first example of a relation of simple iconism is the likeness of the letters *p* and *b*; his first example of an index is the murder (W 2:4, p. 53). The second list of examples gives a portrait, for the likeness, and a weathercock, for the index. The examples from the second list recur regularly in Peirce's later work, in a move that simply includes them with the general class of signs. The examples from the first list do not recur. Yet the issue raised by the example of the murder does not simply disappear; it becomes central to the deployment of the theory of indexicality in Peirce's account of scientific experiment.[17] The existence of a murdered person is a sign that there exists a murderer: is this index the same sort of thing as, for example, the weathercock? Is the heterogeneity of the examples of indexicality itself an index of a problem in the very conception of the class? I shall consider this problem in Chapter 4.

Both icons and indices will come to be fully included in the signs required by logic, and both will be used, substantively and instrumentally, to solve problems in Peirce's philosophy. In the pages to follow, as we watch Peirce move to theorize this inclusion, we will see a shift in the criteria used for making several distinctions. First, pure thought, or "reason," will cease to define the scope of logic as Peirce defines logical notations and their constitutive signs as technical instruments. Second, it will follow from this that symbols cannot be set off against the other two kinds on the basis of their ground in thought or their special fitness for the work of logic. Third, therefore, the criteria for the classes of signs will be forced to change.

Yet boundaries lie both outside and inside that which they bound. The problem associated with the ambiguous zone in which some things both are, and are not, signs will not be perfectly solved by the inclusion of icons and indices. The boundary itself will move, and the zone will become

much narrower, more like a trip wire that things can tumble over in an
inattentive moment; this is the very boundary that must constitute them
as signs—as *p* is constituted as *p* and not *b* and hence acquires its functions
in a given system of marks through the operation of the line of writing:

> Suppose we wish to compare the letters *p* and *b*. We may imagine one of them to
> be turned over on the line of writing as an axis, then laid upon the other, and fi-
> nally to become transparent so that the other can be seen through it. In this way
> we shall form a new image which mediates between the images of the two letters,
> inasmuch as it represents one of them to be (when turned over) the likeness of the
> other. (W 2:4, p. 53)

This is the boundary of semiotic, where signs fade into mere marks, the very
one that Aristotle excludes as nonsemantic when he excludes the *phonè*. Yet
not "the very one," for these marks are marks of writing—they are not
speech; they do not issue forth to express a soul, a subject, or the objects it
knows. They are empty shapes, constituted as signs by their diacritical relation with one another, and by the utterly asemantic line of writing. As a
mark left by an event, in the form of a bullet hole, or a corpse, or the turning of a weathervane, come to count as fully semiotic in the category of the
"index," so do written marks that, in and of themselves may not be "semantic," come to count as signs when the philosopher embarks on a technical manipulation of pieces of type, and when the logician turns to the
semiotics of a formal notation. Such signs are not defined by their thought
content, by the thought space of their emergence, or by their function in the
making of arguments. To accommodate them, Peirce will cease to define
them on the criterion of "imputation" and will use the term *convention*.

Hence, at the turn of the century, discovering phonic iconicity at the
heart of a particular language, Peirce will select a most telling example and
will analyze it not as a natural sign, but as an artifact the conditions of
whose signhood rest in the local instrumentality of English:

> the word "cuckoo" does present a resemblance to the bird; but its onomatopoeia is
> a mere accident of its origin. It is further most used when cuckoos, or some effects
> of cuckoos, are really present; but that slight real connection with the birds is in-
> significant. It is constituted a name for the genus of birds exclusively by the circum-
> stance that an English-speaking hearer of the word will so understand it. (CP 8:119)

Dictated by the topos of thought, a project to regulate thought,
Peirce's engagement with the sign hypothesis will not be dictated *to, by*
"thought." The boundary of semiotic will shift depending on whether he is

writing philosophy—conducted under the sign of pure reason—or logic—conducted under the sign of the *tekhnè*.

The Instruments of Logic

The position taken in the "New List" is subject to a significant modification in a review Peirce wrote in 1885 of Royce's early work, *The Religious Aspect of Philosophy* (W 5:33, pp. 221–34). The review clarifies the connection between fallibilism and the detranscendentalizing of the sign hypothesis; the inclusion of icons and indices follows from it. Indeed, Peirce will claim that the inclusion of icons and indices—these latter, especially—provides the solution to an otherwise insoluble problem in transcendental metaphysics.[18] The generic distinction between "philosophy" and "logic" is both formally and empirically implied by Peirce's procedures in this review: if Royce has not used formal logic, it is simply because he does not read it. That it *bears on* the problems of philosophy will be a persistent theme in the debate between the two colleagues over the decades, and we discern in its appearance in 1885 the beginning of Peirce's campaign to bring the two kinds of inquiry together. But the techniques—indeed, the substantive preoccupations, not to mention the languages required to pursue them—are no longer held in common. Peirce will take it on himself first to teach the philosophers logic, then to teach the logicians philosophy.

Peirce states his explicit disagreement with Royce on two major issues, one being his thoroughgoing Hegelianism, and the other Royce's dismissal of Peirce's own pragmatic account of truth as the end of inquiry.[19] As he was to do in his review of Royce's later work, *The World and the Individual* (CP 8:100–31), Peirce invokes the technicalities of formal logic to explain the source of Royce's defective arguments; just as Hegel overlooks the role of secondness in cognition, so does Royce fail to acknowledge the encounter with the real; hence, he cannot account for error:

Dr Royce's main argument . . . is drawn from the existence of error. Namely, the subject of an erroneous proposition could not be identified with the subject of the corresponding true proposition, except by being completely known, and in that knowledge, no error would be possible. The truth must, therefore, be present to the actual consciousness of a living being. (W 5:33, p. 223)

Peirce cannot accept that "the truth" is so present; it is the horizon of inquiry. Instead, acts of cognition do encounter the real, and in that encounter, they discover doubt and error. Such moments of doubt do not produce positive contents; they have a purely negative effect.[20] Royce's argument, Peirce continues, "is drawn from Formal Logic, for Formal Logic it is which inquires how different propositions are made to refer to the same subject and the like" (W 5:33, p. 223). But Royce, like all the German metaphysicians, fails to draw on the most recent advances in formal logic, and Peirce laments that such writers have not, as one would suppose they might, "postponed their venturesome flights into the thin air of theology and the vacuum of pure reason, until they had carefully tried the strength of every part of that logical machine on which they were to depend." Note the term *machine* here: it indicates the crucial point of difference between the position Peirce has come to take and that of the "theological" philosophers. The starting point is not to be a metaphysical foundation; it is simply technical and procedural. "Logic" in Peirce's work is instrumental, it is not speculative.

We must not, therefore, wonder that Dr. Royce's argument from formal logic overlooks one of the most important discoveries that have lately resulted from the study of that exact branch of philosophy. He seems to think that the real subject of a proposition can be denoted by a general term of the proposition; that is, that precisely what it is that you are talking about can be distinguished from other things by giving a general description of it. Kant already showed, in a celebrated passage of his cataclysmic work, that this is not so; and recent studies in formal logic have put it in a clearer light. (W 5:33, p. 224)

On the basis of these "important discoveries" made in "recent studies" in formal logic (a "branch" of philosophy), Peirce proposes a solution to the logical problem that he discerns in Royce's work:

We now find that, besides general terms, two other kinds of signs are perfectly indispensable in all reasoning. One of these kinds is the index, which like a pointing finger, exercises a real physiological force over the attention, like the power of a mesmerizer, and directs it to a particular object of sense. One such index at least must enter into every proposition, its function being to designate the subject of discourse. (W 5:33, p. 224)

This solves the problem, because

If the subject of discourse had to be distinguished from other things, if at all, by a general term, that is, by its peculiar characters, it would be quite true that its complete segregation would require a full knowledge of its characters and would preclude ignorance. But the index, which in point of fact alone can designate the subject of a proposition, designates it without implying any characters at all. (W 5:33, p. 224)

Peirce then goes on to argue that the function of the index distinguishes "dates and position" and therefore dispenses with the Kantian intuitions of time and space; they can be construed as the effects of semiotic operations.

Peirce's critique is directed both at a metaphysics that deals only with the thin air of pure reason, and at the version of "formal logic" that that metaphysics relies on. Modern formal logic is proposed as a corrective. Within the recent research in modern formal logic, it has been shown that logic cannot deal exclusively with "general signs," that is, symbols; it needs "two other kinds," and Royce would not have made the philosophical error for which he is taken to task had he understood one of these, the index, "which designates [the subject of a proposition] without implying any characters at all." But remarkably, Peirce does not complete his assertion, that "two other kinds of signs are perfectly indispensable for all reasoning." The second kind, the icon, is apparently quite dispensable in the argument he is having with Royce, which bears on the Hegelian tendency to "ignore . . . the Outward Clash."[21] It is not yet explained how the issues raised by iconicity can be brought to bear on the big philosophical themes.

The important discoveries, the recent studies, that Peirce mentions here refer to two of his own publications, *Studies in Logic by Members of the Johns Hopkins University* (1883), edited by Peirce, in which O. H. Mitchell introduced a system of quantification into a formal notation[22]; and Peirce's own "On the Algebra of Logic: A Contribution to the Philosophy of Notation" (W 5:30, pp. 162–90), dated 1885, where he also refers to Mitchell's work. In this latter paper, Peirce counts quantifiers as indices alongside the pointing function, and he uses the icon to analyze the diagrammatic function of notational syntax. It is in this paper that Peirce first modifies the semiotic of the "New List," and it is on the basis of his deployment of it here that the modified hypothesis will be brought to bear, as it is in the 1885 Royce review, on the problems of philosophy. The integration of indices and, eventually, icons, into the problematic of inquiry (cognition, in Royce's work) is of the greatest significance in taking semiotic beyond the topic of "representation," with the whole tradition of philosophy that is brought into play by that topic, toward issues mobilized by a different word, "the sign."

Peirce introduces his aims in "On the Algebra of Logic" as follows:

In this paper, I purpose to develop an algebra adequate to the treatment of all problems of deductive logic, showing as I proceed what kinds of signs have necessarily to be employed at each stage of the development. I shall thus attain three objects. The first is the extension of the power of logical algebra over the whole of its proper realm. The second is the illustration of principles which underlie all algebraic notation. The third is the enumeration of the essentially different kinds of necessary inference. (W 5:30, p. 165)

It is the second of these objects that interests me. As far as I can tell, this is the first time Peirce applies his theory of signs to the analysis of a notation. What is remarkable about it at the outset is that a notation is a rule-governed system of arbitrary signs. To investigate its semiotics is therefore very like what Saussure was to do with natural language some thirty years later. But note, that if a notation is a system of rule-governed arbitrary signs, all the signs of the system conform to Peirce's original definition of the subclass of symbols: if, in a notation, there are no "natural" signs, then "imputation" will not suffice to demarcate the class of symbols, and Peirce will be forced for the first time to acknowledge the possibility, that some examples of each class are not "pure" (W 5:30, p. 163).[23]

Just why Peirce decided to take the step of providing a semiotic description of his algebra can speculatively be explained by referring to some passages from George Boole's *An Investigation of the Laws of Thought*.[24] This is a major text in the development of mathematical logic, and it states the paradigm within which Peirce was working. For my purposes, the most interesting thing in Boole's work is that its introductory chapter on the "Design of the Work" is followed by a chapter devoted to "Signs and their Laws." Notice first of all that "Language" is conceived to be an "instrument," "not merely a medium for the expression of thought" (p. 24), but that the differences between particular "natural" languages are deemed to be irrelevant to the logician, who seeks to discover in their commonality and their universality "some deep foundation of their agreement." This deep foundation he takes to be "the laws of the mind itself." In order to investigate this foundation, Boole will take it to be some universal form of language; he proposes "to give expression in this treatise to the fundamental laws of reasoning in the symbolic language of a Calculus" (p. 5). If "Language" is the general instrument of thought, this particular language is the special instrument of the method of logic. It can be investigated so as to identify its elements, and "to seek to determine their mutual relation and dependence" (p. 24). "The notation of the science of Number" (p. 6) has "a peculiar and exclusive fitness for the ends in view" (p. 5), so to investigate the instrument of human reason is to "inquire in what manner [its elements] contribute to the attainment of the end to which, as co-ordinate parts of a system, they have respect" (p. 24). Note Boole's view of the relation of method, instrument, and the object of inquiry; it is classically positivist: "the laws [of reasoning] are such as to suggest this mode of expression, and to give it" its peculiar fitness to reveal the laws of the mind.[25]

Now notice that the focus on instrument and method means that for Boole, certain metaphysical problems are in practice irrelevant. First, it makes no difference whether "Language is to be regarded as an *essential* instrument of reasoning, or whether, on the other hand, it is possible for us to reason without its aid" (p. 24). Whichever of these doctrines one adopts, "the results obtained" from the actual investigation "are formally equivalent" (p. 25). This is because the logician is investigating "the laws of signs," and because "the immediate subject of examination is Language, with the rules which govern its use." Ultimately, although Boole claims to be investigating the laws of the mind, the ontology of mind, or its transcendental condition, "is beside the design" of his work. Second, he can afford to be agnostic about "a dispute as to the precise nature of the representative office of words or symbols . . . in the processes of reasoning. By some it is maintained, that they represent the conceptions of the mind alone; by others, that they represent things" (p. 26). This is a version of the dispute between nominalism and realism; but again the logician declares that "the question is of no great importance here, as its decision cannot affect the laws according to which signs are employed" (p. 26). With these two declarations of irrelevance, Boole sets aside the topics which Peirce has used most explicitly to introduce semiotic. What is "impertinent" is *atopical*, not on the agenda. Boole has marked for us the boundary conditions for formal logic as a specific discipline, and these boundaries are drawn so as to mark it off from metaphysics. Broadly stated, these are the rules of the genre.

The quotations from Boole serve to show that the classic topic of "representation," mobilized by Peirce to theorize cognition or inquiry, and the topic of "signs" are not the same. The topic of representation is the topic whereby the constitution and knowledge of objects are investigated; classically, and even under the anthropological generalization of Kant, "cognition" is cognition by a subjective instance. Peirce inflects this historically with "inquiry," making true knowledge statements dependent on the long run, rather than on individual apprehension. Representation is inflected accordingly but is still designed to deal with the mediation between acts of knowing and the test of experience. Entrained by this topic are the problems of the ontology and the metaphysics of the mind and its objects.

Such questions as these do not need to be decided in order to do the new logic; nor, if we were to believe Boole, can this new logic contribute to any metaphysical doctrine concerning them. But this is where Peirce will part company with the new paradigm.[26] For him, the problem of "representation" continues to matter, and he will pursue the technically conceived topic of "signs" in order to bring it to bear on philosophy. Eventually, at the turn of the century, this will result in Peirce's retrieval of phenomenology as the foundation of substantive ideas, but even then, he will insist that phenomenology rest on logic, rather than the other way around. Boole makes the distinction between the two topics quite clear in the very first sentence of his second chapter: the logician considers language as an instrument; as such, he investigates its elements, their systematicity, its fittedness to its end. This, he says, is wholly different from considering language merely as "a medium for the expression of thought" (p. 24).

Another way of stating the difference between the topic of "representation" and the topic of "signs" is this: insofar as "representation" is involved in the metaphysics of the mind and its objects, the question of "representation" is the question of its content. What does a representation represent, and is it true? Implied is a "why?" question: to ask why we have, or produce, representations is to seek the nature of the human in its capacity for true knowledge, and to ask why we might investigate representation is to seek the telos of philosophy itself. By contrast, the rhetoric of instruments and methods is the rhetoric of a technology: to ask "why?" of an instrument is to ask what pragmatic need it meets. Then again, to ask "how?" of representation is to seek the transcendental conditions of knowledge; this is Kant's project. To ask "how?" of signs is to inquire into the techniques of reasoning and the rules of a system; this is Boole's, and after him, Peirce's. It is for this reason, I shall argue in the pages that follow, that it is more likely that issues connected with the formal and material properties of the representamen itself should arise in the logic than in the philosophy.

I wish to call attention to another point of interest in Boole's project. He writes that "the elements of which all language consists are signs or symbols. Words are signs" (p. 25). However, they are not the only sort of sign. "Arbitrary marks, which speak only to the eye, and arbitrary sounds or actions" are also signs, and "In the mathematical sciences, letters, and the symbols +, −, =, &c., are used as signs" (p. 25). He then invokes a distinction between "signs" and "symbols": in the conventional usage of mathematics, "the term 'sign' is applied to the latter class of symbols, which represent operations or relations, rather than to the former [that is, the 'letters'], which represent the elements of number and quantity." But he proposes to overlook this distinction and uses "sign" as an overarching category, stipulating its usage by means of the definition. "A sign is an arbitrary mark, having a fixed interpretation, and susceptible of combination with other signs in subjection to fixed laws dependent upon their mutual interpretation" (p. 25). Notice that the laws of interpretation are governed by the systemic relations of the signs among themselves; this is a crucial issue in the Saussurean paradigm, and one that, I have no doubt, derives directly from the practices and techniques of formal logic. Boole's decision to use "sign" in this way is a theoretical synthesis that disregards two conventional boundaries. One is the distinction between "numbers" and "operators," and the other is the distinction between numerical notations and so-called natural, that is discursive, language. These two oversights together construct the site for a general semiotics by constructing its theoretical object. This object classifies together, as "language," what we would usually think of as two quite distinct instruments, "numbers" and "words"; it also classifies together, as "signs," this first grouping with such things as the operators and "arbitrary marks . . . arbitrary sounds [and] actions."

Note in particular that when marks of all sorts are brought together as "signs," they are different from "language" traditionally conceived in one crucial, indeed radical, particular. They are arbitrary; they "speak only to the eye"; they are a contrivance of writing.[27]

It is Peirce who will take up the suggestion of this extension of the category of "sign," not Boole; he construes this category as his category of representation. Then, in place of the no longer useful distinction between "signs" and "symbols," "marks," "numerals," "letters," and so on—all of which would count as discrete classes under the classical terminological regime—he elaborates a classification or "division" of the class into three— all of which count as subclasses of the overarching "sign"—the symbol, the icon, and the index. While this classification is familiar to all readers of primers in semiotics, the highly technical use Peirce makes of it in "On the Algebra of Logic" relies on a complexity unsuspected by theorists of the "iconicity of the image" or the "indexicality of the photograph." I shall return to this use of the index in Chapter 4 and to this use of the icon in Chapter 6. Here, my more restricted purpose is just to show that these classes take on technical functions in logic, and that it is on this basis that they will thereafter be adapted to the needs of philosophy.

"Thereafter" is a little misleading, for it is the case that Peirce sets out in this paper to write a "philosophy of notation," and that in this respect, he is already adapting his philosophical work on representation to "signs," that is, to the requirements of a metadescription of his algebra. Of particular interest is the fact that the "rules" for deriving the three classes in the "New List" are modified. Recall that in the "New List," the theory of signs is based on a kind of speculative psychology and derives from a procedure whereby Peirce teases out the presuppositions of "comparison." He shows that of the necessary elements of "comparison," there are only three possible combinations, and these combinations give the three classes of sign. They are distinguished on the criterion of whether or not the reference to a ground can be "prescinded" from the reference to an interpretant; if it can, a pair of relates remains, and then a further distinction according to the internal constitution of this pair is made (W 2:4, pp. 55–56). The procedure at work in "On the Algebra of Logic" is not dissimilar to this in some respects, but it is significantly different in others: it has itself been formalized. "A sign is in a conjoint relation to the thing denoted and to the mind" (W 5:30, p. 162)—that is, it is a triple relation. The relates can combine in only three ways without violating the rules of the definition, and each of these ways is a kind or class of sign. There are two "degenerate forms" of this relation, in which pairs of terms "are in dual relations which constitute the triple relation" (W 5:30, p. 163); "a plural character or conjoint relation is to be called degenerate if it is a mere compound of dual characters" (W 5:30, p. 162). This idea of degeneracy is borrowed from geometry, whereas the analysis of the constitutive relations of the class in general, to give the subclasses, is a direct application of the relative logic. The derivation of the classes of signs has thus been taken out of the speculative psychological framework that governs it in the "New List" and provided with a vocabulary and an analytical syntax that suits its new setting. We might say that there has been a translation from philosophy to logic, but it is important to note the extent to which this translation has changed the model.

Peirce sets up his introduction to the topic of signs first by saying what he means by a "relation," then by showing why the concept of "sign" is properly analyzed as a three-term relation. Then he derives the classes and goes on to illustrate them. The examples fall neatly into two groups: those that are standard in his treatments of "representation," and those that he introduces for the purposes of this paper (marked with asterisks in Figure 1.1). Figure 1.1 shows examples from the two texts in question.

I note first a feature of the philosophical model that is retained in the

1867	1885
Index	
(murder)	natural signs
weathercock	physical symptoms
	pointing finger
	*demonstrative and relative pronouns
	*letters on a geometrical diagram
	*subscript numbers in algebra
Icon	
(b/p)	*diagrams of geometry
portrait	painting
Symbol	
(man/homme)	general words
word, proposition,	speech
judgment/any mode	

Figure 1.1 . Comparison of examples from the "New List" (1867) and the "Algebra of Logic" (1885).

1885 account. The examples for the class of the "symbol" remain constant here and in all Peirce's writings on semiotic, whether logical or philosophical. These are the "words" or "speech," the "propositions," the "modes of conveying a judgment"; contrasted with the "natural signs and physical symptoms," the distinction appears to be quoted from the old tradition that distinguishes between "natural" and "rational" signs. The assumptions underpinning this distinction are subject to questions arising both from Peirce's reading of Darwin and from the new work on signs introduced in this paper.[28] That it stands apparently intact in this passage functions as an index to the traditional philosophical source of Peirce's inquiry into signs. The symbol, too, will undergo some revision in the course of Peirce's career, yet the symbol will emerge as the place reserved for a signhood that is not "natural" or "physical."[29]

However, there are some interesting adjustments to the standard examples in this paper. First, the "weathercock" is replaced by the "pointing finger." Both are similar in that they "point" to indicate a location in experiential space. But what appears to be lost from the weathercock by focusing on this aspect is its status as a piece of technology; this raises an interesting problem pertaining to the relation of the body with its tools, which I shall discuss in the Conclusion. The second important change is in the breadth of the class of the symbol. In the 1867 paper, Peirce does not discriminate between the functions of words: they are all words and all "rational" signs; in the 1885 paper, however, this class is restricted to "the main body of speech," and it explicitly excludes "demonstrative and relative pronouns," which are now examples of the index. The "words" that continue to be symbols are "general words," that is, predicate words. In the 1885 text, he generalizes the proposition; it is now "any mode of conveying a judgment," that is, I suppose, it includes mathematical propositions at least. The "word" is losing its prestige as a general model for the sign, both because the class of "words" is now found to be heterogeneous and because a variety of things are found to do similar jobs to "general"—that is, predicate—words.

Crucially, all the new examples fall into the classes of the index and the icon. This necessitates some deep adjustments to the criteria for all the classes, as well as for the class of signs as a whole. Consider the criteria for the icon. The first is the standard one that subsists in almost all Peirce's expositions of the classification: the relation of sign to object "consists in a mere resemblance between them" (W 5:30, p. 163). We might recall that it is for this reason in the "New List" that icons cannot be sufficiently clearly disentangled from their objects, and again for this reason, that they have themselves sensory qualities and hence do not count as pure thought. Yet it is for the self-same reasons that they are counted as signs in this paper: "icons are so completely substituted for their objects as hardly to be distinguished from them. Such are the diagrams of geometry" (W 5:30, p. 163).

This description depends upon the icon's sharing some salient sensory qualities with its object. Does this necessarily mean that we replace the object with the icon? Certainly we do, with the diagrams of geometry, and there is a limited sense in which this is also the case with maps and architectural plans, when we use them to plan a journey or a building. But in all these cases, the second intentionality of the icon must be kept firmly in mind; and in all these cases, the substitution of the icon for its object ceases under specifiable conditions. Now let us consider the portrait. There may be cases—for example, portraits of monarchs in ceremonial settings—that genuinely do "substitute" for their objects, but this is peculiar to specific genres. This is a rather different matter from assessing how precise a resemblance is; evaluation of the degree or quality of iconicity requires us *not* to substitute the copy for the object. So let us suppose that Peirce is pointing us toward the issue of use; but if this is so, it is precisely because we *do* distinguish the icon from the object that we *can* use it in certain ways. This is what Peirce goes on to elucidate: in order to use the diagram, we have to forget that it is not the very thing. Then he tries to extend that argument to the painting: "So in contemplating a painting, there is a moment when we lose the consciousness that it is not the thing, the distinction of the real and the copy disappears, and it is for the moment a pure dream—not any particular existence, and yet not general. At that moment we are contemplating an *icon*" (W 5:30, pp. 163).

Let us dwell on—perhaps in—this dream: whereas Peirce wrote that in the case of the diagram, the diagram is for us "the very thing," in the case of the painting, we seem to treat the painting itself as transparent. We do not operate on the painting; we dream, he says, its object. In the example of the painting, "icon" names a pure mental content that results from *forgetting* the difference between reality and representation; in the example of the diagram, "icon" names a representational technique that makes appear an abstraction that cannot appear without it. Indeed, in order to use icons such as geometrical diagrams, the material reality of the diagram must take on thinghood in order to permit the observation and manipulation of the relations it displays. In marked contrast with this, Peirce uses the term *icon* elsewhere to say what he means by the idea evoked by a predicate word. So the question arises whether the icon is a dematerialized mental content or a material form governed by representational protocols. Peirce's answer differs, depending on the generic environment in which the "icon" is deployed. In mathematics and formal logic, and most significantly in his own topological diagrams, "icon" names a material form; in philosophy, however, it names a dematerialized content of the mind that is barely represented at all. As if "philosophy," as a genre, is still governed by the issues of thought that are of such marginal interest for Boole.

These implications are already available when Peirce adds algebraic icons to the geometrical ones. Consider the following passage:

For instance, take the syllogistic formula,

> All M is P
> S is M
> hence S is P

This is really a diagram of the relations of *S*, *M*, and *P*. The fact that the middle term occurs in the two premisses is actually exhibited, and this must be done or the notation will be of no value. As for algebra, the very idea of the art is that it presents formulae which can be manipulated, and that by observing the effects of such manipulation we find properties not to be otherwise discerned. In such discoveries we are guided by previous discoveries which are embodied in general formulae. These are patterns which we have the right to imitate in our procedure, and are the *icons par excellence* of algebra. The letters of applied algebra are usually tokens, but the *x*, *y*, *z*, etc., of a general formula, such as

$$(x + y)z = xz + yz$$

are blanks to be filled in with tokens, they are indices of tokens. Such a formula might, it is true, be replaced by an abstractly stated rule (say that multiplication is distributive); but no application could be made of such an abstract statement without translating it into a sensible image. (W 5:30, pp. 163–65)

Icons have the power to exhibit relations where other kinds of sign do not; they do so because they are "sensible," that is, they have a material form on the page. Some properties cannot otherwise be displayed, and no application can be made of the abstractly stated rule that uses discursive language rather than the formula.

Had Peirce left his discussion of iconicity at the example of the painting, with its capacity to evoke a "dream," a pure mental content, none of these implications would have emerged. This is partly because the investigation of the properties of a notation must make the explicit assumption that diagrams have both formal and material properties. Boole, we remember, is concerned to specify notational signs as "written," and it is the arrangement on the page of the letters, not the properties of the letters themselves, that does the work. Peirce's decision to use his semiotic to describe a notation allows him to apply the assumptions of iconicity to it; Boole does not. It is this that allows him to focus on, rather than disregard, the materiality of the sign and to show that its formal properties are dependent on this materiality.

The implications are far-reaching: when he philosophizes "representation," as in the painting example, he continues to disregard the materiality of signs, the formal material differences of different languages, and to go on talking about pure mental contents. Is it the painting, or its object, that ceases momentarily to be a thing? Is a diagram a thing? Or its object? What is it, to do with icons as he has instructed us in the "New List," to "represent them as representations"? What properties *distinguish them*, as signs, from their objects? I point out that the structural distinction between first and second intentionality cannot answer this question because it cannot tell us why it is possible to manipulate diagrams and so on, whereas it is not possible to manipulate their Platonic abstractions or the abstract formulation of their rules. Icons as such dematerialize so readily in Peirce's philosophical work that the mere decision to bring icons into the fold does not explain how Peirce comes to acknowledge, or to theorize, the formal-material thinghood of signs in general or of the icon in particular.

To find an answer to this question, we need to turn to the criteria for indexicality. The familiar criterion of "real connection" also widens its meaning so as to apply to the new examples that are adduced. Certainly the letters on a geometrical diagram are really connected with the points that they label, as are algebraic subscripts: both depend on immediate contiguity. But "real connection" is only true of the demonstrative and relative pronouns in a restricted set of cases of oral discourse. Notice, then, that "real" covers *causality*, as in the case of physical symptoms, *spatial contiguity*, as in geometry, and *spatiotemporal connection*, as in the case of the demonstratives. Now if we consider written, as distinct from oral, discourse, spatial contiguity is hardly the question, and the guarantee of connection is made not by anything like space or time but by the rules of connected discourse and some rather more formal rules of grammar, such as the anaphoric and cataphoric determination of person and number and gender. If this counts as "real connection" in Peirce's account of indexicality, then "real" has again been dissociated from the "natural." There is a "reality" of the domain of operation of a language just as compelling as is physical space. This holds true also of the classification of quantifiers as indices: what they refer to is the universe of discourse, and this must be specified in order for the quantifiers to function. To learn a language is to learn the rules that govern this sense of a "conventional real."

Now this is a consequence of extending the class of the index to particular signs in a notation, all of which, it is clear, are governed by precise rules and conventions. There is indeed a reality established by the conventions of such languages, and again, it is the reality of the material and formal medium on which a notation depends. The rules governing indexicals in, say, discursive language, are rules that make the particular occurrence of some indexical sign establish a referring relation with another particular occurrence of some sign. This class, then, also implies the thinghood—or the eventhood—of a sign. A long-term consequence of this will be that Peirce distinguishes between the rules of the material form of the sign itself (the type/token distinction) from the rules of its relation with its object.

So *where* and *when* an index occurs is what makes it indexical, but the where and the when are governed by rules, and these are rules that pertain to the materiality of the medium of the language. Notice, then, that once Peirce applies his classification to a formal notation, both the icon and the index are rule governed. The crucial consequence of this is that it is impossible to specify the symbol by its conventionality. As Vincent Colapietro argues, it is the noncoincidence of "arbitrary" with "conventional" in Peirce's work that marks a major difference with Saussure.[30] *All* the signs of the system are conventional; they are simply distinguished by different conventions governing the criteria of their functionality. Only the symbol is conventional *and* arbitrary.

Peirce adds further criteria to his specification of the index, and they are of the greatest interest. The first of these is that an index "denotes without describing." What this means is that an index has the capacity to establish a referring relation, to install something as object, without predicating anything of that object, save that it is there. It is this property in particular that he uses in his critique of Royce's account of error. The index is a device for conferring objecthood on occasion; nothing is known of its objects save that they are objects, posited by virtue of the referring relation itself. This seems to be an uptake of Kant, in that it distinguishes the problem of the ontology of objects from the concept, or operation, of objecthood. But instead of relying on the mental representation of objecthood, Peirce says that objecthood is a function of certain rules governing certain signs in particular languages.

The second criterion Peirce adds seems to be congruent with the first. In order to accommodate algebraic subscripts, he writes that they "distinguish one value from another without saying what those values are" (W 5:30, p. 163). This is apparently analogous to "denoting without describing," but if so, it construes "denote" in an altogether unexpected way. For whereas "denote" would ordinarily denote the relation of a sign with its object, its construal by "distinguish" reorients it to mean the relation of notness between two objects. Something is not something else. So, since both the thinghood of the sign and the thinghood of the object are mutually entailed in the definition of the index, this construal states the condition of possibility of something's being a sign, of its being an indexical sign, as well as of its being the object of such a sign. Likewise, since the classification of signs is a "distinction of icons, indices and tokens," the same principle accounts for the possibility of being any sort of sign, and of being a sign as distinct, say, from a particle (W 5:30, p. 162). Further, the condition of possibility of repetition—that is, of the difference of a sign from itself on two occurrences—must also be the same, since, as Peirce writes elsewhere, "it is not in the least necessary that the spots should be of different kinds, so long as each is distinguishable from the others" (CP 3:423). It seems to follow, then, that difference is itself the *index of signhood* and that the "index" is the theory of this principle.

The index is the theory of the principle that allows Peirce to distinguish signs from other sorts of three-way relations and that allows him to distinguish each of the three terms of the sign relation, even though they are all of the nature of signs; for it is clear that this relation is construed through a diagram and that the points of that diagram are relationally, but not essentially, distinct. The not-ness principle must be at work whenever Peirce alters his classifications and whenever he considers particular examples for inclusion under them. These developments of indexicality and their consequences will be considered in Chapter 4.

For its part, the icon will become the principle of translation between languages. I shall discuss this issue in Chapter 6. Only on some such principle as this can an algebra count as showing something important for logic in the propositions of natural language that the natural language expressions cannot show. The diagrams of geometry, the formal syntax of an algebraic notation, are manipulated in order to reveal formal, or abstract, relational properties that cannot be represented otherwise. Such diagrams can then be used to compare the properties of two objects that may not otherwise seem alike, for example, the typeface of *p* and *b* considered as spatially displayed forms. This is a technicized version of the issue of comparison. Generalizations that do not hold—misleading metaphors, inaccurate models, mistranslations—can be subjected to the not-ness principle. In order for the index to be mobilized as the instrument of this test, it will be important for Peirce to investigate how the classes of sign work together. As he already begins to do in "On the Algebra of Logic," he will discover why it is important not to seek pure examples of each class, but rather to investigate his examples for their interaction.

Peirce does not always respect the distinction I have drawn between "sign" and "representation," and my distinction may not reliably account for his usage. Frequently we see him hesitate between the two and sometimes attempt to draw a technical distinction between them. Nevertheless, it is the case that "sign" is characteristic of the language of mathematical logic and "representation" of the traditional problematic of philosophy. Furthermore, it remains the case that topics come up for consideration under the sign hypothesis in one of these genres that do not come up in the other. This is true in general because "representation" is a philosophical topic that comes to be applied in the logic for the purposes of a "philosophy of notation"; it is also true for the technical issues concerning the icon and the index that I have been discussing, and in particular for the inclusion of these two classes within the domain of logic. In both cases, the findings are transported across the generic boundary. That there is such a boundary operating in practice is shown by the fact that Peirce devotes considerable effort to eliminating it, and it is no doubt this fact that is responsible for the terminological hesitations mentioned above.

It is this effort that motivates him to accept the challenges that arise for the philosophical investigation of semiotic from the technical application he makes of it in his work on notational systems. The challenges emerge from the examples. Consistently throughout his work, Peirce defines philosophy as needing to draw on no special materials from the special sciences. It considers what we know from common experience. This is true of the examples he uses in the strictly philosophical texts. This range of examples—weathercocks, pointing fingers, paintings, words—is expanded to include such things as algebraic notations and their sub- and superscripts as these enter the common knowledge of philosophy. The special sciences, Peirce will say when he comes to write his "ladders of the sciences," have special objects and techniques, and part of what they must do is to classify them. In this respect, the work he does in formal logic is of the nature of a special science.[31] We see him reflect upon, and analyze, its techniques and their formal competencies, and in "On the Algebra of Logic," for example, we see him classify them under the criteria provided by semiotic. The whole of the notation, in this case, becomes a case study. It is an example, a singular example, and it is used as an exemplar. By this means, it changes irretrievably the definition of the class of things semiotic is concerned with. Take these things as signs, he says; remark how they operate. From that operation of exemplification, something new is learned.

A Vagabond Sign

Route à la campagne, avec arbre.

Country road with tree.
    —Samuel Beckett, *En attendant Godot*

Remembering, then, that philosophy is a science based upon everyday experience, we must not fall into the absurdity of setting down as a datum and
starting-point of philosophy any abstract and simple idea, as Hegel did
when he began his logic with pure Being; but we must set out from ideas familiar and complex, as Hegel began his great masterpiece by considering a
man sitting under a tree in a garden in the afternoon. We must not begin by
talking of pure ideas,—vagabond thoughts that tramp the public roads
without any human habitation,—but must begin with men and their conversation. (CP 8.112)

In 1897–98, Peirce wrote a two-part review of the *Vorlesungen über die
Algebra der Logik* by his close colleague Schröder (CP 3.425–55; 3.456–552).[1]
The review is detailed and technical, but it is framed by the philosophical
issues Peirce needed to raise concerning the paradigm within which he and
Schröder had collaborated. Peirce now repudiates this paradigm on the
grounds that it is formalistic: as such, it relegates content to the outside of
its notations, and hence, Peirce argues, it returns logic to a dualistic—
hence nominalistic—account of signhood. Logic therefore cannot include
within itself the semiosis of representation. In Max Fisch's formulation, this
means that insofar as it entails a theory of reference, that theory is confined
to the backward reference of the sign.[2] The interpretability of formal notations is simply a matter of the recursive application of their own rules; any
change in the knowledge base is effected outside the system of these rules,

and neither affects nor is affected by the system of signs. On Peirce's view, where the object is always already of the nature of a sign, this is unacceptable. If the project of philosophy is to account for the relation between the practical business of inquiry and truth, then it is only by including within the purview of the sign system the whole issue of substantive representation that logic can come to grips with the deep demands of its service to philosophy.

To this end, Peirce renews his attention to "logic viewed as semiotic" and gives up his work in algebraic logic to embark on the development of the existential graphs. These are a system of notation designed to analyze the representational claims of real sentences in real settings. In practice, Peirce is only interested in one specific subset of such sentences, those that constitute the events that advance scientific inquiry; but he chooses to class these sentences as events of "conversation," and he models conversation on the daily interactions that make up ordinary social intercourse. Hence, these reviews can be seen as pursuing the line of inquiry opened by the cognition series and further developed in the work on the logic of science in the period 1873–78.[3] This strategy determines the appearance of a construct that was to become extremely influential: this is "ordinary language." It predates the appearance of the parallel "ordinary experience" that Peirce counts as the material for phenomenology in the work of 1903 and after.

Parallel with his critique of formalism in logic, Peirce was also developing his work in pragmatism. Another review, dated 1901–2, serves to identify these issues (CP 8.100–31). Josiah Royce was a neo-Hegelian idealist whose work was, in Peirce's view, "pragmatical" or "pragmatistical" but not truly "pragmatic," let alone "pragmaticist." Peirce takes him to task on two scores: he has not learned the lessons of logic that Peirce has been trying to teach him since 1885, and he has not come to terms with the difference made by modern scientific practice to the philosophical problem of "cognition." Here too the topic of "conversation" takes its place: never mind "pure ideas," he scolds; philosophical pragmatism must deal in the conversations of men. This is the move that Ian Hacking has identified as the move from "ideas" to "sentences" and hence to a "public" account of knowledge.[4] The two lines of Peirce's work in this period join at this point: pragmatism deals in conversations, and it needs a logic adequate to this task. This logic must be designed to integrate the truth claims of content-laden propositions with an account of the logical instruments that condition them.

In this chapter, I turn my attention to the emerging figure of "ordinary language," to the effects it has on the distinction on which I have relied to this point, between philosophy and logic and to the attendant distinction between "thought" and its "instruments." Is ordinary language an instrument like logical languages? Or does it, on the contrary, give unmediated access to the contents of the mind and hence require no semiotic investigation or description of its own? Since Peirce's project at this point involves a convergence of logic with philosophy, we might hope, as Peirce clearly did, that "ordinary language" will serve to obviate the distinction. To do so, however, Peirce will have to eliminate some deep presuppositions from each of the two genres in which he worked, and it is not clear that this was ever fully achieved. The Schröder reviews are remarkable for demonstrating the difficulty of this task. They are marked by the inevitable tensions that attend a radical enterprise such as this.

To demonstrate these difficulties, I focus on an example from the Schröder review, which can be found in various forms throughout Peirce's writing. This is the vagabond, the tramp, or the traveler, the opposite of the sedentary thinker. The source of this figure is a very long tradition of talk about talk: this is the rhetorical tradition, repudiated by Descartes when he leaves the road and goes home to meditate beside the fire. The tramp is the very figure of semiosis. In Peirce's anti-Cartesian papers, conversation displaces solitary meditation, and the day-to-day practices of inquiry are undertaken, as Peirce will put it in the Harvard Lectures of 1903, on the road.[5] The Peircean scholar walks and talks, making the mistakes that he must make and learning to correct them with further searching. However, the tramp is subject to contradictory valorizations: in the review of Royce's metaphysics, where it appears casually as a metaphor, the "vagabond thoughts that tramp the public roads" are Royce's "pure ideas," and as such, they are rejected as idle, for they do no philosophical work. In the Schröder review, by contrast, it is tramps who provide Peirce's key example of "conversation," the very thing that must command the attention of philosophy. Furthermore, the figure of the tramp appears in a technical setting in Peirce's work, well beyond the range of "ordinary language" and "conversation." Here we find the metaphorics of vagabondage used to describe relatives and continuity, and here we learn that the first condition of signs is errancy—that a sign is not a sign without a touch of the tramp.

"A relative," writes Peirce, "is . . . an icon, or image, without attachments to experience, 'without a local habitation or a name'" (CP 3.459).

> . . . oublier qui je suis, et le nom
> de la ville qui m'abrita hier. . . .

> . . . forgetting who I am, and the name
> of the town that gave me shelter yesterday. . . .
>   (Colette, *La vagabonde*)

But he adds that it does have "indications of the need of such attachments" (CP 3.459), "places where hecceities, denoted by indexical words, may be attached" (CP 3.461). Now, "whether or not there be in the reality any definite separation between the hecceity-element and the idea-element is a question of metaphysics, not of logic" (CP 3.462); with this disclaimer, Peirce marks the party wall between the two genres that he nevertheless attempts to bring together. He does so by getting "logic" to mediate between "mathematics" and "philosophy."

I

> Du fermé à l'ouvert, de l'habitat au passage, de l'asile à l'errance. Ainsi du penseur, ainsi de la pensée.

> From the enclosed to the unclosed, from home to the road, from refuge to roving. So goes it with the thinker, and with thought.
>   —Michel Serres, *Statues: Le second livie des fondations*

A significant aspect of Peirce's review of Schröder's *Vorlesungen* is devoted to redrawing the disciplinary map to this end, with the result that each member of the trio—logic, mathematics, and philosophy—will be assigned its proper object. Peirce opens by discussing some precise technical issues entailed in Schröder's treatment of particular problems.

The third volume of Professor Schröder's *Exact Logic*, which volume bears separately the title I have chosen for this paper, is exciting some interest even in this country. There are in America a few inquirers into logic, sincere and diligent, who are not of the genus that buries its head in the sand—men who devote their thoughts to the study with a view to learning something that they do not yet know, and not for the sake of upholding orthodoxy or any other foregone conclusion. For them this article is written as a kind of popular exposition of the work that is now being done in the field of logic. To them I desire to convey some idea of what the new logic is, how two "algebras," that is, systems of diagrammatical representation by means of letters and other characters, more or less analogous to the algebra of arithmetic, have been invented for the study of relatives, and how Schröder uses one of these (with some aid from the other and from other notations) to solve some interesting problems of reasoning. (CP 3.456)

The reviews are "logic" because they are written as a popular exposition of logic construed as a field of "interesting problems of reasoning" and the notational technologies designed for their solution. But they are also "philosophy," because they raise the eminently philosophical question of the relation of philosophy to logic (CP 3.425). This relation is contentious:

The appearance of Schröder's *Exact Logic* has afforded much gratification to all those homely thinkers who . . . opine that questions of logic ought *not* to be decided on philosophical principles, but on the contrary, that questions of philosophy ought to be decided upon logical principles. (CP 3.425)

"Philosophy" and "logic" do not join in an ideal unity: the pure continuity that the topos of reason should provide them with is rent by genre. And it is rent, too, by time, for Peirce writes that rhetoric is "the study of those general conditions under which a problem presents itself for solution" (is present, becomes present, presents its objects) "and those under which one question leads on from another" (CP 3.430). Research, he goes on, is a "process"; it "advance[s] toward truth," but in its "early stages," this advance may be halted, or slowed, by the prevalence of false opinions. But the "spirit of the age" changes, and history has a "logic" that can force the issue, although "it is not to be expected that any rational opinion about logic will become prevalent among philosophers within a generation" (CP 3.425 passim). Note that "time" is no pure or abstract dimension; it conditions the dynamics of research. Further, not only does research take time to stage its disputes and resolve them; the dispute that most particularly interests Peirce, exemplifying as it does an "epoch of transition" (CP 3.425) in logic, is between two groups, or schools, of philosophers, whose point of contention concerns the question of priority between philosophy and logic. Whether logic, or philosophy, should act as foundation for the other is a question that itself introduces a temporal dimension into the space of reason. So Peirce argues that logic, and thereafter metaphysics, must rest on mathematics, the only science in which "there has never been a prolonged dispute," because the "proper objects" of mathematics being continua and their interruptions, only mathematics can posit, or know, a single dimension innocent of the fall into time (CP 3.425).

Innocent, too, of another fall, for the fall into time is the fall into rhetoric, into the practices of history and of the road of inquiry. Mathematics represents the dream of a certain Platonic transcendence, and its condition in notations, the dream of a language without history or rhetoric, a language whose interpretation does not exceed its rules. This is the dream of transparent representation, neither acting as, nor requiring, an advocate. Perfectly abstract, as if pure form, applicable to anything: having no local habitation; not "positive," and therefore having no stake in empirical truth: neither naming nor named. It is on the basis of these topoi that mathematics is contrasted with logic. Mathematics

is not a positive science. . . .

But logic *begins to be* a positive science, since there are some things in regard to which the logician is not free to suppose that they are or are not. (CP 3.428)

At logic, beginning begins; so too does unfreedom and the rent of negation. Its site is the site of transitions, surprises, questions, disputes. Accordingly, Peirce will make logic include a grammar of assertions and a rhetoric of their interpretation and use. He will also come to recognize that the class of "assertions" is too restricted to include such acts as commands: indeed, it has long been recognized that the work of this period includes the development of a rudimentary account of speech acts.[6] Under these circumstances, grammar and rhetoric cannot be disintricated: the "grammar" of a concept will be elaborated as the grammar of it *taken as act.* The beginnings of these developments can be discerned in the Schröder reviews. This is the framework for logic viewed as semiotic that will include what mathematics excludes: the conversations of men.

On this terrain, philosophy and mathematics themselves converse, and both, being here, are vagrants in their own ways. Peirce will write that mathematical ideas, like poetical ones, "have no habitation and no name," that it is up to the positive sciences to anchor them both in experience; yet he also writes, in the Schröder reviews, that, undisciplined by "exact" logic, philosophy is just talk, that it is the mission of semiotic to settle its endless disputes. Such settlements are the task of the "homely thinker."

But what makes us specially at home with the Greeks is that they made their world their home; the common spirit of homeliness unites us both. In ordinary life we like best the men and families that are homely and contented in themselves, not desiring what is outside. (Hegel, *Lectures on the History of Philosophy*)

Where there is no dispute, there is no barrister,[7] nor any need of one, and Peirce berates with considerable scorn "the way in which certain opinions—or rather a certain verdict—becomes prevalent among philosophical thinkers"; where opinions are arrived at in this way, "reason takes hardly the leading part in the performance" (CP 3.425). The principles of logic and philosophy should be based, Peirce declares in the Schröder reviews, on the only "science in which there has never been a prolonged dispute concerning the proper object of that science" (CP 3.426). That science is mathematics, and despite the fact that mistakes occur not uncommonly and from time to time give rise to veritable disputes, these disputes are not prolonged (CP 3.426). The reason for the "immunity of mathematics . . . arises from the fact that the objects which the mathematician observes and to which his conclusions relate are objects of his mind's own creation" (CP 3.426). Yet it is the use of mathematics as an "exemplar in reasoning" that is the "greatest fault" of Royce and his ilk (CP 8.110).[8] This is why the derided "pure ideas" of Royce and the indispensable icons or images of Peirce can share the same metaphors: in the narrative of cognition, both are located prior to their attachment to experience. There is, then, an "essential difference" between mathematics and metaphysics: mathematical reasoning deals only in hypotheticals, whereas "the metaphysician . . . is engaged in the investigation of matters of fact, and the only way to matters of fact is the way of experience" (CP 8.110). The Roycian philosopher uses mathematics as exemplar; the homely thinker uses it as starting point and guide but must also know its limits. The metaphysician needs the methods of mathematics. But the mathematician can do nothing without the metaphysician, whose province is matters of fact. These facts are to be found on the road of inquiry, whatever the risks entailed. Unlike Hegel's view of the homely philosopher, the Peircean inquirer does desire what lies outside. If safety there be for our two vagabonds on this road, it is only to be found in each other's company.

> Incredibly, in the evening the frail old scholars wander out for a breath of fresh air. They prod the pavement with their sticks like blind wanderers on a snowy steppe. Michael and I encountered a pair of them that evening in Luntz Street, behind Sansur House. They were strolling arm in arm, as if lending each other support in their hostile surroundings. (Amos Oz, *My Michael*)

The "essential difference" between mathematics and metaphysics is "not": the proper object of philosophical inquiry is to discover the difference between what is, and what is not. This is the site of logic, located and mapped by the problematic of the copula. Without this difference, logic is "paradisaical" (CP 3.488); with it, logic serves philosophy, which is concerned not with mathematical, but with *discursive* reason. This is the language spoken by the "homely thinker."

> Logic in this stage of its development may be called *paradisaical logic*, because it represents the state of Man's cognition before the Fall. For although, with this apparatus, it is easy to write propositions necessarily true, it is absolutely impossible to write any which is necessarily false, or, in any way which that stage of logic affords, to find out that anything is false . . . plainly without a knowledge of falsehood no development of discursive reason can take place. (CP 3.488)

Not, we might say, is the condition of philosophy; it is a condition that is otherwise known as rhetoric, for it is the terrain of dispute. And note that the object is not pure reason but "discursive reason": dealing in conversation, logic necessarily deals in error.

Fr. *errer*: to wander, roam, or rove. (Harrap's *French–English Dictionary*)

Engl. *err*: (1) to wander from the right way, to deviate from the true course; to fail morally. . . . (2) to blunder; to be mistaken or wrong; to fall into error. (3) to wander, to ramble, to go astray (obs.). (Webster's dictionary)

errancy: (1) the state of being in error; containing errors. (2) a tendency to fall into error; fallibility. (Webster's dictionary)

errand: (1) a verbal message; a communication to be carried to some person at a distance (arch.) (2) a trip to carry a message or do a definite thing. . . . (3) the thing to be done on such a trip, e.g., buying or selling some item. (Webster's dictionary)

errant: (1) wandering, roving, as of knights seeking adventure. (2) in zoology, of or pertaining to the errantia (= free-swimming annelids) (3) deviating from the regular course; erring; wrong. (4) itinerant, formerly applied to judges who travelled on a circuit. (Webster's dictionary)

erratic: (1) wandering, having no certain course, roving about without a fixed destination, irregular. (etc.) (Webster's dictionary)

erratum: an error or mistake in writing or printing. The list of errata of a book is usually printed at the beginning or end, with references indicating the pages of lines on which they occur. "A single erratum may knock out the brains of a whole passage"—Cowper. (Webster's dictionary)

error: (1) the state of believing what is untrue, incorrect, or wrong. (2) a mistake in judgment. . . . (3) something incorrectly done through ignorance. (4) a transgression of law or duty. . . . (5) in law, a mistake in the proceedings of a court of record either in fact or in law, frequently of such a nature as to entitle the unsuccessful party to have the case reviewed. (6) a wandering, excursion, irregular course (obs.). (7) the difference between the approximate or computed result of an operation and the true value, as in mathematics; also called "true error." (Webster's dictionary)

law of error: a law which connects the relative magnitude of errors with their frequency. (Webster's dictionary)

unerring: (1) free from error. (2) not missing or failing; sure, certain, exact. (Webster's dictionary)

Mistakes in mathematics occur not infrequently, and not being detected give rise to false doctrine, which may continue for a long time. Thus, a mistake in the evaluation of a definite integral by Laplace, in his *Mécanique céleste*, led to an erroneous doctrine.

So, several demonstrations in the first book of Euclid, notably that of the sixteenth proposition, are vitiated by the erroneous assumption that a part is necessarily less than its whole. These remained undetected until after the theory of the non-Euclidian geometry had been completely worked out; but since that time, no mathematician has defended them. (CP 3.426)

Hence, we homely thinkers believe that, considering the immense amount of disputation there has always been concerning the doctrines of logic, and especially concerning those which would otherwise be applicable to settle disputes concerning the accuracy of reasonings in metaphysics, the safest way is to appeal for our logical principles to the science of mathematics, where error can only long go unexploded on condition of its not being suspected. (CP 3.427)

Logic may be defined as the science of the laws of the stable establishment of beliefs. Then, *exact* logic will be that doctrine of the conditions of establishment of stable belief which rests upon perfectly undoubted observations and upon mathematical, that is, upon *diagrammatical*, or, *iconic*, thought. We, who are sectaries of "exact" logic, and of "exact" philosophy, in general, maintain that those who follow such methods will, so far as they follow them, escape all error except such as will be speedily corrected after it is once suspected. (CP 3.429)

Professor Schröder and I have a common method which we shall ultimately succeed in applying to our differences, and we shall settle them to our common satisfaction; and when that method is pouring in upon us new and incontrovertible positively valuable results, it will be as nothing to either of us to confess that where he had not yet been able to apply that method he has fallen into error. (CP 3.455)

It may be doubted whether many of the lower animals have any clear and steady conception of falsehood; for their instincts work so unerringly that there is little to

force it upon their attention. Yet plainly without a knowledge of falsehood no development of discursive reason can take place. (CP 3.488)

So much of the general logical doctrine of quantity has been here given, in order to
illustrate the power of the logic of relatives in enabling us to treat with unerring
confidence the most difficult conceptions, before which mathematicians have
heretofore shrunk appalled. (CP 3.551)

—et nous errions, nourris du vin des cavernes et du biscuit de la route, moi pressé
de trouver le lieu et la formule.

—and we wandered, with tavern wine from caverns and ship's biscuit for the road,
mine was a hurried search for the place and for its word. (Arthur Rimbaud,
"Vagabonds")

A mathematician, one might be led to suppose, is the human returned to
paradise, and like the lower animals, innocent of falsehood. Peirce holds
that "logic ought to draw upon mathematics for control of disputed principles;" this would establish on a firm basis those "doctrines of logic . . .
which would be applicable to settle disputes concerning the accuracy of
reasonings in metaphysics" (CP 3.427).

The argument for this precept relies on more than the claim that
mathematics is "immune" (CP 3.426) from dispute. The sciences are
species of the genus science, and "if anything is true of a whole genus of
objects, this truth may be adopted as a principle in studying every species
of that genus. Whatever is true of a species will form a datum for the discovery of the wider truth which holds of the whole genus" (CP 3.427). The
differentia of the sciences are their levels of abstractness. Now if mathematics is the most abstract, Peirce argues, it provides the abstract principles
informing "science"—all of science, any science—all the way down the
track: an unerring path for getting home. The species may go off this track
when they introduce "observations," dealing with "experience," "reality,"
"every-day life," or just the "applicability of language" (CP 3.428). Off the
track of abstract mathematical certainty lie assertion and denial, doubt and
falsehood. Yet it is exactly this track of mathematical argument that Peirce
decides to leave when he rejects the principles of Cartesian rigor in favor of
the multiform arguments of empirical science.[9]

The differentia introduced by the species—by the very fact that
there are species, that most of the sciences are in some particular *not* mathematics—introduce differences of opinion, questions, doubts, inquiry, disputes, that cannot be settled on mathematical principles. Hence the relatively modest place accorded by Peirce to deduction in scientific inquiry,

and the relatively greater importance in the design and calculation of data of probability theory and hypothesis formation.

But probability theory does not settle all the disputes left over after the mathematics of continua has done its work, and the experimental method and hypothesis have done theirs. Some questions may still persist—for example, questions that arise at the threshold of philosophy, the beginning of discursive reason, which logic investigates by investigating the "unlimited applicability of language." Does this mean that Peirce will investigate language? No, and yes. Writing about Peirce at the end of the century of linguistics, we might seek some parallel for ordinary language in Peirce's work to the "philosophy of notation" that he uses to elucidate the algebra of 1885 or the existential graphs thereafter. We find it only after the developments of 1903, when Peirce insists on the indexical properties of certain parts of speech; but he goes no further. Attention to the applicability of language is not necessarily attention to language. Yet the move he announces in these papers, to treat assertions as acts rather than as propositions, entails a move to reconceive the project of "grammar" so as to account for the machinery of talk. Language becomes visible under this regime, though it sometimes slips from view. This is a difficulty in the Schröder papers, one that we can watch at work.

A difference between Peirce and Schröder concerns the meaning of the phrase "exact logic." Is it coextensive with mathematics, or is it "positive" and hence capable of dealing with negation and falsehood? Peirce's view is spelled out in two forms, in both of which he returns to his work of the 1870s in which inquiry is analyzed in terms of "doubt" and "belief." Hence, he takes the object of logic as "beliefs." Of these two formulations, the first serves his argument concerning the reliance of logic upon mathematics:

Logic may be defined as the science of the laws of the stable establishment of beliefs. Then, *exact* logic will be that doctrine of the conditions of establishment of stable belief which rests upon perfectly undoubted observations and upon mathematical, that is, upon *diagrammatical*, or, *iconic*, thought. (CP 3.429)

The second raises the problem of language; it is this formulation that makes of the threshold of philosophy the *abri* of semiotic:

"Exact" logic, in its widest sense, will (as I apprehend) consist of three parts. For it will be necessary, first of all, to study those properties of beliefs which belong to them as beliefs, irrespective of their stability. This will amount to what Duns Scotus called *speculative grammar*. For it must analyse an assertion into its essential elements, independently of the structure of the language in which it may happen to be expressed. It will also divide assertions into categories according to their essential differences. The second part will consider to what conditions an assertion must conform in order that it correspond to the "reality," that is, in order that the belief it expresses may be stable. This is what is more particularly understood by the word *logic*. It must consider, first, *necessary*, and second, *probable* reasoning. Thirdly, the general doctrine must embrace the study of those general conditions under which a problem presents itself for solution and those under which one question leads to another. As this completes a triad of studies, or trivium, we might, not inappropriately, term the last study *Speculative rhetoric*. This division was proposed in 1867 by me, but I have often designated this third part as *objective logic*. (CP 3.430)

Of these two formulations of the scope of "exact logic," the second, "proposed in 1867" and maintained with minor modifications throughout his writing, is the one that Peirce uses to sign his difference with his colleague: "Dr. Schröder's Logic is not intended to cover all this ground."

By the phrase "exact logic" upon his title page, he means logic treated algebraically. Although such treatment is an aid to exact logic, as defined on the last page, it is certainly not synonymous with it. The principal utility of the algebraic treatment is stated by him with admirable terseness: it is "to set this discipline free from the fetters in which language, by force of custom, has bound the human mind." (CP 3.431)

Contrast Peirce's belief in the safety and stability offered by a home base for logic in mathematics, with Schröder's view that algebra "sets this discipline free"; contrast, more pointedly, Schröder's view that it is "language" that binds the human mind in "fetters" with Peirce's view that this very same language, its "unlimited applicability," furnishes the very facts with which logic is concerned (CP 3.428). This is a contrast between the status of language in the Peirce–Schröder paradigm and the status it comes to acquire in Peirce's "logic viewed as semiotic." Yet Peirce is not saying here that an assertion is a discursive sequence, a melodic form and a string of phonemes; he is not saying that the words used and their order are what matter to the philosopher. He is concerned with the "properties of beliefs" independently of the structure of the language in which they happen to be expressed. I reiterate: *independently* of the structure of the language in which they happen to be expressed.

This difficulty with the status of language can be attributed to the generic habits of philosophy: there is something about the philosophical *place* of logic that prevents "language" from being an object of investigation, that prevents us asking of language, as we do of notations and telescopes, how it works, what it enables, and what it constrains. Somehow philosophy has us believe—makes it impossible not to believe—that the mind is born free, though everywhere it be in chains. Philosophy's dream that logic might loose these fetters is the persistence of the governance of logic, even "exact" logic, by the rhetorical topoi of metaphysics and the place they give to "mind" or "reason." Belief is a mere variant of this topos. The material conditions of the practice of human language come to be, as Stanley Cavell has put it, "lost in thought."[10]

Philosophy's dream is Schröder's, and it appears to be Peirce's. Yet we must doubt this, for language, though notwithstanding that it is to be stripped away, is also the very stuff upon which the philosopher of signs will go to work. Let us pursue the detail of his differences with Schröder.

One of these differences will serve as a case study in the problem:

Professor Schröder endeavours to give the most general formula of a logical problem. It is in dealing with such very general and fundamental matters that the exact logician is most in danger of violating his own principles of exactitude. To seek a formula for all logical problems is to ask what it is, in general terms, that men inquire. To answer that question, my own logical proceeding would be—

(note, here, how Peirce shifts the generality of Schröder's project into the specificity of a form of language—)

to note that it asks what the essence of a question, in general, is. Now a question is a rational contrivance or device, and in order to understand any rational contrivance,—

(notice, here, the focus on the instruments of reasoning, as distinct from the nature of reason—)

experience shows that the best way is to begin by considering what circumstances of need prompted the contrivance,—

(and note the pragmatism of the shift, the analogy one might draw between language and, for example, weathercocks—)

and then upon what general principle its action is designed to fill that need. (CP 3.515)

Schröder looks for "general formulas," while Peirce finds little "virtue" in them (CP 3.515). Rather, a question is a "rational contrivance or device"—like a microscope, or an algebraic icon—that is "designed to fill a need." It is "an indication suggestive . . . of what has to be thought about in order to satisfy some more or less pressing want." It is, therefore, governed by the practice from which it emerges; moreover, it is "hypnotic" (CP 3.515), that is, it takes charge of the work of the mind. "Different questions," he goes on "are so very unlike that the only way to get much idea of the nature of the problem is to consider the different cases separately" (CP 3.516). It would seem that the upshot of Peirce's disagreement with Schröder is to suggest that there is no such thing as a "general formula," that "the essence of a question, in general" is that it is never general, that it arises in specific forms for specific needs. Now, although Peirce does not "think [that this] answer . . . affords any particularly precious suggestion"—that is, it does not, he thinks, lead to a further question as to the nature of questions—we may well wonder if the "action" of questions is not crucially bound up with the "forms of [their] expressions" (CP 3.516), and whether this means, for example, the terms that suggest "what has to be thought about." Peirce does not take up this further question, except to characterize his answer as "ordinary" (CP 3.515) and then to contrast it with Schröder's "very different ideas upon these matters" (CP 3.517–19). Peirce's conclusion is that

the invention of [Schröder's] solution exhibits in a high degree that very effective ingenuity which the solution itself so utterly lacks, owing to its resting on no correct conception of the nature of problems in general and of their solutions and of the meaning of a proposition. (CP 3.519)

Peirce's critique of Schröder is an early example of what has come to be known as the "linguistic turn,"[11] that technique of pragmatism also known as ordinary language philosophy which so disturbs the foundationalism of any architectonic project that would ground the *prima philosophia* in an unmediated first principle such as intuition or sensation. Peirce's objection to Schröder is that mathematical language is so specialized that it is incapable of formulating the kind of generality Schröder aspires to. Peirce, on the other hand, uses ordinary language, and his claim is that his method captures the specificity of kinds of problems in their pragmatic settings.

Following his reformulation of the question of the general form of a question, in ordinary language, Peirce feels compelled to defend himself against the charge that it is incompatible with the work of a mathematical logician:

Ideas like those of this statement, and not talk about ⱷx, and "roots," and the like, must, in my opinion, form the staple of a logical analysis and useful description of a problem, in general. I am none the less a mathematical logician for that. If of two students of the theory of numbers one should insist upon considering numbers as expressed in a system of notation like the Arabic (though using now one number as base of the numeration, and now another), while the other student should maintain that all that was foreign to the theory of numbers, which ought not to consider upon what system the numbers with which it deals are expressed, those two students would, to my apprehension, occupy positions analogous to that of Schröder and mine in regard to this matter of the formulation of the problems of logic; and supposing the student who wished to consider the forms of expression of numbers were to accuse the other of being wanting in the spirit of an arithmetician, that charge would be unjust in quite the same way in which it would be unjust to charge me with deficiency in the mathematical spirit on account of my regarding the conceptions of "values," and "roots," and all that as very special ideas, which can only lumber up the field of consciousness with such hindrances as it is the very end and aim of that diagrammatic method of thinking that characterises the mathematician to get rid of. (CP 3.515)

The simple form of this defense is that nothing turns on the use of algebraic formulas. The "very special ideas" attached to algebras are not the sine qua non of mathematical work. This is the same point as Peirce relies on to distinguish his definition of "exact logic" from Schröder's:

By the phrase "exact logic" upon his title page, he means logic treated algebraically. Although such treatment is an aid to exact logic, . . . it is certainly not synonymous with it. (CP 3.431)

Exactly what is "language" in the ordinary language strategy? To gauge the force of this question, we need to reconsider the details of the defense, which relies on an analogy. "The student who wished to consider the forms of expression of numbers" is correlated with Schröder; the one for whom those forms are "foreign to the theory" is correlated with Peirce. But the analogy is a little problematic. For here, the "Peirce" figure is in the position of *disregarding* the "forms of expression of numbers," just as, in his own definition of exact logic, Peirce says its first branch "must analyse an assertion into its essential elements, independently of the structure of the language in which it may happen to be expressed" (CP 3.430). Yet elsewhere, "By *logical* reflection, I mean thoughts in their expressions" (CP 3.490), not "vagabond thought" but "the conversations of men." And here, when considering a question as "a rational contrivance or device," Peirce begins "by considering what circumstances of need prompted the contrivance, and then upon what general principle its action is designed to fill that need." Its action is designed.

At first glance, the dispute between Schröder and Peirce is merely a dispute between two forms of notation—the algebra and the topological notation that Peirce is beginning to develop. In Peirce's view, algebras confine investigation by restricting its matter to mathematical ideas, whereas the virtue of the topological option is that it works on the material provided by familiar "conversation." The existential graphs, on this view, are a very simple procedure, since their business is just to analyze the relative properties of ordinary language predicates. Thus Peirce can claim to marry the certainties of mathematical method with the scope of ordinary language, and to provide the desideratum of the "homely thinker." This is the stability, the certainty, of the unerring procedures of mathematics, applied to the familiar, undoubted observations of ordinary language. But Peirce shares with Schröder the desire to "set the human mind free"; it is merely their methods that differ. Peirce's method frees the mind from the "very special ideas, which can only lumber up the field of consciousness with . . . hindrances." He appears to be claiming that "the diagrammatic method of thinking" gives the human mind unencumbered access to itself and to its contents. Just as the theory of numbers is independent of any particular "form of expression of numbers," so is speculative grammar independent of the structure of any language and, it would appear, of the diagrammatical techniques of its own analytical method. But the intertextualities of Peirce's writings question this view, because the premises established by the anti-Cartesian papers include "that we have no power of thinking without signs" (W 2:22, p. 213). So in the process of answering the charge that he is not acting in conformity with the ideals of a mathematician, Peirce's defense raises two questions, which are perhaps the same: (1) is "the diagrammatic method of thinking" primarily *thinking*?—or is it an "action designed" by the principles of diagrammatization, a contrivance and a device? And (2) what is the relation of the structure of thought to which it gives access to the "structure of language" from which it is said to be independent? What kind of thing is a "thought-sign"? Is "independence" an adequate description of its relation with the language which can be stripped from it by an alternative form of representation, say, a graph? Would this not be, rather, the "translation" discussed by the "philosopher of notation"? This is a question, but it is not, here, Peirce's question. It is mine, and it is the same question as the one that emerged from consideration of the dream of iconicity, where Peirce loses, momentarily, his grasp on the difference between the sign and its object. In the text of the Schröder reviews, this question has neither design nor action. It is an ambiguity, a difficulty, perhaps what he would call a "need," although it has not begun to press. Let us call it a question nonetheless, since that is what it has become through the work of reading. It is a question that appears to disappear under certain conditions.

Appears, only to disappear—

at length he appeared again pennyless as before; but never informed even those whom he seemed to regard most, where he had been nor was his Retreat ever discovered. (Dr. Johnson, *The Life of Richard Savage*)

—and doing so, at once reveals and conceals something of a conundrum.

Let us take the matter of its conditions first. They are generic, but paradoxically so, for while it is in formal logic that the philosopher of signs is drawn to attend to the "forms of expression" of his language, whether algebraical or topological, this logician is intent on retrieving ordinary language from the stripping away that it suffers under a formal notation. At the same time, the logical graphs are designed as an alternative tool with which to grasp the "forms of expression" of thoughts, yet it is in philosophy, conducted *in* and *on* ordinary language that "thoughts in their expressions" become once more mere thoughts.

The question of language is confined by the question of its applicability: "the logician is forced by positive observation to admit that there is such a thing as doubt, that some propositions are false, etc." (CP 3.428). Logic—philosophical logic—is not free not to ask this question. It is determined to it, and thereafter by it, by its place in customary philosophy. Before he defines logic, Peirce defines philosophy:

it makes no special observations, as every other positive science does, yet it does deal with reality. It confines itself, however, to the universal phenomena of experience; and these are, generally speaking, sufficiently revealed in the ordinary observations of every-day life. (CP 3.428)

Thereafter, "reality" and "experience" are construed through "belief" (CP 3.429) and can come under investigation in the form of "assertions" and "questions" by a general—that is, speculative—semiotic, but only under the conditions required by a speculative philosophy: stripped of language to reveal the universal structure of "the experience of reality." Universal.

The general form of an assertion or a question. And it is this question that, Peirce tells us in the second Schröder paper, is meaningless (CP 3.514).

How does this inconsistency arise? The movement of the passage is complex: from the "abstract" (anything goes) to the "positive" (not anything goes), then back from the positive ("concrete reality"; CP 3.428) to reveal the universal. This universal is available for "algebraic treatment," as if the "abstractness" of mathematics and the universality posited by metaphysics are joined in the absence of language. Together, they form the claim to generality that Peirce so berates in Schröder, a bedrock, indubitable generality that would overlook exactly what, elsewhere, he insists we look at: "the forms of expression," the systems of notation in which, for example, the "interesting problems" of logic emerge and can be solved.

Let us consider, again, this passage, this threshold, where logic leaves mathematics to become philosophy—the very same threshold where mathematics meets up with philosophy, to found semiotic logic in their conversation: "The principal utility of the algebraic treatment . . . is 'to set this discipline free from the fetters in which language, by force of custom, has bound the human mind.'" Notice the slippage: is it the "discipline of logic" that is to be set free, or is it "the human mind"? The difference between them is elided by the habits of philosophy. When the logician accepts the identity between the discipline of logic and the mind, he is invoking the figure of Reason, finding in metaphysics the topos that has always set his topics. This topos elides language—language in general, the accidents, the aberrant behavior, the constraining power of particular languages, their customs—elides it from the topics of logic, even in the widest sense. This topos is the sign of Philosophy—not just its sign, but its motor, the constraining force of its custom.

The customs of mathematics have their own force: they make the forms of particular languages appear. But at this threshold, they appear, to disappear. Which, at the liminal spaces of their errant routes—doorways, gateways, fences, and frontiers—is exactly what tramps do, leaving behind them, if we can believe Peirce's description of rural Pennsylvania, a minute, but significant, trace of their passing.

II

Logic "does not concern itself with any facts not implied in the supposition of an unlimited applicability of language" (CP 3.428). Nor does it concern itself with "the structure of the language in which [an assertion] may happen to be expressed" (CP 3.430). What it does concern itself with is "the applicability of language"; truth is something that we *say*. "We": it has its history and its pragmatics, which Peirce defines as the problematic of belief and its assertion. And "say": it has an empirical material form; it is not an "idea" or a disembodied "thought" or even a "proposition." But Peirce abstracts away from the empirical material form, its history, its morphophonetics, its syntax, its lexicon, to discover behind them, though given by them, its "essential elements" (CP 3.430), a "nature," "certain properties" of which the student of logic is "conscious, in some out-of-focus fashion" (CP 3.432). To bring these into focus is the task of logic in its widest sense, that is, of semiotic. It consists of logic proper, of grammar, and of rhetoric.

Logic, in its familiar, narrow, sense, "will consider to what conditions an assertion must conform in order that it may correspond with the 'reality,' that is, in order that the belief it expresses may be stable" (CP 3.430). Detached from its place in the broad scope of speculative semiotic, the "belief" expressed could just as well be a "proposition." But it is not so detached. In its place, within the project of "logic, in its widest sense," it is a "belief," held by people "in situation," as Sartre would put it, located in pragmatic circumstances. Among these people "familiar with the use of language . . . able to converse . . . and so to express . . . doubt" (CP 3.432), propositions have no place. Literally. They have no local habitation. The conversations of these people consist—among a range of other speech acts[12]—of assertions and questions, the latter of which, as we now know, are rhetorical devices designed for particular needs. When logic in its widest sense includes grammar and rhetoric, logic in its narrow, disciplinary sense must lend itself to this broader project. It must, that is to say, do business with language.

> But tell me,
> who are they
> these vagabonds? (Rilke, "Fifth Elegy" from *Duino Elegies*)

> We coted them on the way, and
> hither are they coming to offer you service.
> (Shakespeare, *Hamlet*)

"Language" is an itinerant word, and language has a peripatetic history across a range of disciplines. As I have been using it, it is misleading, suggesting a unified object and hence a contradiction in Peirce's discussion of that object. But it is at least two objects, each elaborated through a different history. On the one hand, "language" is elaborated in the philological tradition and in mathematics by the notion of "a" language, an "algebra," different from some other algebra and able to be mapped on to it only on the basis of explicitly elaborated protocols of translation. A language in this tradition is described semio-logically as a rule-governed system of signs, each a formal–material unit distinct from the others and formally—that is, functionally—related with them. The "meaning" of any sign is just what it can do in the system. On the other hand, "language" is elaborated in the scholastic and Aristotelian tradition as the problem of predication. We might say, abbreviating wildly, that the first of these provides the ground for the structuralist project to describe linguistic systems, whereas the latter provides the ground for the much older tradition of subject–predicate grammars.

This distinction comes to correlate approximately with the distinction between "the system" and its "use." Working within the structuralist paradigm, Benveniste, to take just this example, seeks to articulate the two by separating *langue* from *discours*, making the former the object of a semio-logical description and the latter the object of a "semantics" that retrieves the whole Aristotelian problematic of the attribution of predicates to subjects by an act of enunciation.[13]

On the assumption that the concept of *langue* is developed on the model of the construction and description of formal notations as systems of functional differential values, it is remarkable that to describe what a language is, Saussure produces on one occasion a seriously reductive analogy. A language, he writes, is "something like a dictionary" of which identical copies are deposited in the brains of its speakers.[14] Already possible for Saussure, this became one of the standard construals of the model, representing it primarily as a theory of the lexicon. A further reduction allows this lexicon to consist only of the categorematics.[15] Under this interpretation, "a language" is not a system of negative differences; it is primarily a classification of the *ideas* of a culture, and they can be arranged in a system by a simple method of dichotomization.[16] This is a Ramist reading, and a Ramist project,[17] because it relies on dichotomies and is a method of analysis of ideas. Ramism and its long inheritance make a language a set of words, and this set a "topical logic"; they make the meanings of words the ideas they conjure up or denote; they make the "system" of those ideas the mentality of an age, a people, or a nation.

Saussure's very careful development elsewhere of the notion of the "signified" works against this kind of reading with admirable precision,[18] but it could not prevent it. Without the structuralist overlay of the system of binary oppositions signifying a structured cultural content, it is not significantly different from what Wittgenstein calls the "picture theory" of language and is disabled by the same limitations.[19]

That aspect of the picture theory that relies on the notion of definable mental contents, or ideas, is no doubt as old as Plato; but such things receive a particular inflection as "pictures" under the neoplatonist Ramist influence. Under that influence, too, with the reduction of logic to the general topoi and the consequent marginalization of the problem of the proposition, this becomes the model for the lexicon, and the lexicon takes on the status of the only question of language that arises in philosophy when the base *in discourse* of the problems of metaphysics becomes invisible. Lexical items are thought of as translating mental contents, and the issues for philosophy are how we form these contents and whether they are true. In place of this, Wittgenstein proposes that languages are social games, the playing of which relies on learned behavior.[20] At times Peirce, too, refuses the reduction, claiming, for example, to retrieve the Aristotelian orthodoxy by insisting on the discursive condition of predication (W 2:22, p. 231). But Peirce is no proto-Wittgenstein, despite his insistence on the communal conduct of science, and he retains within his proposal for a general semiotic a theory of the predicate word, the "term," in which the Ramist inheritance persists intact. What it is that we "apply" or attribute to an object by means of a proposition is

familiar images, pictures, or, we might almost say, *dreams*—that is, reminiscences of sights, sounds, feelings, tastes, smells, or other sensations, now quite detached from the original circumstances of their first occurrence, so that they are free to be attached to new occasions.

The "image which [the assertion] is expected to excite in the mind of the receiver" is also

a sign by resemblance, or, as we say, an *icon*—of the similar image in the mind of the deliverer, and through that also a sign of the real quality of the thing. But instead of a single *icon*, or sign by resemblance of a familiar image or "dream," evocable at will, there may be a complexus of such icons, forming a composite image of which the whole is not familiar. But though the whole is not familiar, yet not only are the parts familiar images, but there will also be a familiar image of its mode of composition. (CP 3.433)

"Language" as the universal, or even as the culturally constrained capacity, of the human mind to form ideas; "language" as the general form of discourse; "languages" as technologies of translation; language as both what logic must account for, and what it must strip away. . . . Language, as I have said, is a vagabond word, an itinerant worker that turns up in each of these domains to tinker with their problems.

Similar remarks apply to "sign." Most of its odd jobs, in Peirce's writing, are involved in contesting idealism and Cartesianism. This is so, whether it is insisting that science is the "businesses of living men" conversing together, or whether it is objecting to "setting down as a datum and starting-point of philosophy any abstract and simple idea" (CP 8.112) such as "complete doubt" (W 2:22, p. 212) or "pure Being" (CP 8.112). We set out—we cannot do otherwise—from where we are "with all the prejudices which we actually have when we enter upon the study of philosophy" (W 2:22, p. 212); and the road of inquiry cannot be traveled alone (W 2:22, pp. 241–42) or in silence (W 2:22, p. 231). But in that case, we must inquire into what "language" is for the pragmatic philosopher. For the "grammar" of the Schröder papers is a theory of assertions conducted "independently of the structure of the language in which [they] may happen to be expressed" (CP 3.430).[21] Perhaps it is a theory of the "beliefs" (CP 3.429) those assertions express,[22] an object that, like "thoughts" and "ideas," has no notation, an object the notational conditions of whose existence can be overlooked by the "homely thinker" who shares the philosophers' dream of setting the discipline of logic free from the fetters in which language, by force of custom, has bound the human mind.

Some of the odd jobs performed by "sign" are involved in this very task, of freeing the mind of "language" by asserting the primacy of its ties with "ideas." The paradox of Peirce's semiotic lies in this fact: at the heart of his categorial system, firstness is—and remains throughout his writings—the universe of

mere Ideas, those airy nothings to which the mind of poet, pure mathematician, or another, *might* give local habitation and a name within that mind. Their very airy-nothingness, the fact that their Being consists in mere capability of getting thought, not in anybody's Actually thinking them, saves their Reality. (CP 6.455)

Of course, icons are not examples of pure firstness, since they are signs and as such have the specificity, the constrained particularity needed to serve as "contrivances and devices" in inquiry. Yet their analysis in terms of the categorial system guarantees this tie with the universe of "ideas" in the form of "images, pictures . . . dreams . . . reminiscences of . . . sensations." Such things are the meaning of an icon; they are lodged in minds.

Nevertheless, we can question the "airy-nothingness" of these very same "ideas"; Peirce does so himself by calling them "vagabond thoughts that tramp the public roads" (CP 8.112). Nothing ethereal or Platonic here: very down to earth and in the world. Public, too, unlike the *cogito*, and, like as not, carried along by, acting in, and sometimes making history. But vagabond, yes, undisciplined and therefore outlawed by the "candid and disciplined minds" that settle the disputes of science. These tramps give us an alternative way of construing the troublesome terms and mental icons that Peirce clings to as he clings to a whole tradition of philosophy that in other ways he contests so vigorously. They make us attend, not to the fact that they are "dreams—reminiscences of sights, sounds, feelings, tastes, smells and other sensations," but to the fact that they are "quite detached from the original circumstances of their first occurrence, so that they are free to be attached to new occasions" (CP 3.433). Tramps, like "writing,"[23] do not belong in any one place: they can be pinned down neither to any particular habitation—a "context"—nor to any given name—a "signature."[24] The condition of language is *citation, iterability*. Notwithstanding certain habits, customary ways of formulating its problems, that we find characteristic of philosophy, the pragmatic philosopher has taken language out of the ideal realm, out of the mind, and set it on the road.

For the purposes of pragmatism, walking and talking are paired as a result of the focus on consequences arising in real time. However, in the Royce review, Peirce tries to separate walking from talking, for the "vagabond thoughts" are undisciplined: pragmatism is interested solely, it seems, in trained and purposive talking, in a laboratory, or on the road of inquiry. But *undisciplined* walking, indeed, *strolling*, also reappears, as does a certain kind of urbane but not purposive conversation, as if the very separation of one from the other—of research from reflective musing—would undermine the project of pragmatism. This is because in Peirce's account of inquiry, the whole process rests on the creative lateralities of hypothesis and iconicity. The errancy of signs is playful:

There is a certain agreeable occupation of mind which, from its having no distinctive name, I infer is not as commonly practiced as it deserves to be; for indulged in moderately—say through some five or six percent of one's waking time, perhaps during a stroll—it is refreshing enough more than to repay the expenditure. Because it involves no purpose save that of casting aside all serious purpose, I have sometimes been half-inclined to call it reverie with some qualification; but for a frame of mind so antipodal to vacancy and dreaminess such a designation would be too excruciating a misfit. In fact, it is Pure Play. Now, Play, we all know, is a lively exercise of one's powers. Pure Play has no rules, except this very law of liberty. It bloweth where it listeth. . . . If one's observations and reflections are allowed to specialize themselves too much, the Play will be converted into scientific study; and that cannot be pursued in odd half hours. (CP 6.458–59)

If opposition there be between "musement" (CP 6.458–59) and "scientific study," it is the opposition between "strolling" and walking purposefully down the straight, Cartesian way out of the forest. It is between the errant and the disciplined. Peirce does not outlaw the former; on the contrary, both are ways of finding things. But he knows he can't get very far in solitary wordless meditation "dans un poêle."[25]

He also knows he must start out from where he is, with all the baggage of complex and familiar ideas with which he is always already laden:

Remembering, then, that philosophy is a science based on everyday experience, we must not fall into the absurdity of setting down as a datum and starting-point of philosophy any abstract and simple idea, as Hegel did when he began his logic with pure Being; but we must set out from ideas familiar and complex, as Hegel began his greater masterpiece by considering a man sitting under a tree in a garden in the afternoon. (CP 8.112)

Setting out, then, from an idea familiar and complex, Peirce quotes from Hegel: is the man he finds in the pages of the greater masterpiece sitting, like Descartes, in the pose of solitary meditation? Is he a sedentary dreamer? In Hegel, he is not *sitting* at all; nor is he self-evidently in a garden[26]:

"Here" is, e.g., the tree. If I turn round, this truth has vanished and is converted into its opposite: "No tree is here, but a house instead." "Here" itself does not vanish; on the contrary, it abides constant in the vanishing of the house, the tree, etc., and is indifferently house or tree. Again, therefore, the "This" shows itself to be a *mediated simplicity*, or a *universality*.

Pure being remains, therefore, as the essence of this sense-certainty, since sense-certainty has demonstrated in its own self that the truth of its object is the universal.

Peirce has misremembered Hegel's text, with its abundance of pure ideas— pure being and the like—and has quoted it as if it represented the "homely thinker." So homely, indeed, that it more closely resembles Hegel's ideal of the Greeks, who stay at home, than the people of the road.

Because quotations and citations, reminiscences and the like, "are free to be attached to new occasions," let us take this thinker out of his place in Peirce's text, out of the context provided by the opposition between the garden and the road. Let us set him down closer to the fence, where he might cease to be the picture of a middle-class gentleman taking a postprandial nap. Detached from the circumstances not only of his first, but of his second occurrence, he is now free to appear as a *sans-abri*, stopped in the shade for a spell, or a yarn.

> Route à la campagne, avec arbre.
>
> Country road with tree. (Beckett, *En attendant Godot*)

> —Je dormais. Pourquoi tu ne me laisses jamais dormir?
> —Je me sentais seul.

> —I was asleep. Why don't you ever let me sleep?
> —I was lonely. (Beckett, *En attendant Godot*)

It is not in the habits of such people—or at least, not in the literary tradition that I quote—to travel the roads alone: even Peirce's "musement" is a "communion of the self and the self," a "lively give and take" (CP 6.459). But Peirce is a singular old fellow, with a singular nonsingular idea of the self.[27] Tramps, like scientists and philosophers, converse in the language of their common business. Peirce uses them as an example, in his conversation with Schröder.

This conversation, it will be recalled, concerns among other things the scope of "exact logic." Peirce makes his claim for logic viewed as semiotic by invoking a dispute current among philosophical logicians of the day: the dispute as to the foundations of logic. He quotes Schröder's view derisively: "the last anchor-hold of logic he makes to lie in the correctness of a feeling!" (CP 3.432); then, in answer to the question why such a foolish view would be adopted, he quotes Schröder's use of Sigwart's justification: "in this way Sigwart escapes the necessity of founding logic upon the theory of cognition" (CP 3.432). Now if by the theory of cognition is meant a psychological theory, the two logicians agree: Peirce's view by this time is set firmly against the psychological construal of logic and its tasks. But they agree only on that minimal position: Peirce finds Sigwart's solution inadequate, and he supplies an alternative:

there is a much more general doctrine to which the name theory of cognition might be applied. Namely, it is that speculative grammar, or analysis of the nature of assertion, which rests upon observations, indeed, but upon observations of the rudest kind, open to the eye of every attentive person who is familiar with the use of language, and which, we may be sure, no rational being, able to converse at all with his fellows, and so to express a doubt of anything, will ever have any doubt. (CP 3.432)

To what does "grammar" attend, if not to the morphology, the lexicon, the phonology and the syntax of the language in which some assertion happens to be expressed? It is to the use of language for the purposes of conversation, to the use of conversation as the site of doubt. Notice, then, that doubt, and hence belief, do not arise in minds but in conversations, and notice too, that in order to be useful, a "doubt" is formulated as a "question," which is a "contrivance or device" designed to fit some specific need. It is these facts that open "assertion" to observation. Second only to mathematics, speculative grammar is the first of the logical sciences because

the student would never have had a desire to learn logic if he had not paid some little attention to assertion, so as at least to attach a definite signification to assertion. So that, if he has not thought more accurately about assertions, he must at least be conscious, in some out-of-focus fashion, of certain properties of assertion. (CP 3.432)

Whether or not this is true of the motivation of "students" or even of logicians in general, students we have, so teacher is what the reviewer will become. Pragmatism does not need to know the formal properties of assertion; it needs to know its functional machinery:

When he comes to the study, if he has a good teacher, these already dimly recognised facts will be placed before him in accurate formulation, and will be accepted as soon as he can clearly apprehend their statements.

　　Let us see what some of these are. When an assertion is made, there really is some speaker, writer, or other sign-maker who delivers it; and he supposes there is, or will be, some hearer, reader, or other interpreter who will receive it. It may be a stranger upon a different planet, an aeon later; or it may be that very same man as he will be a second after. In any case, the deliverer makes signals to the receiver. (CP 3.432–33)

A genre, a rhetoric, is simply a kind of "conversation," or of writing, such as, for example, the one that takes place between teachers and students. We might recognize it by its tics: "let us see what some of these are" followed by a generalization, then by an exemplification of the points raised. Within this genre, Peirce tells us the business of "grammar." The grammar of (the concept of) assertion is a structure of pragmatic relations: it necessarily involves a "deliverer" and a "receiver" and the making of signals. These "dimly recognized facts" are obscured by the discursive habits associated with "proposition" in the traditional practices of philosophy, which focus primarily on propositional content, on the "belief" that an assertion expresses. The lateral habits of this teacher bring to light the condition in conversation of an assertion and thus alert his student to the nature of assertion taken as act. The difference lies in its focus on the act in real time and on the consequences *for the receiver*, as distinct from the conventional focus on correspondence between the contents of a mind with the world. Yet the teacher's focus on these dimly recognized facts tends to waver.

Consistently with the didactic tone appropriate to the teacher whose student he has evoked in his conversation with Schröder, Peirce illustrates "assertion" with an example:

For instance, tramps have the habit of carrying bits of chalk and making marks on the fences to indicate the habits of the people that live there for the benefit of other tramps who may come on later. If in this way a tramp leaves an assertion that the people are stingy, he supposes the reader of the signal will have met stingy people before, and will be able to call up an image of such a person attachable to a person whose acquaintance he has not yet made. (CP 3.433)

This example is designed to illustrate only one of the elements of assertion, the one, it so happens, that I have called "Ramist." The deliverer and the receiver have in their minds the same "picture" or image, free to be attached to a new occasion. The picture theory is designed to account for the interpretability of a sign by its receiver. But it takes for granted exactly those elements of "assertion" that the word *assertion* is designed to bring into focus. What is it, exactly, to *make* a sign, thereafter to *deliver* it to "some hearer, reader, or other interpreter"? Peirce provides the beginning of an answer: "Tramps have the habit of carrying bits of chalk and making marks on fences." What is it, exactly, to *receive* a sign? It is written on a fence, on a road traveled by others. To "receive" a sign, we must know its language, and this includes the know-how of the technology it relies on, knowing how to make the same sign for the next fellow, ensuring, first of all, that it work *as* sign, that it address him, interpellate him, be there to be found by him when he looks for it, that it possess, too, no doubt, its secrets and its secrecy so as to exclude those for whom it is not intended, who should not, or have no need to, take it up.

In this case, it is a mark—Peirce leaves its material form unde-scribed—on a fence, written with a piece of chalk which the sign maker is bound by the habits of his form of life,[28] the force of its customs, to carry with him.

A mark that appears to disappear:

> If in this way a tramp leaves an assertion that the people are stingy, he supposes the reader of the signal will have met stingy people before, and will be able to call up an image of such a person attachable to a person whose acquaintance he has not yet made. Not only is the outward significant word or mark a sign, but the im-age which it is expected to excite in the mind of the receiver will likewise be a sign—a sign by resemblance, or, as we say, an *icon*—of the similar image in the mind of the deliverer, and through that also a sign of the real quality of the thing. (CP 3.433)

An interesting disappearance, of the mark, in favor of the image it excites, a fascinating forgetting of the mark, in the face of the "real quality of the thing." An effortless erasure of the whole business of signs, their making, their grammar, their rhetoric, by a dream, a pure idea. Not only the dream, the reminiscence, the Platonic form of stingy people, but the dream of re-semblance, similarity, unmediated sameness whereby what is in my mind is also in yours and is the same as what is remembered—unmediated by time, by history, by practice—its origin in the real qualities of things. A dream in which the "gap" between mind and world,[29] between one mind and other minds, is closed by the dream of metaphysics, which is the end of philosophy.

> En attendant, essayons de converser sans nous exalter, puisque nous sommes inca-pables de nous taire. (Beckett, *En attendant Godot*)
>
> While we wait, let's try to converse without getting upset, since we can't stay silent.

It disappears, this mark; then, though fleetingly, it makes its mark again:

Not only is the outward significant word or mark a sign . . .

For this sign to be a sign, used and interpreted by its receiver, the next tramp in the infinite series that walks the road must have come across something other than stingy people before, something radically heteroge-neous with the images of such things: he must have come across the "outward significant word or mark," the sign itself, its qualities—its shape or its sounds, it size, its color, its length, or its rhythms—its materials and its medium; its use—where, when, with whom, under what circumstances, and for what purposes it is sign; its usage, that is, a predictive generalization over all these factors and more. Peirce will systematize considerations such as these in the first trichotomy of his entirely overhauled or "second" classification of signs (CP 2.243–46) (see Chapter 3). For a mark to be a sign, its "deliverer" and its "receiver" must hold in common, and behave according to, the customs—grammatical and rhetorical—within which— *and only within which*—that mark is a sign.

Such matters are not forgotten when Peirce pursues the project of a "philosophy of notation." Knowing a language, reflecting on what it means to know a language, teaching the "grammar" of the language, will become explicit concerns of the textbooks he plans for the exposition and the propagation of the "existential graphs."[30] But we are not there yet. Where we are is in a review of Schröder's logic, a reviewing of its introduction, which Peirce finds "fragmentary and wanting in a unifying idea"; where we are is in a previewing of an alternative introduction to logic, the place where "a man first comes to the study of logic," and, taken in hand by a good teacher, is led to a clear apprehension of facts that he has already dimly recognized by virtue of "observations of the rudest kind" (CP 3.432). We are at a threshold space between the dark and the clear, where dim recognition is "open to the eye of every attentive person who is familiar with the use of language," and the facts so discovered are not doubted by "any rational being able to converse at all with his fellows." In this liminal space—a review of an introduction—looking back at mathematical logic and forward to a regenerated philosophical logic, Peirce attends to conversation. This is not where language starts; it is where the noticing of it starts.

We are at a fence. On this fence, a sign appears, only to disappear. It disappears when it is used. In use, for the deliverer as for its receiver, its stake is the useful information it transmits; its disappearance is contingent on its uptake, its transformation by, its interpretation in, another sign. It appears, is brought into focus, in mention,[31] when it is not taken up so much as taken as sign. It is noticed by an attentive neighbor, used by him as an example of the properties of an assertion. But this neighbor is only attending to certain of these properties; his attention is deflected from the "outward significant word or mark" to "the image it is expected to excite." Because the neighbor is a philosopher, with the habits of his kind.

This fence stands between the two genres that Peirce is writing, between the "philosophical logic" inherited and regenerated, and the "mathematical logic" that is kept in its place outside the gates of philosophy, rather than let loose to change the assumptions, or the terms, of metaphysical inquiry. At this fence, a semiotician might notice a notation for philosophy and accompany it with a philosophy of notation. But it is also the fence where he might turn away from "the pure mathematical point of view" and momentarily forget to notice what it brings into focus. This fence, then, is of the utmost importance in constituting semiotics, its project, and its writing: it is what distinguishes "the outward significant word or mark" from "the image which it is expected to excite," the "signifier" from the "signified." It is what distinguishes one construal of the predicate—what is *said*—from another—"the sign of the real quality of the thing"—and it is this fence, too, that operates the distinction of "use" and "mention." This fence marks the "gap" between representation and the real and situates in it philosophy itself, determining the shape of its question and of the impossibility of its answer. Here, a logic of conversation is a conversation about logic, and a philosophy of rhetoric is read, or written, by another tramp, in the form of a rhetoric of philosophy. This fence, this gap, this indeterminate betweenhood, is the discursive condition of semiotics, as the semiotic is the condition of all conversation.

Faced with this fence, Peirce will formalize it as the distinction between the first and the second trichotomies—the trichotomy of the sign "in itself" and the trichotomy of the relation of sign to object. Then the project of semiotic will become the articulation of the formal–material conditions and instruments of signhood on the one hand, with the conditions and mechanisms of interpretation on the other. Peirce will come to write that grammar is a condition of rhetoric, that the chalk, the fence, the well-formed mark—their knowing—are a condition of conversation. As conversation is the condition of signs.

PART TWO

THINGS AND EVENTS

3

Around 1903

In 1903, Peirce wrote two major pieces of work. The first, the Harvard Lectures on Pragmatism, were delivered from March to May, and the second, the Lowell Lectures, at the Lowell Institute in October of the same year.[1] This later series was accompanied by a Syllabus, a brochure for which was published. In both the Harvard Lectures and the Syllabus, we find major revisions to the theory of signs, but the differences between them are significant. The Harvard Lectures are Peirce's major contribution to a pragmatic metaphysics; the Lowell Lectures, and hence the Syllabus, are devoted to logic. In part, the differences between the two versions of the sign hypothesis are attributable to this generic difference. This is the shift to what I have called elsewhere Peirce's "second classification" of signs, in which the rules for division and the derivation of classes are quite new in relation with the familiar model.[2] This could have effected a radical change in the detail as well as in the global form of the sign hypothesis, but it remains a hypothesis whose practical utility is never put to the test. In some measure, this is because the Syllabus is somewhat eccentric to the dichotomy between logic and philosophy, and it brings to the theory a feature that is particular to its own genre and that will not recur. What is retained from the work of 1903 is a pragmatic account of signs *in actu*. In my description of this work, I shall press the argument that I have pursued thus far and that now has three distinct elements: (1) in Peirce's formal logic, he uses the sign hypothesis to describe the properties of real signs in real settings, such that those properties either raise problems for, or solve problems in, the hypothesis as it stood prior to the introduction of those examples; (2) the range of examples adduced in the philosophy expands to take account of that work, applying it to more familiar or everyday examples; (3) while the application of the sign hypothesis—whose genesis is in a philosophical setting—to the metadescription of logical notations is the first move of this process, thereafter the direction is most frequently *from* logic *to* philosophy. Nevertheless, Peirce does not always import every insight he gains in logic to philosophy; there are certain points at which philosophy asserts some crucial boundary conditions on the material it sees fit to consider. What these boundary conditions are, and what material is thereby excluded, will emerge as I proceed.

We have seen something like this operating in the pair of texts from 1885: the logical discoveries precede their application in philosophy and are not yet fully integrated, Peirce seeing no place at that time for his account of the icon in the problems of philosophy that he discusses in Royce's work. The pair of texts from 1903 arises in the reverse order. As we read across this pair, we shall observe the completion of the process initiated in 1885, but we shall also see the direction of importation reversed. The Harvard Lectures raise a new problem for sign theory; the attempt to solve it there is not successful. But there is a solution implied in a technical issue in formal logic. Peirce makes it explicit in his work in logic of this period, then systematizes it and integrates it with the rest of sign theory, first in the Syllabus, then in all the major texts following.

Prior to these important texts, in 1898, Peirce had delivered a series of lectures, at William James' invitation, for the Cambridge Conferences.[3] The recent editors of these lectures wished to call their volume "the consequences of mathematics," meaning in particular the mathematical "ways of studying consequences." They point out that, partly because James wanted Peirce to use the lectures to give a popular introduction to his work, the lectures "apply the ideas of mathematics in philosophy." As such, they demonstrate one direction of the intergeneric commerce I am exploring. The editors explain that they did not have their way, but all the proposed titles are felicitous. Peirce had wanted this series to explore "the logic of events"; as we read the title it finally received, we should allow the intonational stress to fall on "the logic of *things*." "The Sign, in general, is the third member of a triad; first a thing as thing, second a thing as reacting with another thing; and third a thing as representing another to a third."[4] The 1898 series prepares the philosophical way for the work Peirce was to do five years later, again at Harvard, where the issue of the eventhood and the thinghood of signs becomes a special focus.

The Harvard Lectures of 1903

The Harvard series of 1903 was a thoroughgoing revision of Peirce's system and is given the status, by Karl-Otto Apel, of the "final revision."[5] Turrisi links the organization of these lectures with the events following Peirce's application for funds to the Carnegie Institution the previous year.[6] Peirce had written to William James lamenting his failure and explaining the extent to which he had been depending on a successful outcome to solve his financial difficulties. James arranged for the lecture series, with a handsome fee, in response to this information. The grant application had included an ambitious plan to complete a work in logic consisting of "three dozen memoirs" in which his logic and his philosophy would be articulated into a unitary system.[7] The Harvard Lectures are what we have instead. Their ambition to present a unified architectonic is reoriented in line with the focus on pragmatism (designed, it is usually presumed, as a way of pursuing his debate with James himself): he would present topics that would allow him to discuss "the 'foundation, definition and limitation' of pragmatism, as well as its 'application to philosophy, to the sciences, and to the conduct of life.'"[8] Part of the difficulty of these lectures derives from the compression of the argument; part derives from the topical arrangement, which seeks to present a whole philosophical system under the head of pragmatism.[9]

What, then, is the "place" of semiotic in this design? Apel responds to this question by seeing it as foundational, as it had been in "On a New List of Categories," but as it had ceased to be during the period in which Peirce worked most intensively on formal logic and in which he developed and applied the pragmatic maxim to the particular context of the logic of inquiry. But what sort of foundation is this? Is it transcendental, as Apel supposes, or is it merely the "formal basis" of empirical science in general, as Oehler would have it?[10] "Peirce's foundation of pragmatism," writes Oehler, "relates the problem of sign-function to the problem of sign use, in other words, the action produced by the sign," thus obviating the need to have "recourse to higher, final truths such as 'reason,' 'language,' or, society.'"[11] As against this, Apel grants to the phenomenology a quasi-transcendental status. He claims that the system of 1903 solves the problem created for Peirce by the assumed discontinuity between the precognitive and the cognitive realm. He argues that the Harvard Lectures establish an "iconic contact between nature and cognition—understood in semiotic terms, between unconscious and conscious argumentation."[12] This iconic contact is the foundation. Apel sees Peirce as moving from a *symbolic* account of cognition, in 1868, which focuses on inference, to an *indexical* account, in 1885, focusing on denotation, and finally to this *iconic* account of 1903, which focuses on "the decisive connection between the qualitative features of nature and the predicates of human perceptual judgment." The metaphysics of 1903 presents a full integration of the three classes of sign to account for the deep continuity of mind with the world. As Apel puts the objective of the system,

[Peirce] aims for a philosophy of continuity in which perception and its objects are to be conceived on the one hand, as the limiting case of rationality (EP 2:16; pp. 226–28 (CP 5.181–85)), while rationality itself is to be conceived, on the other hand, as an object of sensory perception (EP 2:16; pp. 233; p. 238; p. 240 (CP 5.194; 5.205; 5.209)). (Apel's references)[13]

What it means for rationality to be available to sensory perception is explained by the use Peirce makes of the icon, which holds together its construal as "mental content"—the icon as the form of a thought—with its construal as "material form"—the icon as real thing on a page, available for manipulation and indeed observation by the work of reason. On Apel's argument, the three classes of signs are now fully integrated into philosophy. Not only can it use them all from time to time, but they are also structurally integrated into its very foundation. Apel seems to consider this the end of the story. Were we to follow him, this is where we would have to conclude that the sign hypothesis ends up, so integrated into the foundations of the system that it would have no special place elsewhere, so presupposed that it could no longer be an object for scientific investigation. Yet phenomenology *is not* the foundation in the Harvard Lectures or elsewhere: "if it is to be properly grounded, [it must] be made to depend upon the conditional or Hypothetical Science of *Pure Mathematics*. . . . A Phenomenology which does not reckon with pure mathematics . . . will be the same pitiful club-footed affair that Hegel produced" (EP 2:10, p. 144 [CP 5.40]). This returns us to Oehler's view. The iconicity of phenomenology is based on the pure formal icons—indeed, the *theory* of pure formal icons—that Peirce develops throughout his metanotational work.[14] We must distinguish between the icon in these two senses, because without this distinction, the phenomenological icon takes on the aura of a mystical unity of mind with world, and hence transcendental status. Mathematics is the formal foundation for the observation of icons *in actu*, and indeed, for their generation.[15] This formal foundation is procedural and technical, not transcendental (cf. EP 2:15, pp. 212–13 [CP 5.162]). It is found in the real deployment of signs in real situations: it is not derived from a transcendental deduction.

The Lowell Lectures situate their topics on the formal side of this boundary, the Harvard Lectures on the phenomenological side in order to theorize the "positive" sciences. Phenomenology must be

a science that does *not* draw any distinction of good and bad . . . but just contemplates phenomena as they are, simply opens its eyes and describes what it sees. Not what it sees in the real as distinguished from figment,—not regarding any such dichotomy—but simply describing the object, as a phenomenon, and stating what it finds in all phenomena alike. . . . I will so far follow Hegel as to call this science *Phenomenology* although I will not restrict it to the observation and analysis of *experience* but extend it to describing all the features that are common to whatever is *experienced* or might conceivably be experienced or become an object of study in any way direct or indirect. (EP 2:10, p. 143 [CP 5.37])

It is this phenomenology that gives the *ratio* for the categories, which are now considered to be conceptual hypotheses concerning the nature of experience. If they fulfill the role of a metaphysics, this role is not ultimate; it rests on mathematics. The categories are reformulated but are not radically changed. They are "presentness," "struggle," and "law" or representation, and the hypotheses formulating them are submitted to mathematical analysis.[16] This principle of division will produce hypothetical subclasses within each of the categories. It follows the model set out in "On the Algebra of Logic": subdivisions are found by means of the principle, that "Category the First owing to its Extremely Rudimentary character, is not susceptible of any degenerate or weakened modification" (EP 2:12, p. 160 [CP 5.68]), whereas Category the Second has one Degenerate Form (EP 2:12, p. 160 [CP 5.69]), and Category the Third, two (EP 2:12, p. 161 [CP 5.70]).

Peirce then uses the representamen as the exemplar of a subdivision by trichotomy, but we can expect that this example, like others, will take on a life, and examples, of its own:

The representamen, for example, divides by trichotomy into the general sign, or *symbol*, the *index*, and the *icon*. An *icon* is a representamen . . . by virtue of a character which it possesses in itself, and would possess just the same though its object did not exist. Thus, the statue of a centaur is not, it is true, a representamen if there be no such thing as a centaur. Still, if it represents a centaur, it is by virtue of its shape; and this shape it will have, just as much, whether there be a centaur or not. (EP 2:12, p. 163 [CP 5.73])

The centaur is a new example (Figure 3.1), and Peirce is unsure whether he should admit it into the domain of genuine representamens, because its object is a fiction. On the principle enunciated in the phenomenology (not distinguishing between a figment and the real), he both does and does not. This is not the first time *in these lectures*, nor indeed the last, where he uses a fiction in order to argue a point: "Imagine," he writes, "that upon the soil of a country that has a single boundary line, . . . there lies a map of that same country. . . . I shall suppose that it represents every part of that country. . . . Let us further suppose. . . . " (EP 2:12, p. 161 [CP 5.71]). Indeed, not only is the map a useful fiction, it is used to illustrate a notion of "self-consciousness" that he has introduced through a bit of "buffoonery":

I remember a lady's averring that her father had heard a minister, of what complexion she did not say, open a prayer as follows: "O Thou, All-sufficient, Self-sufficient, Insufficient God." Now pure Self-consciousness is Self-sufficient, and if it is also regarded as All-sufficient, it would seem to follow that it must be Insufficient. I ought to apologize for introducing such buffoonery into serious lectures. I do so because I seriously believe that a bit of fun helps thought and tends to keep it pragmatical. (EP 2:12, p. 161 [CP 5.71])

Peirce may, or may not, be self-conscious about his deferred narrator here, but we can suppose that he is: it is a familiar joke for passing off a fiction as an authorized report. But pragmatism is about the "logical goodness, or truth" (EP 2:14, p. 204 [CP 5.142]) of a belief or judgment, and Peirce insists throughout the lectures that such things are of the nature of assertions (or at least assertibles) (EP 2:10, p. 141 [CP 5.29 ff.]).[17] Deferred narration, or more generally deferred authority, is precisely a device for not taking the responsibility for the truth of one's statements; belief, which is suspended in the case of fiction, depends upon such taking of responsibility (EP 2:10, p. 141 [CP 5.29 ff.]). Nothing can be asserted of a fictional entity, and Peirce raises the problem of fiction explicitly in order to be able to include apparently fictional signs within the broad domain of semiotic. The example again involves a chain of deferred narration:

All propositions relate to the same ever-reacting singular; namely, to the totality of all real objects. It is true that when the Arabian romancer tells us that there was a lady named Scherherazade [*sic*], he does not mean to be understood as speaking of the world of outward realities, and there is a good deal of fiction in what he is talking about. For the *fictive* is that whose characters depend upon what characters somebody attributes to it; and the story is, of course, the mere creation of the poet's thought. Nevertheless, once he has imagined Scherherazade and made her young, beautiful, and endowed with a gift for spinning stories, it becomes a real fact that so he has imagined her, which fact he cannot destroy by pretending or thinking that he imagined her to be otherwise. What he wishes us to understand is what he might have expressed in plain prose by saying, "I have imagined a lady, Scherherazade by name, young, beautiful and a tireless teller of tales, and I am going on to imagine what tales she told." This would have been a plain expression of professed fact relating to the sum total of realities. (EP 2:15, p. 209 [CP 5.152])

The solution Peirce proposes has become standard in analytic philosophy for dissolving the problem of fiction; its merits or otherwise will not detain me here. For the thing that interests me is that, like the lady who averred that her father had told her of an unidentifiable minister who said . . . , the Scherherazade example relies on a trajectory upstream, so to say, of the device of deferred authority. Anchored in a transcendental source, these two examples contrast with the centaur, which is referred neither to object nor to author, simply—but infinitely—to other icons. The upstream trajectory is evident in one further example:

Analogy suggests that the laws of nature are ideas or resolutions in the mind of some vast consciousness. (EP 2:13, p. 184 [CP 5.107])

The Universe is a vast representamen, a great symbol of God's purpose, working out its conclusions in living realities. (EP 2:13, pp. 193–94 [CP 5.119])

The Universe as an argument is necessarily a great work of art, a great poem,—for every fine argument is a poem and a symphony,—just as every true poem is a sound argument. But let us compare it rather with a painting. (EP 2:13, pp. 193–94 [CP 5.119])

This analogy finds the Author at the end of the chain, but since Peirce distrusts it as scientific procedure, so may we. Philosophy finds it reassuring to reduce all fictions to some form of true event in some consciousness, but this maneuver does not solve the problem from which he started with the centaur. For if it is the case, that some sculptor imagined and then executed the shape of the centaur, it does not bestow on the centaur the status of object that Peirce appears to need in order for the statue to count as a representamen.

The lectures propose a far more satisfactory solution to the problem of fiction than the postulate of authority at the end of the chain. Fictional objects have the same status as the objects of hypotheses, and indeed, this status is explained by the fact that the whole point about the icon is that it can say nothing at all about the ontology of its objects. This is true of both the mathematical icon and the phenomenological icon. The distinction between fictional objects and assertible objects is made by the index, or more substantively, by submitting the results of abductions to the test of the pragmatic maxim: what are the real consequences of the sign? The issue for Peirce will be to establish a rule whereby he can distinguish one from the other—those hypotheses that do, and those that do not, deserve admission as hypotheses into the particular kind of semiotic chain that is scientific inquiry (EP 2:16, pp. 234–35 [CP 5.196]). The argument is introduced in Lecture 6, following the Scherherazade example:

In deduction . . . we set out from a hypothetical state of things which we define in certain abstracted respects. Among the characters to which we pay no attention in this mode of argument is whether or not the hypothesis of our premises conforms more or less to the state of things in the outward world. . . . We construct an icon of our hypothetical state of things and proceed to observe it . . . we proceed to inquire whether it is true or not. (EP 2:15, p. 212 [CP 5.161–62])

Peirce's hesitation about fiction, whether or not the statue of a centaur is a genuine representamen, is a hesitation concerning the boundary of the domain to which logic viewed as semiotic will apply. Whether or not the representation of an object can be asserted is the domain of logic proper, or "critic." This is the part of logic that considers the truth values of representations. But logic "considered as semiotic" is broader than critic; it includes "grammar," which treats of the properties of signs themselves, whether or not those signs represent assertible facts or even hypotheses regarding assertible facts. Semiotic must be able to consider signs such as the centaur, the self-reflecting map, and the stories of Scherherazade, if only to supply them for any account of how we make the distinction between fiction and fact in the first place. This kind of test, we have seen, depends on the index, the principle of not-ness, and in general, the category of secondness which distinguishes between the "inner" and the "outer" worlds.

The centaur example serves the purpose of exemplifying an icon that is not anchored by an index to some *centaur other than another statue-of-a-centaur (or a painting, etc.). The world of culture is pervaded by such things—poems, symphonies, stories, paintings—and the philosopher must know about them, have descriptions of their grammar available, in order to know under what conditions they do, and do not, enter his domain of business. But that is all that he will do with them.

Peirce goes on with his kinds of signs, the next one being, as we might expect, the index:

> An *index* is a representamen which fulfills the function of a representamen by virtue of a character which it could not have if its object did not exist, but which it will continue to have just the same whether it be interpreted as a representamen or not. For instance, an old-fashioned hygrometer is an *index*. For it is so contrived as to have a physical reaction with dryness and moisture in the air, so that the little man will come out if it is wet, and this would happen just the same if the use of the instrument should be entirely forgotten, so that it ceased actually to convey any information. (EP 2:12, p. 163 [CP 5.73])

The definition is contrived so as to be the exact opposite of the icon, and the example is a scientific instrument, albeit a primitive one. The hygrometer is of the same nature as the weathercock: it points to, and is determined by, some fact of meteorology. Notice that it is of a quite different order from the examples drawn from algebraic and geometrical notations, but that it has the same sort of status as "physical symptoms," that is, it is an index by causality. This is what Peirce will identify as the "relatively genuine form of Index," and on the model of subdivision by degeneracy, he will set alongside it a relatively degenerate form: "any mere land-mark by which a particular thing may be recognized because it is as a matter of fact associated with that thing, a proper name without signification, a pointing finger, is a degenerate index." We have seen the finger before; it inheres in the name of the class itself; we have not seen the landmark, nor have we seen Peirce adduce proper names. The features of these three examples are brought together in the Bunker Hill Monument (EP 2:12, p. 163 [CP 5.75]).

The examples deployed in the Harvard Lectures continue to play out the distinction between assertible and nonassertible signs, for where the key example of the icon, the centaur, represents an object that exists only as a product of the imagination, the "inner world"—all the examples of the index participate not only in "reality" but in existence: as things in themselves, they exist in time and space, as do their objects. This is what Peirce means by "factual connection," and his examples of the index are perspicuous for this criterion. As the superscript letters to the diagram, the subject to the propositional form and the quantifiers to the universe of discourse, so is the landmark to the map. It orients infinite semiosis, anchoring it to existential experience by interpellating the body in space.

The new account of the functional complementarity of the icon and the index completes the analysis of the proposition that was begun in 1885. Peirce takes the proposition as the key example of the symbol, then analyzes this as follows:

The *Symbol,* or relatively genuine form of Representamen, divides by trichotomy into the Term, the Proposition, and the Argument. The term corresponds to the icon and to the degenerate index. It does excite an icon in the imagination. The proposition conveys definite information like the genuine index, by having two parts of which the function of the one is to indicate the object meant while that of the other is to represent the representamen by exciting an icon of its quality. The argument is a representamen which does not leave the interpretant to be determined as it may by the person to whom the symbol is addressed; but separately represents what is the interpreting representation that it is intended to determine. This interpreting representation is, of course, the conclusion. (EP 2:12, p. 164 [CP 5.76])

Notice that the symbol is now analyzed by means of the icon and the index, which are here integrated into the symbolic function, rather than standing outside of it. This allows me to return to the issue of how inclusive semiotic is. We have seen examples of pure indices and icons that, in their simplicity, are quite distinct from the class of symbols. These examples are adduced for didactic purposes, to illustrate the definitions. When Peirce goes on to *use* his sign hypothesis in the further stages of his argument, all the signs will be complex and mixed. They will be the kind of things that produce beliefs. These are of the general nature of propositions, which join indices to "general symbols" whose content is sometimes represented to be an icon. This is amply demonstrated by the "Logical Goodness" section of Lecture 5, where Peirce announces rather surprisingly that "a representamen is either a *rhema,* a *proposition,* or an *argument*" (EP 2:14, p. 204). The surprise is registered by the original editors of the *Collected Papers,* who supply in brackets an explanation: "A representamen [as symbol]" (CP 5.139); but the gloss, although correct in its assumptions, deflects attention away from what is really going on here. Peirce writes: "Esthetic goodness . . . may . . . must be possessed, by any kind of representamen: rhema, proposition, or argument,"[18] as if the whole field of representation were occupied by a familiar, quite particular, class of symbols, defined entirely in traditional terms.

I suggest that Peirce's attention to the field of signs has been entirely captured by, and confined to, the signs of particular relevance to particular demands of the topic at hand, which does not need to consider such things as centaurs or the tales of Scherherazade, and feels more at ease considering the documents of history than its commemoration by a monument. There are several occasions in his writing where a similar confinement takes place, and I shall point them out as they arise in my discussion. On this basis, I claim that the boundary is now no longer drawn between classes of signs, as in the "New List," but that it is drawn between those representations that integrate the properties of the three classes of signs and those that do not. In practice, this will work out to correspond with the class of assertible or asserted propositions, broadened to include pictorial representations that join an index to the iconic form (for example, portraits), as well as propositions of geometry and algebra. These are the representations used in inquiry; many other sorts of signs are not. The vocation of pragmatism is to deal with this class.

The passage on the symbol is disappointing in two respects. First, it is difficult to see in what Peirce is offering something new over and above the most classic analysis of the proposition into subject and predicate. Second, the traditional triad of term, proposition, and argument appears in this passage to be coextensive with a class that we know, from his other examples, to be far broader than this. In both these respects, Peirce's analysis is a regression to the version of the problematic that gave rise to the sign hypothesis in the first place. Can he discover no new examples of symbols, and is there nothing to be discovered about their grammar? Well, yes, to both questions, as it happens.

Although the definition given in Lecture 3 (EP 2:12, p. 164 [CP 5.76]) is indeed limited to the traditional terms, there are other points where Peirce gives instances rather than definitions and where these instances have properties that are obscured by the name "proposition." In fact, elsewhere he has written, instead of "term, proposition and argument," "word, sentence or book" (EP 2:12, p. 163 [CP 5.73]). Such things have a materiality quite different from that of the referents of the logical names: words are in sentences which are, for example, in books,[19] although not books such as *The Arabian Nights*, I presume; the issue they raise is that of *assertion*. Peirce always means "seriously assertible"; unlike the proposition, which is merely a logical form, the assertion is an act with practical consequences: it entrains belief or doubt, and from both, further action. It produces "physical effects":

Nobody can deny that words do produce such effects. Take, for example, that sentence of Patrick Henry which, at the time of our revolution, was repeated by every man to his neighbor:

"Three millions of people, armed in the holy cause of Liberty, and in such a country as we possess, are invincible against any force that the enemy can bring against us."

Those words present this character of the general law of nature, that they might have produced effects indefinitely transcending any that circumstances allowed them to produce. It might, for example, have happened that some American schoolboy, sailing as a passenger in the Pacific Ocean, should have idly written down those words on a slip of paper. The paper might have been tossed overboard and might have been picked up by some Tagala on a beach of the island of Luzon; and if he had had them translated to him they might easily have passed from mouth to mouth there as they did in this country, and with similar effect. (EP 2:13, p. 184 [CP 5.105])

When Peirce asks himself "But *how* do they produce their effects?", he gives what appears to be a lame response:

They certainly do not . . . *directly* react upon matter. Such action that they have is merely logical. It is not even psychological. It is merely that one symbol would justify another. However, suppose that first difficulty to have been surmounted,—

which, plainly, it has not been . . .

—and that they do act upon actual thoughts. That thoughts act on the physical world and *conversely*, is one of the most familiar of facts. (EP 2:13, p. 184 [CP 5.106])

Familiar it may be; explained it evidently is not. The significant word is "actual": symbols act on actual thoughts. Events of thought; symbolic events: these are not logical forms. Peirce cannot account for the power to produce interpretants if he cannot account for the mode of action of a sign.

The form of the problem is similar to the issue that Peirce raises concerning the mode of action of a law. No court can implement its decisions without a sheriff, just as no law can act in the absence of secondness. But what does this mean in the case of signs? Peirce will ask this question in the terms appropriate to the genre of his lectures; he will inquire into the ontology of signs themselves:

The mode of being of a representamen is such that it is capable of repetition. Take, for example, any proverb. "Evil communications corrupt good manners." Every time this is written or spoken in English, Greek, or any other language, and every time it is thought of, it is one and the same representamen. It is the same with a diagram or picture. It is the same with a physical sign or symptom. If two weathercocks are different signs, it is only in so far as they refer to different parts of the air. A representamen which should have a unique embodiment, incapable of repetition, would not be a representamen, but part of the very fact represented. (EP 2:14, p. 203 [CP 5.138])

Notice first that proverbs are very unlike the propositions of inquiry. It is the saying of them in particular circumstances that has effects, their local applicability rather than the truth of their propositional content. Notice second that Peirce has started his lectures to these students of William James by repeating what is to all intents and purposes a proverb—the pragmatic maxim—which he translates from its original 1878 formulation, in French, into a near equivalent in English (EP 2:10, p. 135 [CP 5.18]), and then proceeds to explore, sometimes reformulating it, throughout the lectures, gradually transforming it as it is modified or enriched through the effects of the topics to which he applies it. It ends up all but unrecognizable when he puts "the edge on the maxim of pragmatism" (Lecture 7, passim). Notice, third, that the particular proverb that he chooses is a moralized version of the pragmatic maxim. Presuming that signs are events of "communication," we can translate his proverb thus: all signs have effects; make sure that they are not corrupting ones. Repeating his maxim in this form reflects upon the ethical basis of the pragmatism he is expounding. This is no mere proverb idly cited: the lectures are intended to prove it, to provide it with a foundation, and hence to establish its truth. What follows for "good signs"?—that they must be logically sound, certainly, but that their enunciation have consequences and that these consequences be desirable. This cannot be assessed without assessing their action in relation with their aim:

If the meaning of a symbol consists in *how* it might cause us to act, it is plain that this "how" cannot refer to the description of mechanical motions that it might cause, but must intend to refer to a description of the action as having this or that *aim*. (EP 2:14, p. 202 [CP 5.135])

The proverb Peirce cites suggests that this aim must be the maintenance and furtherance of "good manners," but what are the "good manners" that would be corrupted by bad communications? The proverb may in fact be cited from Montaigne: "The first step in the corruption of morals is the banishment of truth."[20] Peirce would add his gloss: that the conversations of "men" should further the aims of inquiry, that they should seek truth.

Peirce's account of "how" the proverb acts on occasion is unsatisfactory and inconclusive: "This repetitory character of the representamen involves as a consequence that it is essential to a representamen that it should contribute to the determination of another representamen distinct from itself," he would have us believe; "every representamen must be capable of contributing to the determination of a representamen different from itself" (EP 2:14, p. 203 [CP 5.138]). He conflates here two issues that we know him to have distinguished sharply in his later work. These are the "significate effects" of the sign—its interpretant—with the issue of the repetition of the sign itself. The interpretation of a sign cannot be limited to the repetition of the same sign: the interpretant is a different, or second, sign of the same object. Rather than dwell on the confusion of this passage now, I prefer to return to it when I consider how Peirce was to solve the problem. I shall also consider at that point why the solution was available only when he turned his attention again to the description of a formal language.

Nevertheless, it is of the greatest interest that the problem first arises qua problem, in the philosophical setting. The aim of the lectures is to elucidate the topic of pragmatism, and pragmatism is a philosophy that articulates a logic of representation with inquiry considered as real actions with consequences, in the real world, in existential and historical time. It is therefore also of genuine interest that two of the examples adduced in the Harvard Lectures are examples from, and represent events in, the history of the country—now no longer merely mapped, but narrated—that was to claim "Pragmatism" as its native philosophy. The theory of signs must itself be pragmatic. Peirce has always assumed *that* signs act, and that they do so through their interpretants; in these two examples, he has begun to attend to this action as the stuff of history.[21] *How* they act is the new question. In order to answer it, a pragmatic semiotic must subject signs to the same kind of analysis that any phenomenon receives: all have qualities, all have a mode of existence, all are governed by laws. This amounts to the requirement that semiotic have an empirical and a descriptive dimension: if signs have real effects in the world, we'd better investigate their properties. When Peirce chooses an example from history to raise this issue, he can count on his audience not to contest his premiss: Patrick Henry's call did have effects, and those effects were—are—part of the lived experience of the United States citizen. The sign hypothesis must be able to account for that sort of thing, just as it must be able to account for the inhibiting or guiding effects of maxims and proverbs on day-to-day behavior. If Peirce can come up with an answer to his question "how?", the sign hypothesis will serve to delineate the domain of inquiry of pragmatism, first by distinguishing signs from other sorts of things, though the knowledge of all things depends on signs, and second by distinguishing inquiry from fiction, though the fictional constructs of phenomenology and mathematics are its indispensable starting point. In this, semiotic will serve as a map of the system; like the infinitely self-reflecting map Peirce has cited (from Royce, as it happens), this map will contain a map of itself, a theory of signs that reflects upon the condition of possibility of the map itself—indeed, of the system. This map is Peirce's fantasy of the totalizing mastery of knowledge; it is a fiction.

A Digression

Following the "Algebra of Logic," and increasingly when he was developing his alternative to algebraic notation, the "existential graphs," Peirce regularly resorted to semiotic terminology to describe his procedures. In one example of this practice, the terminology is used in the introduction as if he could presume its familiarity to the reader (CP 4.418 ff.). This is in marked contrast with the technical terminology of the graphs themselves, which needs careful explication.

A *diagram* is a representamen which is predominantly an icon of relations and is aided to be so by conventions. Indices are also more or less used . . . etc. (CP 4.418)

In this paper, Peirce spends most of his time expounding the conventions of the system. Convention No. 6 reads as follows:

A heavy line, called a *line of identity*, shall be a graph asserting the numerical identity of the individuals denoted by its two extremities. (CP 4.444)

Then, two paragraphs later, quite unexpectedly, the exposition digresses. The digression lasts for two paragraphs (CP 4.447–48) that occupy three full pages of the *Collected Papers*.

Remark how peculiar a sign the line of identity is. A sign, or to use a more general and more definite term, a *representamen*, is of one or other of three kinds: it is either an *icon*, an *index*, or a *symbol.* An icon is a representamen of what it represents and for the mind that interprets it as such, by virtue of its being an immediate image, that is to say by virtue of characters which belong to it in itself as a sensible object, and which it would possess just the same were there no object in nature that it resembled, and though it never were interpreted as a sign. It is of the nature of an appearance, and as such, strictly speaking, exists only in consciousness, although for convenience in ordinary parlance and when extreme precision is not called for, we extend the term *icon* to the outward objects which excite in consciousness the image itself. A geometrical diagram is a good example of an icon. A pure icon can convey no factual information; for it affords no assurance that there is any such thing in nature. But it is of the utmost value for enabling its interpreter to study what would be the character of such an object in case any such did exist. Geometry sufficiently illustrates that. (CP 4.447)

We note in this passage a number of features that the "Algebra of Logic" has led us to expect. (1) Peirce uses the term *sign* as if it were natural to his discourse, then restates it with his technical term *representamen*.[22] The representamen brings the object into relation with its interpretant; it is, so to say, the mechanism of the sign relation. (2) The icon must be a "sensible object," but almost immediately, and certainly without noticing the difficulty, Peirce claims that "strictly speaking [it] exists only in consciousness," and that it is an "extension" of the term to apply it to the "outward objects which excite in consciousness the image itself." Here we have a trace of the "mental image" construal of the icon, which we saw in the example of the painting, intersecting with the difficult issue of the ontology of geometrical figures. Because he is too careful a mathematician, Peirce cannot say that the "mental image" is the object of the sign; the object of a geometrical figure is absolutely ideal, a pure form, of which any mental image is itself only a representation. Nor can he say that the sign is entirely subsumed in its material form on the page; this would make of the figures of geometry fictional *entia*, which is unacceptable. In fact, as we have seen, the crucial issue in the icon is that it cannot tell us anything at all about the ontology of its objects and hence cannot tell us how to distinguish between fictional objects, mental contents, and ideal objects. (3) Give or take its existence in the mind or on the page, the icon has its own "sensible" characters, thus giving us a way of knowing them, hence of knowing the hypothetical properties of its object and of manipulating their relations.

   Peirce continues his digression. Before he can tell us why the line of identity is so remarkable, so "peculiar," he must give us a whole theory, or at least a whole classification, of signs, against which to consider it:

Of a completely opposite nature is the kind of representamen termed an *index*. This is a real thing or fact which is a sign of its object by virtue of being connected with it as a matter of fact and by also forcibly intruding upon the mind, quite regardless of its being interpreted as a sign. It may simply serve to identify its object and to assure us of its existence and presence. But very often the nature of the factual connexion of the index with its object is such as to excite in consciousness an image of some features of the object, and in that way affords evidence from which positive assurance as to truth of fact may be drawn. A photograph, for example, not only excites an image, has an appearance, but, owing to its optical connexion with the object, is evidence that that appearance corresponds to a reality. (CP 4.447)

Previously, the index has been opposed both to the icon and to the symbol, on the grounds that it "designates its object without implying any characters at all"; here, that criterion appears to be troubled by the fact that the photograph "excites an image." However, the significant criterion of indexicality remains that the index "may simply serve to identify its object and to assure us of its existence and presence." The example appears to be mixed over two classes. Note that "presence" is consistent with the idea of "struggle" between two positive contents, but is inconsistent with the idea drawn by implication from the "Algebra of Logic," whereby the index is the principle of distinction and difference, of not-ness. And the photograph displays a further feature of the index, perennially implicit in Peirce's discussions of this class, and explicit in the "Algebra of Logic," that it must necessarily be "a real thing" itself, alongside and in factual connection with the reality of its object.

Peirce then turns to the symbol:

A *symbol* is a representamen whose special significance or fitness to represent just what it does represent lies in nothing but the very fact of there being a habit, disposition, or other effective general rule that it will be so interpreted. Take, for example, the word "*man*." These three letters are not in the least like a man; nor is the sound with which they are associated. (CP 4.447)

Semioticians brought up principally on a diet of Saussure will recognize this issue as the arbitrary nature of the sign, which, when allied to the conventional rules of the system, is the principle Saussure uses to account both for the repeatability of the sign and for its capacity to change its value over time. Furthermore, the issue Peirce is about to raise is precisely the issue of repeatability:

Neither is the word existentially connected with any man as an index. It cannot be so, since the word is not an existence at all. The word does not consist of three films of ink. If the word "man" occurs hundreds of times in a book of which myriads of copies are printed, all those millions of triplets of patches of ink are embodiments of one and the same word. I call each of those embodiments a *replica* of the symbol. This shows that the word is not a thing. What is its nature? It consists in the really working general rule that three such patches seen by a person who knows English will affect his conduct and thoughts according to a rule. Thus the mode of being of a symbol is different from that of the icon and from that of the index. (CP 4.447)

In this passage, Peirce sorts out the confusion evident in the commentary of the proverb in the Harvard Lectures: he distinguishes the issue of the repeatability of the sign itself from the issue of its interpretant. The symbol is a law—that we have known since 1867—but it is a law that governs its own instantiation as well as its interpretability. Peirce here makes the interpretability of a symbol depend on both parts of this premiss. We do not interpret a law: the law governs our interpretation of its instantiations.

The philosophical source of Peirce's question is also the source of its solution. Peirce imports his pragmatism into the heart of his logic in order to answer the question of *how* a sign acts. The answer must be consistent with his metaphysics; it must not resort to psychology, nor can it suppose "mechanical" explanations. There must be a logic of action that seeks to articulate real sign events with their laws. In order to answer his question, signs must be phenomena, graspable as objects of a knowledge. Hence, they must themselves be analyzable in terms of the three categories, as qualities, events, and laws, and hence no longer confined to the category of generality. At the site of this requirement, Peirce will introduce the "first trichotomy"; he will do so in the Syllabus. But the elements of the solution are provided by the Harvard Lectures. Symbols will no longer merely be signs *of* generality—that is, predicates; they will themselves be general, and by this Peirce now means that they are like any class: their members are alike, "repeated," but subject to infinite difference in their instantiation (cf. EP 2:13, p. 183 [CP 5.103]). Hence, not only each class of sign, but each example of a sign, is a class. The words of Patrick Henry are a class of events; it can be predicted—he tells his story in the future tense—to have certain kinds of effects if the conditions are favorable; likewise, the proverb is a class of events, as are "ordinary common nouns or verbs"—the word *man*, for example—whole books, and even the indexical words "*that, this, I, you, which, here, now, yonder*" and "pure symbols" such as "*and, or, if*" (CP 4.447). Notice that the definition of the symbol has now been firmly detached from the definition of the predicate. Certainly, predicate words are symbols, but the class of predicates and the class of symbols are not coextensive. This is consistent with his description of the signs of algebra in the "Algebra of Logic," where far from allowing only the variables to count as symbols, Peirce includes the operators. All the signs of a formal notation are governed by conventions; all are to this extent symbolic. And it is the conventions of his "Existential System of 1897" (CP 4.422) that he is here expounding.

This point is of the greatest significance. We might say that the definition of the symbol that Peirce has relied on throughout his work on signs to this date has actually failed, and it has failed on empirical grounds. The assumptions built into the definition of the symbol fail to describe the "nature," the "mode of being" of signs in a notation. These assumptions are inherited from a very traditional logic indeed, a logic that works directly with natural language, and that describes the words of a natural language as being "categorematic" or "syncategorematic," but never both at once. This logic gives the distinction between "subject" and "predicate," which Peirce continues to use (CP 4.438), but it is the relation between subject and predicate, not just in one proposition, but in a complex of propositions, that is subject to diagrammatic analysis in the existential graphs. That distinction is no longer simply the assumption of the sign hypothesis. It is itself the material that signs must analyze, and Peirce goes to some pains to use his diagrams to tighten it up so that the analysis can reveal the logical structure of propositions, which are now its objects.

In other words, at least in respect of the description of signs in a formal notation, the topic of signs has broken out of the place of its emergence; this place was defined by the problem of names in an Aristotelian framework. Names install the very problem of metaphysics to which Peirce addresses himself, the problem of universals, and at the outset, provide the topos of the issue of "comparison." The breakout occurs as a result of including all three kinds of signs within the domain of logic and is confirmed when, in the description of a formal notation, all three are defined by means of their conventions. Peirce will need to restate the *differentia specifica* of the symbol: no longer defined by the properties of general words, symbols are defined by the fact that there is a "habit, disposition, or other effective general rule that it will be so interpreted," and that this is the *only* thing that guarantees their interpretability. This criterion holds alongside others (factual connection, sensible or structural similarity) for the index and the icon respectively, but because the three classes all share "conventionality" in the case of a notation, Peirce attempts to sharpen the distinctions among them by resorting here to a temporal criterion:

The mode of being of the symbol is different from that of the icon and from that of the index. An icon has such being as belongs to past experience. It exists only as an image in the mind. An index has the being of present experience. The being of a symbol consists in the real fact that something surely will be experienced if certain conditions be satisfied. (CP 4.447)

Readers attentive to the categorial dimension of this argument will have noticed that it does not conform to the definitions of the categories as given in the Harvard Lectures. There, "presence" and presentness are attributed to category the first, and conflict between two presentations, "struggle," is the attribute of category the second. Struggle, presumably, is the becoming-past of one of these presentations; but it is also the category that accounts for the kind of validity adhering to inductive inference, which is the accumulation of real experiences of a certain kind. Therefore, says Peirce, it is knowledge of the past and allows for the prediction of future similar events only on the basis of a hypothesis concerning a law governing those events. Granted, all signs, of whatever class, are "thirds," but the icon is a firstness of thirdness, and an index a secondness of thirdness, so the attribution of presentness to the index and of pastness to the icon is inconsistent. I suggest that this inconsistency points to the wholesale breaking down of the way in which the categorial scheme has hitherto been applied to signs. Peirce cannot find his way out of the difficulty without undertaking a thoroughgoing revision of the principle underlying the classification of signs. This he will do in the Syllabus.

Not entirely satisfied with the criterion he has proposed, Peirce makes a second attempt:

The value of an icon consists in its exhibiting the features of a state of things regarded as if it were purely imaginary. The value of an index is that it assures us of positive fact. The value of a symbol is that it serves to make thought and conduct rational and enables us to predict the future. (CP 4.448)

Here, Peirce has moved away from asking the metaphysical question regarding the "nature" or the "mode of being" of the three classes: instead, he asks their *value*, that is, their practical competences. The pragmatic definition of a thing, and of the concept of that thing, is not its essence; it must be a full description of the work it does. For the sign, this is representational work: the differences among the three classes have to do with the kind of knowledge of the objects that each affords. This is both more precise and technical, and more adequate to the purposes of this paper, than the standard definitions, because the ontology of the classes is not really an issue in this setting. Peirce will ask what kind of representational work each class of signs does and how it acquires these specific competencies.

As in the "Algebra of Logic," Peirce is interested in the division of the signs "in order to enunciate [a] proposition": there, it was that "in a perfect system of logical notation signs of these several kinds must all be employed" (W 5:30, pp. 163–64); here, it is altered subtly but significantly. The point of interest is the principle of the mixed sign:

It is frequently desirable that a representamen should exercise one of those three functions to the exclusion of the other two, or two of them to the exclusion of the third; but the most perfect of signs are those in which the iconic, indicative, and symbolic characters are blended as equally as possible.

—with which he returns us to the point of his digression:

Of this sort of signs the line of identity is an interesting example. As a conventional sign, it is a symbol; and the symbolic character, when present in a sign, is of its nature predominant over the others. The line of identity is not, however, arbitrarily conventional nor purely conventional.

Peirce goes on to show that the line of identity has both indexical features and iconic features and concludes on a triumphant note: "Thus uniting, as the line of identity does, the natures of symbol, index, and icon, it is fitted for playing an extraordinary part in this system of representation" (CP 4.448). The line of identity is the exemplary example of an exception to the rule of classification.

However, this move would have been impossible without the distinction between the sign and its replicas, which has been introduced, apparently accidentally, close to the beginning of the paper, prior to the formulation of any of the conventions:

[the graph] may be considered as the expression of whatever must be well-understood between the graphist and the interpreter of the graph before the latter can understand what to expect of the graph. There must be an interpreter, since the graph, like every sign founded on convention, only has the sort of being that it has if it is interpreted; for a conventional sign is neither a mass of ink on a piece of paper or any other individual existence, nor is it an image present to consciousness, but is a special habit or rule of interpretation and consists precisely in the fact that certain sorts of ink spots—which I shall call its *replicas*—will have certain effects on the conduct, mental and bodily, of the interpreter. (CP 4.431)

"Effects on the conduct": these are the traces of the pragmatic maxim brought to bear on the technicalities of an instrument of logic. In order to have such effects, the graphs must be asserted, and in a text probably contemporary with the one I am considering, Peirce makes the equivalence explicit: a graph "is to be distinguished from a graph-replica" and remains a graph, "though not actually asserted" (CP 4.395). Instantiation is the condition of the sign *event*, and the sign event is the condition of the production of real consequences. When instantiated, all signs take on instrumental status, functioning to some end on occasion.

I close my digression by bringing together two strands of the argument. I have made a case to the effect that the problem Peirce puts in the Harvard Lectures, concerning the mode of real action of signs, is determined by its setting in the philosophical project of those lectures. That project is to develop a pragmatist foundation for pragmatism as a method, to rationalize the methods of science, and to provide a critique of their outcomes. The sign hypothesis has a function in each one of these aspects, but in order to fulfill those three functions, it must itself be subject to the pragmatic maxim and the methods it dictates. This requires that it be something quite other than the transcendental condition of knowledge in general: it must be a self-reflecting knowledge of itself taken as object. This object, moreover, must participate fully in reality as analyzed phenomenologically by the categories: it must have qualities, it must have laws, and it must be capable of existence. Under these conditions, exemplification takes on the role not merely of providing handy didactic illustrations of a definition, but of providing "peculiar" or particularly "interesting" examples of signs at work. This is what Peirce finds when he turns his attention to the real work of particular signs in a particular "system of representation" (CP 4.421). I have suggested, moreover, that all the elements of the solution are available philosophically in the Harvard Lectures, but that Peirce fails in his commentary of the proverb example to provide a satisfactory answer to his question. What is it, then, about the description of a formal notation that helps him to provide a better one? The answer I propose to this question is that such descriptions are of their very nature empirical: they are case studies of signs at work. What work they do, and how they do it, is the question. Peirce does not, because he cannot, study the action of the proverb as a series of real-time events[23]: he cannot show it changing anything, although, as with the call of Patrick Henry, he is sure that it must. But what happens as a real consequence of the introduction of the line of identity into the system of existential graphs is the very point of the part of the exposition that follows this digression (CP 4.449 ff.), and this, he can show.

I further suggest that the distinction between the symbol and its replica has become inevitable and is consistent with several other features of this paper. Consider the introductory general definition:

An *existential graph* is a logical graph governed by a system of representation founded upon the idea that the sheet upon which it is written, as well as every portion of that sheet, represents one recognized universe, real or fictive, and that every graph drawn on that sheet, and not cut off from the main body of it by an enclosure, represents some fact existing in that universe, and represents it independently of the representation of another such fact . . . written upon another part of the sheet, these graphs, however, forming one composite graph. (CP 4.421)

I note the insistence on the materiality of the system. It is, writes Peirce a little later, a "system of expression," not (as Boole wrote of the algebra) a "representation of thought," and this system has a particular function not assimilable to attempts to construct, for example "a universal language for mathematicians" or intended to serve as "a calculus, or apparatus by which conclusions can be reached and problems solved with greater facility than by more familiar forms of expression." On the contrary, "the whole effort has been to dissect the operations of inference into as many distinct steps as possible" (CP 4.424). It is an analytical tool designed to reveal, inter alia, the "nature of mathematical reasoning" (CP 4.428):

Our purpose, then, is to study the workings of necessary inference. What we want, in order to do this, is a method of representing diagrammatically any possible set of premises, this diagram to be such that we can observe the transformation of these premises into the conclusion by the series of steps each of the utmost possible simplicity.

What we have to do, therefore, is to form a perfectly consistent method of expressing any assertion diagrammatically. The diagram must then evidently be something we can see and contemplate. Now what we see appears spread out as upon a sheet. Consequently our diagram must be drawn upon a sheet. We must appropriate a sheet to the purpose, and the diagram drawn or written on the sheet is to express an assertion. We can, then, approximately call this sheet our *sheet of assertion*. (CP 4.428–30)

Notice the materiality of Peirce's desiderata: the diagram must permit usual observation, and hence be "drawn upon a sheet." It "appears," and its function is to "express an assertion."

The Harvard Lectures established the need, under pragmatism, to deal with assertions (or assertibles) rather than confine logic to the abstract structure of propositions; here, this is taken for granted, and the next step follows directly. The representation of an assertion in some other form of expression must itself have material existence. This in turn accounts for the apparently gratuitous first convention, where Peirce distinguishes between the "grapheus," responsible for imagining the universe, and the "graphist" responsible for appropriating the sheet of assertion and inscribing the graph on it. The graphist represents the state of real knowledge of the universe created by the grapheus.[24] This is analogous to the work of inquiry at any given point in its continuing development; some of the purported facts may be wrong, or may require further modification, and so on (CP 4.431). Inquiry is a practice, material, historical, social; its work occurs in real time, through events, in assertions.

It is important to stress that Peirce does not claim that any particular graph, or any particular proposition drawn from the current state of play in the work of science, represents true knowledge or any particular proposition drawn from the current state of play in the work of science. Rather, the relation between the graphist and the grapheus, between the graphs and their objects, is itself a metaphor of Peirce's account of the relation between inquiry and (ultimate) truth. A metaphor, note, or an icon. Hence, its own truth claims are suspended. But importantly, the development of the existential graphs accompanies a move on his part to distinguish the project of his work from that of his formalist colleagues Kempe and Schröder. His objections to logical formalism are parallel to his objections to Royce's Platonist idealism; they are supported in the same way by recourse to indexicality. No diagram, no map, no algebraic formula can perform an identification without some form of collateral experience (CP 3.419); no diagram has meaning without a system for connecting it with nature (CP 3.420). This is the indexical requirement; it contrasts with Kempe's "conception [that] depends upon considering the diagram purely in its self-contained relations" (CP 3.423). The existential graphs—and we should take due note of their name—are devised as a method of analyzing assertions made concerning facts, whether these assertions be drawn from mathematics or more broadly. The first convention, then, represents the fundamental assumption of Peirce's work in this period: the objects of logical analysis are assertions, and their objects are hypothetical material truths concerning a state of affairs. The graphs themselves are icons; they bear a metaphorical relation to the processes of inquiry. Applied to that branch of inquiry called semiotic, the indexicality requirement will work out as a requirement to pick out "*this* sign" and to investigate its properties in practice. This is laboratory work, on samples, on examples. Where better to start than on the signs that constitute the instrument that he is devising for the analysis of the assertions of inquiry?

One further feature of this paper can be taken to determine the fact that in it, Peirce makes explicit the need to distinguish between the sign and its replicas. Quite unlike his work on logical algebras, the rhetoric of any of the expositions of the existential graphs is devised for the purpose of teaching them. In the algebras, Peirce can presuppose a readership that shares his assumptions, that has so much collateral experience of the matter in hand that he does not need to spell them out. This was not the case for Boole, who had to spell out some basic assumptions concerning the use of an algebraic notation to solve certain kinds of problems. In Peirce's work on formal logic through the 1880s, he is working in active conversation with a group of like-minded scholars, all of whom are seeking to solve similar sorts of problems with similar instruments, and who are equally likely to extend or modify the properties of these instruments as appropriate. The genre of a paper in formal logic—like any genre—is governed by what it does not need to say. But in the expositions of the existential graphs, Peirce is working alone. Their point is to invent the notation and to demonstrate its capacities: to instruct others in its ways and means. This is why he must spell out exactly what it is, and what it is not, intended to do; this is why so much of the writing is taken over by the rationale of the conventions; this is also why the exposition is didactic, stopping frequently to illustrate the techniques of the system; this is also why he insists that there must be an interpreter, a fact not in doubt for the algebras; this is why, indeed, expositions for the papers on the existential graphs differ widely from those on the algebras in exactly this point, that the latter are written in view of solving particular technical problems, whereas the former are written to establish them and to get them into circulation. This rhetorical fact is responsible for a presupposition both trivial and highly significant: Peirce's own reader is learning how to reproduce the signs of

1867	1885	1903
Index		
Weathercock	natural signs	hygrometer
	Physical symptoms	
		Pointing finger
		*landmark
	pointing finger	
	*demonstrative and	
	relative pronouns	*proper names
	*letters on a geometrical	
	diagram	
	*subscript numbers in	
	algebra	
Icon		
Portrait	painting	*statue of centaur
	*diagrams of geometry	
	*general formulae of	
	algebra	
Symbol		
word		
proposition		
	general words, the main	
	body of speech, any mode	general word
	of conveying	sentence
	judgment	book
		*P. Henry's call
		*the proverb

Figure 3.1. Comparison of examples from the Harvard Lectures (1903) with those from the "New List" and the "Algebra of Logic."

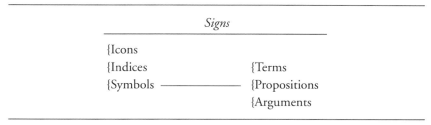

Figure 3.2. The first classification of signs.

the system. "I place a high valuation upon my Existential Graphs," he writes to Welby, "and I hope you will persevere in the study of the system; and if you do so, I desire to aid you."[25] Hence the rhetoric—let us say the genre of these expositions—is based on the assumption of replication—exact duplication, in the first instance, then adaptation and modification as the system is, Peirce hopes, taken up and applied to real problems.

The Syllabus of Topics in Logic

Following the introduction of some key examples in the Harvard Lectures, the table of the three kinds of signs now looks like Figure 3.2, which is based on the standard classification. Remark that the line of identity cannot be classified in it.

If the standard classification cannot be said to preclude mixed kinds a priori, it does have a tendency to illustrate its definitions as if pure examples of each case were the norm. But if the "most perfect signs" are now perfect blends of the three classes, then the task facing Peirce is to account for such blending. This is achieved in what I shall call the "second classification," which is based on three trichotomies and results in ten classes. I give this classification in the terminology of the Syllabus in Figure 3.3.

The second classification of signs, and the theory that it implies, are different from the first in some crucial particulars.[26] First, the second classification comprises a new trichotomy, which becomes the first. This is the trichotomy of the sign taken as a thing and an event. Note that this is not a sign "in itself," but the sign as *object* of a theoretical representation under the protocol of "grammar"; its task is to analyze the formal and material conditions for something to act as a sign. Under the standard theory, Peirce displays considerable reluctance to take these conditions of signhood seri-

	I	II	III
I	Qualisign	Icon	Term
II	Sinsign	Index	Proposition/dicent
III	Legisign	Symbol	Argument

Figure 3.3. The three trichotomies, from the Syllabus (1903).

ously. That is to say, under the standard theory, there is not, nor could there be, a theory of what the continental tradition of semiotics has called the "signifier." While it is discernibly a presupposition of the representamen in Peirce's early work, and notably a condition sine qua non of the icon (for example, CP 2.304), it is sometimes overlooked entirely (for example, CP 2.228) and sometimes counted as "superficial" (CP 4.535) or as secondary to the mental content (for example, CP 2.303). More frequently, it is noted but set aside as not being part of the significant character of the sign (for example, W 3:38, p. 107). The second classification is remarkable for asserting, on the contrary, that the material and formal properties of the sign taken as a thing are as much a part of the signhood of the sign as the representation relation and the interpretant relation. While this is implied in the relational analysis of the triad—the sign itself is the first correlate— the new classification proposes an analysis of the properties of the first correlate that is entirely unprecedented in Peirce's work.

The second difference between the first and the second classifications is that in the latter, the subdivisions thrown up by the trichotomies have a changed status. Under the standard theory, it is the terms of the trichotomy that are the classes, or "genera," of signs; under the second classification, they are components of signs. Signs are formed by combining them with one another (Figure 3.4).[27]

Combinations within the one trichotomy do not appear, and the system of the ten classes also implies other preclusions (EP 2:21; p. 296 [CP 2.264]).[28] It should be noted that this restriction, if applied, would preclude both the analysis of the line of identity discussed above, and the analysis of the proposition used in the Harvard Lectures. These examples would have to be analyzed under the protocols of the new system.[29] In order to produce the ten classes, the categorial analysis is applied three times.[30] The first time, it is applied to the general notion of the sign relation, to produce the three relata; the second time, it is applied to each of these in turn, to produce the three trichotomies. In each of these applica-

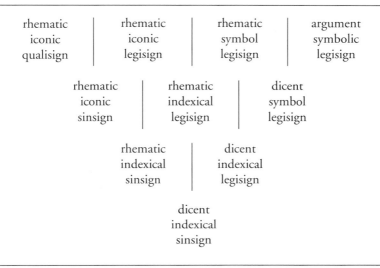

Figure 3.4. The second classification of signs, The Ten Classes (EP 2.21, p. 296 [CP 2.264], 1903).

tions, division into three is achieved through the procedure of prescission, the point of which is to state the presuppositions of each definition. By contrast, the third application of the categories reverses the procedure: it *adds* secondness to firstness, and thirdness to the product, such that each of the ten classes conforms to the general triadic structure of signhood from which the analysis starts.

The second classification is first formulated in some late pages of the draft *Syllabus of Some Topics in Logic*, under a section headed "Nomenclature and Divisions of Triadic Relations, So Far as They Have Been Determined" (MS 540; EP 2:21, p. 289 [CP 2.233 ff.]). The Syllabus was to have accompanied Peirce's Lowell Institute Lectures of 1903. The Lowell Lectures allude to the standard form of the sign hypothesis and to the analysis by "degeneracy" of the categories. This is also the case for the early parts of the Syllabus (MS 478). In the chapter devoted to the classification of the sciences, in the section headed "Speculative Rhetoric," Peirce presents the familiar two trichotomies, stating that speculative grammar is concerned with the "physiology" of signs (MS 478, p. 42) and with giving to the icon the status of "firstness of thirdness" (MS 478, p. 45). Somewhere between this part of the Syllabus and that part contained in MS 540, Something

Seems to Have Happened. There is some indication in the Logic Notebook (MS 339) that this event can be dated to late July or early August 1903, because in that notebook, between a page dated July 10 and one dated August 4, we find an undated page of jottings concerning the standard divisions of signs. At the bottom of this page, unannounced and undescribed, there is a scribbled tabular array of the *three* trichotomies. I think that this is the first such occurrence in the notebooks.

Early work on Peirce's classifications of signs has focused either on the number of classes and the rules for yielding them[31] or on the theoretical adequacy of those classes.[32] More recently, the focus has shifted to explicating the implications of the classification through different styles of diagrammatization.[33] I shall not go over the terrain of those questions here. I am interested in the changes and in the conditions of their emergence. In large measure, the broad conditions have been established in the foregoing argument, but the picture can be filled out by attending to some further features of the changes.

The manuscript text of the Syllabus itself is instructive. It is a remarkable fact about the passage in which speculative rhetoric is expounded (MS 478, pp. 40–51) that the theory of signs is somewhat less stable than the repetition, or recitation, of its habitual form would seem to suggest. The first indication of this instability occurs in the following sentence: "Representamens are divided by two trichotomies" (MS 478, p. 45)." On the face of it, this is a mere variation on the formula according to which "the representamen . . . divides by trichotomy into the general sign, or *symbol*, the *index*, and the *icon*" (EP 2:12, p. 163 [CP 5.73]) and "the symbol divides by Trichotomy into the Term, the Proposition, and the Argument" (EP 2:12, p. 164 [CP 5.76]). Each of these, the broad class of signs, and the symbol within it, is the "genuine" form, to which triadic subdivision can apply.[34] But the claim that there are "two" trichotomies of signs is unexpected, given Peirce's "triadomic" proclivities. The strangeness of this move becomes explicit a little further on (MS 478, p. 51), where Peirce refers to the trichotomy of the term, proposition, and argument as the "second" trichotomy. This is entirely consistent with there being two trichotomies, but the original editors of the *Collected Papers* found it so strange that they amended it, first by writing over "second" on the manuscript page with a penciled "third," like teachers correcting a mistake in a student's essay, and second by providing the amended version in the published text: "Of the three classes of the [third] trichotomy of representamens" [CP 2.309]). But "two" was, although problematical, truer of the standard classification than "three"; and "three" was about to be, but *was not yet*, true of the revisions effected in the Syllabus. There were not "three trichotomies" until a later stage of the draft (MS 540, p. 5).

The second indication of instability comes in the passage defining the icon in the same part of the manuscript. Peirce finds himself in something of a dilemma regarding whether the icon is "a thing" or a "mere possibility" (MS 478, p. 45–46). The dilemma arises when Peirce apparently fails to grasp his own very paradoxical notion of a "firstness of thirdness," construing the firstness of the icon in the same way as he construes category the first. What he needed was to distinguish *material possibility* from "an idea" (EP 2:20, p. 273 [CP 2.276]), which he does in this passage by distinguishing an "iconic sign" from "an icon," and exemplifying the former by "any material image, [such] as a painting." The solution rests on two moves, each of which points toward the creation of the first trichotomy: the first is to acknowledge that the very notion of an iconic sign implies that "*quâ* thing," an iconic sign has material qualities that "[render] it fit to act as a sign," and the second is to give to these iconic qualities the status of components combinable with conventions that make them significant (MS 478, p. 45–46).

The third point of instability in this passage is involved in the discussion of replicas of symbols. The replica is "only an embodiment" of a symbol that, in itself, has no existence. This discussion (reproduced at EP 2:20, p. 274 [CP 2.292]) gives two divergent definitions of the symbol. In the first place, it is "a rule that will determine its Interpretant"; in the second, this is found to require specification of the replica:

The word [*man*] has no existence although it has a real being, *consisting in* the fact that existents *will* conform to it. It is a general mode of succession of three sounds or representamens of sounds, which becomes a sign only in the fact that a habit, or acquired law, will cause replicas of it to be interpreted as meaning a man or men. (EP 2:20, p. 274 [CP 2.292])

Notice that the "succession of sounds" refers to material qualities rendered significant by convention. The word is just such a convention, and its replica is what enables it to "act as a sign." All the ingredients of the first trichotomy are in place in the discussion, although they are not distinguished as such. The symbol is defined both as the symbol and as what will become the legisign or type, but Peirce hesitates as to whether these are distinct functions:

The word and its meaning are both general rules; but the word alone of the two prescribes the qualities of its replicas in themselves. Otherwise the "word" and its "meaning" do not differ, unless some special sense be attached to "meaning." (EP 2:20, p. 274 [CP 2.292])

What the first trichotomy eventually does is to attach a "special sense" not to "meaning" but to "word."

Peirce writes elsewhere (MS 728) that a class is a solution to a problem; presumably, then, a system of classes is a solution to a systematic problem (cf. CP 4.116). My reading of this section of the Syllabus has sought to show that a systematic problem is exactly what we have: the difficulties Peirce has with the definitions of both the icon and the symbol will be resolved by specifying the functions of the first trichotomy. Likewise, the oddity involved in asserting that "representamens are divided by two trichotomies" can be read with hindsight, and in the light of the categories, as an incompleteness: the "two trichotomies" of the early part of the Syllabus leave open the place that will be filled by the triad of qualisign, sinsign, and legisign. Further, the task of this place is to state the presuppositions of the issue of assertion, here called the dicent sign.

Peirce does not appear to have solved his problem by pondering on his past mistakes, nor even to have identified them as such: he appears to discover the problem only when a lateral move into mathematics throws up the solution. The continuation of the draft Syllabus consists of two chapters, one (MSS 538, 539) on the "Nomenclature and Divisions of Dyadic Relations . . . ," and the other on triadic relations (MS 540). Both are formalizations of the classes so named. Peirce works out several systems of divisions for dyadic relations, two of which are of particular interest for what he will afterward propose for triadic relations. One of these is the matrix (CP 3.591 ff.). The other consists of eight parameters which are "cross-classified" to produce nine classes (CP 3.581, 584). It is a similar model of cross-classification that he uses to produce the ten classes of sign (cf. Figures 3.3 and 3.4).

Prior to this, in 1902, Peirce had distinguished two models of classification: the biological model of "hierarchical classification," which derives from the Aristotelian tradition, and the models of classification available from mathematics and chemistry (MS 427, pp. 142 ff.). "Why should the biologists impose upon nature a hierarchical classification as the only form?" he had asked (p. 142)—but not for the first time. In 1898, he had already drawn a sharp distinction between the "ordinary logic" and the "relative logic" in terms of what model of classification each implies:

[The ordinary logic] is tied down to the matter of a single special relation of similarity.

Thus, the ordinary logic has a great deal to say about *genera* and *species*, or in our nineteenth century dialect, about *classes*. Now a *class* is a set of objects comprising all that stand to one another in a special relation of similarity. But where ordinary logic talks of classes the logic of relatives talks of *systems*. A *system* is a set of objects comprising all that stand to one another in a group of connected relations. (CP 4.5)

The distinction is of some moment for the theory of signs because what I have called the first classification is modeled on the logic of genera and species, whereas the second is modeled on the logic of systems. The analogy Peirce used for this new project was not biology, but chemistry. Concepts, he had been arguing since the late 1890s, had "valency," that is, were best analyzed by a relational structure explicitly compared to that of an atom (for example, CP 3.470 ff.). The concept "sign" could be analyzed in just this way and is consequently found to be structurally triadic. In one manuscript (MS 482), dated by Robin as circa 1896–98, he returns on more than one occasion to the problem of the validity of the analogy of chemistry with the logical graphs he was devising at the time. At times he pursues the analogy substantively, comparing monads with particular elements (alt. p. 11); at others, he gives it the status of mere metaphor, "simply used to fix the ideas" (alt. p. 8). Yet he writes, "I confess that the comparison often recurs to my mind," and even though he hesitates, he concludes that "the suggestions of chemical graphs have directly caused important advances in modern algebra" (MS 482, alt. p. 11).

The problem seems to be definable as a question of levels. The analogy of logical graphs with the graphs of chemistry is unable to be generalized beyond the fact that they both are graphs. But if concepts have valency, then it can also be said that they are part of a larger system (cf. CP 3.454) and that the logical analysis of the concepts of a science, for example, will not be an attempt to define their indecomposable abstractions, but rather an attempt to define their systemic relations. It is in these terms that Peirce is eventually led to reconstrue the interpretant as an explanatory system (CP 4.116, 2.230). But it is also the case that the concepts whereby another concept is analyzed are themselves systemically related. The three trichotomies that provide the basis for the second classification of signs are a system of terms in just this sense; their task is to give the analytic definition of the concept "sign."

One of the achievements of chemistry that most fascinated Peirce was the periodic table, and his admiration for Mendeleev was very often expressed during the years immediately preceding and following the turn of the century. The periodic table is interesting because it is an example of the very kind of system that Peirce proposes as an alternative to hierarchical classifications such as those of the "Aristotelian tradition." It is also able to be analyzed as a mathematical formalization. Describing the workings of the table (in undated MS 693), Peirce uses similar terms to those he had used to describe the matrix of dyadic relations (MS 593), and he goes on to construe the functions and arguments of the table as approximate mathematical relations. The important points to note are these: the classifications of chemistry and mathematics, although not necessarily the same, come together in his contestation of the predominance of the biological model, because both admit cross-classifications (MS 427, p. 142–43). The principles of systems are explicated by mathematics and exemplified empirically by the periodic table. The second classification of signs is Peirce's contribution of a second example of this procedure.

The implications of this move for the class of signs are considerable. First, it gives a system of triadic relations, rather than, as in 1885, for example (W 5:30, p. 162 ff.), an ordered triplet of dual relations. The result is to formalize the hypothesis that operates throughout the theory of signs. All classes of sign are formally and materially determined by this triadicity: all are defined with, and not to the exclusion of, the interpretant relation. Second, as a consequence of the previous point, the first relatum—the sign taken in itself—is accorded full status in the analysis of the structure of signhood. It is as a consequence of this move that questions of the "quality of the sign *quâ* thing," of the material existence of the sign, and of the rule of the sign, as distinct from the rule of its object relation, are no longer out of bounds. This is the place of the first trichotomy. Nevertheless, despite the exigencies of the systematization of the class of signs, it could not have been included had it not been, in some sense, ready to go. I have proposed a story of how it came to be ready to go in the preceding part of this chapter: it tells how Peirce came to treat the sign hypothesis as a hypothesis regarding empirical facts, requiring observation of real examples of signs at work. The convenient examples of real signs at work that were available to him were provided by the language he was constructing de novo (CP 2.290 n.).

Notwithstanding Peirce's commitment to analyzing assertions concerning matters of fact, it is possible and indeed necessary to the description of a formal system that the issue of particular meanings be set aside, and that the signs of that system be defined purely in terms of the logical transformations that are possible on them (MS 455, p. 16v; CP 4.530; MS 466, p. 17; MS 693, p. 278, etc.). This is what Peirce will identify as the "Pure Mathematical point of view" (MS 455, p. 16v, p. 17; MS 478, p. 151, etc.), and he confesses that it is "a point of view far from easy to a person as imbued with logical notions as I am" (MS 455). Indeed, to give an idea of what pure mathematics is, Peirce suggests we "imagine [the graphs] described without any allusion whatever to their interpretation, [and] defined as symbols subject to the fundamental rules of transformation," (MS 466, p. 9). Likewise, the "archegetic rules" of the system are also defined as examples of the purely mathematical, and the question arises whether they are representamens at all (MS 478, p. 151). We recall the centaur: is it a representamen if its object does not exist? This case is more radical: is it a representamen if it *has no object*? But just as "mathematics appears . . . to be a science, as much as any science, although it may not contain all the ingredients of the complete idea of a science" (EP 2:8, p. 86 (CP 7.186), so may the formal signs of any "algebra" count as "signs" (CP 3.418), regardless of whether they are meaningful or "meaningless" (MS 466, p. 17). If formal, nonrepresentational signs are signs, then so too must the formal, nonrepresentational *condition* of all signs be part of their signhood. It is this decision that is represented by the first trichotomy, and in particular by the distinction between the legisign and the symbol.

For some time, Peirce maintains a formal distinction between his use of the term *sinsign* and the term *replica*. This is because the sinsign is supposed to capture the possibility that there are absolute singulars, "peculiar occurrences that are regarded as significant." Replicas replicate something governed by a law:

A Legisign is a law that is a sign. This law is usually established by men. Every conventional sign is a legisign [but not conversely]. It is not a single object, but a general type which, it has been agreed, shall be significant. Every legisign signifies through an instance of its application, which may be termed a *Replica* of it. Thus, the word "the" will usually occur from fifteen to twenty-five times on a page. It is in all these occurrences one and the same word, the same legisign. Each single instance of it is a replica. The replica is a sinsign. Thus, every legisign requires sinsigns. But these are not ordinary Sinsigns, such as are peculiar occurrences that are regarded as significant. Nor would the replica be significant if it were not for the law which renders it so. (EP 2:21, p. 291 [CP 2.246])

New examples, such as "the ring of a telephone-bell" (EP 2:21, p. 295 [CP 2.261]), are adduced to demonstrate the eventhood of a sinsign. Yet even this is not an absolute singular since recognition of the kind of event it is requires the assumption of a class of similar events. In the later versions of the second classification, although the words *replica* and *instance* continue to be used, the distinction Peirce is seeking here appears to lapse.[35] Notwithstanding these terminological hesitations, the major breakthrough has been achieved: the eventhood and the thinghood of signs can now be integrated into the theory, without this in any way compromising the "representative office" of the sign, and in such a way as to clarify how a sign acts on occasion to produce real effects.

The qualisign is a necessary corollary of the relation between the legisign and the sinsign:

A *Sinsign* . . . is an actual existent thing or event which is a sign. It can only be so through its qualities; so that it involves a qualisign, or rather, several qualisigns. But these qualisigns are of a peculiar kind and only form a sign through being actually embodied. (EP 2:21, p. 291 [CP 2.245])

We need seek no further explanation of its emergence. Nevertheless, it is tempting to speculate that the "qualities of the sign *quâ* thing" became explicitly thinkable for Peirce also as a result of the existential graphs. This is because they are icons; as such, it is their *material* properties (MS 491, pp. 1–2) that render them fit to represent whatever they do represent. Accordingly, Peirce dwells at some length on the conventions for "drawing" and "reading" them (CP 3.475) and on the material conditions of their capacity to perform their task. We find, for example, that he attends to the dimensionality of the graphs (for example, MS 484; MS 490; cf. also MS 455, p. 10). We find considerations of line, of surface, and of position; we find color and other modes of qualitative distinction (MS 482). We find him developing the notion of the sheet of assertion, using it to represent the universe of discourse (for example, CP 4.512–15; MS 280, pp. 30, 31) and the book of sheets representing alternative possible universes. We also find him including in the interpretation rules questions concerning the material implications of reading the graphs in different sequences enabled and constrained by different spatial arrangements (CP 3.475). In all of this work, Peirce is behaving like a scrupulous craftsman, and in all of it, the details he attends to acquire the status of signs, both representational and operational. I suggest that it is this work that allows Peirce to understand what the qualities of a sign taken as thing might be in concrete fact, and it is this that will make the first trichotomy more than a mere list of items established by the rule of the categories. When the ambiguities of the sinsign are sorted out, the first trichotomy is a tightly organized system of relations according to which the legisign or type is the rule governing the qualities of replicas and their capacity to act as signs (EP 2:20, p. 274 [CP 2.245–46; 2.292]).[36]

Digression on an Issue of Chronology

The passage on the "line of identity" is drawn from a manuscript entitled "Logical Tracts No. 2." In the *Collected Papers*, the editors date it at "c. 1903," which would put it in the same year as the Harvard Lectures and the Syllabus. Its discussion of signs does not coincide with that of the Harvard Lectures, and its analysis of the replica solves the problem of the repetition of signs that arose in relation with the proverb example. The passage is written as a digression, and its rhetoric might suggest that Peirce stumbles across a new problem as he deals with that example. A neat narrative account of the "development" of Peirce's theory of signs might run as follows: Peirce made this discovery while he was writing the "Logical Tracts No. 2," some time following his return from Cambridge, in the late spring or summer of 1903; then, in the course of writing the Syllabus, he reflected on the general problems associated with it, following which he produced the second classification to deal with it. That narrative has the added attraction of conforming to his narrative model of the sequence of events that change scientific generalizations. However, it runs into an empirical problem: the dating of the passage is uncertain. My story requires that it was written *between* the Harvard Lectures and the Syllabus, and this is dubious. I quote the response I received to my query from the generous and attentive scholars who run the Peirce Edition Project:

In his copy of the Collected Papers, Max Fisch dated (in his own hand) ms. 492 (which the text comes from) "c. 1903," and Robin followed suit. However this date puzzles me a lot. When on earth would Peirce have had enough time to compose such an elaborate and patient piece in 1903? He had virtually no time between the Harvard Lectures and the Lowell Lectures: almost immediately after he finished the Harvard lectures he began preparing the Lowell Lectures, the Syllabus of which was composed at a tremendous pace in October 1903. You need to make a careful comparison of the last (sixth) section of the Syllabus on Existential Graphs with ms. 492 to see whether the latter is not later. I strongly suspect that ms. 492 is later. The handwriting, for one thing, doesn't seem to allow it: it has a tinge or tone not seen in the Harvard or Lowell lectures, not to speak of the 1902 papers. The paper itself (Crane's 1900 Japanese Linen) is the same as in ms. 517 ("Kaina Stoicheia"), which we have dated early 1904, and both documents bear formal similarities. But Peirce used that same paper to write "Minute Logic" in 1902, so that is not conclusive. The handwriting is distinct enough, though. My present guess/feeling is thus that ms. 492 was composed sometime in 1904, but of course this needs to be supported much more strongly than I can do at the moment.[37]

Supposing 1904 to be right, no story at all concerning the "development" of the theory of signs can be hung on this digression. Simply, Peirce's attention is taken by an interesting sign, and he takes time off from the exposition of the conventions of the existential graphs to provide a succinct and elegant summary of semiotic. But this summary does not include most of the findings available from a key passage of the Syllabus. If Fisch, Robin, and the original editors were right about 1903, however unlikely that might seem given the hyperactivity it implies, then this noninclusion is easily explicable, and indeed, the description of the properties of the "line of identity" becomes available for generalization and inclusion in the later classification.[38] According to this hypothesis, after the Harvard Lectures, Peirce resumed work on the existential graphs, drafting introductions to them intended for an uninitiated readership: "Well, I'll be!" we can imagine him exclaiming; "Just look at that!" But we can equally well imagine him reflecting carefully on his rhetorical strategies: he might have asked as he sat quietly in his attic with the ladder retracted, "However can I convince people that signs are important? How can I get them to notice the topic, even, let alone to study the sign qua sign?" And he may have chuckled as he found the answer: stop them in their tracks when they think they're on the way somewhere else; get them to encounter the unexpected. "Remark!" he writes, as the boys on Boston Common call "Hi!" and Horatio Greenough proclaims "here!"[39]

It may be wise to enter a caveat concerning dating at this point. The Syllabus is a very long piece of work and carries evidence of some interesting shifts and even inconsistencies that suggest that it corresponds to a period of intense intellectual inquiry over some little time, possibly interspersed with other writing projects. It must be false, I believe, to date the whole of this text at some point before or after the completion of "Logical

Tracts No. 2." This must also hold in reverse. The digression from "Logical Tracts No. 2" that I have been discussing takes no account of the new work available from the revised classification worked out in the Syllabus. On a chronological account, we would have to suppose that the new work was not in fact yet available to Peirce when he was writing it. This does not support the conclusions drawn by André de Tienne from the material analysis of the manuscripts.

However, it may be that a chronological account is not the best way to explain the material in this collection of texts. Two features distinguish the work on signs in the Syllabus from previous work: one is the range of distinctions it makes available, and the other is the model of classification that organizes them. This model is a combinatory: its protocols are such as to describe particular signs as combinations of features from each of three trichotomies. While the *need* to combine features of different classes of sign with one another is demonstrated in the passage from "Logical Tracts No. 2," the actual combination we saw at work there is a combination of three kinds from a single trichotomy and is in principle ruled out by the combinatorial rules proposed in the Syllabus. In the work following 1903, we will find that, in practice, Peirce makes very little use of the combinatorial model. While certain significant distinctions among and within the trichotomies are integrated into later work, the classification itself is not.

As I have argued, Peirce's work on signs does not take the form of a general speculative theory but of the application of the sign hypothesis to some precise purpose in philosophy or in logic. Each such application throws up issues to be dealt with in, or by, semiotic. The one text of which this is not true is the Syllabus. Two factors distinguish it: (1) it is not that some observable fact becomes an example in and for the semiotic, but that the semiotic itself has become an example for a classificatory experiment; and (2) the genre of the Syllabus is determined by the need, arising from the Lowell Lectures, to give a reasoned summary of the sequence of the argument, which is, as always, ramified to an extreme. Obedient to the genre of a syllabus, Peirce classifies the sciences; then, within "logic," he gives the branches of semiotic, followed by the classes of sign. We might have expected, here, in what was intended as a table of contents, three points, one each devoted to the three classes recognized in the standard classification. But what we get is a new classification, and the reason we get it is that the very genre of the Syllabus has drawn Peirce toward reflection on the nature of classification, its means, and its competences. This Syllabus does not so much list the topics of its object discourse as acquire a topic of its own. This is the logic of classification exemplified. The "second classification of signs" is not, therefore, determined by the foundational (or antifoundational) place of semiotic in the architectonic; nor is it determined by the demands of a metasemiotic description of a formal notation. It is an exercise in classificatory techniques, and its *ratio* is given by the method, the rhetoric, of the piece of writing in which it arises.

4

Traveler, Stay Awhile

All signs have a touch of the tramp; but they can be pinned down awhile. This is the task of the special class of signs called the index, which is the kind of sign that transforms qualities and relations into "matters of fact" by connecting them to experience:

No matter of fact can be stated without the use of some sign serving as an index. If A says to B, "There is a fire," B will ask, "Where?" Thereupon A is forced to resort to an index, even if he only means somewhere in the real universe, past and future. Otherwise, he has only said that there is such an idea as fire, which would give no information, since unless it were known already, the word "fire" would be unintelligible. If A points his finger to the fire, his finger is dynamically connected with the fire, as much as if a self-acting fire-alarm had directly turned it in that direction; while it also forces the eyes of B to turn that way, his attention to be riveted upon it, and his understanding to recognize that his question is answered. If A's reply is, "Within a thousand yards of here," the word "here" is an index; for it has precisely the same force as if he had pointed energetically to the ground between him and B. (CP 2.305)

The index here is the force that directs attention to the surrounding concrete reality. It does so by establishing the relation between the here and now of the use of the sign with the location in space and time of the object identified in that reality. However, concerned that this might be construed in too restricted a manner, Peirce goes on to insist that mathematics, "and even dreams," make some use of indices. Reality is not here to be construed as conferred by physics, but by "a certain degree of fixity, in consequence of which [certain imaginary constructions] can be recognized and identified as individuals" (CP 2.305).

The achievement of "fixity" and "individuality" are the functional characteristics of the class of the index; these—and hence the index itself—are restricted to the "backward reference" of a sign.[1]

Indices may be distinguished from other signs, or representations, by three characteristic marks: first, that they have no significant resemblance to their objects; second, that they refer to individuals, single units, single collections of units, or single continua; third, that they direct the attention to their objects by blind compulsion. But it would be difficult if not impossible, to instance an absolutely pure index, or to find any sign absolutely devoid of the indexical quality. Psychologically, the action of indices depends upon association by contiguity, and not upon association by resemblance or upon intellectual operations. (CP 2.306)

It will be noted—the consequences of this point will be discussed at greater length presently—that the passage moves from "distinguishing marks" in the constitution of the index as form to its functional characteristics.

Now consider the following passage, which summarizes the example of the "map of the map." Although it does not discuss it explicitly, it is apparent that the example cannot work without implying the indexical function:

On a map of an island laid down upon the soil of that island there must, under all ordinary circumstances, be some position, some point, marked or not, that represents qua place on the map, the very same point qua place on the island. (CP 2.230)

The distinction between backward and forward reference is evident here. Each new version of the map is an icon that represents the point upon which it stands as a space, while each previous version points to that spot and locates it in relation with others. Iconicity (the map) refers *in futuro*, indexicality (the point) refers *in praeterito*. Indexicality, then, is the countervailing force to the infinite regress represented by the map of the map. It does so by individuating, and "fixing," its object, but it can only do so on a temporary basis. This is demonstrated in a recurrence of the fire example, in which the restrictedly local efficacy of the index is a problem for travelers on the road:

Suppose two men meet upon a country road and one of them says to the other, "The chimney of that house is on fire." The other looks about him and descries a house with green blinds and a verandah having a smoking chimney. He walks on a few miles and meets a second traveller. Like a Simple Simon he says, "The chimney of that house is on fire." "What house?" asks the other. "Oh, a house with green blinds and a verandah," replies the simpleton. "Where is the house?" asks the stranger. He desires some index which shall connect his apprehension with the house meant. (CP 2.287)

This is the need for "attachment." As I have stressed throughout, the road is to conversation as the hearth is to "thought," a metaphor for its conditioning circumstance and the determinant of the issues raised once it is taken as the focal figure of a philosophical problematic. What the traveler wants is what he does not have, as a direct result of being on the road: the presence of things absented by the passage of "experience" through time and space. It should be borne firmly in mind that this is no mere caprice associated with a metaphor: Pragmatism is by definition on the road, because its vocation is to be a philosophy in, and about, experience. Peirce's insight here is very modern, recognized as a contemporary preoccupation under the slogan of the "loss" of the referent. This slogan should be understood pragmatically rather than metaphysically. It arises in the inevitable gap between "presentation" and "re-presentation." Peirce bridges this gap by articulating the nominalist insistence that true reference is secure only for individuals with the realist insistence that some generalizations can be submitted to the test of reality and shown to endure. This articulation is achieved by the "contrivances and devices" of indexicality.

Fixing and individuating; backward reference; arresting for a moment the essential mobility of the objects of knowledge: broadly, these are the functions of the index. However, on closer inspection, the class of the index—its inclusiveness and the analyses that underpin it—appears itself to elude these conditions: an index, Peirce sometimes writes, is a "fragment torn away from its object" (CP 2.230), so that either part of some whole "indicates" the existence of the other. And again, the index is the "common environment of the interlocutors" (CP 2.318). It works by "contiguity," by "blind compulsion"; it "connects the apprehension with the [thing] meant" (CP 2.287). It is difficult to identify the principle of coherence that gives to a *kind of sign* the function of being—not "referring to"—the common environment of the interlocutors, and at the same time permits the solution to quite abstract problems in logic (CP 8.41; 2.305). Peirce would certainly retort that this objection relies on the nominalist assumption that there is an ontological difference between signs and bits of reality; but this retort goes no way toward finding the needed principle. Furthermore, the examples adduced to elucidate the index display a somewhat challenging heterogeneity. Over the years, the class of the index comes to contain a weathercock, a pointing finger, exclamations, pronouns and prepositions, natural signs and physical symptoms, labeling devices on diagrams, landmarks, proper names,[2] quantifiers and some other logical operators, and the arrangement of cards in card tricks. What could be the criteria that would underpin a class that contains this range and more?

It would be open to us simply to dismiss Peirce's attempt to treat this diversity as a single class: we could argue that Peirce indulged in taxonomies with excessive enthusiasm, and there is nothing that compels us to do likewise. The contemporary usage of the term *index* is such as to favor an objection along these lines.[3] The range of things that Peirce classes as indices is simply too heterogeneous to be accommodated within a single class, or to be adequately or nontrivially described by a single criterion or set of criteria. The index is a useful category only if it designates a class of like-minded signs, and we should proceed to formulate some definition that achieves a precise purpose. For example, we could count the index as the device that secures reference, then rule out those examples of "indexicality" given by Peirce that do not "secure reference." One proposal along these lines might be that the scientific instruments do not "refer," on the grounds that "to refer" is a language act. Then the class of the index would be constrained by the class of linguistic signs or their formal equivalents. A second proposal might take the following form: Peirce is wrong to count the quantifiers as indices; the scholastics did so, but they were mistaken because the quantifiers do not refer.[4] This objection does not ask what it is about the quantifiers and other examples of the index that makes Peirce class them together. It starts from a differentiation of kinds of meaning in which "reference" is distinguished from "sense"; anything that is neither the one nor the other is an operator. By contrast, Peirce differentiates *kinds of signs* on the basis of their modus operandi. He counts as "indices" signs whose function is to "select" that to which a general sign is applied. In this case, even quantifiers such as "something" or "nothing" select that to which the predicate applies, even if that selection is vague and inapplicable to a state of affairs.

While the foregoing proposals rest on the assumption that indices are verbal/discursive or formal notational signs, an alternative position amounts to counting indexicality as a nonsemiotic adjunct to language; only symbolic signs, on this view, count as signs (or as language), and reference is that act of joining the nonsemantic with the semantic. Hence, as in the previous objection, the quantifiers would count as nonreferential because they are nonsemantic. On this view, it would be consistent to class together the technical instruments with the verbal indexical devices; but to do so on the grounds that this class is ipso facto nonsemiotic runs counter to the systematic inclusion of the index alongside the icon and the symbol within the general class of signs. It would correspond with the position taken by Peirce in "On a New List of Categories," but not with his later work. Peirce argues that any system of signs must include all three classes, without which stipulation, logic falls into a sterile formalism which it is his express purpose to avoid. The driving force of Peirce's semiotic, I recall, is to establish a domain in which reason and experience, logic and science, are not ontologically or methodologically separate.

By contrast with these accounts, I am here to learn about Peirce. The upshot is to clean up Peirce's class by excluding from it those signs that do not refer on some definition of reference; none tells us anything about what Peirce might have been trying to do by including as indices the apparently heterogeneous examples. However, all such attempts to clean up Peirce's class are predicated on the assumption that classes are homogeneous. I have argued in the previous chapter that Peirce came to question this conception of classification. Wittgenstein too rejects it, replacing it with the "family resemblances" theory of class membership, and it is certainly heuristically convenient to treat Peirce's classes of signs as "families" in this sense, held together by a "set of connected relations."

However, families are fractious things. In the following section, I examine the class of the index by attending more closely to three groups of examples, the natural signs, the scientific instruments, and the conventional indices such as quantifiers and pronouns. My purpose is to see what can be learned from Peirce's refusal to class these separately.

I

Let us start with the "natural signs and physical symptoms." (W 5:30, p. 163)[5]

Every physical force reacts between a pair of particles, either of which may serve as an index of the other. (EP 2:2, p. 9 [CP 2.300])

To take this sort of sign as a simple fact of nature is to overlook a crucial principle of Peirce's work: semiotic is a theory of second intentions as they apply to first, and as such, must differentiate between them; this is the difference between the relation of cause and effect (a first intention), and this relation taken to be a sign (a second intention). The crucial words are "may serve as." First intentions may be theoretically independent of second intentions, but they can only be known through them, and Peirce's semiotic is a theory of this knowing. Science treats as signs events of nature: what happens, what is involved, when it does so? First intentions and second intentions behave according to a different temporality. I take this difference to correspond (approximately) to the difference between "evolution" and "history." Sebeok's account of the index has the consequence of collapsing history back into evolution, hence reducing knowledge of nature to nature itself. On Peirce's view, knowledge thus conceived is a knowledge that cannot differentiate itself from instinct, and therefore cannot give an account of error.

Peirce himself appears not always to have attended to this distinction. This usually occurs when the three classes of sign are obtained through the analysis by degeneracy. Take this example:

A sign is either an icon, an index, or a symbol. An icon is a sign which would possess the character which renders it significant, even though its object had no existence; such as a lead-pencil streak as representing a geometrical line. An index is a sign which would, at once, lose the character which makes it a sign if its object were removed, but would not lose that character if there were no interpretant. Such, for instance, is a piece of mould with a bullet-hole in it as sign of a shot; for without the shot there would have been no hole; but there is a hole there, whether anybody has the sense to attribute it to a shot or not. A symbol is a sign which would lose the character which renders it a sign if there were no interpretant. Such is any utterance of speech which signifies what it does only by virtue of its being understood to have that signification. (CP 2.304)

Under this style of analysis, it is important to Peirce to "prove" that only the symbol is a fully genuine sign, that is, that it displays the three-term relation. Here, the icon has a virtual but not a real object, and the index is an index whether or not it is interpreted. However, we should beware of a confusion: Peirce does not claim that the bullet hole is not taken to be a sign; he merely claims that it is not interpreted. The passage does not overlook the principle of second intentionality so much as take it for granted. Taking something as a sign is a necessary, but not a sufficient, condition for interpretation or semiosis, which is the transformative dynamic of second intentions. Even under the analysis by degeneracy, second intentionality is what makes the difference between mere secondness, and indexicality: "A

Sign does not function as a sign unless it be understood as a sign" (MS 599, quoted from Marty).

It is for this reason that the apparently natural signs are continuous with the scientific instruments. Technical aids enhance perception and direct it toward precise scientific purposes; they are devised as means of taking bits of nature as signs and are thus the technical realization of second intentionality:[6]

A sun-dial or a clock *indicates* the time of day. (EP 2:2, p. 8 [CP 2.285])

a low barometer with a moist air [*sic*] is an index of rain; that is we suppose that the forces of nature establish a probable connection between the low barometer with moist air and coming rain. A weathercock is an index of the direction of the wind; because in the first place it really takes the self-same direction as the wind, so that there is a real connection between them, and in the second place we are so constituted that when we see a weathercock pointing in a certain direction it draws our attention to that direction, and when we see the weathercock veering with the wind, we are forced by the law of mind to think that direction is connected with the wind. The pole star is an index, or pointing finger, to show us which way is north. A spirit-level, or a plumb bob, is an index of the vertical direction. (CP 2.286)

This second passage is remarkable for its principled refusal to distinguish between the "pole star" (given by nature), the "pointing finger" (a human practice), and weathercocks and barometers (technical devices). Taking, making, and using signs are equally and on the same grounds ways of effecting second intentionality from first.

However, there remains a nagging doubt concerning the technical instruments. It is one thing for them to count as ways of making signs out of the givens of the natural world, and quite another to claim that they themselves are signs. They are not signs if they are considered merely as pieces of machinery, and there are plenty of examples one could adduce to illustrate this distinction. They are signs when considered from the point of view of their representational function. What is a sign that a barometer might count as a member of this class? If it is indeed the case that taking, making, and using signs are all equally ways of effecting second intentionality, the beginning of an answer is provided in the "New List":

second intentions are the objects of the understanding considered as representations, and the first intentions to which they apply are the objects of those representations. (W 2:4, p. 56)

The definition is commutative: second intentions are representations, and representations are second intentions whose objects are first intentions. It would be hard to exclude weathercocks and barometers from this definition. On the contrary, such things are technical devices for doing what all signs do, that is, converting their objects into the kind of stuff with which semiosis deals, or deals further. This suggests that the index is the semiotic device par excellence. As distinct from the suggestion discussed above, that indices are nonsemantic adjuncts to language, this analysis suggests that indices—and a fortiori the scientific instruments—are "semiotic" precisely because their function is to convert first intentions into second.

Now it is clear that this may also be the case for the other kinds of sign, since the object of any second intention is a first intention, and first intentions are not necessarily raw stuff. So this account does not get to the specific character of indices as distinct from icons or symbols. Indeed, if, as I suggested above, the instruments are the paradigm case of second intentionality, they are such for the whole class of signs. This suggests that from this point of view, the specificity of the classes may not be particularly important. Further, as Umberto Eco has pointed out, not only is it the case that signs are unlikely to be pure examples of one kind or another, but it is also likely that the very project of a semiotic taxonomy is ultimately not useful.[7]

Nevertheless, indices are posited as a class in much of Peirce's writing, and we need to find out if this class is indeed doing particular kinds of work in pursuit of some aspect of the sign hypothesis. Let us move on to the group of notational and verbal linguistic indices. Recall that these are the examples that effected (in 1885) a major modification in the definitions of the three kinds. Their inclusion as indices entails that at least this large group of signs is mixed over the criteria that had heretofore distinguished indices from symbols, that is, convention. These are conventional signs that function as indices:

Geometricians mark letters against the different parts of their diagrams and then use these letters to indicate those parts. Letters are similarly used by lawyers and others. Thus, we may say: If A and B are married to one another and C is their child while D is brother of A, then D is uncle of C. Here A, B, C, and D fulfil the office of relative pronouns, but are more convenient since they require no special collocation of words. (EP 2:2, p. 8 [CP 2.285])

It is not the nature or the form of the letters themselves that makes them indices, but the way they are used. These are devices whose constitution is conventional, but whose function is indexical. In the case of the passage above, it is clear that such things as "letters" are conventional symbols that may sometimes be, but are not always, used as indexical devices. This is not always so. Some words are conventionally constituted to fulfill an indexical function. Unlike the letters in the above example, their use does not vary, and their nature as indices seems as it were to be built in:

The demonstrative pronouns, "this" and "that," are indices. For they call upon the hearer to use his powers of observation, and so establish a real connection between his mind and the object; and if the demonstrative pronoun does that—without which its meaning is not understood—it goes to establish such a connection; and so is an index. The relative pronouns, who and which, demand observational activity in much the same way, only with them the observation has to be directed to the words that have gone before. (CP 2.287)

The terminations which in any inflected language are attached to words "governed" by other words, and which serve to show which the governing word is, by repeating what is elsewhere expressed in the same form, are likewise indices of the same relative pronoun character. (CP 2.287)

A possessive pronoun is two ways an index: first it indicates the possessor, and, second, it has a modification which syntactically carries the attention to the word denoting the thing possessed. (CP 2.287)

Other indexical words are prepositions, and prepositional phrases, such as, "on the right (or left) of." Right and left cannot be distinguished by any general description. Other prepositions signify relations which may, perhaps, be described; but when they refer, as they do oftener than would be supposed, to a situation relative to the observed, or assumed to be experientially known, place and attitude of the speaker relatively to that of the hearer, then the indexical element is the dominant element. (CP 2.290)

Supplied by the grammar of some language, or constructed from its resources (as is the case for any algebraic notation), such things "fulfill offices" or functions. Let us consider further examples: is "a rap on the door" (EP 2:2, p. 8 [CP 2.285]) a different kind of index from a "ring on the telephone" or an exclamation? What about a thunderclap? (EP 2:2, p. 8 [CP 2.285]). Is our temptation to class them separately due to some genuine difference or to a long-held habit of distinguishing nature from artifice? And if we hold to this latter distinction, on which side of it does language fall?

The following example of a verbal index is "intended to act upon the hearer's nervous system":

When a driver to attract the attention of a foot passenger and cause him to save himself, calls out "Hi!" so far as this is a significant word, it is, as will be seen below, something more than an index; but so far as it is simply intended to act upon the hearer's nervous system and to rouse him to get out of the way, it is an index, because it is meant to put him in real connection with the object, which is his situation relative to the approaching horse. (CP 2.287)

Peirce classes this example together with pronouns and prepositions as all indifferently connecting one piece of experience with another: we must acknowledge that the analysis is a trifle reductive. It will help to consider a feature of the verbal signs that I have so far not discussed: they all to some degree function to establish the relationship between interlocutors and use it for some precise purpose. Thus, the prepositions establish the situation of the hearer relative to the speaker and to the observed object, the relative pronouns provide the framework within which certain possible objects are excluded from the interpretational range of some piece of discourse, and so on. This explains the "rap on the door" and the "ring on the telephone," both establishing the channel of communication on which the relation of speaker and hearer depends. It also explains the following collection, apparently disparate, but held together by one of the most illuminating principles used by Peirce to explain indexicality:

Some indices are more or less detailed directions for what the hearer is to do in order to place himself in direct experiential or other connection with the thing meant. Thus, the Coast Survey issues "Notices to Mariners," giving the latitude and longitude, four or five bearings of prominent objects, etc., and saying there is a rock, or shoal, or buoy, or lightship. Although there will be other elements in such directions, yet in the main they are indices. (CP 2.288)

Along with such indexical *directions of what to do to find the object* meant, ought to be classed those pronouns which should be entitled selective pronouns [or quantifiers] because they inform the hearer how he is to pick out one of the objects intended, but which grammarians call by the very indefinite designation of indefinite pronouns. Two varieties of these are particularly important in logic, the universal selectives, such as quivis, quilibet, quisquam, ullus, nullus, nemo, quisque, uterque, and in English, any, every, all, no, none, whatever, whoever, everybody, anybody, nobody. These mean that the hearer is at liberty to select any instance he likes within limits expressed or understood, and the assertion is intended to apply to that one. The other logically important variety consists of the particular selectives, quis, quispiam, nescio quis, aliquis, quidam, and in English, some, something, somebody, a, a certain, some or other, a suitable, one.

Allied to the above pronouns are such expressions as all but one, one or two, a few, nearly all, every other one, etc. Along with pronouns are to be classed adverbs of place and time, etc. Not very unlike these are, the first, the last, the seventh, two-thirds of, thousands of, etc. (CP 2.289)

All these indices "give directions for finding" their objects, that is, for establishing a relationship of selective attention between the interlocutors and the object. This is a performative construal of indexicality, consistent with the pragmatic turn of Peirce's late work in which he sought to theorize the action of signs and through that, their power to produce action.

At the "the gate of perception," some indices fix their object, individuate it, and do so "without implying any characters at all." They present it *to* re-cognition but do not "recognize it." At "the gate of action," some others tell us how to find that object. In both cases, the index is incapable of generalization. Its task is to bring some thing to interpretation, and for that reason it is also the mechanism of "surprise" in which some interpretation is found to fail.

The index therefore plays a crucial role in Peirce's pragmatism, especially in two respects. First fallibilism: it is the index that connects representation with experience; hence, it secures the conditions under which some judgment can be shown to be in error; and it is the device whereby logic can acknowledge ignorance, or error, concerning some object, without entailing the nonexistence of that object (CP 8.41). Moreover, since pragmatism as Peirce elaborated it requires the entailment of logic with empirical science in order to build a "truly scientific philosophy," experience and logic must be strictly entailed with one another. The class of operations needed to achieve this entailment must be performed by a single class of sign; if this requirement could not be met by a single class, the entailment would be defective. No less than Peirce's account of truth and truth seeking depends upon this project.

Second, the relation of knowledge and action: made, taken, or simply used as given, indices are devices for interpreting a bit of the world in such a way as to guide action (the thunderclap, the rap on the door, "Hi!", the notices to mariners); some are devices for establishing the conditions of communication, others for using communication to some particular effect, and still others for converting "experience" into the data for theory.

As long as they are not confused with the raw stuff of nature and construed strictly as second intentions, all indices are devices. I include fevers and claps of thunder under this description, since they are used in ways extraneous to their constitution as effects of some natural cause. The range of the examples is striking because it acknowledges the range of tasks that these devices are engaged in. It is not yet clear, however, that the specificity of the class of the index can be secured. If all signs are instruments when they are instantiated, the difference between classes would have to be sought in the clear distinction between one range of tasks and another. At this stage, all we can say is that this distinction is commanded by the vocation of pragmatism: this is the *purpose* of the class, it is not yet an account of the modus operandi of indices as distinct from icons or symbols.

II

Sometimes Peirce's difficulties in defining the index consist in too great a breadth, in which case they capture very little about the operation of indexicality; sometimes, by contrast, they are too narrowly determined by the particular features of a set of examples. The most interesting difficulties, however, occur when the definitions are hijacked by criteria used for distinguishing the fundamental categories. In these cases, a tendency to apriorism in Peirce's reliance on the categories allows metaphysical fundamentals to take over from the design of a tool—a theoretical definition—orienting it toward illustration of these fundamentals rather than devising it for any particular task in semiotic. It is this kind of difficulty that has the gravest consequences. For if we were to conflate secondness with indexicality, we would fail to account for the signhood of the index and hence for its capacity to enter into, and to orient, semiosis. This would lead to the following dilemma.

If it is the case, as Peirce holds until 1903, that indices are indices even in the absence of interpretation, then it would follow from his definition of the three branches of semiotic that there is no rhetoric of the index. This would be consistent with holding that indices are given by nature. But if it is the case, as I argued above, that the second intentionality of the index secures its status as a sign, then, qua sign, it must meet the minimum condition on signhood, which is that it is a three-term relation of representamen, object, and interpretant. Formalized by the relational analysis into *n* terms, the categorial analysis flouts this requirement, on the grounds that an index is "degenerate in the second degree," that is, is constituted by a two-term relation. The difficulty is clear: if signs are defined *ex hypothesi* by a three-term relation, and the index is a two-term relation, the index is not a sign. The same problem arises for the icon. Peirce's answer to this is that only symbols are "genuine" signs; the other two classes are "degenerate" in that they exhibit some, but not all, of the features of signhood. But this is unsatisfactory, for the three-term relation that defines signhood is a structure of relations, not a list of features. If one of the terms of that relational structure is eliminated, the structure changes. On any definition of the sign that Peirce produces, that modified structure would be incapable of identification, or use, as a sign.

The retrieval of the principle of second intentionality resolves this difficulty. When some fragment of reality serves as a sign of some other fragment of reality as Peirce puts it, it is taken as, hence interpreted as, a sign. In order to interpret that fragment of reality—say, a clap of thunder—we have first to interpret it as something more than a loud noise issuing from the heavens. Then the interpretant is restored to the relational structure, and the sign functions as sign and not merely as a discharge of energy in a low-pressure system. Now if the two-term relational analysis of the index were right, this solution would imply a further step: the index would cease to be an index and become a symbol as a result of retrieving its structural interpretability. This conclusion is implied in the following passage:

A weather-cock, which is a sign of the direction of the wind, must really turn with the wind. This word in this connection is an indirect one; but unless there be some way or other which shall connect words with the things they signify, and shall ensure their correspondence with them, they have no value as signs of those things. Whatever has these two characters is fit to become a sign. It is at least a symptom, but it is not actually a sign unless it is used as such; that is unless it is interpreted to thought and addresses itself to some mind. As thought is itself a sign we may express this by saying that the sign must be interpreted as another sign. (W 3:27, p. 76)

This de facto synonymy of "sign" with "symbol" has the consequence that the classes of sign no longer accomplish any real work to pursue or elaborate the sign hypothesis. Further, it relegates the significance of the differences among classes of sign to their constitutive origins, effectively deleting them from the moment of interpretation or its further effects and consequences. It is clear that this outcome does not correspond with Peirce's practice, since, for instance in formal logic, the pursuit of interpretation is achieved principally through the manipulation of icons and indices. It also violates the pragmatic maxim.

This difficulty inheres in a habit of Peirce's work, the source of which can be traced to the "New List." In the passage where he introduces the classifications of kinds of representation (W 2:4; pp. 55–59), Peirce uses prescission to derive the three fundamental categories; he then reapplies it to produce the three divisions of signs. Relates whose "reference to a ground is prescindible" are opposed to those whose reference to a ground is "unprescindible." This opposition produces the distinction between "likenesses" and "indices," respectively. It is based on the opposition between "internal" and "relative," and "correspondence in fact," which is presumably "external." The third class is based on "imputation," and it accounts for all "general signs." The division then corresponds to the division between "internal to the representation" (the likeness or icon), external to the representation (the index), and produced by the work of reason (the symbol). Only this last is relevant to logic, for it is logic that deals with the work of reason, and in this schema, this corresponds with the work of interpretation (W 2:4, p. 56). Interpretation is construed through argument, argument is a division of symbols where the other divisions are constituents thereof, and argument is the province of logic.

The moves Peirce goes through in this passage produce a precise correlation between the classes of sign and the categories, with the effect that "argument" and hence interpretation are denied to the first two classes. Yet it was on this very criterion that representation *as a category* had been distinguished from the other categories. The homology risks reducing the differentiation among kinds of representation to a repetition of the categories in general: symbols = thirdness, indices = secondness, icons = firstness. Peirce attempts—and his commentators have followed him in this—to correct for this reduction by introducing the ideas of "firstness of thirdness" and "secondness of thirdness," but I put it that this correction does not solve the problem so much as disguise it. If the sign is not a three-term relation based on the structural centrality of the interpretant, it fails to be a sign and cannot account for semiosis or for inquiry. *Pace* the commentators: if the semiotic of Peirce's pragmatism is confined to the symbol, it does no work other than what can be done by the most orthodox philosophy of language. Surely, writes the semiotician, the classes of sign end up more fruitfully than in their own irrelevance?

Now, as we know, Peirce's later work comes to include icons and indices in the work of logic. Nevertheless, the effects of the denial I have outlined pervade even the argument of the Harvard Lectures of 1903, where the inclusion of indices and icons within propositions effects a similar reduction. The divergence between these two directions of Peirce's work amounts to a serious inconsistency, which demands that the three classes be redefined on some other basis. This does not occur until the new work outlined in the Syllabus, in which, as I have argued in the previous chapter, the division into kinds is aligned with the definition of signhood as such. When this happens, all signs, of whatever class, are defined triadically; the interpretant is structurally inherent to each, and hence, the branch of semiotic that attends to the effectivity of signs—that is, rhetoric—pertains to all classes. It further follows that the interpretant is not restricted to the class of symbols, but that any class of sign can act as an interpretant to any other.[8] Peirce then turns this into a principle: if symbols are interpreted only by other symbols, then they do not achieve the purpose of signs, which is to orient signs toward action.

However, it also follows from the second classification and its later developments that there are no "pure" icons, indices, or symbols, and it would seem to follow from this that the issue of definition and exemplification for any of the classes must lapse. In fact, however, in place of definitions of classes of sign, we find attempts to define the indexical, or the iconic, or the symbolic function: this means both its *purpose* and the *mode of operation* by which that purpose is to be achieved. Any particular instance of a sign might now fulfill all three (or more), but each function continues to require attention. I have already considered the pragmatic purpose of the index. I now turn to its mode or modes of operation—that is, I ask *how* an index works to do what it must do.

III

The answer to this question depends in part on the distinction between a type and its tokens and therefore becomes available only after the important work of 1903—or rather, more accurately, the distinction between the type and the token—clarifies a somewhat perplexing point in Peirce's earlier discussions of the index. As we have seen, Peirce insists from the outset that the index is "real," that it forms part of the reality of which its object is the other part. "If the Sign be an Index, we may think of it as a fragment torn away from the Object, the two in their Existence being one whole or a part of such whole" (CP 2.230). The difficulty in formulations such as this is that they appear to conflate the first intentionality of the "fragment of reality" with its second intentionality, its function as sign. The introduction of the first trichotomy amounts to an analysis of the formal conditions of second intentionality. When this is in place, Peirce intuits a special relationship between indices and tokens, over and above the necessary condition of the use of any sign. A sign will function indexically if its representative character depends on its own thinghood and eventhood: this sign in this place used at this time under these circumstances to indicate this particular object. The other two classes of sign have their objects attached to them, by convention or by resemblance. Another way of putting this is that the index is the traveling sign par excellence, moving on after every use, carrying no bags.

In many of the examples considered above, the function of the index has something important to do with establishing the relation of speaker and hearer; some others are explicitly performative. Consider the function of indexicality in the operations of assertion:

> In every assertion we may distinguish a speaker and a listener. The latter, it is true, need have only a problematical existence, as when during a shipwreck an account of the accident is sealed in a bottle and thrown upon the water. The problematical "listener" may be within the same person as the "speaker"; as when we mentally register a judgment, to be remembered later. . . .
>
> The assertion consists in the furnishing of evidence by the speaker to the listener that the speaker believes something, that is, finds a certain idea to be definitively compulsory on a certain occasion. There ought, therefore, to be three parts in every assertion, a sign of the occasion of the compulsion, a sign of the enforced idea, and a sign evidential of the compulsion affecting the speaker in so far as he identifies himself with the scientific intelligence.
>
> Because compulsion is essentially *hic et nunc*, the occasion of the compulsion can only be represented to the listener by compelling him to have experience of that same occasion. Hence it is requisite that there should be a kind of sign which shall act dynamically upon the hearer's attention and direct it to a special object or occasion. Such a sign I call an Index. It is true that there may, instead of a simple sign of this kind, be a precept describing how the listener is to act in order to gain the occasion of experience to which the assertion relates. But since this precept tells him how he is to act, and since acting and being acted on are one and the same, and thus action is also *hic et nunc*, the precept must itself employ an Index or Indices. That to which the index directs attention may be called the subject of the assertion. (CP 2.334–36)

We should attend to the following points in this passage: (1) the generalized assumption of the communicative frame of assertion; (2) the performativity of the assertion, in that it acts on the listener's attention in such a way as to "compel him to have [an] experience"; (3) the assumption that the uptake, or the interpretant, of that act must itself be (or involve) an act; (4) the local effectivity of the assertion, in that it is limited to a particular occasion; (5) the local effectivity of the index, in that it acts to connect this listener's apprehension to this object or occasion; and (6) the functional equivalence of a "simple sign" and a "precept." Of particular interest is the fact that this passage is an analysis of an assertion, not of a "proposition." Where a proposition is a logical form, an assertion is a sign *in actu*, that is, a token, significant as occurring just when and where it does. When an assertion is considered as a token, this implies something over and above the necessary condition of the use of any sign, and the same is true of the index. We are not talking about the "realization" of a form here: we are talking about the meaning of the act, which does not inhere in its formal components or their relations. This sequence of consequences is implied in points 4 and 5. The index has only local effectivity as a representamen, in that its object is occasional, and this effectivity is tied to the local effectivity of its act, in that it has power only within the conditions of a particular event of semiosis.[9]

Peirce's analysis delineates three "parts" to an assertion. These are informed by two aspects of his semiotic: the division of signs, and the branches of semiotic. On the one hand, the "enforced idea" can be construed as an icon, a qualisign, or a term,[10] while the sign of the occasion is explicitly the index. On the other hand, to take the sign as an assertion, that is, as an act, commands an element that spells out the rhetorical dimension: an assertion requires "a sign evidential of the compulsion affecting the speaker in so far as he identifies himself with the scientific intelligence." The entailment of the operations of indexicality with the operations of the communicative frame of the assertion suggests that rhetoric may provide the key to the "problem" of the index.[11]

This suggestion is supported by the example of the "notices to mariners," and by Peirce's account of the construction of a domain of experience shared between interlocutors for the purposes of reference. In the former, the performative is more in the nature of advice, whereas in the latter, the indices of assertions are construed as "directions." It receives further support from the case of the card trick, where the role of the players is close to that of the traveler who "desires some index which shall connect his apprehension with the house meant" (CP 2.287):

But whichever of these methods you employ, you should not touch the row of black cards until the red cards having been regathered after the last dealing, you have said something like this: "Now I think that all these dealings and cuttings and exchanges of the last cards have sufficiently mixed up the red cards to give a certain interest to the fact that I am going to show you; namely, that this row of black cards forms an index showing where any red card you would like to see is to be found in the red pack. But since there is no black king in the row, of course the place of the red king cannot be indicated; and for that reason, I shall just cut the pack of red cards so as to bring the king to the face of it, and so render any searching for that card needless." You then cut the red cards. That speech is quite important as restraining the minds of the company from reflecting upon the relation between the effect of your cutting and that of theirs. Without much pause you go on to say that you shall leave the row of black cards just as they are, simply putting so many of them from one end of the row to the other. You now ask some one, "Now, what red card would you like to find?" On his naming the face-value of a card, you begin at the left-hand end of the row of black cards and count them aloud and deliberately, pointing to each one as you count it, until you come to the ordinal number which equals the face-value of the red card called for; and in case that card is the knave or queen, you call "knave" instead of "eleven" on pointing at the eleventh card, and "queen" on pointing at the last card. When you come to call the number that equals that of the red card called for, you turn the card you are pointing at face up. Suppose it is the six, for example. Then you say, naming the card called for, that that card will be the sixth; or if the card turned up was the knave, you say that the card called for will be "in the knave-place," and so in other cases. You then take up the red packet, and counting them out, aloud and deliberately, from one hand to the other, and from the back toward the face of the packet, when you come to the number that equals the face-value of the black card turned, you turn over this card as soon as you have counted it, and lo! it will be the card called for. (CP 4.591)

The red cards are an index not because they are a sign given by nature, or causally related, but because they are a "fragment torn away from its object" (CP 2.230). In this, they resemble the relation of smoke to fire or of symptoms to a syndrome.

"Evidently," as Peirce writes, "our conception of rhetoric has got to be generalized" (EP 2:23, p. 326). There is rhetoric involved in the arrangement of the cards, in the accompanying gestures, and in the speech (including its delivery). The arrangement of the cards gives the dealer "instructions" for locating the cards that have purportedly been shuffled, while the gestures are designed both to accomplish this task for the dealer, and to disguise those instructions for the other players. Peirce makes it very clear that the speech thwarts the standard indexical function of giving "in-structions" or "directions" for finding the object meant; but it is also clear that this contrast illuminates the standard case.

Here is a second example of a similar use of indices to thwart refer-ence: it comes from a story I heard on Australian radio not long ago. Some researchers—an archeologist, a geographer, and an anthropologist—de-cided to retrace the journey recorded in the diary of a nineteenth-century explorer named Hodgkins who himself had been attempting to map an important Aboriginal trade route. In itself, this is an indexical exercise. Their predecessor had wanted to find a particular plant with narcotic prop-erties that was extremely valuable in the preinvasion Aboriginal economy. The Aboriginal guides he had used kept telling him "it's just over there," but he quickly realized that they were systematically misleading him so that he wouldn't find it. Their means were entirely indexical: they lit signal fires that were picked up by people ahead, who would respond by setting a signal fire in a direction that led away from the trail. As in the previous case, this use of indexical signs is simply the opposite of the standard one, which it serves to illuminate.

Referring is an act, supported by the indexical devices that we have considered: they ensure shared reference, or, in these two special cases, en-sure that it is not shared. Rhetoric is involved throughout in that, as Peirce puts it, rhetoric is the art of rendering signs effective (EP 2:23, p. 326). This leads me to recall that Peirce has drawn our attention (in CP 2.336) to the fact that the range of devices that might serve as indices does not stop at simple or single signs such as letters or exclamations; rather, it must extend to include quite complex rhetorical devices, like the instructions to mariners and the speech that accompanies the card trick. It also suggests a further inference that warrants attention: that the conditions under which things serve as indices are usefully described as rhetorical conditions. I want to explore this inference in the form of a hypothesis concerning genre, where genre counts as a postulate concerning the performativity of semiosis. This postulate involves (at least) the following elements: the con-struction of particular forms of relationship between the interlocutors, by the medium of communication and the social situation in which that com-munication has a function[12]; the use of that relationship to some end, and hence relevance criteria such as those discussed by Grice for "conversation" but constrained by the specificities of that function[13]; hence, constraints and requirements on topic, register, arrangement of materials[14]; what can be done to make the communication achieve its end under these constraints, and hence, protocols of reference and proof,[15] as well as turn-taking and so on; and uptake, that is, what happens next.[16] Significantly, any genre operates on the basis of presuppositions concerning all of these factors, which do not need to be explicit in the exchange itself but which come to the fore with mistakes and transgressions, or the deliberate counteruses I have discussed. I shall seek to sustain two arguments: first, that indices function in terms of these presuppositions, and hence that the presuppositions are the conditions of intelligibility of the indices they use; and second, that some genres require the construction and deployment of particular indices for their operation, and some things function as indices only in particular generic settings. For each argument, I shall draw on Peirce's own examples, sometimes expanding them. In general, I hope to account for the heterogeneity of Peirce's examples of indexicality by means of these arguments; the classhood of the index is largely clarified once these extra premises are introduced, but there will be some exceptions.

In the exposition of the card trick, the term *index* is used in the sense of an index in, say, a printed book; each black card refers to a "place" in the collection of red cards, where both collections are deemed to be systems, and places are identified relative to one another. So each black card *in position* is also an "index" to a red card. I suggest that it is only within card tricks such as the one Peirce describes that any card can be taken as functioning as an index. In other card games, indexicality operates in other ways—for example, through the cards discarded by some player operating to indicate those that s/he is building on. This is my first example: the indexicality of the cards is specific to the genre, the game, that Peirce is expounding.[17] Is this the case for any other examples Peirce adduces of the index?

For a second example, let us recall the indexical functions performed by "letters" under various circumstances (CP 2.285). Peirce distinguishes two genres, geometry and legal documents, in which "letters" are used to "fulfill the office" of indices—of names in the former, and of relative pronouns in the latter. These letters are intelligible in these settings only because the conventions of the genres function as interpretive protocols.

My third example is one I have not yet discussed for other purposes:

any mere land-mark by which a particular thing may be recognized because it is as a matter of fact associated with that thing, a proper name without signification, a pointing finger, is a degenerate index. Horatio Greenough, who designed Bunker

Hill Monument, tells us in his book that he meant it to say simply "Here!" It just stands on that ground and plainly is not movable. So if we are looking for the battle-field, it will tell us whither to direct our steps. (EP 2:12, p. 163 [CP 5.75])

I want to dwell on—or at—the Bunker Hill Monument, and its generalization as a "land-mark." It says "here!" and tells us "whither to direct our steps," if, and only if, we "are looking for the battlefield," that is, if and only if, we know what we are looking for. We must know what the object of the sign is before we can find it, before the sign can operate as a sign. This must be true of scientific instrumentation as well, though in not quite the same way. But what Peirce fails to point out in his use of the monument is that we also have to know what landmarks and monuments are. This is generic knowledge. When I gave as my title "traveler, stay awhile," I was punting on your recognition of this genre. We write on monuments, and even when we do not, we consider them to be written on by some such mark as this, which refers to the genre, to its mode of address, to how we use it for the purposes of commemoration, to what we are supposed to do when we come across it. "Directing our steps thither" is necessary to this function, but it is not sufficient. Why would we want to do so? What is the meaning of what we do at monuments? How do they interpellate us and who are we when we heed their call? A genre is a kind of occasion, with all that that entails. I invite you to bring your awareness of the generic competence that defines this kind of information to the following conundrum:

On a peak still unnamed by the non-indigenous, but no more than 30 km as the crow flies from Gudgenby, lies a stone arrangement which determined and well-informed bushwalkers can reach only after seven hours of difficult hiking. Over 40 m long, and oriented south and north, three mysterious lines of stones on sloping granite slabs seem connected to huge rocky outcrops. Granville Crawford did not know of it; today nobody knows its origin or purpose.[18]

Is this stone arrangement a monument? It says "here," certainly, and the specification of "here" is one of the things that indexicality can achieve; I shall return to this. But the informational void is so radical as a result of the cultural discontinuity that this book is about, that all we can say about the stone arrangement is that it is "mysterious"—which means precisely that we are ignorant of its very genre. Note that this is different from not knowing what in particular is commemorated by some monument. We can look at monuments where the writing is erased or weathered beyond legibility and still know they are monuments, know what kind of job they are doing, what kind of rhetoric they are involved in, how they address the passerby, what "staying awhile" might entail. But in the absence of this knowledge, we know nothing bar the designation of the place as place. It must be a sign, we say, but what sign? What kind of sign? To whom is it addressed, and why? Formally indexical at the very most, it would fail even to have the pure deictic value of "here," because "here" is dysfunctional when it no longer operates as the center of a set of coordinates.

An opposite example is available in the grounds of the University of Queensland. The university occupies a site bordered by a river; the land is river flat, some of which is subject to flooding, and it has been contoured by landscaping work designed to minimize the danger, but there is some naturally occurring high ground. On one of the hillocks in the park, we find a mysterious stone arrangement. Many years ago, there was a plaque that informed the passerby that it was an "aboriginal totem" that had been found somewhere north of Brisbane and reconstructed in this place. Hence, its (original) indexicality has been rendered inoperative; but the early anthropologists were convinced that they knew its genre, and they labeled it accordingly. It is offensive to the local indigenous population on both counts, because "totem" describes nothing at all in their culture, and the displacement is the very sign of dispossession. The plaque has long since been removed, and the stone arrangement is now just decoration, stripped of its very capacity to be a sign.[19] Notice, moreover, that the crucial criteria for indexicality—individuality and fixity—are exactly what has been deleted in this example, and that the deletion occurs precisely as a result of the generic attribution.[20]

I should add here that it is now part of common knowledge that such stone arrangements may well have been "marker stones," neither "totemic" nor monumental in their intention but rather the marks of a complex mapping system in which certain places were designated stopping places for various purposes—storytelling and ritual, trading and other intergroup negotiations, or for food gathering at particular seasons. The system of such markers thus worked as the mediation of the relation among person, tradition, and place and hence were crucial in the construction of identity. You can see how significant their uprooting and displacement must be.[21] Notice that to call such things "marker stones" is to assign them to a genre but to understand that genre in terms of its principal function, which is unambiguously indexical. Hence, it is not generic attribution as such that is at issue in this example, but a wrong generic attribution. As a genre, totems have a classificatory, and hence symbolic, function in Peirce's terms; marker stones are places to stay awhile.

These Australian examples help us to discern some features of monuments and landmarks that Peirce must have relied on in order to invoke the Bunker Hill Monument as an example of indexicality: that they commemorate or celebrate something that occurred in a certain place; that they are constructed in, and work as marks of, that place; that we visit them in order to rehearse the story which gives that place its meaning; and that rehearsing that story constructs the relational continuity of personal identity with collective history. Repetition and return are of the essence here. That relational continuity constitutes the deictic coordinates—I/here/now—they/there/then—on which certain kinds of narratives that sustain identity depend. This is what is missing from the other stone arrangements I have mentioned. But notice that I have said "certain kinds of narratives." Monuments are not genres merely because they are certain kinds of stone arrangement at certain points of the earth's surface; monuments are glossed by narratives—certain kinds of narratives—they are genre "all the way down." Knowing about the battle is knowing the story of Bunker Hill, and to visit the monument is to elicit its telling.

Reading Horatio Greenough's book—chance reading, or reading for one of his reviewing jobs, in any case not technical, philosophical reading—Peirce chances upon this explanation of the intentions of this particular monument.[22] By great good fortune, Greenough uses exactly that criterion—"here"—that Peirce often uses to define the index; this is the criterion that he sometimes calls an object's "hecceity," its "thisness." On the basis of this coincidence, he includes the architect's explanation of the monument as an example of the index. Notice that the example has traveled, despite its individuality, despite its fixity in the ground, from Greenough's memoirs to a lecture hall in Harvard, from Bunker Hill to a classification under speculative grammar, from its materiality in stone, its concrete particularity, to the generalization of an idea. From architecture to philosophy, from Boston to Australia and back again, when, on a brief visit to Boston some years ago, I wanted to visit the monument but was prevented by the itinerary of the tour bus. (However, its displacement is now complete: pictures of it, period and contemporary, are available on the Internet.[23]) Of course, I was not seeking to stay awhile in order to rehearse the story of the battle; I'd have gone to rehearse the story of Peirce's example. My purpose was to import it out of Peirce's philosophy, across another border, into a place where I could make it the example of an example, as I did, back off the bus and walking around old Boston, with this next one:

"Hi!" or "Hullah," . . . in my boyhood days the signal to get out of the way of a coaster's sled on Boston common, where I suppose coasting has long since been prohibited. (PW appx. G, p. 193)

Boston Common is there, of course, but the planting is such that I could find no space on it where boys might have ridden their sleds downhill and endangered passing philosophers, who of course were not required to "stay awhile," but to jump out of the way.

I can make broadly the same point about the monument and the call of "Hi!": they cannot work if we don't know their genres, and they cannot work as examples of indexicality unless we presuppose that knowledge. Otherwise, as the examples of lost Aboriginal places have shown us, they lose their very capacity to be classified as signs, except insofar as their displacement produces new conditions for their signhood to be remobilized.[24] But it is true that "Hi!" works deictically, that is, that its genre is mobilized at the moment of its utterance, just as the monument mobilizes its genre at the place it occupies. The stone arrangement in the high country near Canberra at least declares its pure formal indexicality and hence declares that it is a sign: it tells us that we have lost a genre, that it is lost from that place, and that from that place are also lost the cultural conditions under which that genre could operate. That is telling us a great deal; it has become a monument to that loss and hence can function in its grieving. But the stone arrangement at the University of Queensland cannot tell us even this; it is no longer a sign, and only for those of us who remember that once there was a plaque can it count as the loss of signhood itself. Traveler, stay awhile.

The foregoing examples sustain the claim that the rhetorical conditions under which indexicality functions as such are generic conditions. This is also clearly true of the scientific instruments, some of which, it is true, such as clocks, weathervanes, and telephones, have entered into general usage, but many of which operate in highly specialized environments for highly specialized purposes. Scientific instruments are designed exclusively to produce particular sorts of information, which takes more or less constrained forms; moreover, to use the information is to use the information in ways consonant with its design. Whether restricted to specialized use or more widely available, we must learn not only to read them but to set them, we are, as it were, trained by them to their purposes.

Some other examples of the index sustain a slightly modified version of the claim concerning genre, namely, that the pertinent rhetorical conditions are the ones known usually as speech acts. For Wittgenstein genres and speech acts are all indifferently "language games," and for Bakhtin, too, the only difference is whether they are "little speech genres" or larger ones.[25] Their performative dimension is what makes them similar sorts of things, since in each case saying is doing and demands a doing as its appropriate response. Take the example of "Hullah!" Peirce registers the fact that social conditions regulating its occasion have changed so radically that it may no longer be intelligible. If that occasion no longer arises, neither does the call or the interpretive rule guiding our actions in response to it. Other clear examples are the instructions to mariners and Peirce's generalization of them to a range of further cases: "more or less detailed directions" (CP 2.288); instructions as to "how to pick out one of the objects intended" (CP 2.289); a "virtual precept stating how the hearer is to proceed in order to find an object to which the proposition is intended to refer" (CP 2.357). This represents a modification of the position we saw in CP 2.334–36 above, where Peirce gives "simple signs" and "precepts" as two alternative forms of index. Here, any index is construed performatively on the model of the precept. This performative construal emerges at about the same time as Peirce produces a performative account of assertion.[26]

My examples thus far have sustained the argument that interpretability is governed by performative considerations such as genres or speech acts,[27] and Peirce's own construal of the index in these terms lends weight to this proposal. I am tempted to extrapolate from these examples to the effect that genre is presupposed in the selection of examples of indexicality, and hence in the constitution of the class. Yet there is a clear set of examples of indexicality of which this statement appears to be false. These are the empty, or purely formal signs, that grammarians such as Benveniste, or Fillmore, call the "deictics"; Jakobson calls them the shifters, and it is usual among philosophers to call them the "indexicals": this class includes the relational systems of the pronouns, the tenses, and other devices for locating points of time and space, including the pure example of "here" as it travels from monument to interior decorating, from storytelling to conversation, from geometry to geography, stopping in each as they will in order to anchor their frame of reference. For these cases, all we can say is that the generic settings in which we find them require their deployment for the achievement of their performativity, but not that they themselves are specific to any setting or settings.

In the passage where Peirce lists the collections of signs that work in this way (CP 2.289–90), they are listed as freestanding items, as if they were recognizable as indices under all and any generic circumstances. The issue of repetition and return, so salient in the example of the monument, is exactly what is denied for these grammatical indexicals: they mean, says everyone from Peirce through Jakobson, something different every time they are used. Yet Derrida has reminded us that such things cannot function unless they are indeed repeated, that, like the monument and like signatures, their general function is to fix and to individuate their objects, but that they can only do so from the heart of the paradox whereby singularity is constituted by that very generality—by habit and convention.[28] This paradox is acknowledged in Peirce's analysis: these indices are governed by conventions that fit them to work as they do. They are "indexical legisigns" or, *in actu*, indexical sinsigns.

The usual assessment of this group is just that they are general devices provided by the language, and there is no need for the further hypothesis concerning genre in order to understand how they work. However, I wish to reexamine them in the light of my suggestion that indices function in terms of generic presuppositions, and hence that these presuppositions are the conditions of intelligibility of the indices they use. This is self-evident in the following example:

If, for example, a man remarks, "Why, it is raining!" it is only by some such circumstances as that he is now standing here looking out at a window as he speaks, which would serve as an Index (not, however, as a Symbol) that he is speaking of this place at this time, whereby we can be assured that he cannot be speaking of the weather on the satellite of Procyon, fifty centuries ago. (CP 4.544)

Note that Peirce assumes identity between the circumstances of the utterance and its indexicality. These circumstances are deictic (now, here, as he speaks) and hence particular to the utterance in question; but note that deixis does not operate apart from generic considerations. In this case, these are very general—that is, face-to-face communication—and the unmarked use of deictic operators is such as to be interpreted through face-to-face communication by default. By contrast, exactly the same lexical items can be used in marked ways. Take, for example, "I am 'here' to learn about Peirce," as used in the introduction to this chapter. "Here" does not mean, in this case, at my desk in suburban Brisbane, and the present tense does not mean the now of writing. "Here" signifies a conceptual and discursive space in which I read Peirce, where "reading" is generically mixed over my studying the texts with the questions I bring to them from my other reading and my providing those questions and answers derived from the texts, in writing, for the readers of my text. It is a particularly complex, hence marked, use of "here," as of the present tense, because it identifies a time–space complex in which face-to-face communication does not provide a model for the interface between my uptake of Peirce, and yours of my work.[29]

Although there are generic differences within each of these groups that operate far more specifically and locally, the distinction between face-to-face communication and various forms of communication at a distance can be said to operate generically. It is responsible for shifts in the conditions of intelligibility, not only of "here" and "now," but of any of the deictic operators, including tense. This is because each one of the factors listed above is conditioned by the spatiotemporal relation of the interlocutors and the medium of communication. The same cannot be said for the quantifiers, which "mean that the hearer is at liberty to select any instance he likes within limits expressed or understood, and the assertion is intended to apply to that one" (CP 2.289). In this case, the "limits expressed or understood" appear not to be generic; they correspond to the "universe of discourse," the pertinent domain of reference established or presupposed by *single* utterances, or by collections of utterances whose relation with one another is constituted by an interpretive sequence. This supports the intuition, discussed briefly above, that the quantifiers do not belong with the deictics, but as I mentioned then ("then"), it does not follow from this distinction that Peirce is wrong to class both groups together as indices on the grounds that both groups "select" that to which general signs apply.

Peirce's claim is that the index is a precept for securing reference, and mine is that this precept works in particular ways according to the genre that uses it. With the apparent exception of the quantifiers, genre is a condition on indexicality. If the performative construal of indexicality is accepted, then "instructions for finding" is a performative generalization, a genre, maybe called the "precept," for construing the whole class. This amounts to the same thing as "the constative is a performative" or "referring is a speech act." The scope of such claims is the whole class.

IV

It may well be the case, then, that the performative construal of indexicality accounts for Peirce's insight, that all the signs he classes as indices in fact function in the same sort of way. I wish to consider one last group of examples in order to test this conclusion. If it holds, then it provides a satisfactory gloss on Peirce's intuition concerning the class of the index. It would then give succor to atomistic theories of the sign that hold that the meaning, or value, of some sign inheres in its place in its system, and that uses of the sign are explained by the system but do not explain it. This thesis seems especially to hold for formal signs such as indices. This consequence would provide a severe test not only of the argument of this chapter, but of this book as a whole. What explanatory value does the genre postulate have?

From time to time, and especially when he is writing "philosophy," which is, he argues, the genre that investigates "ordinary experience," Peirce appears to rely on face-to-face communication for the typical cases of the index. Thus the example of the Simpleton who does not provide the indexical signs that are needed by his chance acquaintance to identify the object of the information. The criteria that Peirce has used to delineate the class for these cases are summed up in this: "An index has nothing to do with meanings; it has to bring the hearer to share the experience of the speaker by *showing* what he is talking about. The words this and that are indicative words. They apply to different things every time they occur" (CP 4.56). The important point, one that I have not attended to until now, is the idea of "shared experience," and Peirce adverts to it frequently. But what is it, to share experience? Peirce tells us, as the grammarians have done, that it depends on deixis:

Other indexical words are prepositions, and prepositional phrases, such as, "on the right (or left) of." Right and left cannot be distinguished by any general description. Other prepositions signify relations which may, perhaps, be described; but when they refer, as they do oftener than would be supposed, to a situation relative to the observed, or assumed to be experientially known, place and attitude of the speaker relatively to that of the hearer, then the indexical element is the dominant element. (CP 2.290)

But this answer holds only for a fairly restricted range of cases, and notably does not hold for the indexical signs required in a formal notation. What is the logical equivalent of "shared experience"?[30] Peirce follows De Morgan and Boole on this matter: it is a designated "universe of discourse" which may be wide or narrow, hypothetical or empirical, imaginary or real (CP 2.536). The assumption of "some recognized range of experience or thought . . . referred to" (CP 2.360) is the necessary condition for referring to some object. This holds equally for "ordinary conversation."

Notice, then, that there is required an index of the pertinent "range of experience" in order for the indices of objects within that range to be interpretable (cf. CP 2.369). Indeed, as we have seen, the "common environment" is itself an index whose function is to guarantee the operation of other indices (CP 2.318). And so it comes to pass that the index is required to make the most important of distinctions: between "fiction" and "reality," for example (CP 2.337), "the imaginary worlds of plays and novels" and the range of other possibilities thrown up by hypothetical propositions and the pure formal possibilities of mathematical constructs.

In every proposition the circumstances of its enunciation show that it refers to some collection of individuals or of possibilities, which cannot be adequately described, but can only be indicated as something familiar to both speaker and auditor. At one time it may be the physical universe, at another it may be the imaginary "world" of some play or novel, at another a range of possibilities. (CP 2.536)[31]

Nothing could be more significant for the distinction among genres than the distinctions—sometimes quite informal, but always operative—among the sets of objects to which they might on occasion refer: the sciences, for example, or history, speculative metaphysics, formal logic, neighborhood gossip, political debate, institutional administration, medical practice, the branches of semiotic, not to mention the exegesis and commentary of texts of philosophy, history, science, poetry . . . or the rest. These informal sets are presupposed. My claim, that the presuppositions of any genre operate as conditions on the intelligibility and use of indices, seems then to be sustained. Likewise, my further claim that it is generic variety that explains the heterogeneity of the class of the index.

In the formal notations, Peirce has used the index not merely to pick out substantive items, but also to achieve pure diacritical differentiation. Hence, the index is exemplified in a description of a logical algebra by "the subscript numbers which in algebra distinguish one value from another without saying what those values are" (W 5:30, p. 163). One instant is distinguished from another, one day from another, solely by means of indexicals, for otherwise they differ not one whit. This being the case, the index is the very sign of difference, and hence, the formal condition for any classification—

But of superior importance in Logic is the use of Indices to denote Categories and Universes, which are classes that, being enormously large, very promiscuous, and known but in small part, cannot be satisfactorily defined, and therefore can only be denoted by Indices. (CP 4.544)

—and this must hold for the classifications of signs themselves, as well as for that competing scheme of classification for the conditions of semiosis, the genres.

I could go on, following the trail of the index to the point where we find that examples themselves have an indexical function in just those situations where it is difficult or impossible to refer directly to a class. But I think by now that you have got the point, that you are tired, and that you need a stopping point. You might think that the form of my argument was a simple reversal: in the early days of a field of inquiry now called semiotics, we thought that simple signs were the building blocks of discourse and that generic determination was a set of contextual constraints that supervened over these signs but did not condition them. This proposition seemed most secure when applied to the purely formal sign, the index, and is consistent with Peirce's claim that grammar underpins rhetoric. I came to challenge this proposition when I chanced—not in Boston but in Peirce—upon the Bunker Hill Monument: I found that genre underpins the very class of the index in such a way that the property of indexicality depends upon the variety of generic determination. Is genre, then, the foundation of the whole box and dice? Well, no, actually. For the surprises of the road have brought me to this, that indexicality is a formal condition on the very postulate of genre itself. This genre, I might say, or that; this example, or that; this question, this road, this halt.

This circularity—this aporia—is important. I think it means that in order to know anything at all about semiotic practices, we need two systems of classification, that neither grounds nor founds the other, but that both claim to do so: signs, and genres; language, and communication; grammar, and rhetoric. The point where they meet has been the site of significant, albeit entirely inconclusive, battles. All we can do is mark it, and rehearse the story. Traveler, stay awhile.

PART THREE

"MY WHOLE THEORY"

5

1904–1909

The work on signs following 1903 is drawn from generically mixed sources. There is a draft exposition from 1904 entitled "New Elements" (EP 2:22) and the unfinished "Ideas Stray or Stolen on the Rhetoric of Science" (EP 2:23) (both from 1904); there is the series of articles for the *Monist* (1906), and there is the correspondence with Welby (1903–11). The first of these is clearly philosophical in its concerns and situates itself in polemical relation with the mathematical way of doing logic; the second, "Ideas Stray or Stolen," sets out to describe as a rhetorical practice what it is to write, indeed, to *do*, science; in the *Monist*, Peirce expounds the existential graphs as a preliminary to his prolegomena to Pragmatism. All three suppose that the reader needs to be convinced of the importance of semiotic before they embark on their specific arguments, and they establish their ground by outlining the general theory of signs. By contrast, the correspondence takes for granted that signs are important: on the assumption that this ground is shared with Welby, Peirce takes the opportunity to try out further distinctions and definitions. All are explicitly framed by their relation with disciplinarity: "New Elements" contests the methods and objectives of mathematical logic, referring to the Euclidean model to do so; the *Monist* paper debates with a nominalist who contests the need for diagrams of thought in philosophical research; the essay on rhetoric, also written in polemical intent, is framed as a conversation between cultivated nonspecialists; and the correspondence with Welby is a genuine exchange with a brilliant autodidact whose incapacity—or refusal—to write within the confines of specialist disciplines fitted her, perhaps uniquely, to read Peirce, whose writing is both a desperate attempt to do so and a demonstration that every gesture of such writing raises a substantive problem that takes it off the track.[1]

Peirce outlived Welby by only two years, and there is little of substance on semiotic from that final desolate time.[2] The correspondence with her traverses the period from 1903 to 1911 and hence accompanies all the major work on signs discussed in the previous chapter and in this one. In the letters, Peirce uses Welby as a sounding board for the further extensions of the second classification, and it is important not to treat them as if they were definitive theoretical pronouncements. In an unsent draft from 1905, Peirce says as much: "I have been overhauling my classification of signs with the result of throwing the matter into a state of confusion which I hope with time will heal up into some connective tissue" (appx. G, PW, July 1905, p. 189). Peirce boasts that he now has a "whole theory," yet what he writes is an outline sketch of his classifications; much of the theoretical rationale is therefore left out, as is systematic reflection on the implications of these extensions. Indeed, the almost exclusive focus on classificatory distinctions has, I believe, a deleterious effect on the consistency of the work on signs in the letters. At the end of this chapter, I shall offer a diagnosis of this effect. Before I get to that, however, I shall trace the series of modifications Peirce brought to his classifications in chronological order. We shall note that some rather loose formulations in the letters are tightened up for publication, and that the letters, and drafts for further letters, sometimes indulge a taste for trial runs that, I am bound to say, lead up blind alleys. We all do likewise. It would do Peirce an injustice to read his theory from these assays. But, as with any manuscript source, it is possible to read this work as revealing the issues that sign theory was encountering. I shall suggest that the ever more elaborate classifications represent attempts to override these problems in a rationale deriving from the most general account of the three categories, that sometimes does, and sometimes does not, forget the lessons of "things and events." A sign, if I may put it this way, of the amnesia to which I refer, is the almost total absence of exemplification for many of the new trichotomies invented during this time.

Yet the lesson of "things and events" is not entirely forgotten. In some important respects, the "pragmatization" of the sign that we have seen developed in the work from 1903 is Peirce's starting point here, and his reflections on the further requirements of his theory largely stem from it.

These relate to the development of "logical critic," or the theory of the semiosis of objects, and "speculative rhetoric," the theory of interpretation. Articulated with the grammar as formulated in the Syllabus, this will be the "whole theory." It is still programmatic, but the pragmatism of this program informs what I take to be the most perspicuous—and most suggestive—definition of the sign Peirce ever formulated:

It appears to me that the essential function of a sign is to render inefficient relations efficient,—not to set them into action, but to establish a habit or general rule whereby they will act on occasion. According to the physical doctrine, nothing ever happens but the continued rectilinear velocities with the accelerations that accompany different relative positions of the particles. All other relations, of which we know so many, are inefficient. Knowledge in some way renders them efficient; and a sign is something by knowing which we know something more. (PW, October 12, 1904, p. 31)

To do this passage justice, we must read together the point concerning the function of signs—their capacity to effect real action—with the point concerning the generation of new knowledge. The deep connection between these points is underwritten by the relation of grammar with logic and rhetoric. It is an account of this relation that Peirce was seeking in his final years.

Before these developments, however, "probably early in 1904,"[3] Peirce wrote a significant exposition of the theory of signs entitled "New Elements" (EP 2:22), deemed by Max Fisch to be his "best statement so far of his general theory of signs" and by the editors of the *Essential Peirce*[4] to "deepen" the theory by "linking it with the mathematical conception of 'degrees of degeneracy.'" As we have seen, this conception had been expounded in detail in the Harvard Lectures of 1903. Indeed, the curious feature of this work is that it takes no account at all of the second classification, and that it harks back to the early chapters of the Syllabus—that is, those written before the breakdown of the conceptual logic that informs them (see Chapter 3)—in respect of the topics it treats and the terms in which it frames them. Supposing the dating of the manuscript to be correct, this poses a problem of interpretation. There are two possible hypotheses: first, the classifications of 1903 and later are merely experimental, having no consequences; this is clearly not the case, because Peirce continued to refine the late classifications in all the writings of this last period; or second, the work recorded in "New Elements" is understood by Peirce to have a separate function from that of the work on the classifications. This latter hypothesis is the more plausible, but the fact that that function remains so separate as to be unaffected by the other work is of the greatest interest. What we find is that Peirce has distanced himself from the "mathematical style" of doing logic, and hence that the writing of logic can be brought within the fold of philosophy; there is now a distinction between a "general theory of signs" represented by the classifications, broad enough to deal with the full range of examples Peirce has considered—this includes, but is not restricted to, the notational examples—and a "special theory" required specifically for philosophy. This corresponds with Peirce's distinction between "grammar," and "critic," spelled out in his account of "the three essential branches of semeiotics,"

> Of which the first, called *speculative grammar* by Duns Scotus, studies the ways in which an object can be a sign; the second, the leading part of logic, best termed *speculative critic*, studies the ways in which a sign can be related to the object independent of it that it represents; while the third is . . . speculative rhetoric. (EP 2:23, p. 327)[5]

The focus of "New Elements" is critic, which deals almost exclusively with symbols, because only symbols can be arguments that can be tested for their truth, and only symbols depend on the interpreting mind. The generic distinction I have worked with thus far is obscured, but it is not erased, and the special demands put on logic by philosophy continue to draw the familiar boundary around symbols to separate them out from all other kinds. For this reason, I shall reserve material from "New Elements" for my discussion of the symbol, in the Conclusion. Here, I confine myself to Peirce's late work on the classifications.[6]

October 12, 1904

> But I wanted to write to you about signs, which in your opinion and mine are matters of so much concern. More in mine, I think, than in yours. For in mine, the highest grade of reality is only reached by signs; that is by such ideas as those of Truth and Right and the rest. It sounds paradoxical; but when I have devolved to you my whole theory of signs, it will seem less so. I think that I will today explain the outlines of my classification of signs. (PW, October 12, 1904, p. 23)

In this letter to Welby, Peirce gives the basis for the classification. The three trichotomies discerned in the Syllabus are these: "signs may be divided as to their own material nature, as to their relations to their objects, and as to their relation to their interpretants." But further to these divisions, there are two kinds of object, and there are three kinds of interpretant.[7] There are sporadic attempts by Peirce to articulate the divisions of one trichotomy with those of others, but these attempts are not systematic, and the full combinatory is nowhere apparent.[8] At the end of the letter, Peirce apologizes for sending "such a dissertation," but immediately adds a postscript in which he lists the "ten principal classes of signs." These are close, but do not correspond precisely, to the ten classes outlined in the Syllabus; they appear to be derived from the rule of degeneracy, not from the combinatory. In the second classification, each class of sign is constituted by the combination of one element from each of the three trichotomies. Under this rule, no constituent element—for example, a "qualisign"—corresponds to a class of sign. In the postscript list, by contrast, this rule is broken, so that both qualisigns and arguments appear as classes, not as constituent elements. Moreover, several classes in the postscript list are formed from two, not three, elements from the trichotomic table.

This is not the only difference between the outline written to Welby and that given in the Syllabus. More significant is the decision to distinguish between the "immediate" and the "dynamic" objects, and among three kinds of interpretant. However, the question arises, what are these trichotomies *of*? In the late work, Peirce multiplies his distinctions of "kinds of objects" and "kinds of interpretants," but it is not clear that all the classes thus distinguished are defined by the sign relation.

This problem is particularly acute in the case of the object. In order to avoid the Scylla and Charybdis of standard accounts of representation—that is, idealism on the one hand, and nominalism on the other—Peirce needs the sign to mediate between the "outer world" and the "inner world." For this reason, he suggests that signs have "two objects," which he defines as the "object as it is represented" and the object "in itself." This is deeply perplexing for a philosopher who has devoted most of his metaphysics to a critique of the very idea of a "thing in itself." This formulation, and others like it, explain why this distinction has been construed according to the Fregean pair of sense and reference, and the structuralist distinction of the signified and the referent. But this reading is difficult to justify in Peircean terms, since the whole effort of his work is to provide an alternative to dyadic accounts of representation. The positing of two distinct objects appears to reproduce the metaphysical problem, rather than to provide an account of the mediatory competence of the sign.

We must ask, furthermore, if this distinction, between the "object in itself" and the "object as represented," is the same as the following:

In respect to their relations to their dynamic objects, I divide signs into Icons, Indices, and Symbols. . . .

In respect to its immediate object a sign may either be a sign of a quality, of an existent, or of a law. (p. 33)

The structuralist reading of Peirce assimilates the "dynamic" object to the "object in itself" or "referent" and the "immediate object" with the *signifié*, the object as it is represented by the sign.[9] Let us suppose temporarily that this is right, to see where it takes us in our reading of this letter. If it is the case, then I can discern only six, not ten, trichotomies in the classification given.[10] On the other hand, we may separate the two passages, allowing one to be a division of the object and the other to be a division of the sign's relation with its object. But this second reading compounds the difficulty I am discussing, because what is an object if it is not an object of a sign? Peirce admits of no such thing.

Truth is the conformity of a representamen to its object,—*its* object, ITS object. (EP 2:27, p. 380 [CP 5.554])

The difficulty is acknowledged by Peirce in the unsent draft of 1905:

The Form, (and the Form is the Object of the Sign), . . . is quite independent of the sign; yet we may and indeed must say that the object of a sign can be nothing but what that sign represents it to be. Therefore, in order to reconcile these apparently conflicting Truths, it is indispensable to distinguish the *immediate* object from the *dynamical* object. (appx. G, PW, July 1905, p. 196)

So we cannot admit an object entirely dissociated from representation, but the alternative, an object having no independent ontology apart from its projection by its sign, is the *differentia specifica* of the icon exclusively. This means that the "immediate object" should be a trichotomy of the objects of icons only. Peirce does not restrict it in this way, and I am far from persuaded by this reading. If a division corresponds only to the properties of a single class of signs, it is effectively redundant. An alternative reading is to suppose that he is considering propositions exclusively: propositions do have two objects, in the sense that their predicates are sometimes construed by Peirce as iconic of possible objects, and their subjects as indexical of something in the real. Again, mapping the *für uns/an sich* dichotomy on to, respectively, the "immediate" and the "dynamic" objects, the predicated object would be the object "as represented," and the indicated object would be dynamic. Again, this reading, although plausible, is redundant, for two reasons: first, Peirce presents the dynamic object as a defining property of the whole of the second trichotomy, and presumably therefore of each of its members; and second, he does not need a further division to do something already achieved by the analysis of propositions as combining the properties of icons and indices.

A perusal of the list of objects comprising this trichotomy sheds further light still: the "immediate object" is the kind of object that the sign claims to represent—a quality, an existent, or a law. As it happens, these are exactly the objects of the hypotheses that posit the three phenomenological categories. As such, the "immediate object" returns us to the most general formulation of the metaphysics, prior to the derivation of sign theory from that metaphysics. The "immediate object," in this letter, is not a hypothesis concerning signs; even less is it a classification of subdivisions of the general, let alone a specific, class of signs. It collapses signhood into phenomenology. The problem is not merely that this reduces the specificity of signs into the generality of the categories, but that this reduction neglects the formal properties of signs, as well as their materiality. I suggest that when Peirce does this, he is neglecting semiotic in favor of "meaning." The object, one might say, adopting Welby's distinctions, is the "meaning" of a sign, irrespective of the formal and material conditions of signhood and of semiosis. This can be explained very simply. "Semiotic" is Peirce's field; that of his interlocutor is "meaning." As Gérard Deledalle points out, it is predictable that both Peirce and Welby should seek to "read their own theory in each other's writings"; but this leads to a general, and sustained, misunderstanding between them in the correspondence.[11] Conversation with neighbors sometimes requires translation in order to produce mutual understanding; but translation comes at a risk and is bound to be shadowed by misunderstanding.

The tension between a focus on meaning and a focus on signs is evident in all Peirce's correspondence with Welby. There is also evidence of it elsewhere, and one must suppose that it was fostered by the turn to phenomenology as much as by the generic environment of these letters. However, in the distinctions among kinds of interpretants, this tension does not override another drive of Peirce's work: this is the pragmatic construal of semiosis. As we have seen, the question concerning "how" a sign acts to produce real consequences has led, first of all, to the identification of the thinghood and the eventhood of the sign itself. In the further extensions to the classification, Peirce follows through the implications of this solution for the interpretant. If the sign is followed by an interpretant, there must be features of that sign that determine or elicit some interpretants and preclude or discourage others.[12] Some of these features are grammatical properties, and some are rhetorical. Further, the interpretant itself must potentially be embodied and have some reality as an event.

Peirce opens his considerations with the familiar division:

In regard to its relation to its signified interpretant, a sign is either a Rheme, a Dicent, or an Argument. This corresponds to the old division Term, Proposition, & Argument, modified so as to be applicable to signs generally. (PW October 12, 1904, p. 33)

It is implied in this account that certain forms of interpretant are precluded from certain kinds of signs—truth claims from class names, formal inferences from single propositions. I take it that this is what is meant by the "signified interpretant": each of these forms is a rule governing what can follow from it. A *term* "is simply a class-name or proper-name"—it is a potential description, but it is not applied to anything. Nothing follows from it except the qualities that inhere in the hypothesis of the class (the connotations accreted from its class of usage).[13] A *proposition* asserts a predicate of something and hence is interpreted as making truth claims; it can be contested or confirmed. An *argument* displays the interpretant that follows from its premises. These are formal, "grammatical" properties of the signs themselves, and it is in this sense that the sign "determines" its interpretant.

Following the "signified interpretant," Peirce gives a brief account of the way in which "a sign may appeal to its dynamic interpretant." Note "appeal to": this is the domain of rhetoric in the familiar sense. It is not presumed necessarily that the interpretant will turn out as expected. Here, "dynamic" refers to the pragmatics of the act: this interpretant is an event.

1st, an argument only may be *submitted* to its interpretant, as something the reasonableness of which will be acknowledged.

2nd an argument or dicent may be *urged* upon the interpretant by an act of *insistence*.

3rd Argument or dicent may be and a rheme (=term) can only be, presented to the interpretant for *contemplation*. (PW, October 12, 1904, pp. 34–35)

Notice that "contemplation" connotes an immobilization of the sign, the suspension of its action. The sign *is presented*, qua sign. The interpretant in this case is not the "uptake" of speech act theory; nor is it the inference that follows from the sign. I suggest that the "needed commentary upon the syntax" is of this order. But it is of the greatest interest that Peirce includes this within the "dynamic" interpretant. This division bears on what we do with signs, and one of those things is to read them, or analyze them, or draw a diagram of their relational grammar, or tease out their implications by means of other exegetical techniques. The division assumes that the sign is structured in such a way as to elicit the acts that interpret it.

The third division of the interpretant bears on the ontological properties of the interpretant sign: is it a feeling, an actual experience, or an infinite series of thoughts or other signs of the same kind? We can relate this with Peirce's change of terminology for the "signified interpretant." Peirce is concerned here to generalize signs beyond the cognitive and beyond the model of linguistic signs. Actions, thoughts, feelings, appearances, diagrams, words . . . may be signs; so then, may any sign be interpreted by an action, a thought, a feeling, a word, a diagram. . . . Semiotic now occupies a space far broader than the "space of thought"; and signs, although they be governed by laws, are rhetorical events. Semiotic is process, not space; the pragmatic construal of the interpretant charts how the sign effects particular kinds of changes in the real.

It is at least plausible that the choice of the term *dynamic* as applied to one "kind" of object and one "kind" of interpretant is motivated by the pragmatic construal of semiosis. In this letter to Welby, Peirce elaborates this construal in respect of three features. One is the reconstrual of the second trichotomy, where the structure, the signifying properties of the sign are counted as crucial to its capacity to act; the second is the addition of the rhetorical action of the sign in eliciting an interpretant; and the third is the broadening of interpretation from being modeled on inference, to being potentially an action or an experience, or a feeling. This third feature corresponds to the thinghood and eventhood of the sign itself, and it is on this that Teresa de Lauretis relies for her argument that Peirce provides the premises for a semiotics of experience.[14] An account of events of semiosis requires an account of signs, and hence of interpretants themselves; the distinction between the signified and the dynamic interpretant investigates the nature of the process itself; and—once its ambiguities are sorted out— the distinction between the "immediate" and the "dynamic" object will address the question of pragmatic epistemology, the requirement that the action produced involve verifiable or falsifiable descriptions of real things.

"Prologomena to an Apology for Pragmatism"—1906

The interest of this paper for semiotic lies specifically in its reflections on the first trichotomy and in its clarification of the divisions of the object. It locates the topic of signs as preliminary to any elaboration of a pragmatic philosophy: the subtitle of the opening section, "Signs," announces a topic in its own right, and the third section, entitled "Graphs and Signs," expounds those parts of his theory of signs that Peirce needs for the purposes of describing his existential graphs. The major part of the article is devoted to an exposition of the graphs, and it closes with the announcement that "the utility of this diagrammatization of thought in the discussion of the truth of Pragmatism" will be demonstrated in the following paper.[15] The arrangement of the exposition thus conforms to the place of mathematics and logic in relation with philosophy, as set out in the ladders of the sciences; and the argument pursues the same goal as that of the Harvard Lectures on Pragmatism. But it spends no time on the phenomenological base of material hypothesis; this is logic, granted devised in the service of philosophy, but logic first and foremost.

As such, we can expect that what Peirce uses from the "whole theory" is calculated for the instrumental use he makes of it in the description of the notation. The Lowell Lectures allow us to predict the status of the first trichotomy in this project. We can also expect that the instrumentality of the notation in "the discussion of the truth of Pragmatism" will dictate any further feature required of signs and sign theory. The Harvard Lectures have told us that this will be the relation of a sign with its object, this relation being crucial for the development of a "scientific philosophy." Hence, although the paper does not exist, we know that any discussion of "the truth of Pragmatism" will first be a discussion of the conditions of truth in general. Signs will be studied for their "representative office." First among equals, the "second trichotomy"—icons, indices, and symbols—will have the leading role.

The first section of the paper introduces the topic of signs by comparing "diagrams of the general course of thought" with the map that a general might use in a campaign, and then with the sample of a chemical substance as used by a chemist in an experiment. In this latter, the chemist works upon "the Very Object under investigation" (CP 4.530), and Peirce uses it to sustain by analogy the claim that both the map, and the diagrams of thought, are not, as one might have objected, "mere representations," but are "the very object." In each case, this object is "the form of a relation," an abstraction always already designed and manipulated by signs, and the point of the argument is to contest the nominalistic general's separation of "representation" from its objects. This being established, Peirce moves to propose a generalization concerning signs: every sign is "determined by its object," and is so on one of three grounds, either by

> partaking in the characters of the object, when I call the sign an *Icon*; [or] by being really and in its individual existence connected with the individual object, when I call the sign an *Index*; [or] thirdly, by more or less approximate certainty that it will be interpreted as denoting the object, in consequence of a habit (which term I use as including a natural disposition), when I call the sign a *Symbol*. (CP 4.531)

The trichotomy here expounded is the one called the "relation with the dynamic object" in the letter to Welby discussed above; that relation is established between the sign and something outside itself, whether "outside" be in the mind or the imaginary or ideal spaces projected by mathematics, or in the system of conventions regulating a "form of life," or in the existent real. This passage gives a general definition of signs and elaborates on it in such a way as to suggest that the most important aspect of that definition is the representation relation, prescinded from the interpretant. While this trichotomy is "only one of ten," it is especially significant, Peirce tells us, because "that which we can learn from this division is of what sort a Sign must be to represent the sort of Object that reasoning is concerned with." In other words, from his "whole theory," Peirce selects just that part of semiotic that corresponds precisely with the scope given to semiotic globally in "On a New List of Categories." But note: Peirce takes particular care not to identify this as the scope of semiotic; his discussion is carefully confined to a particular "sort of sign."

It is not that there are not other kinds of signs, other kinds of representation, other acts that enter into semiosis. Simply, they are left out, for the purpose at hand. Nor is it that pragmat(ic)ism has no interest in the remainder; pragmat(ic)ism may well require of itself that it develop a fully pragmatic account of the action of signs in a range of situations. This is what the Harvard Lectures gesture toward, and this is what Peirce develops in his correspondence with Welby. But in this article for the *Monist*, Peirce is concerned exclusively with the diagrammatic analysis of thoughts. Thoughts, here, are the objects of the diagrams, and these diagrams will display the property lauded in "Logical Tracts No. 2," in which the "most perfect" signs are those that combine the symbolic, the indexical, and the iconic. Why these and no other classes of signs? "Symbols afford the means of thinking about thoughts in ways in which we could not otherwise think of them" (CP 4.531). But symbols alone are inadequate

since symbols rest exclusively on habits already definitely formed but not furnishing any observation even of themselves, and since knowledge is habit, they do not enable us to add to our knowledge even so much as a necessary consequent, unless by means of a definite preformed habit. (CP 4.531)

The point is made here in respect of the objective Peirce has stipulated for his graphs: they must tell us something about the course of thought that we could otherwise not discover. But it must apply in principle to semiosis in general. Not that semiosis necessarily does always tell us something new or modify our knowledge base definitively, but that any account of semiosis that precludes change, either on the basis of an ultimately closed system of beliefs and assumptions, or on the basis of an ideal community, is bound to be inadequate. It is particularly interesting in this passage that Peirce attributes such preclusions to any account of representation that works exclusively with symbols, that is, conventional signs. Both the index, which effects the encounter with existent reals, and the icon, which represents hypothetical states of affairs, are required in order to open the symbol beyond the system of conventions that constitute it.[16]

Indices . . . furnish positive assurance of the reality and the nearness of their Objects. But with the assurance there goes no insight into the nature of those Objects. . . . Each Icon partakes of some more or less overt character of its Object. (CP 4.531)

Peirce will go on to define his diagrams as primarily iconic, although they have "symbolide" as well as indexical features. This is significant, because alone of the three kinds, the icon

does not stand unequivocally for this or that existing thing, as the Index does. Its Object may be a pure fiction, as to its existence. . . . But there is one assurance that the Icon does afford in the highest degree. Namely, that which is displayed before the mind's gaze—the Form of the Icon, which is also its object—must be *logically possible*. (CP 4.531)

Notice that "the mind's gaze" corresponds with the notion of "contemplation" that we saw in the Welby letter. Icons are presented for a kind of study that in itself is not a pragmatic uptake so much as an analysis of potential interpretability. But notice, too, that the icon can do nothing to distinguish fiction from fact, or truth from lies and deceptions:

Each Icon partakes of some more or less overt character of its Object. They, one and all, partake of the most overt character of all lies and deceptions—their Overtness. Yet they have more to do with the living character of truth than have either Symbols or Indices. (CP 4.531)

Their relation with truth is "living" in that their objects are hypothetically possible and hence productive of unexpected or new understandings. But as truth, it is anything but assured. Indeed, by definition, the objects of icons are fictional, whether or not any such object turns out, in further representations of other kinds, to have some reality. Lies, deception, and fiction are "overt," this overtness itself being their tactic of representation. And just as the icon is centrally constitutive of our engagement with the real, and the principal device of our representation of that engagement, so, I believe Peirce is saying, are lies, deception, and fiction constitutive of our engagement with truth: constitutive; no mere accident that requires deletion, censorship, or correction, but constitutive. They are the risk of new understandings and creative solutions, with the risk of mistake and error that accompanies it, the risk of broken habits, the risk of unshared assumptions and the risk of disturbance in the communities of conversation. To acknowledge this requires that we take seriously the rhetoric of representation. When we turn the "mind's gaze" on our representations, when we "contemplate" them, when we provide the "needed commentary on the syntax," we are suspending the evaluation of their truth claims in order to do just this. We ask if their claims are logically possible, and we ask—prior even to that question—what the nature of that claim is, and how any sign claims competence to make it.

    This requirement to "contemplate" the sign as sign is not restricted to the icon. In the unsent draft of 1905, Peirce applies it to the "dicisign" (the assertible proposition).[17] Referring to the need to distinguish the immediate from the dynamic interpretant, he writes,

The same form of distinction extends to the interpretant; but as applied to the interpretant, it is complicated by the circumstance that the sign not only determines the interpretant to represent (or to take the form of) the *object*, but also determines the interpretant to represent the sign. Indeed in what we may, from one point of view, regard as the principal kind of signs, there is one distinct part appropriated to representing the object, and another to representing how this very sign itself represents that object. (appx. G, PW, July 1905, p. 196)

It is this set of implications from iconicity—the risk of the new, the breaking of habitual and conventional assumptions, the place of the suspension of truth conditional logic, and hence the place of alternative modes of interpretation—that, I believe, has been missed by some of the readings of Peirce's pragmat(ic)ism that seek to bring him back into the fold of orthodox epistemology. It is not that all signs are reduced to iconicity, but that iconicity pervades all of semiotic. This pervasiveness of the icon is of the utmost significance, first because the icon imposes this requirement, to know *it*, in its formal and material constitution and competence, and second because it is in and through iconicity that Peirce theorizes hypothesis and hence preserves the necessarily fallible and provisional condition of all representation.

As I have argued, Peirce selects in this paper only those elements of his "whole theory" that he needs for their application in the description of his existential graphs. He makes this explicit prior to embarking on that description:

> I certainly could not tell you what sort of a Sign an Existential Graph is, without reference to two other divisions of Signs. . . . Consequently, I ought to give such hints as I conveniently can, of my notions of the structure of Signs, even if they are not strictly needed to express my notions of Existential Graphs. (CP 4.535)

Here, sketched but not elaborated, we are told that there are ten trichotomies, deriving from the observation that there are "usually two Objects, and more than two Interpretants." The distinction between the "immediate" and the "dynamic" objects is no longer beset by the ambiguities evident in the Welby letter:

> we have to distinguish the Immediate Object, which is the Object as the Sign itself represents it, and whose Being is thus dependent upon the Representation of it in the Sign, from the Dynamical Object, which is the Reality which by some means contrives to determine the Sign to its Representation. (CP 4.536)

In this formulation, neither the immediate nor the dynamic object is restricted to one class of sign, and both are potentially functions of icons, indices, and symbols. This is because the distinction Peirce draws relies on fallibilism. The "immediate object" is the one that will be corrected by further investigation; the "dynamic object" is the regulative assumption on which that process is based. The object as represented "in" the sign is probably wrong. I refer here to Misak's reading: all scientific propositions are hypothetical and fallible, but science rests on the assumption that any particular representation can be bettered, and hence that its objects can be better or more fully known.[18]

The work on the interpretant has been refined, but is also broadly similar to the formulations given in the letter to Welby:

> In regard to the Interpretant we have equally to distinguish, in the first place, the Immediate Interpretant, which is the interpretant as it is revealed in the right understanding of the Sign itself, and is ordinarily called the *meaning* of the sign; while in the second place, we have to take note of the Dynamical Interpretant which is *the actual effect* which the Sign, as a Sign, really determines. (CP 4.536)

Notice that the word *meaning* is attached to the "immediate interpretant" and is glossed as the "right understanding of the sign itself." That right understanding must involve, minimally, both the constraints on interpretation imposed by the logical status of the sign (as term, proposition, or argument), and the enablements provided by the representational protocols of the sign (as icon, index, or symbol). Hence, "meaning," or the "immediate interpretant," is a function of the formal properties of the sign itself, not "in" itself, but the ground of its relation with its object.[19] The actual effect is the action of the sign on occasion and is the only reference in this paper to this dimension of the question raised in the Harvard Lectures: how does a sign have consequences? Peirce then mentions the third division, the "final interpretant," of which Peirce confesses that his "conception is not quite free from mist." It will be further clarified in later letters to Welby, to which I shall turn presently.

Peirce has sketched three divisions of the interpretant, and two of the object, yet he concludes this sketch by declaring,

> Of the ten divisions of signs which have seemed to me to call for my special study, six turn on the characters of an Interpretant, and three on the characters of the Object. (CP 4.536)

These are not outlined, presumably because they are not needed. But one division, which "involves none but the most superficial considerations" (CP 4.535), "is concerned with the nature of the Sign itself, and this [Peirce] now proceed[s] to state" (CP 4.536). This passage contrasts markedly, and in the most significant way, with the standard accounts of the Saussurean distinction between *langue* and *parole*, as well as the standard accounts of the distinction between type and token.[20]

This is the first trichotomy, now reformulated in what has become its standard terminology: tone, token, and type. Peirce needs it because "The

Term (Existential) *Graph* will be taken in the sense of a Type; and the act of embodying it in a *Graph-Instance* will be termed *scribing* the Graph (not the Instance), whether the Instance be written, drawn, or incised." A tone is "an indefinite significant character such as a tone of voice," but in this paper, the "tones" are such things as lines, scrolls, tinctures, and cuts—the "marks" that constitute the material form of the sign. The distinction between the token and the type is made, as is Peirce's custom, on the basis of two different technologies of counting, the printer's (how many words "should lie visibly on a page or be heard in any voice"), and the lexicographer's, or in this case, the set of distinct signs that comprise the system of existential graphs. A type is a "definite significant Form," whereas a token "is a single event . . . or a single object or thing . . . such event or thing being significant only as occurring just when and where it does" (CP 4.537).

The important thing that Peirce adds to this division is his account of the relation between the type and the token:

In order that a Type may be used, it has to be embodied in a Token which shall be a sign of the Type, and thereby of the object the Type signifies. (CP 4.537)

A token is a sign of its type. This formulation brings with it the whole theory of signs. It has been adumbrated previously, in such formulations as "the being of a sign is merely *being represented*" (EP 2:22, p. 303). If a token is a sign, potentially, formally, and pragmatically:

1. The type is its object. We might ask, then, if a token is, for example, an icon, an index, or a symbol—or some combination of the three—of its type.

2. The token is a sign and hence has its own material properties, print or voice, drawn or written, these not being dictated by the type, but giving it its capacity to act on a particular, materially constrained occasion.

3. The token is a sign, and hence it interprets its object as it represents it. It must have a rhetoric, presumably intricated in the answer to (1) and in the specification of (2).

4. The token is a sign, and hence its rhetoric elicits an interpretant. Certainly, Peirce's definition of the sign in this paper implies recognition of the type.

The essence of a sign, (stretching that word to its widest limits, as *anything which, being determined by an object, determines an interpretation to determination, through it, by the same object*). (CP 4.531)

but the interpretant cannot be limited to recognition; it cannot merely replicate its type. Otherwise, it can produce no real effects or consequences. This has been made clear in Peirce's strictures concerning the incapacity of symbols to "add" anything to knowledge, except on the basis of a "preformed habit." We interpret tokens, significant as occurring just when and where they do, in the form and under the material conditions of their occurrence; we do not interpret types.

Only by accepting the implications of this definition, that the token interprets its object as it represents it, and that to interpret the token involves representing it in a new sign, can Peirce avoid mortgaging the "grammar" of signs to synchronicity. If tokens merely replicated their types, this would make the system of types "themselves" inviolate, resistant to change, at the same time as requiring of it that it explain the mechanism of change in meaning. The implications of this contradiction would be severe. Interpretation would be restricted to the third trichotomy, while the first trichotomy would be handled by replication. Then the issue would arise as to how to handle the representation relation: entirely subject to interpretation (and hence arbitrary)? Entirely determined by the system of signs (and hence purely conventional)? Determined by the real (and hence quarantined from the action of signs)? The contradiction would return Peirce to an account that separates "signs themselves" from their meanings, the system from its history. It would reproduce in Peirce the contradictions that beset the Saussurean project. A synchronic account of the system of signs cannot explain semiosis. Peirce's view of the relation between types and their tokens has the opposite effect: it implies a semiosic account of the sign itself.

The Saussurean account of the relation between *langue* and *parole* not only restricts it to synchronicity, but it does so because it confines it to the space of a single language. *Parole* "realizes" an ideal *material* form—the phonological signifier, say, in a phonetic approximation. If this approximation deviates too greatly from the ideal form, it counts as a mistake, or even as unintelligible. *Langue* is therefore a rule governing that materiality. The most remarkable difference with Peirce lies here. The question that has led to the elaboration of the distinction between type and token was first raised in respect of the translations of a proverb; it is devised in part to handle the passage *between* signifying systems. I shall return to the issue of translation in Chapter 6. For the moment, it is enough to note that though we recognize the proverb in its different forms, those forms have a material effect on its use on occasion. Likewise, the different versions of the pragmatic maxim change the capacity of that maxim to act in particular contexts. Equally, the graphs themselves must have properties that enable discoveries concerning "the course of thought" that other systems of representation cannot enable. The token, then, *represents* the "significant form" of the type; it does not reproduce its material properties. It is no doubt for this reason that the material qualities of the sign are often dismissed as accidental by Peirce, even though they are a sine qua non of the action of any sign. A sign must be "embodied," since types do not act; but any body, potentially, will do. Furthermore, what Peirce has pointed out in respect of the advantages of an algebraic notation also holds for any notational instrument: the conventions governing the materiality of the system make salient the "form," say of a proposition, but different systems make salient different aspects or properties of that form. Hence, Peirce's insistence that the existential graphs do a quite different job from an algebraic notation. Each has a particular interpretability, and what we do with each is a function of this.[21] Indeed, it is the special competence of the icon that it make a hypothesis concerning the form of its object. If the token is a sign of its type, it interprets it, and that is because it *translates* it. It is at this point that any sign is subject to semiosic change as a direct implication of its use on occasion.

Before we leave this most important topic, there are two further points to note. (1) In the first trichotomy reformulated as it now is, Peirce refuses what Saussurean theory requires, that is, an *initial* distinction between signifier and signified. (This would be a reason for counting Saussurean theory as "nominalist" in Peirce's use of this term.) The "tone" can just as well inhere in the object as in the material properties of the sign itself. These two dimensions are not distinguished until the point where a sign is represented to be a sign in a further sign. It is of the utmost importance to acknowledge that all aspects of meaning are the product of semiosis; they are not initial inputs. Only in this way can the problem of perception be made continuous with the problem of representation: the object of a sign is always already a sign, and is so because the perception of a sign is no different from the perception of any other sort of thing. Only at the point where the sign is taken as a sign does the need to distinguish it from its object arise. As I have argued, the distinction between first and second intentions is a necessary assumption in all Peirce's work on signs. (2) The token is the sign of its type and hence of the object of that type, whatever the nature of that object, and whatever the nature of the representation relation. Any interpretant of that token will be an interpretant of that relation. But since that interpretant arises through the process of translational or inferential change, and since it entails the taking of the sign as sign and hence "the needed commentary on the syntax," the interpretant of a token will, of necessity, involve reflection *about* the type, *about* the relation of sign to object, and *about* the object. Peirce's work on the type/token relation places reflection on, and translation of, the type at the center of his account of what it is to use a sign.

There are several drafts, letters, and fragments composed around the period of the *Monist* papers that shed further light on the issues raised by the first trichotomy, and on the move Peirce made to adopt the terminology that is now familiar. Take first this passage from a 1905 letter to William James:

> (Of course, I have not fully defined a proposition, because I have not discriminated the proposition from the individual sign which is the embodiment of the proposition. By a proposition, as something which can be repeated over and over again, translated into another language, embodied in a logical graph or algebraical formula, and still be one and the same proposition, we do not mean any existing individual object but a type, a general, which does not exist but governs existents, to which individuals conform.) (CP 8.313)

The passage takes for granted the point I have raised concerning the inevitability of translation at the point of embodiment of the sign. It also takes for granted a far more contentious proposition, namely, that the type thus translated remains the same object in any embodiment. This is a foundational assumption of translation, since translation must assume that it can posit, outside itself, a self-consistent identical object that subsists, no matter how many versions it is translated into, in how many languages, for how many distinct purposes or social settings. Indeed, for some piece of writing to count as a translation, it must be a translation of some identifiable other piece of writing. This assumption gives the rationale for comparing two translations of the same object, as well as for the criteria for judging their conformity with it. The translations might then stand as members of the same class, precisely on the criterion of standing as translations of the same object; and the type would stand to these translations as the rule that governs them. In construing this claim, then, we should not dismiss it too hastily on the grounds, say, that translations are always unfaithful to some degree, or that a sign always abolishes the previous sign at the point of representing it. On the contrary, the claim that a "token is a sign of its type" entails the assumption that the type is formally distinct from any particular embodiment. If we suppose, no doubt too hastily, that tokens are *iconic* of their types, then the object of a token is, like the object of any icon, a projection. Like triangles, the type is neither independent of its embodiments, nor is it subsumed by them. However, this does not solve all the problems: the formulation Peirce uses elicits a Platonic construal of the type. The type is a "general" thing, to which its tokens must conform. It is, we might be tempted to suggest, an idea, a pure form, a rule that "governs" its tokens. Is Peirce's theory of signs ultimately platonic? To answer this question, we must recall that semiosis has no absolute origin, any more than an absolute end. The platonic construal of the type suggests an origin beyond which there is no previous sign. Hence, it would violate the basic principle of semiosis.

Peirce considers this problem in an unsent draft addressed to Welby. The question of Platonism arises in the course of a curious, but highly instructive, foray into the dictionary. Peirce notes that "The dictionary is rich in words waiting to receive technical definitions as varieties of signs" (p. 194). Among these, he has discovered *token* and *type*:

"Token" is our good old Gothic word, though generally something material, or at least an individual, while a "type," on the contrary,—literally = French *coup*,—is of the nature of a form, an impression. The idea seems to prevail that the Greek word is often used by Plato in the sense of a sculptor's model. I have my doubts whether Greek sculptors of that age used models as ours do. I think the canon and their memory guided them mainly. At any rate, Plato rarely if ever used the word in any such sense. There is a place in the Republic filling 42 pages of the Teubner (C. F. Hermann) edition (Vol IV pp 58–99) in which Plato uses the word no less than 17 times, in every possible sense. Among these there are perhaps two or three instances where it means something to be imitated, though not certainly. . . . But if you look through his works for places in which he would be expected to use the word in that sense, it is very strikingly absent. I infer, therefore, that to his sense of the word, it was somewhat of a stretch so to use it. It usually means a character with the idea of being quite roughly like something, or the rough impression that experience of a thing leaves upon the mind. (appx. G, PW, July 1905)

Whatever faith we put in Peirce's philology, one thing is abundantly clear: in none of his construals of Plato's word *type* does he give to it the status of an origin. It is a form struck, an impression left by experience, and even if it is an imitation, that imitation is always already of something prior to it. The type is itself an imitation, a rough one at that, not of a living model, but of the rules given by the canon, by cultural memory. There is no first sign.

When we look for Peirce's uses of the term *type*, much as he did for Plato's, we find that most conform with the standard use of *type* to mean "kind" or "class." But Peirce also uses the word in a more specialized sense, drawn from the technical lexicon of printing. Doing so, he restores to the word *impression* its full technical sense. A type is a piece of type, and its tokens are the impressions left by it. And that type itself is drawn from a "canon" of forms, or it is newly devised according to the principles of the canon, or it is adapted from that canon for a new purpose. Two passages, exemplary for their display of the technical adaptation of types, show Peirce concerned with the typography of logical notations:

In 1872, Robert Grassmann, brother of the author of the "Ausdehnungslehre," published a work entitled *Die Formenlehre oder Mathematik*, the second book of which gives an algebra of logic identical with that of Jevons. The very notation is reproduced, except that the universe is denoted by T instead of U, and a term is negatived by drawing a line over it, as by Boole, instead of by taking a type from the other case, as Jevons does. Grassmann also uses a sign equivalent to my —<. (W 4:19, p. 182)

The following examples will illustrate the distinction between statistical deduction, induction, and hypothesis. If I wished to order a font of type expressly for the printing of this book, knowing, as I do, that in all English writing the letter *e* occurs oftener than any other letter, I should want more *e*'s in my font than other letters. For what is true of all other English writing is no doubt true of these papers. This is a statistical deduction. But then the words used in logical writings are rather peculiar, and a good deal of use is made of single letters. I might, then, count the number of occurrences of the different letters upon a dozen or so pages of the manuscript, and thence conclude the relative amounts of the different kinds of type required in the font. That would be inductive inference. If now I were to order the font, and if, after some days, I were to receive a box containing a large number of little paper parcels of very different sizes, I should naturally infer that this was the font of types I had ordered; and this would be hypothetic inference. Again, if a dispatch in cipher is captured, and it is found to be written with twenty-six characters, one of which occurs much more frequently than any of the others, we are at once led to suppose that each character represents a letter, and that the one occurring so frequently stands for *e*. This is also hypothetic inference. (W 4:64, p. 420)

If the type itself is an impression, roughly left, say, in memory or in archives, on material supports of one kind or another—collective, cultural, canonical—and in the traditions and conventions of a language, then it is implied that the type itself is the outcome of a translation that yields "types" by abstraction from a series of particular occurrences. This translation makes of a series of roughly similar things or events a model to guide imitations, a rule adaptable to the requirements of particular occasions. It is both the similarity, and its roughness, that inform the rule, which is a rule both of conformity and of adaptability. Noting, as Peirce has done, that it might refer just as easily to sculpture as to typography and to the "impressions left by experience"—and hence to the full range of signs— the type/token distinction, with its constitutive relation, must also apply to such things as genres and disciplines, those "canons" that inform "conversations" and that supply the criteria for interpreting, say, the rhetorical taxis of a theoretical exposition. When we make the necessary commentary on the syntax, it is on this that we comment: the imitation and the adaptation of the type.

This reading of the type displaces "ideas" from the centre of the theory of signs, and it does so by placing at this center the issue of *tekhnè*. Several important recent discussions of the philosophical tradition of inquiry into representation have done likewise.[22] In Peirce, it has been there from the outset, if at times only implicitly. The icon is necessarily a technical contrivance, manipulable for the purposes of mathematics and logic; and the list of examples of the index displays the significance of technical contraptions for the mediation of representation. Logical notations, and hence any specific language, are instruments (CP 3.520, CP 3.620, CP 3.628, W 4:56, pp. 381–82, etc.), methods are instruments (CP 7.276, W 5:33, p. 231), as are concepts and theories, and so on. This is no idle metaphor: to consider something as an instrument is to consider it as a device, designed both materially and formally for a purpose. It is in this sense that Peirce describes the capacities of the human mind:

I hold, for instance, that man is so completely hemmed in by the bounds of his possible practical experience, his mind is so restricted to being the instrument of his needs, that he cannot, in the least, *mean* anything that transcends those limits. The strict consequence of this is, that it is all nonsense to tell him that he must not think in this or that way because to do so would be to transcend the limits of a possible experience. For let him try ever so hard to think anything about what is beyond that limit, it simply cannot be done. (CP 5.536)

Signs are instruments. They are instruments of thought, devised by thought, without which thought is impossible, but they are not modeled on some conception of pure ideas that would transcend their instrumentality, a disembodied *cogito*, a mind defined in relation with God's truth, or any of the usual variants on this theme. When Peirce decides to use the term *type* for what had been the legisign, it is in order to point up this aspect of the signhood of signs; but the ambiguity of the term, the fact that it is indissociable from the connotation of "class," indeed, of "idea of [a] class" allows him to yoke the technicalities of the device with the features of generality and of canonicity—the "laws," "conventions," and "habits" of representation—that govern the tokens that make them operate on occasion.

December 23–28, 1908; March 14, 1909

Peirce writes two further letters to Welby on signs, one dated December 23, 1908 (with its associated drafts, EP 2:32, pp. 481–91 [CP 8.342–76, CP 8.377–79]), and the second, dated March 14, 1909. While the first of these contains some further tentative elaboration of the ten trichotomies, by far the most interesting point it raises is associated with the status Peirce now gives to semiotic. No longer merely a "whole theory" authored by Peirce, it is now a *science*, a discipline with its specialized branches and practitioners; not a "doctrine," but a field of inquiry.

In a draft of the first letter, Peirce quotes from the "New List," outlining the distinctions among the three branches of the study of signs, grammar, logic, and rhetoric. Then he continues:

I should still opine that in the future there probably will be three such sciences. But I have learned that the only natural lines of demarcation between nearly related sciences are the divisions between the social groups of devotees of those sciences; and for the present the cenoscopic studies . . . of all signs remain one undivided science,—a conclusion I had come to before I made your acquaintance, but which the warm interest that you and I have in each other's researches, in spite of the difference in their lines, decidedly confirms. (EP 2:32, p. 482 [CP 8.342])

Peirce's draft, which appears to be dated after the letter he finally sent to Welby, shows a hesitation on this matter. We read a minor but significant difference. Looking over the history of his research in semiotic, he recognizes the limitations of the scope of the field as he had first formulated it in the "New List":

In a paper of 1867 May 14 (Proc. Am. Acad. Arts & Sci. [Boston] VII 295), I defined logic as the doctrine of the formal conditions of the truth of symbols; i.e. of the reference of symbols to their objects. Later, when I had recognized that science consists in *inquiry*, not in "doctrine," . . . and when I accordingly recognized that, in order that the lines of demarcation between what we call "sciences" should be real, . . . those lines of demarcation can only represent the separations between the different groups of men who devote their lives to the advance of different studies, I saw that for a long time those who devoted themselves to discovering the truth about the general reference of symbols to their objects would be obliged to make researches into the reference to their interpretants, too, as well as into other characters of symbols, and not *of symbols alone* but of all sorts of signs. (PW December 23, 1908, pp. 79–80)

Any "man who makes researches" into semiotic "will be forced to make original studies into all branches of the general theory of signs" (PW December 23, 1908, pp. 79–80). Hence, his own studies have considered "logic" as semiotic, a field far broader than "the formal conditions of the truth of symbols." In this broad field, he situates Welby's work in relation with his own, but he begs her to take the step that he has taken, that is, to articulate her specialism with the whole:

"Significs" would appear, from its name, to be that part of Semeiotic which inquires into the relation of signs to their Interpretants. . . . But, assuming this to be your meaning, I should hardly think it possible, in the present state of the subject, to make much headway in a truly scientific investigation of significs in general without devoting a very large share of one's work to inquiries into other questions of semeiotic. (PW December 23, 1908, pp. 79–80)

Evidently, Peirce's considered view is that the difference in "lines" between Welby's work and his own is neither idiosyncratic nor a difference of schools of thought, but a difference between branches of the science. The move affects the rhetoric with which he addresses her. He will not engage with her in dispute or debate; he will organize their work into different territories. Then he will map the territory that contains them both, identifying its issues, its branches, its questions, and its definitions, but he will do so in terms of his own "whole theory." For this purpose, the whole theory will be the architectonic, constructed broadly on the same lines as in the "New List" but updated to include consideration of "all sorts of signs."

The whole theory starts with a definition of the sign, and moves directly to the "three universes" (the categories) in order to give the rationale of any trichotomy. These are given in order: the first trichotomy, now with the terminology Peirce has used in the *Monist* paper, but including a query concerning the use of the term *tone*. *Mark* may be better, for why would he suddenly turn to the voice, when all his work on this trichotomy has derived from issues to do with the technologies of written signs? However, he asks Welby to suggest something better. From there, he moves to the two objects, each of which has a trichotomy. These are, taking the Dynamoid Object first:

a Possible; when I term the Sign an *Abstractive*; . . . an Occurrence . . . [when] I term the sign a *Concretive*; . . . [and] a Necessitant [for which] I have at present no better designation than a "*Collective.*"

and second:

If the Immediate Object is a "Possible," that is, if the Dynamoid Object is indicated . . . by means of its Qualities, etc., I call the Sign a *Descriptive*; if the Immediate [Object] is an Occurrence, I call the Sign a *Designative*; and if the Immediate Object is a Necessitant, I call the sign a *Copulant*. (PW December 23, 1908, pp. 83–84)[23]

It is quite plain that both these trichotomies are "translations" (the word is Peirce's, in the same passage) of the categories, made to look like "kinds of signs." The classifications are potentially endless variations on the very familiar theme: there are triads everywhere, all displaying the distinctions among quality or possibility, fact or actuality, and law or continuity. But these classifications signally fail to do what the invention of the first trichotomy brought off so brilliantly: they do not arise as the response to a theoretical "surprise" and hence cannot represent the solution to a real problem. And so it comes to pass that Peirce again starts to classify "meaning" in place of semiotic devices. This is in line with the 1904 letter to Welby and follows from the 1903 construal of the categories under which the categorial analysis becomes a general phenomenological description of anything at all. It is hard not to see in this move the metaphysical vice par excellence, the one, moreover, that Peirce so frequently denounces: metaphysics tells us what meaning is, prior to, and independently of, the action of signs.

But he does return to the action of signs. This is because he has positioned Welby's work as bearing specifically on the interpretant, and because he reconstrues that work in terms of the direction dictated by pragmatism. In the 1909 letter, he discovers that he may have been influenced by Welby in his groping toward a classification of interpretants:

By the way, I find in my portfolio some part of a letter, if not the whole, dated December 28. I suppose I sent you that. I hope so, because it seems, from the glance I cast upon [it] to be concerned with my gropings after the three kind [*sic*] of Interpretant. I now find that my division nearly coincides with yours, as it ought to do exactly, if both are correct. I am not in the least conscious of having been at all influenced by your book in settling my trichotomy, as nearly as it is settled; . . . But as far as the public goes, I can only point out the agreement, and confess to having read your book. (PW, March 14, 1909, p. 109)

Do they agree closely? Peirce proceeds to inquire and finds that "the greatest discrepancy appears to lie in my Dynamical Interpretant as compared with your 'Meaning.'" Welby, he finds, attends to the intention of the sign, whereas he, Peirce, attends to the "direct effect actually produced by a Sign upon an Interpreter of it" (PW, March 14, 1909, p. 110). And he further diagnoses this difference by pointing out that his "interpretant with its three kinds" is "something essentially attaching to anything that acts as a Sign," unlike Welby's work, which attends only to human signs. Natural signs, writes Peirce, have no "utterer," and hence cannot be analyzed for their "intention." This little difference with Welby has helped him to sort something out:

My Immediate Interpretant is implied in the fact that each Sign must have its peculiar Interpretability before it gets any Interpreter. . . . The Dynamical Interpretant is a single actual event. The Final Interpretant is that toward which the actual tends. (PW, March 14, 1909, p. 111)

Let us return to this strange word *immediate* as Peirce applies it both to objects and to interpretants. There is certainly strong evidence for the construal on which I have based my remarks hitherto, that is, that "immediate" describes some sort of internal property of the sign, and this is undoubted in Johansen's account.[24] For him, the immediate object is of the nature of a "thought," and the dynamic object, of an ontological other to thought. Peirce, he thinks, accepts and confirms Kant's distinction between the *Ding für uns* and the *Ding an sich*. However, "immediate" is clearly the opposite of "mediate" and is thus equivalent to "unmediated." Given this, it *should* mean "direct," as in the following passage: "we have *direct experience of things in themselves*. Nothing can be more completely false than that we can experience only our own ideas" (CP 6.95, quoted by Johansen, p. 288). This direct experience of things is secondness—*experience*, not knowledge, or understanding, or interpretation—it is not semiotic at all. If this is what Peirce means by "immediate," then it is the object *prior to* representation; its complementary opposite, the "dynamic object," is the gradual discovery of that object once it enters semiosis.

Consider the following:

There is, we think, and reasonably think, a limit to this, an ultimate reality, like a zero of temperature. But in the nature of things, it can only be approached; it can only be represented. The *immediate object* which the sign *seeks to represent* is itself a sign. (MS 599:36, quoted by Johansen)

The "immediate object" is not here of the nature of thought at all. It is that which the sign seeks to represent, a presentation that, when re-presented, loses precisely that which we seek, its immediacy. This does indeed support the Kantian distinction, but it reverses the correlation that is usually supposed. It also gives a far more satisfactory reading of the "two kinds of object" than any that relies on the ontological difference of thoughts and things.

Peirce's late classifications are certainly pragmatic in respect of the elaboration of the interpretant as act, but this pragmatism sits ill with the classification of meaning. The point at which the inconsistency is revealed is the distinction of the immediate object from the dynamic object. Whichever way we read it, the distinction harbors within itself the dichotomy of mind and world, internal and external, representation and reality. This division has returned Peircean metaphysics to the problem that he has denounced with nominalism and reconstrued in his interpretation of Kant. In the place of the binarism that opposes an external reality to the contents of the mind, the ungraspable things-in-themselves to the noumena, Peirce had proposed two solutions: one is the fallibilistic philosophy of science, in which the "dynamic" object is the source of surprise, that which is to be known by the work of signs; the other is the distinction between the object of an index and the object of an icon or a symbol. Scientific philosophy, he has told Royce in 1885, must take seriously the work of the index as designating without describing that object which is to be known; with this, the "symbols" of science are fallible but correctible. These two solutions taken together obviate the need for "two kinds" of objects, replacing "two kinds" with two stages of the object of any semiosic sequence. Why, then, did Peirce forget this argument and return to a binarism that repeats the problems to which he had offered such a satisfactory solution? It is no mere slip, because not only did he restate it as a binarism, he consolidated the opposition between internal and external by providing each "kind" of object with its own trichotomy.

In 1900 and 1902, Peirce had reviewed Royce's book, *The World and the Individual*, and had raised exactly this issue:

we shall never have a satisfactory account of what we virtually aim at in seeking to know, until we recognize the individual character of the object of search.

This individual character is what Prof. Royce desires to bring out by his new definition of the object. He reaches this aspect of the matter through the conception of Purpose. Every idea he says has its purpose, which he calls its "internal meaning." We wish that in place of the vague word "idea," he had substituted *judgment* or *virtual judgment*; . . . since . . . only judgments have truth or falsity. . . . Now by the internal meaning or purpose of an idea Prof. Royce . . . understands all the experiments which would verify it. We can hardly believe that he is so entirely won over to the extreme pragmatism of his colleague, James, as to hold that Doing is the ultimate purpose of life. Nor is this necessary; for the purpose of an experiment is to learn, and the performance of it is only a means to that end. This internal meaning calls, then, for more and more definiteness without cessation; and the limit toward which it thus tends but never fully attains is the knowledge of an individual, in short, of God. (CP 8.114–15)

Royce, like Welby, is concerned with "meaning"; he is a pragmatic idealist. Peirce contests his version of pragmatism in the passage above, and pursues this debate in his review of the second volume of Royce's work by quoting to Royce his own pragmatic maxim. Royce, it appears, is relying on an entirely traditional analysis of meaning as "internal" and "external," connotation and denotation, depth and breadth.

Prof. Royce applying this doctrine to Ideas, notices their Internal Meaning and their External Meaning. He conceives of the internal meaning in a peculiar way. Another writer, a quarter of a century ago, laid down this maxim: "Consider what effects that might conceivably have practical bearings, we conceive the object of our conception to have. Then our conception of those effects is the *whole* of our conception of the object." (CP 8.119)

Peirce goes on to show that Royce has reconstrued the tradition in "this same pragmatistic spirit": the internal meaning is an obscure purpose, the external meaning, its fulfillment. Peirce approves of the move to pragmatism but holds that Royce's solution fails to solve the problem because it is governed by an idealist conception of meaning in the first place. He proposes semiotic in its place:

In the opinion of some students who have succeeded in rendering the doctrines of logic more precise than they used to be, it is better to divide the difficulty of defining the meaning of an "idea," by first analyzing the nature of a sign in general. For an "idea," as having a meaning, is of the nature of a sign. . . . But in analyzing the general nature of a sign, it will be needful, to distinguish radically different kinds of signs. A sign may serve as a sign simply because it happens to resemble its object. This resemblance will, then, constitute its internal meaning. But it cannot be said to have any external meaning. There are other signs which become such by virtue of being really connected with their objects. Such is a symptom of disease, or the letters attached to parts of a diagram. The external meaning of such a sign is its most prominent feature. Its internal meaning may be vanishingly small. . . . There is, however, a third totally different order of signs, which become such, not by virtue of any character of their own as things, nor by virtue of any real connection with their objects, but simply by virtue of being represented to be signs. . . . Such signs may have little or much internal meaning and external meaning but they have a third kind of meaning which consists in the character of the interpretant signs which they determine. This is their principal meaning. What Prof. Royce calls an "idea" is a sign of this class. (CP 8.119)[25]

This splendid passage explains why any attempt to provide a theory of "meaning" that is not first a theory of signs is bound to reproduce the general, traditional, problems of metaphysics. Peirce accepts to go on using the terms *internal* and *external*, but they do not here correlate with the "mind" and the world it seeks to know. They are functions of the properties of different kinds of signs. Further, and most notably, "ideas," or even "judgments," are not helpfully analyzed in these terms: their meaning resides in their relation with their interpretants.

When, writing to Welby, Peirce divides the object into two kinds, immediate and dynamic, and when he construes these two kinds as internal and external, he has forgotten these two lessons that he has delivered to Royce. Speaking *to* Welby's idealism, he has adopted her language. But remarkably, in the same period, writing in the *Monist*, Peirce's memory is restored. Writing about pragmatism, and about the need for logic within it, expounding his existential graphs for this purpose, Peirce construes "internal" and "external" in terms of the principle of fallibilism and self-correction—not "two kinds of objects," but two stages of the knowledge of objects, the provisional and the upshot of the sequence. What is it about the conversation with Welby that favors this amnesia in the first place, in 1904, and allows Peirce to repeat it, in 1908–9?

Unlike Royce, Welby is philosophically untrained, but like him, her work has a transcendental reach. It is informed by (an eccentric) Christianity, and it envisages "a new degree of truth, inclusive and comprehensive, raised by the amalgamation of all science to an altogether higher plane of meaning. Her aspiration was always toward this idea of a great composite mind, which would exhaust the knowability of the universe."[26] Notwithstanding Peirce's commitment to the kind of knowledge achieved through empirical scientific investigation, notwithstanding his commitment to fallibilism, this aspiration must have appealed to him, must have confirmed his idea of the highest vocation of philosophy, and must have done so specifically in the context of his deep disagreement with the epistemologically relativist pragmatism of William James. James is rarely mentioned in the correspondence, and given the significance of the relationship with James in Peirce's life at this time, it is quite astonishing that James' death in 1910 does not rate a mention to Welby. So let us suppose that the debate with James is what sets the agenda with Welby, not as debate, but as the ground that they share. This identifies two issues: the architectonic on the one hand, and belief in a truth determined ultimately by external reality on the other.[27] Peirce writes to Welby on this ground, and not on the ground of pragmatism. This is Philosophy with a capital P, in which the difference between a theory of signs and a theory of meaning simply pales into insignificance. Only a theory of meaning can be "whole" in this sense. Peirce's totalizing use of the categories is reductive and overrides the requirement for particularity—his pooh-poohing of the search for a "general form" of a question—in the study of the conditions and outcomes of the semiosic sequences that constitute in practice the processes of inquiry. Wholeness may need to be sacrificed in the study of the means of semiosis—the living businesses of living men—but this latter focus is lost in the generalizations of a global theory.

In the correspondence with Welby, we read a Peirce who will not give up this desire for a global system but who is not, here, challenged on its ground. It requires neither defense nor the philosophical rationale in which Peirce attempts—for example, in the Harvard Lectures, delivered at Royce's invitation, in the forum in which James' philosophical authority was undisputed—to marry realism with pragmatism. Unlike formal philosophical papers, and unlike lectures, both of which enact the dialectical struggle that defines philosophy as a rhetorical practice, the correspondence performs the "fusion" of two minds in a shared language (appx. G, pp. 196–97) and constructs the terrain that they share.[28] But we also read a Peirce who urges Welby, as he urges Royce and James, to take logic seriously. Here he is the teacher and here too, therefore, he is seeking to share a language; he imparts it in the letters in which he hopes she will persevere with his existential graphs, and expounds them to her as if she has embarked on their study. Logic is not, here, "critic" so much as a technique of critic, and that technique involves the technology of signs that I have discussed above. Hence, I suggest, the uneasy mix between a "classification of meaning," corresponding to the shared philosophical ground and restricted, significantly, to the issue of the objects of signs, and the careful attention to signs and their interpretants as semiotic instruments. What Peirce accepts from Welby is her understanding of "meaning" as "philosophy," a metaphysical account of the content of signs; what he wants her to accept from him is this: not only the sign, but also the interpretant is potentially a thing and an event, something that acts, becomes actual, and has actual consequences, rendering "inefficient relations efficient" on occasion.

The late classifications of signs are a very peculiar construct. T. L. Short calls them "darkest semeiotica," describing them as "immense, obscure, crabbed with dense tangles," containing important suggestions, but tentative and difficult to clarify.[29] Scholars from Lieb to Liszka have fought their way through its "thickets," elucidating the broad system, counting the classes, selecting those aspects of the classifications that seem most useful. I agree with Short that the first trichotomy is the richest and most fully developed of them all, and that the distinctions Peirce was drawing within the broad category of the object, and those, likewise, within the interpretant, are fraught with difficulties. I confess that as a descriptive semiotician, there is little from this period of Peirce's work that I am inclined to use. It should be clear from the foregoing what this is: the type/token relation seems to me to illuminate a very difficult issue in semiotic, as does the fallibilistic construal of the distinction between the "immediate" and the "dynamic" object. Some suggestions regarding the interpretant are also promising, but only to the extent that they show where, in a Peircean semiotic, we can accommodate insights into the effectivity of the sign that we know better from other sources.

Rather than dwell longer on the details of these classifications, I want to turn my attention to the very fact that they are classifications. I have suggested that the best way to read the second classification, the combinatory of the Syllabus, is as a "grammar" of the sign, meaning by this what Peirce always meant by "grammar," the study of the conditions fitting some thing to act as a sign. It is proper that this should comprise a trichotomy analyzing the sign itself, another analyzing the relation of the sign with its object, and a third analyzing the structural properties of the sign as they determine its interpretability.[30] What is the function of the further classifications that analyze the "two objects" and the "three (or six . . .) interpretants"? Are they, respectively, a "logic" and a "rhetoric"? Why produce a classification of kinds of object and kinds of interpretant, as if these two relata of the sign were theorizable outside the relation that gives them their function in the sign? And why, given that all three relata—the sign, the object, and the interpretant—are *signs*, why do we need special classifications to deal with each relatum? The question is troubling because it draws our attention to the silent assumption of the further classifications: if each relatum of the sign relation requires its own classification, this implies that each relatum is phenomenologically, or ontologically, or metaphysically, different from the others. This implication violates all Peirce's principles. For the difference between the object, and the sign, and the interpretant, is a structural and a functional one: there is no essence of objects, say, or interpretants, or even of signs, that requires its own theory. They act as they do, fulfill the function that they fulfill, because of the place they occupy in the relation. This relation is dynamic and ever-changing, but all its relata are signs.

To a certain degree, the problem of the late work can be glossed as the result of returning to a classificatory protocol of genus and species, instead of the relational systems that Peirce had entertained at the turn of the century. He takes each relatum of the sign as a genus, then seeks its species, seeming to forget the relational analysis that has generated the terms in the first place. This problem is evident in the difficulty Peirce has with the distinction between the two "kinds of objects." As we have seen, he "forgets" that what he is talking about is the process of inquiry, handling as "kinds" what is easily handled by the account of science as fallibilistic. He does not require a critical logic other than this. A similar analysis holds for the "kinds" of interpretants distinguished as "immediate," "dynamic," and "final." Or take the distinction between the "emotional," the "energetic," and the "logical" interpretant: these are just different material forms for an interpretant and could be handled by the "qualisign" or tone, and the accompanying issue of translation under the first trichotomy. The difference between a sign that presents for "contemplation," or for assessment of its truth conditions, or for its proofs, orients our attention to the protocols of the sign that determine its interpretation, recasting the familiar distinction of term, proposition, and argument in explicitly rhetorical terms. This being the case, I suggest that the classification presented in the Syllabus could have been used to handle the signs that occupy all three structural positions of the sign relation. It would handle them as signs, asking of each what conditions fit it to fulfill its specific function in the relation. This relation is the mechanism of semiosis; outside of it, nothing acts as a sign; only that mechanism "renders inefficient relations efficient." Peirce simply does not need ontological bits and pieces, such as objects "inside and outside" the sign, or "bodies, feelings and minds," for this purpose. Why he did not notice this is a very curious thing indeed. It is as if, having discovered the means to theorize signs as things, Peirce lost his focus on the motivating need for this discovery, which is to give an account of actual events of semiosis. At this point, "things" and "events" part company. The classifications appear to me to immobilize semiosis not on principle, but as an effect, possibly unwanted, of the very fact that they attempt to classify all three branches of semiotic. Until the Syllabus, the classificatory work restricts its scope to grammar, asking what it is in each case that fits some sign to act as a sign. It is as if the very elegance of his 1903 answer to this question has tempted him to extend "grammar" to cover all three branches of semiotic. Neither logic nor rhetoric is susceptible of a grammar, and the semiosis of semiotic is blocked by metaphysics at this point.

6

The Ways of Semiosis

I

Nothing speaks for itself, strictly nothing, speaking strictly. The sign is medium and mediator, the ineliminable third term, "that which is what it is owing to things between which it mediates and which it brings into relation to each other" (W 6:23, p. 170). "Category the Third is the Idea of that which is such as it is as being a Third, or Medium, between a Second and its First. That is to say, it is *Representation* as an element of the Phenomenon" (EP 2:12, p. 160 [CP 5.66]). "It involves a sign, or representamen, of some kind, outward or inward, mediating between an object and an interpreting thought" (CP 1.480). "A Representamen mediates between its Interpretant and its Object, and that which cannot be the object of the Representamen cannot be the Object of the Interpretant" (CP 2.311). Note the location of the sign, *between,* and likewise that of the third term: "By the third, I mean the medium or connecting bond between the absolute first and last. The beginning is first, the end second, the middle third. The end is second, the means third" (CP 1.337). It is here, in the issue of the *means* of representation, that Peirce's semiotic begins.

This mediating structure refers indifferently to the "representamen" and to the "interpretant," to the sign taken as a three-term relation as well as to the middle term of that relation. In "On a New List of Categories," the verbs *to represent* and *to interpret* gloss one another: "a mediating representation may be termed an *interpretant*" (W 2:4, p. 53). However, this structure is not sufficient to explicate the function of the sign. In work following the "New List," the term *interpretant* refers to a sign subsequent to a previous sign. In this case, the term *third* is used ordinally, to refer to the third member of a sequence in which, if the "representamen" is a mediator, the "interpretant" its effect, its consequence, or its uptake. This introduces time into the model, opening the way for it to explicate the eventhood of the sign. Take this famous passage from the cognition papers, in which the dynamic of semiosis is first made explicit. Note the use of "translate or interpret" to explicate the production of an interpretant sign:

When we think, to what thought does that thought-sign which is ourself address itself? It may, through the medium of outward expression, which it reaches perhaps only after considerable internal development, come to address itself to thought of another person. But whether this happens or not, it is always interpreted by a subsequent thought of our own. If, after any thought, the current of ideas flows on freely, it follows the law of mental association. In that case, each former thought suggests something to the thought which follows it, i.e. is the sign of something to this latter. Our train of thought may, it is true, be interrupted. [However,] from our second principle, that there is no intuition or cognition not determined by previous cognitions, it follows that the striking in of a new experience is never an instantaneous affair, but is an *event* occupying time, and coming to pass by a continuous process . . . if a train of thought ceases by gradually dying out, it freely follows its own law of association as long as it lasts, and there is no moment at which there is a thought belonging to this series, subsequently to which there is not a thought which interprets or repeats it. There is no exception, therefore, to the law that every thought-sign is translated or interpreted in a subsequent one, unless it be that all thought comes to an abrupt and final end in death. (W 2:22; pp. 223–24)

We must understand representation as consisting minimally of a sequence of *two* interpreting representamens: the first interprets the object to some further sign; the second is the subsequent sign that reproduces the process, taking as object the previous representation. The focus is now on semiosis as process, rather than on the sign as entity, but these are complementary and mutually entailed. Each sign is defined on the model of mediation. It is precisely because the sign is third and the third is middle that semiosis is infinite. Any sign, therefore, is definitionally incomplete, and given that the subsequent interpretant is a *sign*, then it too is subject to the same condition. And so on, as Peirce will say, ad infinitum:

A *Sign* is anything which is related to a Second thing, its *Object*, in respect to a Quality, in such a way as to bring a Third thing, its *Interpretant*, into relation to the same Object, and that in such a way as to bring a Fourth into relation to that Object in the same form, *ad infinitum*. If the series is broken off, the Sign, in so far, falls short of the perfect significant character. It is not necessary that the Interpretant should actually exist. A being *in futuro* will suffice. (CP 2.92)

Peirce's account of signhood is functional, in the sense that he asks what work a sign does and how it does it: "semiosis" is the answer to the first part of this question, and "mediation" is the answer to the second part. Semiosis is the dynamic of change that operates between the past orientation of the sign and its future orientation; mediation is the mechanism of representation and interpretation.

The difference between the past and the future orientations of the sign relation can be grasped by juxtaposing two analogies for the process of semiosis. One, classical in philosophy, is the metaphor of the veil of truth; the other—the onion metaphor—translates the icon into less transcendental language, where it has other implications. Here is Peirce's version of the veil:

The meaning of a representation can be nothing but a representation. In fact, it is nothing but the representation itself conceived as stripped of irrelevant clothing. But this clothing never can be completely stripped off; it is only changed for something more diaphanous. (CP 1.339)

The idea of the progressive "diaphanization" of knowledge, in Arthur Danto's words,[1] is certainly congruent with Peirce's mathematical construal of the "limit" as an ideal, but unattainable, terminus; but Peirce goes on to transform the metaphor. Semiosis consists of adding layers:

Finally, the interpretant is nothing but another representation to which the torch of truth is handed along; and as representation, it has its interpretant again. Lo, another infinite series. (CP 1.339)

And again:

Anything which determines something else (its *interpretant*) to refer to an object to which itself refers (its *object*) in the same way, the interpretant becoming in turn a sign, and so on *ad infinitum*. (CP 2.303).

Thus, he writes, we have "sign overlying sign" (CP 2.94).

Now this idea, that all we can do is *accumulate* signs, is a problem for standard theories of representation. The business of science, of all inquiry, and certainly of all inquiry into inquiry, as philosophy purports to be, is to *reveal* the truth. The problem is made explicit by the trope of the veil, in any of its guises. However, as I. A. Richards has put it, the idea that language is a dress that thought puts on is a "wretchedly inconvenient metaphor."[2] If language is a dress, a costume or disguise for reality, thought, or truth, then the business of a philosophy must surely be to strip them of their finery and reveal what lies beneath. It will be noticed that if the "sign overlying sign" is forever putting more clothes on, the philosopher is forever engaged in undressing it, though he may sometimes acknowledge his failure to do so *jusqu'au bout*. Peirce is inclined to mockery:

Perhaps the greatest obstacle to conveying a simple statement of what is here meant by a Sign is that, not only owing to the genesis and structure of speech, must it be set forth in figurative expression, but that any initial form that can be given to it independently [?] will perforce be obtrusively figurative. Now in this age of physical science [?] cannot attract notice [?] all in a definition, without even intelligent and educated men, yea, and a large class of young women, exclaiming "Oh, that is poetry: tell us the truth." They seem to consider Poetry to be *per se* false, little thinking that in order to be the genuine thing, its first requisite is to be very true. If they do not know this, what can they know of those regions of thought where truth as it walks abroad is always clothed in figures of which it divests itself for none but its intimates? Let one put up with figurative ideas rather than go without any. (MS 634, pp. 17–19; some words are unreadable)

Peirce replaces the august allegory of Truth with the humble onion, which represents precisely the accumulation of layers through semiosis:

The attempt to divest thought of expression and to get at the naked thought itself, which some logicians have made, is like trying to remove the peel from an onion and get at the naked onion itself. (MS 450, p. 3)

This is because "Expression and thought are one" (PW December 1, 1903, p. 10); yet elsewhere, Peirce conceives of their separateness, only to reject it anew as he pursues his metaphor:

[Thinking] is essentially composed of signs, as its matter, in the sense in which a game of chess has the chessmen for its matter. Not that the particular signs employed are themselves the thought! Oh, no; no whit more than the skins of an onion are the onion. (About as much so, however.) (CP 4.6)

And thus we find, returning to the problem of comparison from whence arose the postulate of the sign, that there is perhaps no truth other than the signhood of signs:

The young chemist precipitates Prussian blue from two nearly colorless fluids a hundred times over without ceasing to marvel at it. Yet he finds no marvel in the fact that any one precipitate when compared in color with the other seems similar every time. It is quite as much a mystery, in truth, and you can no more get at the heart of it, than you can get at the heart of an onion. (CP 4.87)

According to the analogy of the veil, truth is the ultimate object of desire, though we may never have the pleasure of intimacy with it; according to the analogy of the onion, when we get to the end, there is nothing there. At the end of real onions, there are other onions, or dinner. The contrast here is between a transcendental account of inquiry, and a workaday one, "seminary" and "laboratory" philosophies, as Peirce terms them (CP 1.126 ff.); the point of the contrast is to argue for pragmatism.

Unexpectedly—but it is in a letter to a friend—we do find Peirce in the bedchamber one morning. Peirce is writing to William James, attempting to explain to his pragmatist colleague exactly what he means by the three kinds of interpretant. He resorts, as he so often does, to an example from ordinary conversation. With sign overlying sign, Peirce does what the metaphor expects him to do: he peeps through the curtains, but significantly, he looks outward, and—empirical scientist to the last—the object of his inquiries is the weather:

For instance, suppose I awake in the morning before my bedfellow, and that afterwards she wakes up and inquires, "What sort of a day is it?" *This* is a Sign,[3] whose Object, as expressed, is the weather at that time, but whose Dynamical Object is the *impression which I have presumably derived from peeping through the window curtains*. Whose Interpretant, as expressed, is the quality of the weather, but whose Dynamical Interpretant is *my answering her question*. But beyond that, there is a *third* Interpretant. The *Immediate Interpretant* is what the Question expresses, *all* that it immediately expresses, which I have imperfectly restated above. The *Dynamical Interpretant* is the actual effect that it has upon me, its interpreter. But the Significance of it,[4] the *Ultimate* or *Final Interpretant* is her *purpose* in asking it, what effect its answer will have as to her plans for the ensuing day. I reply, let us suppose: "It is a stormy day." Here is another sign. Its *Immediate Object* is the notion of the present weather so far as this is common to her mind and mine,—not the *character* of it, but the *identity* of it. The *Dynamical Object* is the *identity* of the actual and *Real* meteorological conditions at the moment. The *Immediate Interpretant* is the *schema* in her imagination, i.e., the vague Image or what there is in common to the different Images of a stormy day. The *Dynamical Interpretant* is the disappointment or whatever actual effect it at once has upon her. The *Final Interpretant* is the sum of the *Lessons* of the reply, Moral, Scientific, etc. (EP 2:33, p. 498)

These "lessons" are perhaps the clearest statement of what Peirce means by the "final interpretant." They are the implications and practical consequences adumbrated by the pragmatic maxim: "Considérer quels sont les effets pratiques que nous pensons pouvoir être produits par l'objet de notre conception. La conception de tous ces effets est la conception complète de l'objet" (W 3:67, p. 365). The practical consequences that translate information into action are perhaps the meal that we find at the end of real onions.

The difference between the veil and the onion is, I have suggested, the difference between the "backward orientation" of the sign and its "future orientation." By analogy, it is also the difference between two conceptions of truth. In a detailed article on definitions of truth (CP 5.565–73), Peirce draws a clear distinction between "transcendental" and logical truth. The latter is a function of signs:

Truth and falsity are characters confined to propositions. A proposition is a sign which separately indicates its object. Thus, a portrait with the name of the original below it is a proposition. It asserts that if anybody looks at it, he can form a reasonably correct idea of how the original looked. A sign is only a sign *in actu* by virtue of its receiving an interpretation, that is, by virtue of its determining another sign of the same object. This is as true of mental judgments as it is of external signs. To say that a proposition is true is to say that every interpretation of it is true. Two propositions are equivalent when either might have been an interpretant of the other. This equivalence, like others, is by an act of abstraction (in the sense in which forming an abstract noun is abstraction) conceived as identity. And we speak of believing in a proposition, having in mind an entire collection of equivalent propositions with their partial interpretants. Thus, two persons are said to have the same proposition in mind. The interpretant of a proposition is itself a proposition. Any necessary inference from a proposition is an interpretant of it. When we speak of truth and falsity, we refer to the possibility of the proposition being refuted; and this refutation (roughly speaking) takes place in but one way. Namely, an interpretant of the proposition would, if believed, produce the expectation of a certain description of percept on a certain occasion. The occasion arrives: the percept forced upon us is different. This constitutes the falsity of every proposition of which the disappointing prediction was the interpretant.

Thus, a false proposition is a proposition of which some interpretant represents that, on an occasion which it indicates, a percept will have a certain character, while the immediate perceptual judgment on that occasion is that the percept has not that character. A true proposition is a proposition belief in which would never lead to such disappointment so long as the proposition is not understood otherwise than it was intended. (CP 5.569)

However, there are other senses attaching to the word "truth":

But *truth* is also used in senses in which it is not an affection of a sign, but of things as things. Such truth is called *transcendental truth*. The scholastic maxim was *Ens est unum, verum, bonum*. Among the senses in which transcendental truth was spoken of was that in which it was said that all science has for its object the investigation of *truth*, that is to say, of the real characters of things. It was, in other senses, regarded as a subject of metaphysics exclusively. It is sometimes defined so as to be indistinguishable from reality, or real existence. Another common definition is that truth is the conformity, or conformability, of things to reason. Another definition is that truth is the conformity of things to their essential principles. (CP 5.572)

This is the idea of truth that informs the metaphor of the veil. Strip the veils away, it suggests, and the "naked truth" will be revealed, as if things as things, the essential principles of things, would then speak for themselves. "The trouble is," writes Peirce, "nothing does speak for itself, strictly nothing, speaking strictly. One cannot bid his neighbor good morning, really, effectually, unless that neighbor supplies the needed commentary on the syntax. If he does not, I might as well shake a rattle" (MS 427, p. 146). Signs, that is to say, cannot be dispensed with, and understanding how the sign works is part of understanding the thing for which it speaks and whether it does so well.

It has been suggested, however, that the metaphor of the onion speaks for a pre-pragmatic Peirce, and that the Peirce of the mature pragmatism who argues for metaphysical realism opts for the account of inquiry represented by the veil.[5] The question is whether semiosis is infinite: is the "final interpretant" an *interpretant* and hence a sign? Or is it a finality on which the work of interpretation converges, but where it ceases? Does the mature revision to pragmatism require of Peirce that he modify his theory of signs and semiosis, or does the theory of signs require of philosophy that it remain in what Roland Barthes has called "the kitchen of meaning"? As I have done thus far, I shall consider the complexities of this question by attending to an analogy, and some examples.

II

Descartes is the philosopher for whom all the important breakthroughs occur off the road, in the undisturbed solitude and sedentary posture of meditation. Peirce is the philosopher for whom anything of significance—I mean "significance"—happens *on* the road. Take the following example of indexicality, which I discussed in Chapter 4:

Suppose two men meet upon a country road and one of them says to the other, "The chimney of that house is on fire." The other looks about him and descries a house with green blinds and a verandah having a smoking chimney. He walks on a few miles and meets a second traveller. Like a Simple Simon he says, "The chimney of that house is on fire." "What house?" asks the other. "Oh, a house with green blinds and a verandah," replies the simpleton. "Where is the house?" asks the stranger. He desires some index which shall connect his apprehension with the house meant. (EP 2:3, p. 11 [CP 2.287])

What would the Peircean philosopher fail to know if he had not taken to the road? By the fire with old Descartes, he might have assumed a single universe of discourse, in which the referential ambiguities of this example would not have been discernible. Knowledge would arise in the mind, and reference would be a problem of the conformity of representation to the real principles of things; it would not be a problem of the conditions of assertion, in particular insofar as this depends in all these examples on the here and now of a speaking body. On the road, where Simple Simon has a problem of communication only because he has moved farther down the track, he discovers that reference is unstable, needing constantly to be fixed, that the answer to "which?" depends for its intelligibility on the material conditions of utterance and reception, on the answer to "where?" and "when?"

As successive travelers ask their ever more complex string of questions, the eyewitness knowledge of the first informant gives way to "directions," telling their addressees "what to do to find the object meant" (CP 2.288–89). "Perception" gives way to "action." They are the limits of inquiry, the "it" that is there unknown and undefined, and the habits of action attaching to it that are its pragmatic meaning. The principle of indexicality converges with the horizon of empirical science to delineate the scope of pragmatism, where the inquiring I is bound to seek the laws of the object, thereafter to be bound by them in truth.

It is for these reasons that Carl Hausman has argued for a construal of "infinite" semiosis as "indefinite" semiosis. Inquiry is limited in practice by the nature of reality, and if truth is elusive or a long way off, it is a receding limit, a regulative ideal, located in some indefinite future, but nonetheless there and attainable in principle. This construal appears to receive support from the "road of inquiry":

The elements of every concept enter into logical thought at the gate of perception and make their exit at the gate of purposive action; and whatever cannot show its passports at both those two gates is to be arrested as unauthorized by reason. (EP 2:16, p. 241 [CP 5.212])

The "road of inquiry" passage forms the strategically placed conclusion of the Harvard Lectures on Pragmatism. However, Peirce has preempted the capacity even of this metaphor to imply finality. Peirce introduces this passage as the maxim of pragmatism, which is the rule of rational conduct for the position for which he is arguing:

Pragmatism will be more essentially significant for [the man who takes the third position] than for any other logician, for the reason that it is in action that logical energy returns to the uncontrolled and uncriticizable parts of the mind. His maxim will be this:. . . .   (EP 2:16, p. 241 [CP 5.212])

Notice the crucial word *return*. It suggests that there is no exit, for the "uncontrolled and uncriticizable parts of the mind" are exactly those that generate percepts, which are the gate of entry. We may even wonder if the two gates are not a single gate, viewed from either side. It is an implication of this that particular—let us say empirical—investigations do attain answers, but answers are merely the place from which we set out as we ask new questions.

When we leave the road, it is to rest, and unless the rest is silence, the "end" is not only local to a particular line of inquiry, it is also temporary:

And what, then, is belief? It is the demi-cadence which closes a musical phrase in the symphony of our intellectual life. We have seen that it has just three properties: First, it is something that we are aware of; second, it appeases the irritation of doubt; and, third, it involves the establishment in our nature of a rule of action, or, say for short, a habit. As it appeases the irritation of doubt, which is the motive for thinking, thought relaxes, and comes to rest for a moment when belief is reached. But, since belief is a rule for action, the application of which involves further doubt and further thought, at the same time that it is a stopping-place, it is also a new starting-place for thought. That is why I have permitted myself to call it thought at rest, although thought is essentially an action. The final upshot of thinking is the exercise of volition, and of this thought no longer forms a part; but belief is only a stadium of mental action, an effect upon our nature due to thought, which will influence future thinking. (W 3:61, p. 263; 1878)

The stopping place is a new starting point, the exit returns us to the point of entry. This "end" is anything but final; the "final interpretant" does not close off the "future orientation" of the sign.

Peirce has a considerable distrust of any philosophical argument that rests on something "ultimate." This distrust is consistent with his generalized distrust of any metaphysical system not grounded in logic and informed by real science. The claim that some element is "ultimate" is simply a way of blocking the path of inquiry:

The third philosophical stratagem for cutting off inquiry consists in maintaining that this, that, or the other element of science is basic, ultimate, independent of aught else, and utterly inexplicable—not so much from any defect in our knowing as because there is nothing beneath it to know. The only type of reasoning by which such a conclusion could possibly be reached is *retroduction*. Now nothing justifies a retroductive inference except its affording an explanation of the facts. It is, however, no explanation at all of a fact to pronounce it *inexplicable*. That, therefore, is a conclusion which no reasoning can ever justify or excuse. (CP 1.139; 1899)

Why might it be acceptable to invoke an "ultimate end" if it is not acceptable to invoke an ultimate ground? Again, Peirce makes it clear that it is not. In another account of the problem of inexplicable ultimates, Peirce writes that there are certain classes of facts of which it would be unreasonable to expect an explanation: one is indeterminacy, another hecceity:

Indeterminacy, then, or pure firstness, and hæcceity, or pure secondness, are facts not calling for and not capable of explanation. Indeterminacy affords us nothing to ask a question about; hæcceity is the *ultima ratio*, the brutal fact that will not be questioned. But every fact of a general or orderly nature calls for an explanation; and logic forbids us to assume in regard to any given fact of that sort that it is of its own nature absolutely inexplicable. This is what Kant calls a regulative principle, that is to say, an intellectual hope. The sole immediate purpose of thinking is to render things intelligible; and to think and yet in that very act to think a thing unintelligible is a self-stultification. . . . True, there may be facts that will never get explained; but that any given fact is of the number, is what experience can never give us reason to think; far less can it show that any fact is of its own nature unintelligible. We must therefore be guided by the rule of hope, and consequently we must reject every philosophy or general conception of the universe, which could ever lead to the conclusion that any given general fact is an ultimate one. We must look forward to the explanation, not of all things, but of any given thing whatever. There is no contradiction here, any more than there is in our holding each one of our opinions, while we are ready to admit that it is probable that not all are true; or any more than there is in saying that any future time will sometime be past, though there never will be a time when all time is past. (W 6:28, p. 206)

There never will be a time when all time is past, since because semiosis is a process in time, there never will be a sign of the pastness of all semiosis.

Both Quine and Rorty read Peirce as arguing for an End in (what Peirce calls) transcendental truth, and both have written persuasive objections to this position. Hausman rebuts them on the grounds that the End of Inquiry is a regulative ideal for the conduct of inquiry, and while this latter takes place in real time, the former is strictly ideal.[6] However, if it is the case, as we have just read, that "there never will be a time when all time is past," then Hausman's argument fails to connect the regulative principle with the hope that the end is attainable in principle. For to do so would depend on the assumption that what Peirce means by the ideal limit to inquiry is something outside of time. There is no other location for the attainment of a telos.

Rorty has argued that if the end is genuinely the end, then there would be no way of knowing that we had reached it.[7] Hausman sees no way of countering this objection:

if the "we" refers to finite inquirers at any assignable time. . . . it does seem that no *individual* and no finite loci of intelligence would be certain of being in a state of finality with respect to the totality of beliefs, or the opinion that is final. Only a supreme intelligence would be (or come to?) such a state, if such a state is attainable. We are back to the notion of a God's-eye view. For Peirce, such a supreme intelligence would be a supreme community in which individuals are submerged and resistances, Secondnesses, no longer function. I take this community to be at least one of the ideas Peirce has in mind when he writes of God. God would be the final intelligence.[8]

But God is not intelligent in Peirce's sense, and He does not use signs.[9] Even if we accepted Hausman's argument here, we would be left with a difficulty: signs would be regulated by the asemiotic. It is clear that Hausman's view depends on some such assumption as this; it is less clear that this is Peirce's position.

When asked to provide a formal definition of *ultimate* for the *Century Dictionary*, Peirce has this to say:

ULTIMATE:

(1) Last in a series; especially in a series of purposes each, except the last, subsidiary to an ulterior one following it in the arrangement considered, or of actions each of which, except the last, leads to the performance of another. . . . *Ultimate fact* implies that there is a series of facts each explicable by the one following it, until a fact is reached utterly inexplicable. (CP 5.608)

Notice that it is now explicit, that the ultimate—whether we call it "the end of inquiry," the "ultimate opinion," or the "final interpretant"—is exceptional in its capacity to close the series. To claim that some ultimate thing is an interpretant, and hence a sign, brings Peirce up against a dilemma to which he is alert, and which he proposes to solve as follows:

the phrase *ultimate signification* implies that a sign determines another sign of the same object, and this another; and so on until something is reached which is a sign only for itself. (CP 5.608; 1901)

Peirce has preserved the formal property of the interpretant to refer itself to some interpretant. Is this the perfect congruence of object with interpretant for which the naked truth might stand? The sign that is sign "only for itself" recalls the map of the map, which is

the precise analogue of pure self-consciousness. As such it is *self-sufficient*. It is saved from being insufficient, that is, as no representation at all, by the circumstance that it is not *all-sufficient*, that is, is not a complete representation but is only a point upon a continuous map. (EP 2:12, p. 162 [CP 5.71]; 1903)

Notice again that Peirce himself has raised the problem of the semiotic status of this "sign": it would be "insufficient, that is no representation at all" were it claimed to be complete; but it is not, it is only a point, it is very partial. Insufficiency of this sort, it will be recalled, was the point of the joke that Peirce made immediately before expounding the example of the map (CP 5.71): if God is "all-sufficient" he is a "complete representation" and hence, no representation at all. The map, the sign for itself, is sufficient, that is, adequate to some purpose, because it does a particular job of representation.

We might infer that it is a condition of signhood that any representation be partial. Peirce confirms this inference:

Truth is a character which attaches to an abstract proposition, such as a person might utter. It essentially depends upon that proposition's not professing to be exactly true. But we hope that in the progress of science its error will indefinitely diminish. . . . If our hope is vain; if in respect to some question—say that of the freedom of the will—no matter how long the discussion goes on, no matter how scientific our methods may become, there will never be a time when we can fully satisfy ourselves either that the question has no meaning, or that one answer or the other explains the facts, then in regard to that question there certainly is no *truth*. . . . Truth is that concordance of an abstract statement with the ideal limit towards which endless investigation would tend to bring scientific belief, which concordance the abstract statement may possess by virtue of the confession of its inaccuracy and one-sidedness, and this confession is an essential ingredient of truth. (CP 5.565; 1901)

This is a second solution to the problem, because it is this confession that allows any answer to give rise to some further question. Semiosis is infinite because it is part of the definition of signhood that no sign is an island on which the whole universe might stand.[10]

The passages I have adduced thus far in my discussion of the road of inquiry are drawn from writings that span Peirce's career; they do not provide reliable evidence for the argument that Peirce gave up the hypothesis of infinite semiosis as part of his development of pragmatism. Nor do they support the "softer" version of this argument, which is that he reconstrued "infinite" semiosis as "indefinite." It is a better interpretation of the facts to conclude as follows: semiosis and inquiry are not coextensive; inquiry is a certain kind of semiosis—that is, a genre (or field of genres)—a particular form of human endeavor, goal-driven and regulated by any number of contingencies (such as disciplinary norms, funding, institutional arrangements) as well as "inherently" by its own rules (such as the protocols for forming questions, the relation of means to ends). Following the definition of truth cited immediately above, Peirce is careful to distinguish scientific inquiry from the normative sciences, from pure mathematics, and from practical life, on the grounds that "truth" is to some degree a different issue for each of these. In all of these, however, the perfect truth "can neither be stated nor conceived" (CP 5.566), although in each case for different technical reasons. Further, it is relevant to recall the distinction between truth as a "character attaching to a sign" from "transcendental truth," which is indistinguishable from "reality" and a subject of "metaphysics exclusively" (CP 5.572).

Our task, then, is to decide whether the "final interpretant" corresponds to the "metaphysical" conception of truth," or to "truth" as it is defined pragmatically for particular domains of human endeavor. I submit that the verdict is inescapable: Peirce never attempts to speculate as to the end of semiosis. Semiosis is infinite in principle, but scientific inquiry is regulated by its presupposition that it can reach right answers, so that the end of inquiry is always the end of particular inquiries. Peirce asserts—insists, throughout his career—that there are right answers to particular questions, and that they can be discovered with the application of good scientific method and tested against reality. In order to theorize this position, inquiry must be construed as finite in principle; the end of any particular line of inquiry is reached when it can no longer be doubted under any conditions. "Finite in principle" is modeled on, and construed through, practices in history.

So we are brought to this question: do we model semiosis in general on inquiry, and thus on in principle finitude? I have reviewed several major objections to this option. First, as I have argued, the generalization fails, because at every point, the "final interpretant" fails to conform to the definition of the sign. Second, on Rorty's argument, it would follow from this asemiotic nature of the end that it could not count as knowledge. Third, it is crucial to Peirce's fallibilism that inquiry not be closed off by any assumption—or hope—that the currently accepted answer to that question could not be bettered. This leaves us with the second option, which applies the model in reverse: particular inquiries are informed by the principle of infinite semiosis. It is consistent with this reading to construe the end of the road as a stopping place, rather than as an exit from semiosis. It is provisional, in that all answers generate habits of action, and those actions may generate new questions. Furthermore, no inquiry is adequately represented as a single line of questions and answers, any more than material truth can be represented as a single line of argument (W 2:22, p. 212). Networks of facts, systems of explanation, are continually being modified by the introduction of new facts or the integration of one system with another.

Just as continuity is the background condition for the discontinuities necessary to the reality of things and events, so is infinite semiosis the background condition for the boundaries that distinguish one kind of conversation from another, two languages likewise, or that bring one genre to its practical limit or to its encounter with the incomprehensions and questions of another. The conversations of neighbors occur at such points, sometimes to mark them, sometimes to negotiate their differences. This is the work of the intermediary, and it is for this that we need signs. Were it not so, things would speak for themselves, or would have no need to speak (which amounts to the same thing).

I have argued that the very idea of an ultimate sign or final interpretant is self-contradictory. Semiosis is infinite, and there can be "last signs" only in respect of particular series, either contingently last, or last in the sense of best possible answer. This argument rests on the reading I have offered of "the road of inquiry" and conforms with the strictly technical, methodological account of truth as a regulative principle given by Cheryl Misak.[11] I have also argued that what seems to be meant in Hausman's argument by "the final interpretant" confuses two things that Peirce was usually careful to distinguish: a metaphysical account of truth, and a logical one. Metaphysics imagines the naked truth beneath its veils, whereas under logic, truth and falsehood attach to propositions; hence, logic works with the form of the onion, knowing that there is nothing else. There is some evidence that the confusion stems from Peirce's own problems in defining the "final interpretant," as if, at the very point in his research on signs when he was attempting to fuse the findings of logic and philosophy, the generic blurring that resulted made it difficult for him to maintain a distinction that is otherwise crucial to his work on inquiry.

With respect to the narrowly semiotic implications of this issue, I have argued that the cognition series explicates the sign in terms of semiosis, and semiosis in terms of the sign, and that, following this move, it is a misreading of Peirce to separate them. Only when we take the structure of the sign apart from its explication by semiosis is it possible to argue that some sign is last, because it is only under those circumstances that it is not inconsistent to envisage the possibility of a complete sign.[12] Furthermore, while this is made explicit in the cognition series, it is implied by the examples of signhood adduced before that. Signs are definitionally incomplete because they are both structured by, and subject to, mediation.

An objection could be mounted in the following terms: my argument holds for the sign *in actu*, and hence for the dynamical interpretant, but it is restricted to projecting an infinite series of sign events and thus has no purchase on the issue that Peirce himself is attempting to resolve. This is the application of the category of law or thirdness to the interpretant as such. What he is looking for in the "final interpretant" is the law of the interpretation of the sign. This would consist in the sum total of the "lessons" drawn from the sign and the habits of action they would inform. We have to imagine a situation of perfect congruence between the three relates of signhood, or between the backward and the forward orientation of representation. The sign would no longer undergo modification through semiosis; it would repeat itself perpetually. The habits of action would guide action so well that no further doubt could occur. In Naomi Cummings' intelligent construal, interpretation would take the form of predicting a "pattern or rule," and that prediction would continue to be satisfied.[13]

Now, whether in the laboratory, in the repeated experiments that confirm a finding; or outside, in the actions that display the truth of some precept; or indeed, back in the laboratory, when some further representation recasts the questions that may pertain to the first, it is always sign events that do the work. If it be said that the final interpretant is Peirce's attempt to get beyond the "secondness" of the dynamical interpretant into the thirdness of law, then I think we must acknowledge that this place beyond things and events is provisional at best, or at worst chimeric, "that to which the actual tends," perhaps, but of its nature, the elusive object of philosophy's desire. Signs remain subject to semiosis and hence to mediation; they cannot be protected from it.

III

In view of this, "mediation" demands of us a "commentary upon its syntax."

The paradigm examples of mediation are provided in the "New List." The comparison of *b* with *p*, the discernment of the relational structure of /murder/, the translation of *homme* into *man*, Peirce tells us, all require a "mediating representation." He explains what it is to "mediate," then what it is to "represent," by adducing several heterogeneous examples:

Such a mediating representation may be termed an interpretant, because it fulfils the office of an interpreter, who says that a foreigner says the same thing which he himself says. The term representation is here to be understood in a very extended sense, which can be explained by instances better than by a definition. In this sense, a word represents a thing to the conception in the mind of the hearer, a portrait represents the person for whom it is intended to the conception of recognition, a weathercock represents the direction of the wind to the conception of him who understands it, a barrister represents his client to the judge and jury whom he influences. (W 2:4, p. 54)

The barrister is unquestionably the most challenging of these. This is a figure whose professional obligation is to "influence" the judge and the jury before whom he pleads what is acknowledged to be a partisan cause. The barrister introduces the issue of distrust, insincerity, the manipulation of judgment. If we take the barrister as a paradigm case of representation, then we must say that nothing speaks for itself because it needs an advocate, and it has traditionally been the case that philosophy does not want its theories of representation to be tainted by this implication. Consider this view, from Quine:

Rhetoric is the literary technology of persuasion, for good or ill. It is the rallying point for advertisers, trial lawyers, politicians, and debating teams.

Debating teams are promoted in schools as a spur to effective language and incisive thought. They serve that purpose, but only by setting the goal of persuasion above the goal of truth. The debater's strength lies not in intellectual curiosity nor in amenability to rational persuasion by others, but in his skill in defending a preconception come what may. His is a nefarious knack of disregarding all the discrepancies while regarding every crepancy. The same skill, along with legal lore, is the strength of the trial lawyer or barrister, and the strength also of the successful politician, one or the other of which careers the captain of the debating team is clearly destined for. Happily there are lawyers who will take on only such cases as they deem to be just, and politicians who will espouse only a cause that is righteous; but these scruples are not adjuncts of the rhetorical pole, nor are they keys to success in the legal or political profession.[14]

Of course, it is open to us simply to marginalize, or even to disregard, this example, but Peirce lists it together with words, portraits, and weathercocks, so I prefer to take seriously its inclusion in the account of representation. Signs are creative; they provide the conditions for transforming ignorance and error into reliable knowledge. But they do not do so reliably, and they do other things besides—plead a partisan cause, for example. If the class of signs includes the barrister, then the model of signhood that is being proposed cannot preclude false pleading. We have no conception of truth without its accompanying opposite; we have no powers of generating new ideas without—notably—the icon whose truth cannot be guaranteed. Or, as Eco puts the matter, a theory of signs cannot do what Peirce wants it to do without entailing the capacity for lying, as well as fiction, hypothesis, the construction of imaginary objects, fancy, memory, and dreams.[15]

In order to fulfill his brief, the barrister speaks *for* his client *to* the tribunal. In Peirce's early work on the problem of inquiry, he gives the relation between doubt and belief a psychological construal, but the example of the barrister implies an alternative account: doubt can be understood as the coexistence of two conflicting accounts of some event or state of affairs. In this sense, doubt is the structural principle of forensic discourse. A barrister is required to introduce doubt concerning the argument of his opponent and to invite belief concerning his own.

It is of some interest in this connection that Peirce quotes a definition of argument from Cicero, the canonical exemplar of the practice as well as the theory of forensic rhetoric: "There can be little doubt that *argumentum* acquired its logical meaning in the Roman law courts; and Cicero not only uses it as above, but expressly defines it as 'ratio rei dubiae faciens fidem.'" (note appended to CP 2.461). Elsewhere, Peirce makes much of the derivation of the word *doubt*: "Among the inner shapes which binarity assumes are those of the doubts that are forced upon our minds. The very word 'doubt,' or 'dubito,' is the frequentative of 'duhibeo'—that is, *duo habeo*, and thus exhibits its binarity. If we did not struggle against doubt, we should not seek the truth" (CP 2.84). The barrister is the paradigmatic figure for this structure, for there are always two barristers, each aiming to produce belief by disabling the weaker story.

We may hold an opinion, we may judge of that opinion that it has been arrived at most rigorously and that there is no good reason to doubt it; yet we must be ready to admit that we may be mistaken (EP 2:4, p. 31). For Peirce, the "indefinite long run" is less a metaphysical construct than a strategy for deferring the point at which inquiry might stop. This is one of the roles of the barrister, for the forensic skills with which he comes armed are directed not only at persuading the judge of the case he represents, but also at demonstrating that there is reasonable doubt concerning the opposing case. The right answer to a question, the resting place or the stopping point, is not a point where all possible doubt has ceased, but a point modeled on the practices of the law. When Peirce pleads the case for a certain definition of logic and reason, against the ubiquitous theory that it rests on a "feeling of logicality," it is precisely this legal standard of proof that he invokes:

That is the argument which I pronounce a miserable fallacy. If we extend to arguments a just maxim of our law, every argument must be presumed to be sound until it is proved fallacious. Accordingly, I will refer to this argument as the "defendant argument," and to the writers who adhere to it as the "defendants." (EP 2:17, p. 244; 1903)

This is not a chance analogy. Peirce frequently writes of "advocating" an opinion, of arguing against its "opponents," sometimes allowing that conclusions are "verdicts" and for that reason eminently fallible (EP 2:5, p. 44 [CP 5.578]), sometimes identifying the coming to a verdict with conformism (CP 3.425). This is an indication of his ambivalence toward the implications of his own example. However, notwithstanding this ambivalence, he presupposes that rhetoric has its place in the basic training for the liberal professions as well as the academy. This is consistent with the form of the curriculum that governed his own education and that remained in force well into the twentieth century. Indeed, rhetoric is the general science of making signs effective, and knowing about the rhetoric of science is part of the role of semiotic vis-à-vis the practitioners. This is the place of critique, which must understand that which makes signs fit to represent what they claim to represent ("grammar"), that which must understand on what grounds an argument claims validity ("critic"), and the general conditions under which a problem presents itself for solution and those under which one question leads on to another ("rhetoric").

In other words, critique must focus on the means of representation as well as on its outcomes, and it will focus on the outcomes by attending to the means by which they are reached. It would be a very grave step to give up, or even to diminish the importance of, critique by reducing the range of issues with which it deals. Yet it seems to me that this is an implication of a good deal of Peirce scholarship, which is inclined to take "critic" as the full scope of critique. This is exactly what Peirce opposes by elaborating the program for semiotic with its three branches. This exclusion of grammar and rhetoric is no doubt due to the traditional habits of philosophy, but it may also be a consequence of too exclusive a focus on the "end of inquiry," on the task of philosophy as defining this end. A further influence may be the prestige of Kant's metaphor of the tribunal of reason, where reason passes judgment on the case before it. In Peirce's scheme of things, the judge and the jury assess the *representations* that have been made to the court. Without the forensic process as such, the hearing would be conducted on the illusion that judgment is to be passed on the facts "in themselves." Whatever the risks, forensic advocacy is a method for avoiding summary judgment, an outcome that would be open to all the objections Peirce puts to the "method of authority" (W 3:4, p. 60), as well as those that he raises with respect to any claim in philosophy to have discovered an ultimate explanation of anything. It would block the way of inquiry (CP 1.135).

However, we must acknowledge that the choice of the example of the barrister carries implications that do not sit easily with what we might think of as the orthodox view of truth seeking for which "classical pragmatism" is said to stand. This is demonstrated when Susan Haack enlists Peirce in support of her view of "honest inquiry" with its "disinterested . . . respect for evidence" as against "pseudo-inquiry" in which the inquirer "wants . . . to make a case for some proposition determined in advance."[16] The difference between one and the other turns precisely on the status of the forensic, which for Haack has no place in "inquiry"; indeed, for her, the forensic characterizes the practice to which inquiry is most clearly opposed:

In a court of law, there is competition between opposing attorneys: a model which may have encouraged some to suppose that disinterestedness is altogether dispensable. Counsel, however, are not inquirers, nor is a legal proceeding an inquiry into whether the defendant did it. (p. 13)

Neither the philosopher nor the scientist is like legal counsel; Haack compares their work with that of the jury, whereas Peirce's sign is like a barrister who is expected to *influence* the judge and jury. Haack's analogy works this way:

The jury is, however, trying to figure out whether the defendant's guilt is established to the required degree by the admissible evidence presented. And a juror will perform this role better, the closer he approximates the genuine inquirer. (p. 13)

Peirce's barrister is a severe embarrassment to this view, a fact that is demonstrated when we discover Haack quoting Peirce's definition of representation, written for Baldwin's *Century Dictionary of Philosophy and Psychology*. I quote it in Peirce's form:

Represent: To stand for, that is, to be in such a relation to another that for certain purposes it is treated by some mind as if it were that other.

Thus, a spokesman, deputy, attorney, agent, vicar, diagram, symptom, counter, description, concept, premiss, testimony, all represent something else, in their several ways, to minds who consider them in that way. (CP 2.273)[17]

In Haack's version (p. 35), she omits all the examples, the list of which includes the agent, the vicar, the spokesman, and, notably, the attorney. Peirce's sign is not the figure of impartial *judgment*; it is the figure of partial representation. The sign "speaks for" its object as a barrister speaks on behalf of his client. It is partial in both senses—not impartial, and not whole. An example of partial pleading is Haack's own defective quotation of Peirce's account of representation.

   If we give up the place of the barrister, we are left with a sign that can bring inquiry to closure only because it judges itself. For this reason, Peirce does not look kindly on any science that claims to have pronounced a "final word":

such finality is not yet known, thank God, in any modern science; should such ever take possession of scientific minds, it will forebode either the speedy extinction of the human race, or else an era of intellectual epilepsy. (EP 2:31, p. 471)

But Peirce does not forecast the imminent end of the human race (EP 2:31, pp. 466–67); on the contrary, the capacity of intelligent creatures to learn apparently without limit, gives him reason to expect evolution in our reason as well as in our other adaptive capacities. Accordingly, any particular result of inquiry is judged not by itself but by some future judgment. Some "reasoner of the sixteenth century" raises this objection to Peirce's own procedure:

"If you purpose arraigning the very principles of human Ratiocination itself before the bar of judgment, how can they ever be vindicated? Reasoning cannot be allowed to pass judgment on itself."

Peirce concurs. Not only is it not allowed, it is not possible:

it would be powerless to do so, even if it had every conceivable permission, since it is past and gone before any doubt of it can arise, yet there appears no reason why, provided reasoning at all tends to be true, in a more developed state of the growth of reasoning-power, a former reasoning should not be put on trial and be convicted of weakness or utter irrationality. (EP 2:31, p. 466)

The sign that interprets itself is not only solipsistic; it violates the ethics of inquiry. The issue of the self-judging sign is the core of the aporias of philosophy elaborated by Jean-François Lyotard.[18] Traditionally philosophy claims the position of judging all other inquiry—indeed, of passing judgment, if Haack is to be believed, on what does, and what does not, count as worthy of the title of "inquiry." This would be the final interpretant, or in Lyotard's terms, the "universal genre." But there is no such thing, because, as Lyotard describes the problem, there is simply an untidy heterogeneity of genres, each of which functions in terms of its own protocols and presuppositions, each of which stakes its own claim to describe the world according to rules of conduct and interaction that are incommensurate with the others. In this case, no judgment is made from some putative "outside" of the realm of genres, and if some genre judges the conduct and outcomes of another, its judgment is partisan and can do no more than display its own generic stakes. The relation among the genres is either one of indifference or of competition, and the "judge" cannot fail to be party to the cause of his own genre. We are always already in discourse, and we cannot get out.

Further, all discourse, any judgment, is an event in time. It follows, writes François Guibal, that neither we nor our discourse can transcend the time of its event (though that event be protracted or renewed across history), and hence that any attempt to think time is itself time bound. The pattern of this problem is clearly similar to the pattern of the problem that besets Peirce: the means of representation are things in contingency and events in time. If the self-judging sign is a sign, if it is a judgment of any sort, then it is subject to the same aporia. But the alternative is unacceptable: if there is something that can indeed close the process of judgment and is not itself a judgment, then it fails all the tests of logic, of reason, of philosophy itself—especially pragmatism—that Peirce insists upon.

This would seem to leave us in a quandary, in which we are forced to choose between partisanship on the one hand and self-deluding consensus on the other. There is a trap in this for those who seek to denounce the totalizing pretensions of philosophy from a position located within rhetoric. Either way, one genre is seeking to absorb and disempower the other. There is no solution available in a generalization of the forensic. Nor is there a solution in deleting it from our inquiry into signs.

So what place does the figure of the barrister occupy in Peirce's program for semiotic? I have suggested two answers to this question. First, all signs, whether in inquiry narrowly understood or in the broad sweep of semiosis, have a rhetorical dimension or are implicated in a rhetoric, and every scientist and indeed philosopher must be understood as advocating a position. In some very important respects, Peirce's semiotic is concerned with the *force* of signs, not just with their rightness. Rightness is a part of this force, but not its full explanation. This force has real effects. Peirce's insight in this respect is to associate the issue of these effects with the theory of the interpretant; that is to say, in the terms of the rhetoric manuals, he associates an (albeit rudimentary) account of the audience with an account of the formal—"grammatical" and logical—properties of the representamen. It is a clear implication of this account that there can be wrong interpretations, where "wrong" means either "unjustified" by the sign itself, or justified by the sign but not supported by further inquiry. Thus, inquiry into the extent to which a wrong interpretation has force is an implicit aspect of Peirce's program for semiotic. Second, given the rhetoricity of any sign, there is a barrister role for the critical philosopher too. This role is modeled on cross-examination, which Quintilian says is the method of Platonic dialectic. To cross-examine is to cast doubt on the position advocated by the sign that is pleading its cause.[19] This process *defers* belief, requires further research, raises new questions. It is the place from which useful pragmatic forms of doubt emerge. The task of the jury and the judge is to assess how useful, how *reasonable*, such doubts really are. There are always two barristers; doubt arises not from conversation with the people who agree with us, but in conversation with our neighbors who do not. "Even in the most priestridden states," Peirce writes

some individuals . . . possess a wider sort of social feeling; they see that men in other countries and in other ages have held to very different doctrines from those which they themselves have been brought up to believe; and they cannot help seeing that it is the mere accident of their having been taught as they have, and of their having been surrounded with the manners and associations they have, that has caused them to believe as they do and not far differently. And their candor cannot resist the reflection that there is no reason to rate their own views at a higher value than those of other nations and other centuries; and this gives rise to doubts in their minds. (W 3:60, p. 252)

Max Fisch has argued persuasively that discussions of the law have their place in the origins of philosophical pragmatism,[20] partly on the grounds that a large number of the members of the original Metaphysical Club were lawyers, and partly on the evident substantive connections he finds between the early formulations of legal pragmatism and Peirce's development of the pragmatic maxim in his logic of science. In particular, Peirce's lifelong insistence on the continuity between "natural law," jurisprudential decision making, legislation, and "habit" surely owes something to the philosophy of law that was being developed by his close friends from that time, Nicholas St. John Green and Oliver Wendell Holmes Jr. Peirce's obituary for Green lends some support to the view that he showed more interest in the practice of the law than has sometimes been argued (W 3:19, p. 55), and his praise of Green—albeit overdetermined as it must be by its genre—demonstrates that it is the law as an intellectual practice that attracts his attention. Green, he writes, "handled a question of law . . . with the mastery of a logician who easily reduced a case under established principles," but he also counts as the exemplary case of a young man who corrected his tendency to political prejudice through the exercise of reason and the philosophical attitude. Green had been a professor of law, and the obituary was written for the *Proceedings of the American Academy of Arts and Sciences*, of which both he and Peirce were members. But Green was not only an academic lawyer; he had been a barrister, of whom Peirce writes in admiration that "no man at the Suffolk bar produced a greater effect upon the opinions of the Supreme Court . . . than he. His arguments, in addition to the qualities of substance which we have mentioned, had a terseness and simple beauty of form," which Peirce goes on to compare with those of a senior judge. Noting that the barrister's capacity to influence the judge is the point of most fulsome praise in this piece, we might think of Peirce's barrister as an unremarkable example against this background. In Peirce's intellectual milieu, the barrister combined broad culture and deep knowledge of the relevant facts and theories, with the forensic arts, one aspect of which, he tells us, is a mastery of logic and another a mastery of oratorical and rhetorical style. Insofar as a barrister of this caliber might have "effects" on the opinions of the Supreme Court, the genre for which he stands is not an inappropriate model for the marshaling of evidence, the construction of arguments from it, and the dismantling of counterarguments, that go together by the name of "inquiry." As Peirce remarks elsewhere, "training in observation . . . has been pretty much the sum total of the professional training of many very celebrated naturalists, unless we reckon, as part of their professional training, that rhetorical training which enabled them to impress other minds with their ideas" (EP 2:31, p. 471).

An unremarkable example, perhaps. Yet late in his life, Peirce had a moment's hesitation about its implications. The passage occurs in an unsent, and incomplete, draft letter addressed to Welby. For this reason, it is unlikely to represent Peirce's final opinion on the matter, but it is of some interest to inquire whether these hesitations coincide with Haack's objections, and, if they do, how we should assess them. The problem arises when, having formulated a definition of the sign, Peirce finds that the analogy, or example, of the "representative" violates that definition, so he is forced to choose between this definition and a lifelong habit.

I formerly preferred the word *representamen*. But there was no need of this horrid long word. . . . My notion . . . was that it would seem more natural to apply it to representatives in legislatures, to deputies of various kinds, etc. I admit still that it aids the comprehension of the definition to compare it carefully with such cases. But they certainly depart from the definition, in that this requires that the action of the sign as such shall not affect the object represented. A legislative representative is, on the contrary, expected to improve the condition of his constituents; and any kind of attorney, even if he has no discretion, is expected to affect the condition of his principal. . . . I thought of the representation as taking the place of the thing; but a sign is not a substitute. (PW appx. G, p. 193)

Note that Peirce does not abjure the comparison of representation with "representatives of various kinds," but that this comparison now leads to a contrast, in that representatives are active intermediaries, whereas the definition Peirce has tried in the draft requires that the interpretant not act:

A "sign" is anything, A, which

(i) in addition to other characters of its own,
(ii) stands in a dyadic relation, r, to a purely active correlate, B,
(iii) and is also in a triadic relation *to* B *for* a purely passive correlate, C, this triadic relation being such as to determine C to be in a dyadic relation, **R**, to B, the relation **R** corresponding in a recognized way to the relation r. (PW appx. G, p. 192)

This definition formalizes the structure of signhood adumbrated in the "New List"; hence, it returns to a version of semiotic that precedes the introduction of semiosis to the account of signhood. Furthermore, it does so by eliminating from it exactly those features that looked forward to the explicitation of semiosis, the active intermediaries. Has Peirce simply changed his mind? Is the sign active, does it change something in the condition of its object, does it have an effect on its interpretant, or is it a mere vehicle, the humble servant of its object, self-effacing as it brings that object to the interpretant, which itself can do nothing but pass it on again, unchanged? This latter option would make nonsense of the whole theory of inquiry, the account under which progressive representations change our understanding of the world around us, sometimes—in the best of cases— bringing us to an answer that cannot be bettered. I think we must reject it on these grounds, as I believe Peirce did, but the idea that the real object itself would take full charge of the action of signs is, I believe, the assumption that underpins Haack's account of inquiry. For, while her account appears simply to register her distrust of advocacy in the process of judgment, the attempt to eliminate it from "the tribunal of reason" has graver implications.

In order to see what these are, let us return to the definition of representation Peirce provided for Baldwin's dictionary, which is the definition Haack relies on:

Represent: To stand for, that is, to be in such a relation to another that for certain purposes it is treated by some mind as if it were that other.

Thus, a spokesman, deputy, attorney, agent, vicar, diagram, symptom, counter, description, concept, premiss, testimony, all represent something else, in their several ways, to minds who consider them in that way. See Sign. When it is desired to distinguish between that which represents and the act or relation of representing, the former may be termed the "representamen," the latter the "representation." (CP 2.273)

In Haack's use of this definition, it takes this form:

REPRESENT: to stand for, that is, to be in such a relation to another that for certain purposes, it is treated by some mind as if it were that other. . . . When it is desired to distinguish between that which represents and the . . . relation of representing, the former may be termed the "representamen," the latter the "representation." (CP 2.273)

Haack uses this passage to counter Rorty's definition of pragmatism as "anti-representationalism," where Rorty objects to Peirce's "references to 'true representations'" (p. 35). She quotes Rorty's view that "the notion of 'accurate representation' is simply an . . . empty compliment which we pay to those beliefs which are successful in helping us do what we want to do" (p. 35) and positions that view as "nominalist" as against Peirce's realism. Peirce's definition, then, is positioned as a realist account of representation, and what she uses from it to this end is the point that "for certain purposes" the representation is treated by some mind as if it were the thing that it stands for. Implied in the definition, however, is that there exist other purposes. What are they?

Notice that while it may be motivated by a desire for citational economy, Haack's elimination of the examples has the effect of simplifying the issue of representation, reducing the "several ways" in which a "spokesman, deputy, attorney, agent, vicar, diagram, symptom, counter, description, concept, premiss, testimony" can each be said to represent something. This simplification is an abstraction from the range of technical and discursive practices and devices implied by the list of examples; the residue is an abstract account of representation in general. This is the implication of any definition on what Peirce calls the "Aristotelian" model. While Haack presupposes this model, by 1901, Peirce had come to favor the alternative, the system, comprising all those things that stand together in a set of connected relations. Indeed, it must be said that long before he made this distinction, Peirce's habit was to adduce a list of disparate examples before, and sometimes instead of, offering a formal definition. It follows that in Haack's account, there can be no interest in the differences between particular technologies of representation, nor, as it appears, in the range of purposes of signs, of their mechanisms, or of their uses.

What are the other kinds of purpose mentioned by Peirce in his definition? Clearly, we do not eat the concept of a cheese or drink the description of the bouquet of a fine wine; in these cases, substitution does not arise. By contrast, we are obliged to substitute a diagram of a triangle for a triangle, and when a head of state receives an ambassador, the conversation is pursued as if between the states represented. Thus, we might say that to *use* the sign appropriately in such cases, we must treat it as a substitute. Taken together with the belief that signs are not prevented from representing real generals, this is the realist attitude. But Peirce retains from nominalism its refusal to conflate the sign with the thing and its capacity for doubt regarding any particular representation, because it is on this that the possibility of critique must rest. Hence, we must distinguish between the purposes of particular signs, and the purposes of semiotic. The condition of critical philosophy is second intentionality, which requires that we attend to the formal, material, and functional properties of the representamen, asking how it achieves its representation. This is the other kind of purpose mentioned in the part of the definition Haack quotes in place of the examples, but its force is different in their absence. The purpose of semiotic is to study how different kinds of signs achieve their purposes. It follows that the passage deleted by Haack is absolutely crucial, for in it, Peirce attends as he always does to the "several ways" in which each member of his list of examples makes a claim to "represent." What Haack gives up from Peirce is both this range of ways, and the point of semiotic in general. It is unlikely that Peirce would do likewise. Tempted by the formalization of a definition, insisting to Welby that the important issue of signs is their object, Peirce was speaking in the voice of the orthodox philosopher—as Ransdell puts it, attending to "facts" and not to "mere words or symbols"—but it is precisely against this position that he has developed his combination of realism and fallibilism, which depends crucially on his account of the action of signs. The definition in the draft letter would have led him to an impasse; he abandoned it.

Nevertheless, the abandoned draft raises interesting questions: part of the problem with "representamen" is that the analogy it implies is not inclusive enough:

[the word *representamen*] requires some stretching to cover such imperative ejaculations of drivers, as "hi!" or "Hullah," which was in my boyhood days the signal to get out of the way of a coaster's sled on Boston Common, where I suppose coasting has long since been prohibited. (PW, appx. G, p. 193)

The difficulty is plain. While it would not be difficult to argue that "hi!" and "hullah!" work as they do because they "influence"—indeed, move— their interpreters, it is less than clear that those interpreters are something like judges or juries, or that they have "objects" (clear and present danger?) to which they stand as does a barrister to his client.[21] But we should note that Peirce is rejecting the "representatives of various sorts" as if he had intended them to pertain to all cases of signhood: this, he tells us, is the implication of the term *representamen*. However, only if they count as a general analogy that holds for all representation does Peirce's 1905 objection to it carry any weight. Note that the definition from Baldwin's dictionary uses the term *represent* according to standard patterns of English usage. All manner of things "represent," Peirce has always claimed, refusing to distinguish between the "represent" of representatives, and the "represent" of counters and concepts. This range of usage has made it possible for Peirce to reflect on the heterogeneity of signs in general. The draft definition reads as if the "representatives" have taken over, and Peirce has had to set things to rights by eliminating them altogether. It is true that they do not illuminate cases such as "hi!" and "hullah!", but neither can these exclamations say what we mean by the signhood of a word, a portrait, or a weathercock. We must acknowledge that none of Peirce's examples—not the line of identity, not the proverb, not the word *homme*, not Patrick Henry's call, not the marks left by tramps on fences in rural Pennsylvania, none of them is capable of illuminating the semiotic properties of all the others, although many of them bring to light some feature of the action of signs that applies more broadly than to a single case.

In this light, a further, far more interesting question arises. It returns us to Lyotard's challenge to the very project of a systematic semiotic. This is whether a general definition of the class of signs can indeed be given, if that class includes examples as diverse as barristers and "hi!", not to mention fevers and knots in the handkerchief. The general class of signs is established on the basis not of a definition, but on the basis of a cluster of criteria on which something may count as a sign. These clusters of criteria may well be an instance of Wittgenstein's solution to the problem of class membership: a class is a collection of features more like family resemblances than like identity among all members. Not every member would share all of these features, although the family displays them all distributively—hence Peirce's habit of adducing lists of examples rather than definitions. Signs represent "in their several ways." Inclusiveness on the basis of a single criterion, or of a generalizable analogy, is simply not an issue.

The fact that from time to time Peirce attempts to formalize his conception of the class of signs in a definition is not in doubt; nor, however, is it in doubt that he often acknowledges the difficulty, as he does in the following passage:

The general phenomenon throughout mathematics is that almost every strongly marked concept has border concepts which lose the strong characteristics but are included in the broader concept. . . . The same phenomenon presents itself in the realm of phaneroscopy to such an extent that the only successful way of analyzing any of the concepts which belong peculiarly to this realm is not to begin by considering that concept in all its breadth, but rather to confine oneself, at first, to its highly characterized forms, and when that has been thoroughly comprehended, to inquire by what modifications the bordering forms attach themselves to it. . . . However, until special instances are before us, abstract description can hardly be understood. (MS 283, pp. 121–25)

Peirce's solution to the issue of class membership is different from Wittgenstein's: the idea that there are "border concepts" implies that there are also "core" or central concepts that must, we presume, recur in all members. On this assumption, he classifies signs as "relatively genuine" and "relatively degenerate," as in the Harvard Lectures; or he devises the combinatory that results in the ten classes, none of which exactly repeats the features of the others, but all of which are triadic, drawing their features from each of the three trichotomies. These two devices have been discussed in some detail in previous chapters, and there is no need to go over the same ground here. It is enough to point out that Peirce's late work on signs is work on the very problem of class membership, and that although he was tempted also to try to formulate a general definition, none of the general definitions can deal with the range of examples that he adduces from time to time. By contrast with these attempts at definition, the two devices for theorizing classhood, and hence, for representing the classes of signs in their diversity, are far more successful. But it is the lists of examples that actually do the work of exploring the sign hypothesis.

So I return to the barrister, whose status among the examples is established by the position it occupies on its first appearance. Recalling that the "New List" relegates icons and indices outside the purview of logic, we should note that its list of examples consists of four members. The first three represent the three kinds of representation, with the apparently anodyne "word" standing in for the symbol. The central issue of the symbol, however, is elaborated by the barrister. All symbols are taken to work in the context of some argument or another, whether explicit or implicit, whether their material premises "are veracious or not" (MS 283, p. 328). It is implied by the arrangement of the examples in the "New List" that the barrister stands for argument (whether partial—terms and propositions—or complete with premises and conclusions explicit); and of argument, Peirce writes—invoking Cicero's authority—that he prefers that word over the term *inference* because argument implies a discursive, indeed a forensic, practice (CP 2.461; note appended in 1893).

Signs are Peirce's concern, signs *materialiter*—practices, and devices. This is why he is less wary of the implications of the barrister than some of his philosophical colleagues, so unwary—not, I stress, unaware—that the barrister reappears in the unfinished paper on rhetoric as a figure for Peirce himself—"a given advocate" of "a theory of rhetoric"—as he makes a defensive aside concerning the "little grace, dexterity [and] tact" he exhibits in his own "handling of language." In this paper, he is *advocating* a theory of rhetoric, not teaching its art (EP 2:23, p. 329). And we should note a point to which I shall return: advocacy is a sign, not a person, and it is with this sign as such that we do business.

IV

Let us turn, now, to words, which are such a canonical example of signhood that they appear to present no particular feature. Canonically, then, Peirce writes that words are interpreted by concepts in the mind. Yet Peirce's first mention of them is in the context of an unknown or incomprehensible word.

Suppose we look up the word *homme* in a French dictionary; we shall find opposite to it the word *man*, which, so placed, represents *homme* as representing the same two-legged creature which *man* itself represents. (W 2:4, p. 53)

If the barrister brings to the fore one major issue in the theory of representation, the necessary partiality of any sign, the interpreter brings out a second: to interpret is to mediate between two languages. The equation of "interpret" with "translate" is ubiquitous in Peirce to the extent that Roman Jakobson, for one, has read him as saying that "translation" is the *model* for all interpretation.[22] That equation is no doubt an overstatement, particularly in light of the significance of argument; but by the same token, it would be foolhardy to overlook the two parallel examples in the "New List," the bilingual dictionary and the interpreter. These two examples give a technical construal of "comparison" as the equivalence between expressions in two natural languages; the difference between them is simply that the dictionary gives the equivalence as an established habit, whereas the interpreter gives it as the local or punctual solution to a particular problem. This difference corresponds to the difference between the logical interpretant and the dynamical one, where a sequence of the latter may over time become the former. In both cases, the model invoked is interlingual translation or interpretation. By significant contrast with the structuralist tradition, no sign is defined as sign by a single place in a single language. A Peircean sign is a device for translating *between* languages (or places).

The work of the people we call translators and interpreters was a matter of lifelong interest to Peirce, who sometimes translated his own scientific papers and was not above earning money for translations at the stringent end of his life. He seldom works with the texts of the philosophical canon without commenting on the translational problems they present. Often, too, he proposes modifications to the solutions adopted where he deems them to affect issues of substance. Translation is an approximate art, and Peirce's interventions show him to be alert to it as both fallible and open to improvement. Whether concerned with the consequences of anachronistic interpretations of the Aristotelian *épistémè* (CP 1.232; CP 7.250), the appropriateness of borrowing a term from the German to serve in a specialized sense (CP 3.609), or the stylistic depredations consequent on mimicking French translations from the German in English (CP 7.494), the clear implication of Peirce's attention to natural language translation is that equivalence between natural language expressions is not given, but made. This is because languages have different histories (CP 3.609), so that philological similarity may be misleading (CP 7.494). Knowing this history is therefore the first requisite (PW December 23, 1908, p. 79). Significantly, equivalence is context specific ("so placed"), and when the interpreter makes the claim that "a foreigner says the same thing that he himself says," he sustains it on three bases: the appropriateness of a particular choice in the context, the abstract rules of the system, and the history of usage and the regularities that can be discerned in it.

Equivalence, ever more precise, is the aim and the outcome of the translator's art. It therefore returns us to the source problem of sign theory: to count some thing as "the same"—representing "the same" two-legged creature, saying "the same thing"—requires a mediating representation, which is the special responsibility of the intermediary who says it is the same. What is this thing that is common between two forms? In the Harvard Lectures of 1903, when Peirce invokes the example of the proverb (EP 2:14, p. 203 [CP 5.138]), he writes that the proverb remains the same whatever language it is in. This may give the impression that language is epiphenomenal to the signhood of the sign, yet we should recall that this passage is one of Peirce's early attempts to formulate the distinction between type and token. When he achieves clarity in that issue, the issue of the status of the translating form is resolved into the issue of the token:

I have not fully defined a proposition, because I have not discriminated the proposition from the individual sign which is the embodiment of the proposition. By a proposition, as something which can be repeated over and over again, translated into another language, embodied in a logical graph or algebraical formula, and still be one and the same proposition, we do not mean any existing individual object but a type, a general, which does not exist but governs existents, to which individuals conform. (CP 8.313)

What is "the same" is the type; yet all we know of the type is the respect in which two tokens can be said to agree. The type, then, is an ideal object projected by the formal and material properties of its tokens, not of one particular token, since its local particularities may not occur in other tokens, but of the formal properties common to several tokens. How to discern these properties requires specialized skill and training. Under certain theoretical dispensations, it is possible to consider the type as the "meaning" of the signs, but this is ruled out by Peirce on the grounds that the meaning of any sign is the sign into which it is translated (CP 5.427). A token translates its type. On this fact rests the sign's thinghood and its eventhood, its capacity to act on occasion.

My insistence on translation flies in the face of a standard reading of Peirce in this matter. Richard Parmentier presumes without hesitation that in Peirce's account, the sign is transparent, because of his insistence that the particular language of the sign is indifferent to the form of a proposition. This argument is summarized helpfully by Mats Bergman:

As anyone familiar with Peirce's logic knows, he is careful to distinguish the proposition from its accidental expression. That is, a proposition is not supposed to be affected by the material shape it is given for the purposes of outward or inward communication, but remains the same proposition whether it is asserted or denied, stated in English or Finnish, etc. Such a perspective implies that there is a central core to any thought that can be communicated, in spite of the variety of ways that can be used to express it.[23]

Thus, as Bergman puts it, if Parmentier is right, Peirce's conception of the sign conflicts with "a century of linguistic philosophy and semiotics" (p. 233). I shall argue for a dissipation of this conflict. Notwithstanding the ambivalence I have noted in Peirce (Chapter 2) concerning "thoughts in their expression," I shall show that the coherence of Peirce's reflections on semiosis depends on acknowledging that language is not epiphenomenal to signhood. I believe that that acknowledgment is explicit in Peirce, and that we find it in the topic of translation as he considers its place in the technologies of formal logic. Broadly, my argument will be constructed from the following points: first, that types do not act and hence do not participate in semiosis, unless and until they are translated into tokens; second, that this "translation" discovers and represents otherwise "unnoticed or hidden" structural or formal properties of the type; hence, the choice of language is not indifferent; and third, it does this through the offices of iconicity.

In Chapter 5, I raised a question concerning the semiotic relation of type to token. If the token is the sign of its type, what kind of sign is it? The answer is that it is mixed: it is an index in that it is a sample of its class; it is a symbol in that it operates conventionally; and it is an icon in that it must display a resemblance with its object. It is apposite now to return to the issue of its iconicity: the resemblance between token and type is not necessarily material but is necessarily formal. A type can be translated by tokens that take any number of material forms and still remain the same type. This is also the case for the relation between a translation and its source, and I have claimed that a token translates its type. I mean to take seriously this equivalence: iconicity is the principle of translation.

The point is made plain in the key passage of the 1885 paper, "On the Algebra of Logic: A Contribution to the Philosophy of Notation" (W 5:30, esp. pp. 164–65). It will be recalled that this is the paper where Peirce argues that the three kinds of signs are necessary to a "perfect system of notation." Having argued for the particular functions of symbols and indices, Peirce declares that

with these kinds of signs alone any proposition can be expressed; but it cannot be reasoned upon, for reasoning consists in the observation that where certain relations subsist certain others are found, and it accordingly requires the exhibition of the relations reasoned within an icon.

The term *translation* is used by Peirce as he sums up his argument:

[a general formula] might, it is true, be replaced by an abstractly stated rule (say that multiplication is distributive); but no application could be made of such an abstract statement without translating it into a sensible image. (W 5:30, p. 165)

The translation consists in interpreting this relational structure in a new material form.[24] It is this new appearance that displays what would otherwise remain "hidden," and it is this that is contrived in such a way that it can be manipulated. The two material forms must present a "complete analogy" with one another. Previous discoveries, made in this way, can be generalized, "embodied" in "general formulae" that lend themselves to "imitation." They become "patterns" "and are the *icons par excellence* of algebra." Note throughout the use of such terms as *sensible form, exhibit,* and *embody*: translation pervades this process of continuous generalization, abstraction, and transformation. Each such form is an icon of its object, but, since the object of an icon has no independent existence, there is a "type" only insofar as its tokens can be compared in some structural or formal respects which themselves are represented. Furthermore, each such icon transforms that object's powers.

Let us consider this issue first in relation to Peirce's pragmatism. Manuscript 283, entitled "Pragmatism" and dating from 1905, contains an extended reflection on the issue of translation.

What does it mean to speak of the "interpretation" of a sign? Interpretation is merely another word for translation; and if we had the necessary machinery to do it, which we perhaps never shall have, but which is quite conceivable, an English book might be translated into French or German without the interposition of a translation into the imaginary signs of human thoughts. (pp. 100–101)

The point of this elaborate analogy is to demonstrate anew Peirce's insistence that there is no thought without signs. This point had been argued in the cognition papers of 1868–69; its persistence into the mature pragmatism is worth noting. "Thought" is an imaginary construct. Interpretation can be—indeed should be—theorized without it; or rather, thought is *thinking,* and it takes places through the mechanisms of semiosis; thoughts are the objects of thinking (CP 1.27; CP 2.53) and should be reconstrued as "pure possibility" (CP 1.537), a "potentiality" or "form" that "may be embodied in external or internal signs" (p. 102), but is no more than potential without embodiment. "Pure idea[s]," Peirce concludes, are like "an onion without a peel" (p. 132); they have no "efficiency" (CP 1.213). Thought is the accumulation of translations in such a way that its matter displays its history as it reaches outward to a state where it can stop.

He then poses a further question:

Still, supposing there were a machine, or even a growing tree, which, without the interpolation of any imagination were to go on translating and translating from one possible language to a new one, will it be said that the function of signs would therein be fulfilled? (p. 101)

Peirce's answer goes through two moves: one that appears to be affirmative, and then a further move that drives home the pragmatist point. "What are signs for, anyhow," he asks (p. 101), answering that they are designed to "communicate ideas" but they do not fulfill their pragmatic function if they merely transmit "idea-potentiality" from one symbol to another. This is complementary with the principle that signs must translate into different kinds of signs; crucially,

> without embodiment in something else than symbols, the principles of logic show there never could be the least growth in idea-potentiality. (pp. 103–4)

Symbols have no "efficiency" without translation; and they do not "grow" without transformation into other kinds of signs. These two factors are crucial to semiosis. The pragmatist "undertakes to prove," moreover, that the ultimate function of a sign is its capacity to translate into "action or habit of action" (pp. 103–4). This is the "final" interpretant. Yet final though it be, it too is potentially subject to further interpretation. The following passage dates from 1873:

> It may be that I shall finally come to a belief which is a motive for action directly without the intervention of a more special belief. In this case how does the belief address itself to a sign? When a person is said to act upon a certain belief the meaning is that his actions have a certain consistency; that is to say, that they possess a certain intellectual unity. But this implies that they are interpreted in the light of thought. So that even if a belief is a direct motive to action it still is a belief only because that action is interpretable again. And thus the intellectual character of beliefs at least are [*sic*] dependent upon the capability of the endless translation of sign into sign. An inference translates itself directly into a belief. A thought which is not capable of affecting belief in any way, obviously has no signification or intellectual value at all. If it does affect belief it is then translated from one sign to another as the belief itself is interpreted. And therefore this character of signs that they must be capable of interpretation in every sense belongs to every kind of cognition. And consequently no cognition is such or has an intellectual significance for what it is in itself, but only for what it is in its effects upon other thoughts. And the existence of a cognition is not something actual, but consists in the fact that under certain circumstances some other cognition will arise. (CP 7.357)

Again, there is consistency between the mature pragmatism and its earlier formulations. Recall that it is "in action that logical energy returns to the uncontrolled and uncriticizable parts of the mind" (EP 2:16, p. 241 [CP 5.212]). In order to qualify as reasoning, as logical thinking, any interpretant is at least subject to "approval" or self-control (CP 2.773). Where there is no room for further self-control, that is the state known as "fixed belief" and "perfect knowledge" (CP 5.420), but that is "not a sign" (CP 5.476)—

or at least, not in the same way as "that sign of which it is the logical inter-pretant." The distinctions Peirce makes in this issue are fine but important:

> I do not deny that a concept, proposition, or argument may be a logical interpre-tant. I only insist that it cannot be the *final* logical interpretant, for the reason that it is itself a sign of that very kind that has itself a logical interpretant. The habit alone, which though it may be a sign in some other way, is not a sign in that way in which that sign of which it is the logical interpretant is [a] sign.

Now this "final interpretant" is further interpreted, in the sense that it is translated:

> The habit conjoined with the motive and the conditions *has the action for its ener-getic interpretant*; but action cannot be a logical interpretant, because it lacks generality.

Note that Peirce is here relying on the distinctions made among the kinds of interpretant—logical, energetic, and so on. A logical interpretant is translated by an energetic interpretant. Each of these has different func-tions and competences:

> The concept which is a logical interpretant is only imperfectly so. It somewhat partakes of the nature of a verbal definition, and is as inferior to the habit, and much in the same way, as a verbal definition is inferior to the real definition. The deliberately formed, self-analyzing habit—self-analyzing because formed by the aid of analysis of the exercises that nourished it—is the living definition, the veri-table and final logical interpretant.

Yet even at this point, translation does not cease. An interpretant is final only in a paradox: it must be known to be final, and in that knowing, it re-trieves its condition as interpretable:

> Consequently, the most perfect account of a concept that words can convey will consist in a description of the habit which that concept is calculated to produce. But how otherwise can a habit be described than by a description of the kind of action to which it gives rise, with the specification of the conditions and of the motive? (CP 5.491)

There is no exception, therefore, to the law that every thought sign is trans-lated or interpreted in a subsequent one. Pragmatism—the pragmatic def-inition of meaning—relies centrally on this two-way relation between words and actions. It is a relation both theorized and achieved through the process of translation.

However, Peirce's technical interest in translation comes in the first place not from his pragmatism but from his formal logic, specifically, from his interest in the design of notations. In the "Algebra of Logic," it may appear that the units of the language are defined as signs within the rules of that language taken in isolation, thus contradicting the claim I have made that a sign is an intermediary between two languages. But this is illusory. A formal language is an implement of translation. This being so, any item or unit of that language counts as a sign only if it is defined functionally by its capacity to do a particular translational task. Reciprocally, then, any item in some other (usually natural) language is a sign if it is the object of a translation. Learning to manipulate a notation involves "a little practice in translating from ordinary language in this system and back again" (W 5:31, p. 180). Hence Peirce's insistence that the logician has two areas of duty which should not be conflated:

It may be a part of a logician's duty to show how ordinary ways of speaking and of thinking are to be translated into that symbolism of formal logic; but it is no part of syllogistic itself. Logical principles of inference are merely rules for the illative transformation of the symbols of the particular system employed. If the system is essentially changed, they will be quite different. (CP 2.599)

These two "duties" recall the point on the common highway where the mathematician and the logician meet: translation may not be "part of syllogistic itself," but the logician has a duty to see to the translation between systems. Without this duty, the work of logic would be confined to a single system and to the illations possible within it. However, it is not infrequent for commentators of Peirce's logic to overlook this duty, to overlook the differences between systems, and to suppose that a single space of thought was all we had to deal with. This oversight also leaves unnoticed the fact that Peirce has insisted on, that translation into icons is the technical enabling condition of reasoning.

Let us take as an example the early work of Joseph Ransdell.[25] Ransdell takes seriously the model of the sign as intermediary, writing inter alia that the sign "acts as proxy or vicar for the object, i.e. the operation of a sign is actually the operation of the object through or by means of the sign."[26] He construes this as an "ontologically mediating function as vicar for the object to the mind"[27] and distinguishes this from "the mediating function of a sign as between the object . . . and the interpretant" which is a "logical middle term between the subject and predicate term of the judg-

ment." Notice that the vicar is restricted to acting in the representation relation, or the backward reference of the sign: "things" cannot speak for
themselves. But things are different when we turn to the interpretant relation. Once a "thing" has received a symbol, mediation is operated by the
nota notae. This implies that we remain within the space of symbols, and
within the same system of symbols (CP 2.599). There is no *noticed* task
here for the "interpreter."

This very passage (CP 2.599) has been used by Ransdell to argue that
illation is the model for interpretation, and that this somehow transcends
the constraints of particular systems of language. Let us consider Ransdell's
account of the model of inference, which, principally on the evidence of
the "New List" he takes to be the model for interpretation in general.
Ransdell displays a certain nominalistic tendency when he writes that "an
argument is a claim about matters of fact (real or supposed, *not merely
about words or symbols*),"[28] while he acknowledges that Peirce's concern is
with "thoughts in their expression," the business of logic is with "facts,"
not language. He goes on to argue vigorously against the supposition that
Peirce "espous[es] a kind of logical conventionalism through the relativiza-
tion of logical principles to particular symbol systems."[29] I quote Ransdell
in extenso on this point:

> Now when Peirce relativizes logical principles to particular symbol systems this is
> *not* to be construed as meaning that every such system has "its own logic". . . . For
> it is assumed that these are all *languages* within which the *same* thing can receive
> varying symbolic expressions. A given argument can be expressed in any genuine
> language, provided it contains suitable conventional signs, but it is the *same* argu-
> ment because it is concerned with the *same matters of fact*. Naturally, the conven-
> tions for expression are going to vary from language to language, symbol system to
> symbol system, and this is why "if the system is essentially changed, [logical prin-
> ciples] will be quite different." (CP 2.599) However, the varying expressions of
> these principles all alike express the same facts, viz. *those such as are presupposed in
> all discourse.*
>
> What are these facts? Regarded in the most formal way they are, I believe,
> what Peirce tried to epitomize in his many statements of the fundamental and
> generic triadic representation relation. . . . It is . . . *identity*: Peirce intends to iden-
> tify representation and inference.[30]

Now, in the light of CP 2.599 above, the question we must put to Ransdell
is this: if Peirce does indeed intend to "identify representation and inference," does this confine "representation" to a single system? Ransdell can-

not mean this, because he insists that Peirce's semiotic pertains to something far more important than "mere words or symbols." Alternatively, then, if systems of expression are epiphenomenal to systems of facts, does this imply a single system of facts in which all inquiry would ultimately converge?

Exactly what is the relation between the two models for the interpretant relation, formal syllogistic and translation? On the evidence of this passage, the rules of illative transformation pertain to the symbols of a particular system. If it is the case that those rules are "quite different" in different systems, then "translation" is the crucial operation that mediates between systems. Only by translating between systems can we be certain, as Ransdell is, that there are such things as inferential principles that are "presupposed in all discourse," and only by translating can we differentiate them from those that have validity only within the rules of particular systems.

Furthermore, by bringing together the understanding of iconicity we have gleaned from the "Algebra of Logic" with the issues concerning the relation between a token and its type, a more searching answer can be proposed to this question. Recall: (1) no sign is sign without its translation into tokens; (2) interpretation translates one token into another (not into a type). These two facts explain the onion analogy. They explain why there is nothing left when we peel back the layers, and they explain why any attempt to get to the bottom of things actually adds further layers, rather than revealing some hidden truth. The relation between tokens and types is iconic, and iconicity involves material transformation. Recall (3): reasoning involves the translation of general signs into icons, whose relations can be manipulated: "argument"—the work of the barrister—depends on the work of the interpreter. We come, then, to this: if iconicity is the technical condition for "reasoning," then although reasoning reaches conclusions and thus displays the structure of closure, it is based on an "unnoticed and hidden" structure, the structure and the dynamics of translation, which cannot come to an end.

V

The ways of semiosis are heterogeneous. Peirce acknowledges this in the lists of examples and seeks to systematize it in the kinds of signs. Nevertheless, there has been something of a habit in Peirce scholarship to reduce all semiosis to a single mechanism, infinite for some, finite for others.

My argument in this chapter has sought to show that Peirce's work operates on the basis of two models, translation and argument: they model, respectively, open-endedness and closure. However, as we have seen, the open-ended nature of translation stops provisionally when it achieves a useful outcome, and the closure of argument is temporary, returning into the cycle of inquiry.

An apparently similar conclusion is reached by Jørgen Johansen in his careful intervention into the same debate as it was conducted at a conference in 1992.[31] "Man is characterised by an ongoing dialectic between restricted and infinite semioses" (p. 287). Because its conclusion has something in common with mine, but its premises do not, I wish to consider this argument in some detail. This will bring me to a temporary closure of my own.

Johansen acknowledges that there is much in Peirce's work to support the infinity argument, quoting two manuscript passages as evidence:

The life we lead is a life of signs. Sign under sign endlessly. (MS 1334, 1905: 46)

There is, we think, and reasonably think, a limit to this, an ultimate reality like a zero of temperature. But in the nature of things, it can only be approached; it can only be represented. The immediate object which any sign seeks to represent is itself a sign. (MS 599, 1902:35–36).

However, he argues, Peirce also imagined a limit both to the backward and to the forward movement of semiosis (p. 277), the former being an "absolute object" and the latter being "an interpretant that will undergo no further interpretation." Johansen's objective is to moderate the "fascinating idea of infinite, ever-expanding semiosis," which, he claims, is valid only in certain cases (p. 286). These are the "admittedly important and interesting" but exceptional cases, of scientific inquiry and literary and other text-based interpretive practices. We alternate, he declares in an elegant conclusion, between

viewing the elements of our life-world as signs alerting us to begin a quest for interpretation, on the one hand, as familiar stock and fixtures at our disposal and for our convenience, on the other. (p. 295)

In the terms I have used, this alternation is the alternation between second and first intentionality. This is not the way Johansen sets up the problem. Indeed, in an argument contrary to my own, he claims that the "material objects or processes that constitute signs are not themselves semiotic, because they 'have nothing to do with . . . signification'" (p. 282), whereas I have argued that the first trichotomy is Peirce's way of giving to such matters a precise semiotic status. The "molecular properties of lead" (p. 282) are the material condition of translation of a type (the abstraction of the letter) into a typeface that can appear on a printed page. While it is true that their use as a clue for the police gives them a function as indices in a particular sequence of inferences, they do not wait for this sequence in order to acquire semiotic status per se. For Johansen, however, this example supports the claim that there are "nonsemiotic descriptions" of signs; it is the first of four arguments marshaled to distinguish signs from nonsigns. "I do not want," he writes, "to subscribe to the radical thesis that nothing exists but signs" (p. 282). Peirce, of course, has never argued anything remotely like this—the metaphysical categories preserve him from it—although it is true that some commentators have taken his work to authorize this position.

Johansen's next three arguments bear, respectively, on the object, the sign itself, and the interpretant. There is, he argues, a difference between the immediate and the dynamic object, the former being of the nature of a "thought," and the latter, of an ontological other to thought. I have discussed this reading in the previous chapter. An ontological difference also appears to underpin another of Johansen's arguments. Relying on Peirce's distinction among the three kinds of interpretants, emotional, energetic, and logical, and adding to these a fourth, habit, Johansen defines the interpretant as follows:

{a feeling
{an effort

An interpretant is the translation of a sign into

{another sign
{a habit

(p. 285)

He adds that "only one of these four cases actually requires sign action to continue" (p. 285). This conclusion supposes that feelings, habits, and efforts are not signs. To support his view, Johansen elaborates the case of a habit, which, as we have seen previously, is the prime candidate in Peirce's own work for the "final" interpretant, except that all habits must stand ready to be broken.

"A habit," Johansen writes, "is a uniform response to identical or similar semioses, but it does not itself necessarily call forth another semiosis" (p. 285). Following Short, he counts such things as "non-conventional legisigns" and exemplifies them with "genetically programmed colors and mating-behavior[s]"; such things are instinctive and habitual and are semiotic insofar as they consist in the "infinite replication of fixed sequences of sign translations" (p. 287).[32] This is the restricted type of semiosis, essentially different from "infinite semiosis," which is confined to human semiotic practices. This argument depends on a series of correlations: animal is to human as instinct is to thought as behavior is to interpretation as finite is to infinite. Then, to ensure that interpretation comes to an end, Peirce introduces the "ultimate logical interpretant," which is a habit of action (p. 285). This implies a return to nature:

it is easy to agree with Sebeok and Short when they point to the evolutionary aspect of semiosis, and to the decisive step taken by the invention and development of conventional legisigns. It seems to me that the manipulation of legisigns in thought creates the necessary precondition for infinite semiosis. [But this is only a small part of the semiotic competence of the human species] because transformations of signs into habitual actions necessarily play a fundamental part in our lives. (p. 287)

Now I think Peirce agrees with the burden of this argument, but with an important reservation:

All thinking is by signs; and the brutes use signs. But they perhaps rarely think of them as signs. To do so is manifestly a second step in the use of language. (CP 5.534)

Notice the qualification, "rarely," and what follows:

Brutes use language, and seem to exercise some little control over it. But they certainly do not carry this control to anything like the same grade that we do. (CP 5.534)

The issue Peirce is raising is that of the "control" of thought and the difference between the "brutes" and humankind is one of degree, not of kind. The control of thought depends not on conventionality, but on second intentionality. Some animals do recognize the semiotic nature of their messages and are able to manipulate it accordingly.[33] Furthermore, recalling my discussion of the index in Chapter 4, I point out that Sebeok and Short are discussing indexical legisigns. Sign behaviors such as the response to mating colors are indexical, but they are only indexical if one is a semiotician, not if one is a robin, and it is semioticians, not robins, who bestow on such signs their second intentionality. We have found that the index is precisely the point where the brute facts of nature take on the status of signs, but that they do so only as a result of being taken as signs: "second intentions are the objects of the understanding considered as representations, and the first intentions to which they apply are the objects of those representations." It is second intentionality that is the necessary condition for interpretation, that is, for semiosis, and I think it may be misleading to treat genetically programmed behaviors as "semioses," as does Johansen.

This conclusion is mildly troublesome for Peirce's account of habit, but only if we forget that habits are made to be broken and that the ethic of inquiry requires that it do just that. All that is needed for the process to get back on the road is for us to focus on the signhood of our signs. Johansen is not shy of doing so, and much of his argument is taken up with showing exactly how things and actions come to occupy the position of sign in the three-term semiotic relation. Instead of the notion of second intentionality, however, he uses the notion of the frame:

> when an object is displayed for the purposes of advertising that it (and others like it) is itself for sale—say, a car displayed in a car dealer's showroom. . . . The frame is part of the sign: it is not the car that is a sign of "cars for sale"; it is "car displayed in showroom" that is a sign. (p. 291)

I think this is right, and the notion of the frame is useful as a way of bringing together my argument concerning the signhood of signs with my argument concerning genre.[34] Advertising is a genre, with a specific and widely understood rhetorical dynamic that determines both its forms of representation and its modes of address. The frame suspends one uptake of the car (its use) by mentioning it. This is the instigation of its second intentionality, which is functionally equivalent, say, to representing it in a photograph. However, like all advertising, it works to provoke desire for ownership and thus a retranslation into use. If advertising is successful, it abolishes its own signhood. I presume that this is what Johansen means when he goes on to claim that "the interpretant 'cars for sale' of the sign 'car displayed in showroom' will, at one and the same time, end interpretation and confirm the sign's reference to its object" (p. 291). However, there is some confusion in this conclusion: advertising does not want us to behave like literary critics, merely "contemplating" the sign for its "immediate interpretant"; it wants us to take it up. When we do, say by gossiping sneeringly about people who fall for advertising, or who want to own that sort of car; when we do, say by walking into the showroom to inquire about the price and go for a test drive; when, say, we decide to purchase the car, semiosis does not end: we might display the car proudly to our friends, disguise its purchase from the bank manager, allow it to be taken as a sign of our new prosperity, use it as a status symbol or as a sign of group identity, or whatever. The point is that "pure use" is an elusive commodity. Although Johansen is right to draw our attention to the dialectic of use and mention, he is mistaken, I believe, in supposing that when use is achieved, mention ceases. To say that signhood pervades the universe, as Peirce does, is not to say that there is nothing but signs; it is to say that the signhood of things depends on their operating, or being taken as, second intentions.[35]

The ways of semiosis are varied. This fact can be attributed to the variety of signs, or, more restrictedly, to the variety of their kinds; it can also be attributed to the heterogeneity of genres. Since this latter analysis attends both to the forms of representation and the modes of address of any sign, it is more evidently to do with semiosis—with interpretation, with uptake, with the ineluctable eliciting of the next sign—than does the variety of signs. However, consider this: semiosis appears to consist in three interlocking mechanisms. It is set in play by second intentionality, and then, when some thing is taken as a sign, it is transformed, translated into some second sign that purports to bring out in it some hitherto unnoticed or hidden features or structures. Then it is available to argument. This last step, though the most central to inquiry and hence to Peirce's own concerns, is the one that may not occur. When it does, it presupposes, and draws on, the outcome of the previous two. With that, I am drawn to suggest a correlation between these three mechanisms of semiosis and the three preeminent kinds of sign, which we might construe here as three principles of representation. (I am presuming the analyses of icon, index, and symbol that are gradually elaborated after the revisions of 1885; I am also presuming that these three remain the preeminent trichotomy, even following the second and later classifications.[36]) The implications of this suggestion would build rhetorical processes right into the forms of grammar. The index is the principle of second intentionality, whereby things in the world are opened to semiosis; the icon is the principle of translation, whereby signs are transformed into other signs that purport to reveal their properties; and the symbol is the principle of argument, whereby—through surprise, discovery, disappointment, and dispute; through deception and persuasion, and through doubt—men come—sometimes—to agreement.

Conclusion: The Machinery of Talk

Here I sit at my table with my inkstand and paper before me, my pen in my hand, my lamp at my side. (CP 2.141)

Peirce is not a member of that group of philosophers who "have taken human conversation as a matter of course, with rather a remarkable absence of all curiosity about it" (CP 6.3). Theologians, idealist metaphysicians, not to mention many of his own contemporaries, are opposed on this criterion to Pragmatism, which "must begin with men and their conversations" (CP 8.112). However, the notion of conversation is not self-explanatory and should be understood as the site of a significant problem in Peirce studies. First, its scope is not clear: how much of the general domain of semiosis does it occupy? On the basis of the argument I have put in the previous chapter, by no means all. If "inquiry" and "semiosis" are not coextensive, then it is more likely that "conversation" correlates with the former than with the latter. Glossing Max Fisch, who takes conversation as the paradigm of communication, Vincent Colapietro takes "communication" as coextensive with "semiosis."[1] I have to disagree with this gloss. "Conversation," though a generic term covering many kinds of human communication, designates a subset of semiosic phenomena. Klaus Oehler takes a similar view[2]:

The speech situation and the communicative rationality implicit in it should on no account be made to bear the burden of providing the foundation for semeiotic. They represent merely a peculiarly privileged instance through which the basic structures of the sign can be illustrated. (p. 268)

And again:

communicative reason is only a particularly complex case of semeiosis, characterized through goal-oriented production, use, and interpretation of signs. (p. 269)

Second, even supposing, with Oehler, that "conversation" designates a particularly significant and complex subset of semiosic phenomena, what
function does "conversation" have in Peirce's account? Is it a casual term,
broadly coextensive with "inquiry," and simply the name of a vague class?
If not, what exactly is its relation with semiosis?

The following discussion of these issues will start by engaging with
an objection put to Peirce by Jürgen Habermas, whose focus on "communicative rationality" leads him to disregard any form of semiosis that is not
human. I shall then review a reading of Peirce by Peter Skagestad, who argues for a materialist, as distinct from mentalist, account of semiosis. Effectively, Habermas and Skagestad are found to be opposed on the question of whether "conversation" is explicans, or explicandum, of semiosis.[3]
Asking which is the machinery of which, I shall turn to assess the consequences of the shift from "thought" to its "instruments" that I have traced
in the foregoing chapters.

I

Preferring the twentieth-century term *communication* to the enlightenment term *conversation*, Habermas has mounted a significant challenge
to the consistency of Peirce's account of the sign. The argument turns on
the conflict Habermas discerns between Peirce's insistence on dispensing
with the knowing subject in his account of interpretation, on the one
hand, and what Habermas takes to be the telos of sign action on the other,
that is, the "agreement" eventually reached by the "community of investigators" at the end of inquiry. In Habermas' words:

I want to defend the thesis that it is impossible to give a satisfactory explanation
of the interpretant relation of the sign without having recourse to the conditions
for reaching an intersubjective agreement, however rudimentary these may be.
This remains impossible as long as sign-mediated representation is conceived, as
Peirce conceived it, in terms of truth and reality—for these concepts refer in turn
to the regulative idea of a community of investigators.[4]

The "pragmatic turn," he claims, depends upon an "intersubjectively
based semeiotic" (p. 247). Note the crucial assumptions: first, Peirce con-

ceived sign-mediated representation in terms of truth and reality, hence semiosis is coextensive with inquiry; and second, the theory (of this view) of representation must depend on an account of intersubjectivity.

Habermas' critique proceeds in four stages, conceived broadly in terms of an account of the development of Peirce's semiotic, finding that it ends with the abandonment of a social account of signhood in favor of a naturalistic or cosmological account (p. 247). This cosmological reading is supported by Peirce's evident intention to extend the scope of semiotic well beyond the reach of human natural languages. However, as Oehler points out, this is by no means the whole picture. Furthermore, there is ample evidence in the late writings that Peirce's curiosity concerning conversation has not abated. Indeed, manuscript writings from the years following 1903 pursue the pragmatization of the sign, and Peirce introduces into his discussions the concept of the "common ground" needed to explain just how conversation might work in practice. This concept is not highly elaborated, and indeed, Peirce shifts between two poles, the first being some universal conditions on interlocution, and the other, quite particular contextual conditions. Thus, from time to time, it takes the form of the rules of inference, or, in the Syllabus, of the "common environment of the interlocutors" (MS 478, 1903); sometimes it is the "universe of discourse"; at others, "Aryan grammar" (MS 611, 1908). What is it for you to be "my Reader," he asks (MS 339, 1908): the answer is that we share some common ground, for example, the fact that you know English, and you cannot deny it in English (MS 611). Peirce's search for a satisfactory account of this "common ground" is thus not dissimilar to Habermas' requirement that a theory of communication give an account of "initial understanding" (p. 256). Oehler's sardonic aside is therefore justified: "The results of [Peirce's] analysis [of the 'essential ingredients' of the sign relation] would prove not uninteresting to the author of the theory of communicative action" (p. 266).

However, there are three major differences between what Peirce was doing and what Habermas is doing: (1) Habermas is seeking a theory of society, and Peirce was seeking no such thing; therefore (2) Habermas privileges the human and entails the human with the capacity for using language to a particular end—namely, "the cooperative quest for truth" (p. 255); this means that Habermas is concerned actually to theorize the human, whereas for Peirce, the human is continuous with everything in the world and therefore enjoys no privilege as the object of a theory; a fortiori, neither does human language, which cannot, as Oehler points out, be asked to provide the foundation for the whole; and (3) for Habermas, the theory of communicative action rests on the presupposition of intersubjectivity as an account of the fundamental social bond; this entails subjectivity (whether as ground or as effect), whereas for Peirce, no psychological or mentalistic foundation should be presupposed since to presuppose such a foundation is to retrieve an unexplained "ultimate" designed to underpin and to explain the "ultimate interpretant."[5] What Habermas objects to in Peirce is the "anonymization" of the interpretant, the fact that the "interpreter disappear[s] behind the depersonalized interpretant" (p. 263), as in this passage:

I define a Sign as anything which is so determined by something else, called its Object, and so determines an effect upon a person, which effect I call its Interpretant, that the latter is thereby mediately determined by the former. My insertion of "upon a person" is a sop to Cerberus, because I despair of making my own broader conception understood. (PW December 23, 1908, pp. 80–81)

Peirce explains that this is a tactic for avoiding psychologism:

I should like to write a little book on "the conduct of Thoughts" in which the introductory chapter should introduce the reader to my existential graphs, which would then be used throughout as the apparent subject, the parable or metaphor, in terms of which everything would be said,—which would be far more scientific than dragging in the "mind" all the time, in German fashion, when the mind and psychology has no more to do with the substance of the book than if I were to discourse of the ingredients of the ink I use. (PW appx. G, p. 195)

Using the existential graphs as "parable" is an alternative to using human communication, the latter, in Peirce's view, being responsible for assumptions that he prefers to do without. But it is more than a mere tactic; it has a substantive point. By using the graphs in place of the mind, he can focus on their material conditions. Peirce accepts to pursue his exposition in terms of minds and thoughts, but he does so in order to show the limits of these concepts:

Existential graphs are to be conceived as scribed upon the different leaves of a whole book. The whole book represents the thought (upon a given subject) of one mind. (PW appx. G, p. 195)

As he has explained to us, this is a metaphor, just as talk of "the mind" is a convenient fiction. His true interest is in the process of thinking, its minute anatomy, and this he finds in the operations of signs, which may occur, as thoughts, in minds, but which are not defined by this kind of embodiment, since they also take any number of other forms. Again, he despairs that the habits of his readers will lead them to misconstrue his idea:

The blank leaf itself is the quasi-mind. I almost despair of making clear what I mean by a "quasi-mind;" but I will try. A *thought* is not *per se* in any mind or quasi-mind. . . . but a thought, to gain any active mode of being must be embodied in a sign. A thought is a special variety of sign. . . . Now as every thinking requires a mind, so every sign even if external to all minds must be a determination of a quasi-mind. This quasi-mind is itself a sign, a determinable sign. Consider for example a blank book. It is meant to be written in. Words written in that in due order will have quite another force from the same words scattered accidentally upon the ground, even if these should happen to have fallen into collections which would have a meaning if written in the blank-book. (PW appx. G, p. 195)

It is the substantive implications of this strategy that worry Habermas. He thinks it means that persons, real socially situated persons, are volatilized in favor of a cosmological account. That Peirce came to the view that he could not prove Pragmatism without a cosmology is not in doubt: this is the means by which he argues for realism. However, it is not the case that deleting the human from the general laws of semiosis entails deleting human action from the phenomena that semiosis is sometimes called upon to explain. Peirce argues consistently throughout his career that the necessary formal conditions for something's being a sign must not rest on the presupposition of persons engaged in thinking. On the contrary, it has the function of explaining the processes of thinking: it is the "law" that underpins the "event." My argument throughout this book has sought to show that Peirce's research leads him to relinquish the position adopted in "On a New List of Categories" that rests on the assumption of human reason, and to seek an account of the events that effect semiosis. When Peirce describes real cases of semiosis, the thinghood and the eventhood of the sign, and hence of its interpretant, must be specified, and on occasion— particularly those occasions when he is tracing the operations of inquiry— this does indeed involve persons in "conversation"—bodies, things in the world, the locus of experience are the sine qua non of action. This is the machinery of talk.[6]

Because of his concern with this putative anonymization, however, Habermas makes a special point about a passage further on in the same draft. This is the passage in which Peirce experiments with the notion of a "commens" or "commind," the "communicational interpretant." This is "a determination of that Mind into which the minds of utterer and interpreter have to be fused in order that any communication should take place" (PW appx. G, p. 195). This "communicational interpretant" is understood, for example by Jørgen Johansen, as proof not only that Peirce was interested in communication, but that his account of it can dispel the angst he discerns in some quarters concerning whether or not "communication" (presumably in a "big" sense) can be achieved.[7] Again, it is puzzling that Habermas does not find this sympathetic, since it has something in common with his requirement that intersubjectivity be counted as part of the process. But Habermas is preoccupied by the word *fusion*, which suggests, he says, a naturalization of semiosis, an "unforced agreement" in which "the multi-vocal character of intersubjectivity becomes an epiphenomenon" (p. 263). Now I believe Habermas has misread this passage, and that he has done so to the detriment of his own argument. The "cominterpretant," the "commens," the "commind" (the frequent changes in terminology bear witness to the tentative nature of Peirce's draft) is an oddly mentalistic account of the "common ground." It is, writes Peirce,

The *Communicational* Interpretant . . . which is a determination of that mind into which the minds of utterer and interpreter have to be fused in order that any communication should take place. This mind . . . consists of all that is, and must be, well understood between utterer and interpreter at the outset, in order that the sign in question should fulfil its function. (PW appx. C, p. 197)

Now this common ground is not the final interpretant; it is a condition for the pursuit of conversation. Habermas would surely construe it as "the intersubjectivity involved in coming to initial understanding" (p. 256). But note again the crucial difference between Peirce and Habermas. For the former, the common ground is a kind of *interpretant*; that is, it is the outcome of some semiosis. This being so, the logic of Peirce's position is irreproachable: he must be able to theorize semiosis in the abstract in order for it to work as an explanatory factor in concrete cases such as this. Habermas explains semiosis by means of intersubjectivity; Peirce explains (something like) intersubjectivity by means of semiosis, and he is determined for his explanation not to be circular.

Peirce "proceed[s] to explain" the "commens" by means of the now familiar example of the fire:

No object can be denoted unless it be put into relation to the object of the commends. A man, tramping along a weary and solitary road, meets an individual of strange mien, who says, "There was a fire in Megara" (etc.). (PW appx. G, p. 197)

The particular kind of semiosic determination that puts an object into relation with the "commens" is indexicality. Although Peirce's writing in this draft is somewhat confused, it is clear that he is groping his way toward what more recent pragmatics has called "coreference." This, to use Peirce's terminology, is the forcing upon the mind, in perception, of the dynamic object, which is not, he hastens to say, "something out of the mind" but an effect of perception, "including more than perception reveals. It is an object of actual Experience" (PW appx. G, p. 197). The enabling condition for constitution of this common ground is simply the meeting upon a common highway, of two travelers who in other respects are strangers to each other, and who, though they "use English" in this example, might simply have annexed one another's attention—"met"—with rudimentary indexical signs. The sign—semiosis—is the machine of their interaction, and "conversation" is its outcome. Subjectivity, hence intersubjectivity, is dispensable in this account because it has no explanatory function.

The commens is Peirce's admittedly sketchy attempt to supply an explanation for the starting point of conversation. This explanation rests on the capacity of the index to open the "common environment" of the interlocutors to semiosis. These travelers who meet upon a common highway may or may not be members of a community. They may be tramps who share a language and use it to meet needs that they share as a part of their common condition, or they may, as in this draft letter, just pass the time of day, or exchange information concerning the road they have traveled. They may be neighbors, separated by a "party-wall," as in the relationship between logic and mathematics:

A mathematical reasoning may be defined as a reasoning in which the following of the conclusion does not depend on whether the premises represent experience, or represent the state of the real universe, or upon what universe it may be that they apply to. This erects, as we shall see, a definite party-wall between the reasoning of mathematics and much of the reasoning of all the positive sciences, including philosophy. (MS 459, pp. 8–9)

In this case, all they have in common is their differences. This is pernicious for the sciences, for they should be able to work together:

Such being the essence of science, it is obvious that its first offspring will be men,—men whose whole lives are devoted to it. By such devotion each of them acquires a training in making some particular kind of observations and experiments. (Unfortunately, his acquisition of books, instruments, laboratory, etc., depends upon qualifications in which the man of science is usually rather wanting—as wealth, diplomacy, popularity as a teacher—so that he is less likely to be provided with them than are men less qualified to use them for the advancement of science.) He will thus live in quite a different world,—quite a different aggregate of experience,—from unscientific men and even from scientific men pursuing other lines of work than his. He naturally converses with, and reads the writings of, those who, having the same experience, have ideas interpretable into his own. This society develops conceptions of its own. Bring together two men from widely different departments,—say a bacteriologist and astronomer,—and they will hardly know what to say to one another; for neither has seen the world in which the other lives. True, both use optical instruments; but the qualities striven for in a telescopic objective are of no consequence in a microscopical objective; and all the subsidiary parts of telescope and microscope are constructed on principles utterly foreign to one another,—except their stiffness. (EP 2:9, p. 131 [CP 1.236]).

As Peirce remarks elsewhere,

the trouble is that nothing does speak for itself, strictly nothing, speaking strictly. One cannot bid his neighbor good morning, really, effectually, unless that neighbor supplies the needed commentary on the syntax. If he does not, I might as well shake a rattle. (MS 427, p. 146)

How then do our strangers learn to speak together, how do they come to the competence whereby they can "provide the needed commentary on the syntax"? The answer Peirce provides is not that of Habermas, for whom the "community" is presupposed as a common language, used with common goals. Although "the logician assumes no knowledge except that the meaning of language is well-known between himself and the person to whom he is imparting his doctrine" (MS 449, pp. 54–55), this cannot always be presupposed, and Peirce's answer, as he writes to Welby, is that the "word *translating* seems . . . to contain profound truth wrapped up in it" (PW 1909, March 14, p. 111). We need an *interpreter* "who says that a foreigner says the same thing which he himself says." This interpreter is not a subject; it is simply the agentive form that helps Peirce introduce the interpretant; thereafter, it has the same status in the theory as the bilingual dictionary. It is a device.

A further problem with "conversation"—one of the reasons why it cannot provide the answer to a question, but is, rather, the question itself—is that it seems to presuppose cooperation, not merely a common language, a common fund of experience, but also common goals and methods for achieving them. It is the opposite of Cartesian individualism, but its outcomes may be worth no more than the outcomes of solitary meditation. Agreement too easily reached, or reached through methods other than those of inquiry,[8] is not worth more than the absolute certainties of a nonscientific metaphysics.[9] There is nothing to choose between the solitary thinker and the group that thinks in unison. Peirce would have been appalled to learn that it was in the name of pragmatism that Prezzolini had argued, in his *Art of Persuasion*, the power of words to control society.[10] Yet rhetoric has a considerable importance in Peirce's semiotic: it was to provide a theory of how signs—from "a daily newspaper" to "a social movement" (CP 6.455)—have the effects that they do. This importance is not without its risks. Among the pragmatists, it was to be Dewey who would investigate Peirce's assertion that knowledge is essentially social and based in community practice: Peirce was content to emphasize what it did not mean:

Man is essentially a social animal: but to be social is one thing, to be gregarious is another: I decline to serve as bellwether. (CP 1.11)

Gregariousness in philosophy was something that he abhorred. Against it, he came perilously close to retrieving the figure of solitary meditation, asserting the value of independent thinking over "coöperation and solidarity of research" (CP 3.425) in the early stages of a science. In practice, Peirce's solution involves "musement," which is a solitary exercise, in relation with disciplined and purposive research, which is conducted in teams. Nevertheless, this does not resolve the difficulties involved in the concepts of "conversation" and "community," and the problem Peirce points to here is substantial. If conversation takes place only within a like-minded community, it is unlikely to change the patterns and habits of thought that constitute that community as a community; yet solitary scholarship is disabled for the opposite reason.

The opposition between solitude and community cannot resolve this dilemma, because of our habits of thinking about communities as entirely "like-minded" and distinguished from other communities as one enclosure is from another. I suggest that "neighborhoods" may be a more productive metaphor for this purpose, because a neighbor is someone with whom one shares a fence or a boundary of some sort. A neighborhood is not internally total or homogeneous, and we should think, rather, of loose coalitions provisionally formed around specific local purposes. Peirce often uses the term *community*, yet unless we construe it as a neighborhood, we will not understand his refusal of "gregariousness" alongside his condemnation of "thinking in unison." This condemnation is parallel in all respects with his condemnation of "those who believe in their own existence"; "the most balsamic of all the sweets of sweet philosophy is the lesson that personal existence is an illusion and a practical joke . . . neither selves nor neighborselves [are] anything more than vicinities" (CP 4.68).[11] We must not presuppose "community" as the ground of semiotic practices, and if it is the "horizon" of conversation, then like the final consensus itself, it is a counterfactual, used only to define the regulatory principle of inquiry.

There is a theory of neighborhoods in Peirce's work, but it is not a social theory. The term arises in the technical context of his work on the mathematics of continua, and in that context, is connected to words such as "boundary," "region," and "limit" (for example, CP 4.125 ff.). Boundaries are necessarily blurred (CP 4.127), and "it is not really contradictory . . . to say that a boundary is both within and without what it bounds" (W 2:6, p. 83). The conversation of neighbors is a practice of the fence: this involves conflict, negotiation, common pragmatic purposes. This is the place of rhetoric. As I have noted, this turn to rhetoric has its own dangers; yet it is rhetoric that explains both the determination of the interpretation of signs and the capacity of interpretation to produce change. This change occurs in the premisses and the assumptions of the conversation itself, which count among the real effects of sign practices; these real effects cannot be limited to the reaffirmation of the same.[12]

The Peircean imaginary is imbued with mathematical ideas, and it is from them that he draws many of his operative metaphors. Thus, for example, in a discussion of the distinction between the "mind" and the "world," a distinction he prefers to term the "inner" and the "outer" worlds, he writes:

We naturally make all our distinctions too absolute. We are accustomed to speak of an external universe and an inner world of thought. But they are merely vicinities with no real boundary line between them. It comes to this: there are some ideas,—objects, be it remembered,—which will have their own way, and we cannot swerve them much, and the little effect we can produce upon them we only produce indirectly. They make up or indicate the outward world. There are other ideas which seem very docile, they are just as we think they ought to be. They form the inner world. Yet it will be found that the inner world has its surprises for us, sometimes. It isn't so exactly as we would have it as we fancy. It is rather our wishes which conform to it, Mahomet that repairs to the mountain. Neither is the moderate amount of control which we exercise upon the world of ideas nearly so direct as we fancy it to be. We go about instinctively, and without being aware how circuitously we proceed to change the current of thought. There is an intermediate world, our own neighborhood, household, and persons, which belongs to us, which we sometimes feel inclined to class with the outer world and sometimes with the inner world. (CP 7.438)

The generic distinctions Peirce draws among mathematics, logic, and philosophy, and within logic construed as semiotic, among the regions he calls "grammar," "critic," and "rhetoric," can be understood in terms of this metaphor. They all arise, we might say, in the same neighborhood, but "as a contradiction consists in giving to contradictory terms some breadth in common" (W 2:6, p. 83), so that shared neighborhood is the ground of the distinctions among them. Neighbors share boundaries, and the boundaries between them are really operative. Genres are neighbors in this sense; they neither think nor act in unison. They know little about each other, and they know even less about what each other knows. This not knowing is as much the ground of their interactions, including what they can and cannot do for one another, as is what we usually mean by their "common ground."

As I have indicated, this common ground is achieved by the action of signs—by indexicality as well as by translation. It is also achieved by the work of the barrister. For it is the barrister—the figure of forensic rhetoric—that acknowledges in Peirce's theory the immense significance of difference, of party-walls, of the disputes that characterize neighborhoods. Without this acknowledgment, the ideas of common ground, of intersubjectivity, of community, are utopian. The barrister does not, as Habermas puts it, merely indulge in a "contest, in which one side seeks to overpower the other rhetorically" (p. 255). Like the interpreter, the offices of the barrister are an indispensable step in commenting the syntax of difference, prior to interpreting some case into the language of one generalization or another.

Peirce's project, then, is to account for the "grammar," or the syntax, of semiosis irrespective of the particular elements—for example, persons in social situations—needed to account for particular practices. Can it be done? Maybe only metaphorically, but the metaphors are borrowed from physics or mathematics, not social theory. In a famous passage, drawn from Peirce's attempt to find his metaphysical categories at work in all areas of science ("A Guess at the Riddle") (W 6:26, p. 196), Peirce discusses what would be needed to account for the properties of protoplasm, doing so in terms that correspond to his account of the way an organism responds to the "irritation" of doubt and the formation of a habit that appeases it. It can thus quite properly be taken as a parable for the process of interpretation, and it is framed as a hypothesis.

The passage invites close attention in respect of two points. First, words such as *habit, system,* and *neighborhood* are deployed in a technical setting. When Peirce uses these terms in the semiotic, they come informed by this usage. This is no mere point concerning the impossibility of containing words in their original context of usage; rather, it displays in practice the work Peirce does to make philosophy "scientific." As a result, metaphysical postulates such as the mind, and reason—as well as their updated versions, society, consciousness, subjectivity—are thought in continuity with natural phenomena, not posited over against them. The description of the disturbance of the molecules is, furthermore, interpreted in terms of the mathematics of continua and infinitesimals. The parts of this "body" or "substance" are represented in the same way as mathematical points, lines, and surfaces. With this usage comes the very structure of a kind of argument: mathematics, chemistry, physics, and biology are brought together to make philosophical metaphysics converse with foreign herds. It can only do so if it gives up its reliance on metaphysical postulates such as "mind," and accepts to construct its models from an alternative paradigm. Sometimes Peirce proposes his existential graphs for this purpose; at others, as here, he uses the mathematical description of physicochemical change. This is a procedure, Peirce has told us, that is "far more scientific than dragging in the 'mind' all the time, in German fashion." This procedure, I take it, is what Habermas objects to as a cosmology; but we should note carefully the substantive issue at stake for Peirce. Only in some such way as this can he avoid the hated nominalism, which leaves reason and its representational means outside the ambit of nature.

Second, the disturbance of the substance has several effects: particles "shoot" from one system to another, or "wander" among systems; not only does the internal structure of any system change, but the relations among systems are changed, with new ones forming. With the disturbance, we have the breaking up of harmony and its reestablishment, some systems brought closer together, others made more distant, still others abolished altogether. New neighborhoods are formed, their relationships remaining unsettled for a time. This story, or something very like it, is implied in the dynamics of interpretation.[13] With the introduction of doubt comes the breaking of a habit, and the making of a new habit depends upon the formation of a new system within which the object under question is interpreted. All such systems are provisional.

Granted that this hypothesis is, from time to time, anthropomorphic, it is not fully so, and many of the terms of the narrative arise from standard chemical or physical descriptions of the day.[14] This is not so much an "elimination" of personhood as an attempt to demonstrate the continuity of apparently separate domains of natural behavior by means of drawing an analogy *from* physics and chemistry *to* signs. What, then, is the place of the "person" in Peirce's account? Is it merely "absorbed" into the three place relation of the sign, as Habermas fears (p. 246), and is this simply a disguise of the real grammar of signs, which cannot do without a user? An alternative is suggested by Vincent Colapietro, who argues that Peirce's theory of signs provides the basis *for* a theory of the subject (p. 28).

The structure of Colapietro's argument is similar to Habermas', but where Habermas argues against a Peirce who is alleged to abstract sign processes away from the subject, Colapietro enlists Peirce in an argument against Eco whom he accuses likewise of being "unwilling to come to grips with the figure of the subject."[15] Eco, it seems, provides comfort to Habermas by "call[ing] upon Peirce as an ally" (p. 28) in the "case of the vanishing subject" (p. 29). Accordingly, Colapietro seeks in the Peircean opus an account of the self.

The argument proceeds through a demonstration of what is at stake in the choice of "intersubjectivity" over "subjectivity." Where this latter assumes that "the self is a source of thought and action, feeling and dreams" (p. 38), the former accepts a self that is "a medium through which forces and persons other than the subject speak" (p. 38). Then "subjectivity" is construed through intersubjectivity, rather than the other way around. The subject is in the first place a body because, as Peirce writes, "the organism is only an instrument of thought" (W 2:22, p. 241); it is also split by the unconscious and is culturally and historically overdetermined (pp. 40–42). On this basis, it seems that the self is an effect of semiosis: "we cannot fully understand any of these fundamental dimensions of human subjectivity apart from an elaborate theory of semiotic processes" (p. 42).

Let us pause to consider these issues in the light of a certain history of post-Cartesian philosophy proposed by Ian Hacking.[16] As I remarked in Chapter 2, Hacking charts the advent of a "public" account of knowledge, in which the problematic of ideas formed and held in a mind is replaced by a problematic of the circulation of "sentences"; Peirce's focus on "conversation" stresses this public dimension of knowledge, and his attempt to dispense with the mind in favor of a nonmental interpretant is consonant with it. Hacking argues that the "weakest point" of the Cartesian conception of knowledge in terms of "ideas" is its "very starting point, the Cartesian *ego* itself."[17] This was noted by Hume: "The mind has . . . no way to bundle up states of consciousness to form an idea of its self." He goes on to consider various half-measures for the solution of this quandary, based on a "bunch of egos" instead of just one.[18] Although Habermas is a major figure in the move to theorize public, as distinct from mind-based, knowledge, it is difficult to see how his account of intersubjectivity avoids the pitfall of the pluralization of the ego unless it accepts the argument put by Colapietro: that not only intersubjectivity, but also subjectivity itself is an effect of semiosis.

To this point, then, I accept Colapietro's argument. However, Colapietro goes on to ask whether the reverse is true: "Can we understand the nature and varieties of semiosis apart from any consideration of the subject?" (p. 42). Several elements make up his answer: Peirce argues for an identity of sign and self, for an essentially communitarian—hence, communicative—conception of the self, but he also argues for a formal account of the semiotic that does not refer to human thought (p. 44). While this last remains Peirce's aim for "logic," Colapietro takes issue with Eco's adoption of this aim as a constraint in principle on a theory of semiotics. "It is one thing," he writes, "to say that a *general* and *formal* theory of signs does not necessarily take into account the subject of semiosis, and it is quite another to assert that such a theory of signs *cannot* in principle investigate the subject" (p. 44).

Colapietro therefore proceeds to extrapolate from Peirce's work a theory of "the subject of semiosis," doing so developmentally, across the forty-year stretch of the corpus, and structuring his account by means of some standard topoi of philosophical anthropology and philosophical psychology: personality, purpose and will, substance, individuality, mind, and organism in chapter 4, followed in chapter 5 by a discussion of inwardness and autonomy. His aim throughout this exposition is to prove that Peirce's account of the subject evolves into a coherent "vision of the active self," formed through its relationality with others, and developing as "a unity of habits" (p. 91). This is indeed a theory of selfhood construed under the protocols of moral philosophy; I am not sure that this is the same thing as an account of "the subject of semiosis."

The problem that I discern is common to Habermas and to Colapietro: both are inclined to suppose that "semiosis" is a single process and hence that subjectivity, or intersubjectivity, must also be posited in general. I doubt if there is such a thing as the subject of semiosis. My doubts arise partly from Peirce's objective, to give a formal grammar of semiosis in general, abstracted from the description of any particular kind—for example, inquiry—and partly from my own assumption that semiosis is observable only in specific practices. Although I admire and accept Colapietro's semiotic construal of subjectivity, it seems to me that it cannot be sustained without accepting the plurality of practices. Nor, I believe, can he make good his claim that subjectivity is necessary to semiosis. This is the case because, as Johansen, Oehler, and others have argued, "semiosis" has in Peirce's work an extension far broader than "human communication" or "conversation." Hence, in order to provide a theory of this latter, "subjectivity" is an extra principle that is added to "semiosis." This entails, *pace* Habermas, not identifying the interpretant with the interpreter. Furthermore, I take the view that any particular kind—genre—of semiotic practice likewise requires particular elements not common to others. If the "subject" is one of these elements, then that subject is as much an instrument of semiosis as it is its "agent."

II

Where Habermas requires the intersubjective social bond to sustain his theory of communicative rationality, Peter Skagestad looks to the tool kit.[19] His argument is concerned with the status of exosomatic implements in Peirce's account of semiosis, and takes its starting point from what appears to be a joke:

A psychologist cuts out a lobe of my brain (*nihil animale me alienum puto*) and then, when I find I cannot express myself, he says, "You see your faculty of language was localized in that lobe." No doubt it was; and so, if he had filched my inkstand, I should not have been able to continue my discussion until I had got another. Yea, the very thoughts would not come to me. So my faculty of discussion is equally localized in my inkstand. It is localization in a sense in which a thing may be in two places at once. On the theory that the distinction between psychical and physical phenomena is the distinction between final and efficient causation, it is plain enough that the inkstand and the brain-lobe have the same general relation to the functions of the mind. (CP 7.366)

We have already seen Peirce pooh-poohing the idea that "the mind and psychology has [anything] more to do with the substance of the book than if I were to discourse of the ingredients of the ink I use" (PW appx. G, p. 195). But as he himself added with the onion, no more, and no less. "The development of Reason consists, you will observe, in embodiment, that is, in manifestation" (MS 449, p. 48): as the body must be trained to hold the pen, so must the ingredients of ink fit it to its purpose. With respect to the inkstand, Skagestad argues that this is not a joke, but a serious problematization of the thesis that thoughts are in brains. Indeed, on his analysis, this is the radicalization of the "critique of consciousness."[20] It rests on two arguments. First, like the theorists of literacy, Peirce holds that "having writing implements is a condition of having certain thoughts," and that "literacy enables modes of thought, and hence, contents of thought, unavailable to purely oral culture" (p. 551). This is particularly evident in Peirce's account of logical and mathematical notations. His view is similar to that of Karl Popper's account of the role of "exosomatic organs, such as pens, pencils, typewriters, and computers" (p. 552). Second, Peirce is concerned to show the absurdity of holding that "the mind is inside the brain" (p. 553), or indeed, localized in any particular place. This is a more radical thesis than the postulate of intersubjectivity:

You find the mind where there are inkstands or other means of expressing thoughts, paper and other vehicles for preserving and conveying thoughts, and of course, brains capable, through the intermediary of eyes and hands or the equivalent, of interacting with external tools and media. (p. 553)

If this is where "the mind" is, "knowledge" resides "exosomatically, in books, articles, and the like, rather than in the conscious experience of the authors or readers of said books etc. That conscious experience . . . was rendered dispensable for the analysis of knowledge or of mind" (p. 555). This is why the Peircean thinker, even when he is sedentary, is not "meditating," but seated at a table with the tools of his trade to hand.[21] According to Skagestad, Peirce "never denied the existence of consciousness," but because "cognition consists of the manipulation of signs," cognition does not consist of conscious states (p. 554); consciousness has a role in the "self-control" of the reasoning process, but it cannot provide an analysis of the process. Furthermore, writes Peirce, when we seek to give an account of "how we think," we cannot give a direct "description" of the process; rather, "a knowledge of how the brain, or any other physical machine works . . . amounts positively to a *translation* of it, or in some cases, to a 'grammatical', or a 'syntactical' analysis of thought. For the 'signs' in which we think, whatever this may be in any particular case . . . must be subject to rules more or less analogous to the rules of syntax" (MS 678, p. 25 alt.). "The mind is essentially a sign user" (p. 558). Subjectivity—I extrapolate—is therefore in need of specification for particular machines. Machines are designed to meet particular needs and are limited by that design. Likewise, particular kinds of signs have both "efficiencies and inefficiencies" (CP 4.531) for particular purposes. There is no doubt a difference between men and machines, consisting in the fact that machines cannot originate anything beyond the "efficiencies" of their design, but even then, "People are like machines, in that the unaided individual is as limited by his/her design as is the machine . . . [and] people do not think unaided" (p. 559). Formal trainings—literacy, numeracy, as well as the special manual and intellectual techniques required for particular kinds of tasks—must count, I think, as the "designing" of persons: "the organism is an instrument of thought."

Skagestad sums up his argument thus:

> In Peirce's view, to be a reasoner is to be a user of machines, be they soft machines like alphabets, numerals, logical notations, and typefaces, or hard machines, like logic machines, alembics, cucurbits, and inkstands. . . . Reasoning [is] (a type of) sign action, depending for its specific character on the specific material qualities of the signs deployed. (p. 559)

Not only are some machines or instruments signs, but the relation of men with signs is the same as the relation of men with machines. Signs are machines without which there is no mind and without which we can do no work. Effectively, in practice, we cannot theorize semiosis in the absence of this nexus of human skills with instrumental efficiencies. These human skills arise in relation with the design of the machines. For this reason, there can be no account of the cultural and historical overdetermination of subjectivity without an account of the trainings and the instruments that implement specific practices. If man is a toolmaker, it is also the case that tools make the man. If this is the case, then subjectivity is a contingent product of its practices, not a foundational datum for the general theory of semiosis.

III

I want now to consider the implications of this debate for the particular case of the symbol, for the symbol is the event-unit of "conversation." This being so, the symbol appears to entail the classical notion of human subjectivity that, inflected through the theory of the interpretant and its associated "community of inquirers," gives the rationale for Habermas' reading. Is the symbol the sign of mind? And if it is, how does it stand in relation to the consequences of Skagestad's argument? Does it reduce the tool kit paradigm to instrumental status, where an always already fully formed mental power invents freely what it needs? The ambiguities of Peirce's views are nowhere more evident than in the case of the symbol.

The term *conversation* is strategic. It was first introduced in 1868 as a device for translating out of the metaphysical postulate underpinning standard philosophical solutions to the problem of truth, which rely on the assumed discontinuity of mind with world. Peirce approached this problem in two ways. Recall that in the "New List" the dualism of mind and world remains broadly intact: the categorial scheme of that paper rests on five categories, of which two are foundational, and the three "intermediate" ones "accidental." "Being" "arises upon the formation of a proposition" and hence is a functional account of mind, thought, or reason; "substance," is "the present in general," "IT," the real. First, as a means of combating these nominalistic assumptions, he gave up the foundational categories.[22] In subsequent work, the ontological separateness of mind and world is reduced to the point where mind is analyzed as the processes of inquiring into the real, and the real is construed as those tested outcomes that count as true.

Second, allied with the doubt/belief account of inquiry that Peirce worked on during the 1870s, "mind" is transformed into "discussion." Take these passages from 1872:

When two men discuss a question, each first endeavours to raise a doubt in the mind of the other, and that is often half the battle. When the doubt ceases there is no use in further discussion. . . .

The only justification for reasoning is that it settles doubts, and when doubt finally ceases, no matter how, the end of reasoning is attained. Let a man resolve never to change his existing opinions, let him obstinately shut his eyes to all evidence against them, and if his will is strong enough so that he actually does not waver in his faith, he has no motive for reasoning at all. (W 3:4, pp. 14–15)

Let any two minds investigate any question independently and if they carry the process far enough they will come to an agreement which no further investigation will disturb. (W 3:5, p. 17)

As Peirce has concluded in the cognition series, a mind alone cannot engage in serious inquiry, let alone attain truth; the process that interests him requires at minimum *two* minds in "discussion."

Now Peirce also writes that it is the "nature of the mind" that is "undoubtedly" the "origin of the principles" of signhood (W 3:30, p. 83). However,

They are involved in so much of what is true of the mind as is implied in our capability of reasoning at all and which may therefore be said to be implicitly taken for granted by all men, that is, to be deducible from what everybody agrees to and must agree to before we can begin any discussion whatever in a rational way, and which is thus taken out of the special domain of psychology and made the common property of science. These principles might be evolved from a study of the mind and of thought, but they can also be reached by the simple consideration of any signs we please. Now the latter mode of studying them is much the easiest, because the examination of external signs is one of the most simple researches which we can undertake, and least susceptible to error, while the study of mind is one of the most difficult and doubtful. (W 3:30, p. 83)

Peirce's second means of reducing the metaphysical baggage of "mind," then, is to translate the problem of mind into a scientific method of empirical observation. The mind is ontologically continuous with the world it studies; it does not stand outside it; therefore it can be studied in the same way, as a succession of phenomena in real time (W 3:25, p. 26). In other words, Peirce shifts the problem of the first philosophy away from the privacy of mental acts toward a phenomenal account of talk about the world taking place *in* the world.

Talk is the manifestation of mind. In the "New List," the principal criterion of the symbol is that its connection with its object is "imputed," and while this term does not recur, the criterion persists in a generally mentalist account of its constitutive character:

the third is the general name or description which signifies its object by means of an association of ideas or habitual connection between the name and the character signified. (W 5:35, p. 243)

Or there may be a relation which consists in the fact that the mind associates the sign with its object; in that case the sign is a *name*. (W 5:35, p. 245)

Likewise, in 1893, the "symbol is a mental act" (CP 2.438), but this mentalist account is already associated with "habitual connection" in 1885 and again in 1893, where we read "that a symbol is a conventional sign" (CP 4.56; cf. CP 2.292). All this is grist to the mill of Habermas, for whom "reason" and "social consensus" are mutually entailed. The mentalist criterion persists: symbols are "mental signs" (CP 2.302; 1895); they mean what they mean because they "determine, in the mind of the auditor, corresponding signs" (CP 2.92). It is not until 1901 that we find a formalized definition that dispenses entirely with "the mind":

A Sign (q.v.) which is constituted a sign merely or mainly by the fact that it is used and understood as such, whether the habit is natural or conventional, and without regard to the motives which originally governed its selection. (CP 2.307)

And again, in 1902/3:

A symbol is a representamen whose special significance or fitness to represent just what it does represent lies in nothing but the very fact of there being a habit, disposition, or other effective general rule that it will be so interpreted. (CP 4.447)

Yet we would be misled to read such definitions as a wholesale dismissal of the mind from Peirce's account of the symbol.

Symbols have the special capacity sometimes to be true; on this condition, their constitutive laws are not merely contingently human or social; they are not merely the laws of their types. Hence, the predictive capacity of a symbol is predictive both in a strong and in a weak sense. Weakly, it simply predicts its own interpretation and is no better than any nominalism; strongly, it predicts whatever the law it represents predicts. Hence, when Peirce writes that "a Symbol is a law, or regularity of the indefinite future" (EP 2:20, p. 274 [CP 2.293]; 1903), he intends this to refer to the capacity of symbols to be true in the long run. This is the effective *differentia specifica* of the class, since the index is true only on occasion and the icon is neither true nor false. The narrowly mentalist account of the symbol is now the affair of the psychologist (CP 4.479; 1903). Natural or conventional (CP 2.307; 1901), if a symbol is a law in the strong sense, then a law is nothing but a symbol (EP 2:13, p. 184 [CP 5.107]; 1903). It is the outcome of inquiry.

This strong sense of the predictive powers of the symbol derives from Peirce's formulation of the class in the "New List," where it is the proposition that provides the site for the problematic of signs in general. Peirce returns to this formulation in the 1890s, when he writes that a symbol is "the *copula* of the assertion" (CP 3.435; 1896). It states "what is." This explains why the "law" to which the definitions of the symbol refer is equally the law of the object as the law of its signifier. This is a realist definition that does not presuppose the truth of its representation, because propositions (only propositions) may be asserted falsely or in error, but it does posit the capacity of the class of the symbol to represent truths in the long run.

The symbol is an *ens rationis* (CP 4.465; 1903), seeking, indeed stating, the rationality of the universe. Its telos as well as its constitution is Reason: it "serves to make thought and conduct rational and enables us to predict the future" (CP 4.448; 1903). Hence it is crucial to the definition of Pragmatism:

The entire intellectual purport of any symbol consists in the total of all general modes of rational conduct which, conditionally upon all the possible different circumstances and desires, would ensue upon the acceptance of the symbol. (EP 2:25, p. 346 [CP 5.438]; 1905)

These definitions demonstrate the importance that mind continues to have as a, perhaps the, criterion of the symbol. Yet it is precisely in respect of the symbol that mind is construed as talk. Take the standard examples: words, or utterances of speech, sentences, books are manifestations of talk. Accordingly, symbols are also defined by the semiosic dynamic itself:

Symbols grow. . . . A symbol, once in being, spreads among the peoples. In use and in experience, its meaning grows. (CP 2.302; 1895)

A Symbol is a Representamen whose Representative character consists precisely in its being a rule that will determine its Interpretant. (EP 2:20, p. 274 [CP 2.292]; 1893)

A Genuine Sign is a Transuasional Sign, or *Symbol*, which is a sign which owes its significant virtue to a character which can only be realized by the aid of its Interpretant. Any utterance of speech is an example. If the sounds were originally in part iconic, in part indexical, those characters have long since lost their importance. The words only stand for the objects they do, and signify the qualities they do, because they will determine, in the mind of the auditor, corresponding signs. (CP 2.92; 1901)

Importantly, these insights result in the identification of the symbol with the assertion:

Neither the predicate, nor the subjects, nor both together, can make an *assertion*.

The assertion represents a compulsion which experience, meaning the course of life, brings upon the deliverer to attach the predicate to the subjects as a sign of them taken in a particular way. This compulsion strikes him at a certain instant; and he remains under it forever after. It is, therefore, different from the temporary force which the hecceities exert upon his attention. This new compulsion may pass out of mind for the time being; but it continues just the same, and will act whenever the occasion arises, that is, whenever those particular hecceities and that first intention are called to mind together. It is, therefore, a permanent conditional force, or *law*. The deliverer thus requires a kind of sign which shall signify a law that to objects of indices an icon appertains as sign of them in a given way. Such a sign has been called a *symbol*. It is the *copula* of the assertion. (CP 3.435; 1896)

If the symbol is the sign of talk, is talk merely the manifestation of mind, or does it work, so to say, as its machinery? Does the symbol function as explicans to conversation, or alternatively, is conversation the explicans of the symbol? There is some evidence to support the latter view; it flows from the special role of the interpretant in some definitions of the symbol (CP 2.92; CP 2.292; EP 2.22, p. 322). Take this passage, which I discussed in Chapter 4:

A sign is either an *icon*, an *index*, or a *symbol*. An *icon* is a sign which would possess the character which renders it significant, even though its object had no existence; such as a lead-pencil streak as representing a geometrical line. An *index* is a sign which would, at once, lose the character which makes it a sign if its object were removed, but would not lose that character if there were no interpretant. Such, for instance, is a piece of mould with a bullet-hole in it as sign of a shot; for without the shot there would have been no hole; but there is a hole there, whether anybody has the sense to attribute it to a shot or not. A *symbol* is a sign which would lose the character which renders it a sign if there were no interpretant. Such is any utterance of speech which signifies what it does only by virtue of its being understood to have that signification. (CP 2.304)

Now if it is indeed the case that the special criterion of the symbol is its interpretant, then it would follow from this definition that Habermas is right to insist that talk explains semiosis, not the other way about; hence, it would indeed require some factor such as intersubjectivity, or society, or community, to account for its operation. However, I have argued that the definitions formulated in terms of "genuine" and "degenerate" classes do nothing but repeat the logic of the categories; this repetition is significantly less productive than the recursive application of the categorial scheme to thirdness. In the latter process, the interpretant inheres in all the products.

In contrast with this, the analysis "by degeneracy" violates the definition of the sign as necessarily a three-term relation. If the other classes of signs are effectively excluded by their status as "degenerate" on the grounds of not involving mediation by an interpretant, then Peirce's semiotic is restricted to the symbol.

Many influential accounts of Peirce's pragmatism rely on just this construal of the symbol. John Fitzgerald, for example, argues that Peirce was searching for a "unified proof of his pragmatism" and that the premisses for this proof derive from the principles established in the theory of signs.[23] Thus the nub of logic, semiotic, is called on to provide the foundation for pragmatism (CP 2.304). In the following discussion of Fitzgerald's thesis, I shall argue that it rests on the full set of philosophical loci that have commanded my attention thus far: the presupposition of "mind," the explanation of the interpretant in terms of the presence of an interpreter, and a construal of the symbol through thought rather than talk.

Fitzgerald's reading proceeds by locating the theory of signs in the divisions of the sciences Peirce developed between 1895 and 1903; the place of phenomenology gives the rationale for the division of signs into icon, index, and symbol. He then moves to the interpretant, giving this a crucial role for pragmatism. This scheme gives no place to the second classification and hence overlooks the distinction between type and token. However, the later divisions of the interpretant are taken into account, so one feature of what I have called the "pragmatization" of semiotic itself, the dynamic interpretant, does have a function in the thesis.

Central to Fitzgerald's account of the theory of signs is his gloss of the distinction between "genuine" and "degenerate" signs. The specificity of the symbol hangs on this distinction because only "genuine" signs rest upon the act of a mind. While the foundation for the sign relation in degenerate cases is said to "antecede" "the activity of the mind" (pp. 47–48) or is "independent of a knower" (p. 46), "the fitness [of a symbol] comes from the fact that the sign vehicle is related to the object by a mind" (p. 62). It is this that gives a special place to the symbol in pragmatism, which involves a thesis concerning "the meaningfulness of propositions" (p. 70). Notice then, that in Fitzgerald's account, the centrality of mind is associated with a decision to distinguish the pragmatics of assertion from the meaning of propositions.[24] An assertion is a public act, but

Peirce usually moves to a more formal point of view. . . . There is something antecedent to the acceptance of these social responsibilities, something more basic

[than] the act of assent and the act of assertion. A proposition, which lends itself to analysis in terms of the division of signs, is presupposed. (p. 67)

Notice the assumption here: that propositions exclusively, not assertions, are analyzed by the division of signs. When Peirce develops the second classification, it implies a decision not to make the move that Fitzgerald describes; in particular, the "dicent" sign covers the "assertible" as well as the assertion, the distinction between these two corresponding to the "immediate" and the "dynamic," or the virtual and the actual, that is, to the distinction between "first" and "second." This is one feature of the second classification that persists in all the later work, and it is simply not the case that the "division of signs" pertains only to the propositional content and not to the assertion as act. Indeed, the move to take the pertinent event unit of conversation as an assertion simply follows from the requirement that signs themselves be things and events, as well as laws.

Evidently Fitzgerald's analysis rests on the first classification of signs; in this, he is authorized by some passages dating from the period prior to the introduction of the second classification in which Peirce does indeed analyze the proposition as consisting of the adjunction of a symbol whose context is construed as an icon with an index. I shall return to the issues raised by this analysis shortly. Fitzgerald supplements it with the division of the interpretant:

The major division of interpretants is into the immediate, the dynamic and the final . . . there is a further subdivision of the dynamical interpretant into the emotional, the energetic and the logical interpretants. (p. 76)

I think Fitzgerald is right to argue that pragmatism must hinge on the theory of the interpretant, and he is also right to focus on the dynamical interpretant (p. 83). Only in this way can he show the connection between actual interpretations and the business of inquiry. It is simply a pity that he deprives his thesis of a potential strength by dissociating the division of the interpretant from the pragmatization of signs in general. Thus, in glossing the dynamical interpretant, Fitzgerald allows that it is an actual effect, and that one such kind of effect, the "logical interpretant," is a sign. The others are feelings and efforts. This results in a paradoxical conclusion, that I find alien to Peirce's position: "A sign allows for future translations and for future development, whereas a feeling or an actual activity does not" (p. 79). On this view, assertions are signs only insofar as they are analyzed into their propositional content, but not insofar as they are public acts with consequences. Yet we have seen that when Peirce asks the pragmatic question of how signs have effects in the world of things and events, the answer is found in the move from the law to its instantiation, from the proposition to its assertion, the type to its token, this last being "the sign as occurring just when and where it does." The dynamical interpretant with all of its subdivisions is part of this move, and it is not clear why it advances Fitzgerald's argument to reserve signhood for the logical interpretant alone.

We must presume that the answer lies in the privilege of mind. Fitzgerald must presuppose a mentalist account of the symbol in order to guarantee that the symbol address another mind. This, he argues, is the crux of pragmatism. Pragmatism is concerned only with intellectual concepts, and the intellectual, conceptual component of meaning is the "immediate interpretant," the "fitness of the sign to be interpreted in a certain way" (p. 82). Beneath the assertion lies the proposition; beneath the sign lies its intellectual content, analyzed into the symbol plus the index, with the symbol analyzed further as resting on an icon (p. 70). This is an analysis of the proposition, not of the assertion. It follows, then, notwithstanding the focus on the dynamical interpretant, that signhood is the analysis of meaning, not of acts or things or events. Yet it is precisely for confining the question of meaning in this way that Peirce takes Royce to task in 1903 (CP 8.100–31); the pragmatic analysis of the sign is devised in order to dissolve the metaphysical presuppositions of such distinctions as these.

For the kind of pragmatism that is Fitzgerald's concern, the interpretants that matter are meanings that become habitual (p. 167). "The most significant of the effects of the sign will be signs or habits. Of these two, the latter is more fundamental since it constitutes the *raison d'être* of signs themselves" (p. 167). The question that Fitzgerald does not answer is how a logical interpretant becomes a habit, for under Peirce's probabilistic construal of law, habits are series of events. I believe this question cannot be answered without taking into account the thinghood and the eventhood of signs themselves, and hence of interpretants themselves. Fitzgerald attempts to do so by locating the significant event of interpretation in an interpreter, but he undermines the force of this answer by privileging thirdness or law over against qualities and events instead of heeding Peirce's own advice concerning the integration of the three categories in the explanation of phenomena. There is no court without a sheriff, no law if it be not enacted in events, no abstract knowledge without perception.

Mind addresses mind, and mind resides in interpreters. The contents of these minds are true if, and only if, they correspond to the world as it is. The kind of pragmatism Fitzgerald is concerned with seeks to account for the processes whereby such correspondence is achieved. Yet the correspondence theory is structured by the dualism Peirce worked all his life to contest. It follows that the issue of processes—experiment, induction, probabilistic calculations, and the like—is only half the story. Peirce's argument for realism against nominalism could only be made good when the theory of signs ceased to rest on the postulate of a Mind ontologically distinct from the objects it grasps. The first step is achieved when the object is itself construed as a sign; the second is not achieved until the signs in which it emerges through interpretation are construed as things, objects like any others. This involves, most crucially, a radical change in the theory of the symbol whose *differentia specifica* under the first classification, I recall, its "genuineness" in relation with the other signs, rested on the centrality of mind as distinct from qualities and hecceities. So the question arises: what is a symbol under the second classification? What is a symbol if it is no longer the sign by, for, and of the mind? In place of the figure of reason, Peirce introduces that of convention, allowing this to be processual, the dynamic outcome of agreements come to over time and modified likewise. Convention is socially based, and it is in history.[25] This implies that its mechanism consists, minimally, in assertions, not in propositions; hence the late examples: proverbs, newspapers, great social movements. It is this that makes sense of the historicization of inquiry and gives to it its full weight.[26]

However, it would be misleading to assert that this change occurs as a clean break in Peirce's work. The late work is, as I have sought to show, marked by significant conflicts, the most acute of which arises at the site of the symbol. Fifty years of discursive habit cannot be overthrown by one brilliant insight. Furthermore, it is precisely at this site that the radicalism of Peirce's project comes to challenge his own deepest presuppositions. Allow me to circle one last time over the career in order to describe this challenge. I have shown that in the "New List," Peirce delineates the three main divisions of signs in order to set aside both icons and indices, and to attend exclusively to the symbol. This focus changes as a result of his work on the semiotics of formal notations where the special powers of both icons and indices become evident. Further, each of these classes takes on substantive philosophical importance. I have also shown that during the period 1885 to 1903, there is effectively no new work on the symbol, and that all the new work in semiotic either bears directly on the other classes or follows from their elaboration. The symbol returns to center stage only in 1903, when the question of its real effects is raised for, and by, Pragmatism.

We should recall from that early work that "the sign" has a double vocation: it is both end and means. The form of knowledge itself, it must also be known as an empirical or phenomenal object. Truth is mediated by its means, and it is to the nature of these means that Peirce has devoted his attention between 1885 and 1903. Hence the technical work on notations, the analyses first of indexicality, then of iconicity; hence, too, the range of examples of each, notably the material instruments of scientific research; and hence the new question that emerges for the symbol, the question of its real consequences. Following this, in the late work, there is an evident move to focus again on the symbol, but the philosophical vocation of the symbol appears to take over semiotic, the ends of semiotic to override interest in its means.

Insofar as this is the case, it rests on an effective identification of the symbol with the proposition, and an account of it in terms of its formal constitution, rather than on its eventhood. Take the following definition, dating from 1893, as exemplary: a symbol—here coextensive with a proposition—is formed from the combination of an icon with an index.

It is impossible to find a proposition so simple as not to have reference to two signs. Take, for instance, "it rains." Here the icon is the mental composite photograph of all the rainy days the thinker has experienced. The index is all whereby he distinguishes that day, as it is placed in his experience. The symbol is the mental act whereby [he] stamps that day as rainy. (CP 2.438; 1893)

We should scrutinize this insistence of the mind in the explication of the symbol, for the mind is just that metaphysical ultimate that has been eradicated from the other signs.

In the first classification, the symbol is the umbrella term for the trichotomy of term, proposition, and argument, identifying the common feature of its members as the conventionality of their relation with their objects. Under this construal, its paradigm example is the proposition, concatenated to form arguments or awaiting its "attachments" when it is a mere term. In principle, therefore, this construal is incompatible with the logic of the second classification, which combines its terms rather than relating them as genus to species. Yet it seems to be the case that Peirce's account of the symbol continues to be governed by his early work. Indeed, we can speculate that it is the pressure of the symbol that accounts for the fact that Peirce does not persist with the combinatorial logic, although he retains both the terms and the analyses that emerge from it. For under the logic of the combinatory, the symbol loses its raison d'être and can neither act as the general category for the third trichotomy nor be formed from the combination of index and icon.

These conclusions are demonstrated by the argument of the draft entitled "New Elements" (EP 2:22). The text is conceived as a preface to a book on logic, and has the function of a "scholium . . . a comment upon the logical structure of the doctrine" (p. 303). The main subject of this scholium is the proposition, and it is this object that the theory of signs expounded in it is designed to theorize. It does so on the basis of the first classification, derived by degeneracy, the icon, the index, and the symbol: both the definitions and the examples are familiar, with the symbol distinguished as "a sign which is fit to serve as such simply because it will be so interpreted." This character elicits the paradigm examples, all of which "belong to minds who think in words" (p. 307). While the degenerate signs "serve purposes that genuine signs could not" (p. 306), genuine signs— that is, symbols—"have a great power of which the degenerate signs are quite destitute. They alone express laws," and furthermore, "they serve to bring about reasonableness and law" (p. 308). The symbol is thus the sign of Reason. Its three subspecies are again the familiar ones: an argument with the signs of its purposed interpretant erased is a proposition, and a term is a part of a proposition disjoined from its subject. The junction of subject with predicate is the function of the copula, and Peirce goes on to claim that the symbol itself *is* this connection (p. 310). Hence it is clear that all Peirce needs out of his exposition of signs is the symbol, glossed as the proposition because this is the paradigmatic form of all its species: "It is the Proposition which forms the main subject of this whole scholium" (p. 311); the proposition is what it is through the offices of the copula. This is the essence of the symbol.

Peirce has mentioned the special competencies of icons and indices, but in fact used them exclusively in the gloss of the symbol: the copula "is an index" in that it operates on occasion to join what it joins, while it also "involves an icon" in that it signifies that connection even as it effects it (p. 310). Beyond this, icons and indices have no further role in this draft. This outcome is somewhat similar to that of the "New List," although reached by a different route. Logic here deals only in symbols, and preeminently with propositions. Furthermore, although Peirce is careful to distinguish between a sign and its replicas, he sets these latter aside:

Logic is the study of the essential nature of signs. A sign is something that exists in replicas. Whether the sign "it is raining . . . " happens to have a replica in writing, in oral speech, or in silent thought, is a distinction of the very minutest interest in logic, which is a study, not of replicas, but of signs. . . . A *proposition* is . . . that sign of which the judgment is one replica and the lingual expression another. (p. 311)

Notice the implication that a replica is *not* a sign: this implication is in direct conflict with Peirce's decision to integrate the first trichotomy into the classification of kinds of signs. Notice, too, that if a replica is not a sign, it cannot provide any premises that would answer the question of how signs act. Yet how signs have real effects is an insistent question in "New Elements," taking a form similar to the form it takes in the Harvard Lectures.[27] Reducing the class of signs to the symbol, and abstracting from the symbol the form of the proposition, "New Elements" lends itself to a certain reading of Peirce's pragmatism in which the sign itself is volatilized. He attempts in this draft to say what a sign really is, its "being," as distinct from its being represented (p. 311): the implications of this move are shocking for a man who has argued consistently that we can deal with nothing but signs, that the sign is to its meaning as the skins of the onion are to the onion, no more and no less: they *are* the onion, no less than its *esse in praesentia*, no more than the conditions of possibility of its *esse in futuro*. I have shown in the preceding chapters that the position argued in "New Elements" is neither Peirce's last word on signs nor even the leading thread of his research in the final decade. Nevertheless, it is a thread, consistent with many other accounts of the symbol at this time.

It is certainly the case that the second and later classifications are the framework of the general theory of signs, of which a specialized part designed for the special purposes of critic bears on the second trichotomy and preeminently the symbol; but this does not reconcile the logic of the work on the symbol with the logic of the general framework. Suppose that a proposition is the object of its replicas, and that, in line with his search for a realist solution to the problem of true knowledge, Peirce sets out to provide a semiotic analysis of each of the terms of this relation. Nevertheless, he provides a *different* analysis for each: the object of one analysis is the form of thought, the object of the other is its thinghood and its eventhood. The dualism of this purported solution is inescapable: the form of thought is the real being of the sign, replicas mere representations (pp. 303, 311). Not only dualistic, with just a soupçon of nominalism lurking about, the solution is internally contradictory, since it both positions the replica as a representation and sets it aside from the study of logic, which "is the study of the essential nature of signs" (p. 311). This contradiction resembles the difficulties studied in chapter 2, where "thought in its expression" is found to be the ungraspable object of semiotic inquiry. It is clear that Peirce is looking for essences here, and that the replica counts in this metaphysics as accidental; but surely, if the replica is a representation, it too has an essential nature? My analysis of the type/token distinction in Chapter 5 has sought to show that the same semiotic analysis can and should be applied to the token as to the type, and that Peirce's grammar, not his critic, ultimately provides the means to do so. At the risk of repetitiousness, I recall that Peirce was seeking a "truly scientific metaphysics": there is no law without a sheriff, no natural law that can be stated otherwise than as the probability of a certain occurrence, no thirdness in the absence of secondness, no thought without signs. The metaphysics of much of Peirce's late work on the symbol fails this test.

And much of it, too, shows him engaged on the task of reconciling the two analyses. The following definition from the Syllabus attempts to blend the criteria from the first with those of the second classification:

A Symbol is a sign which refers to the Object that it denotes by virtue of a law, usually an association of general ideas, which operates to cause the Symbol to be interpreted as referring to that Object. It is thus itself a general type or law, that is, is a Legisign. As such it acts through a Replica. Not only is it general itself, but the Object to which it refers is of a general nature. Now that which is general has its being in the instances which it will determine. There must, therefore, be existent instances of what the Symbol denotes, although we must here understand by "existent," existent in the possibly imaginary universe to which the Symbol refers. The Symbol will indirectly, through the association or other law, be affected by those instances; and thus the Symbol will involve a sort of Index, although an Index of a peculiar kind. It will not, however, be by any means true that the slight effect upon the Symbol of those instances accounts for the significant character of the Symbol. (EP 2:21, p. 292 [CP 2.249]; 1903)

This definition distinguishes, in order to articulate them, the nominalist focus on the "convention" constituting the type with the realist law of the object. The "association of general ideas" is what Peirce calls the "iconic" dimension of the symbol, whereas the picking out of "instances of what it denotes" corresponds with the indexical element of a proposition. While it acts "through a Replica," what the symbol does, and how it does it, are accounted for by its formal constitution by the icon and the index, and not by the semiosic relation between token and type discussed in Chapter 6.

The theoretical function of this formal analysis of the symbol is the crux of the matter. Is the symbol merely the sum of its parts? If it were, it would be the redundant term of the system. However, Peirce maintains that a symbol is a mental act, different from each of its parts by virtue of the law of the copula. This is highly significant. With this return to the classical conception of the proposition, Peirce retrieves thought; but the law of the copula cannot account for semiosis, because semiosis rests on the relation between two signs, not on the internal structure of one.

Only an assertion can ask the questions that judge a representation[28]: Is it a sign? What is it a sign of? Is it a good sign? This is the principle of doubt, the *duo habeo*. There are two signs, and it is the relation between them that mobilizes semiosis. The interpretant is a second sign that translates its object and becomes object for the next sign; this sequence of signs is the object of the theory, the central question of Peirce's inquiry. Moreover, this sign that is rent by time is doubly split, for it rests on the principle of second intentionality that guarantees that the sign is taken *as sign*. In the absence of these two principles, it is simply not possible to generate an account of the "needed commentary upon the syntax"—that is, a grammar, a critic, and a rhetoric of the sign—from a formal theory of the proposition, no matter how semiotic the terms in which it is couched.

Of the two projects of semiotic—one developed by the logic, one developed for philosophy—the former studies the devices and contrivances of inquiry, whereas the latter takes "the sign" as answer to the philosophers' question: How come we to know? The practical machinery; or the transcendental conditions. What signs do, or what they are. It is to the uneasy tension between these two projects that we must, I have argued, attribute many of the problems discussed throughout this book: the ambiguous status of language and of translation, the analytical function of conversation. These problems could, in their turn, be reanalyzed in terms of the ambiguities of the symbol. The symbol construes thought as talk, but then, distinguished from the assertion, is analyzed for its propositional content. Evidently, the renewed focus on the propositional form is due to the significance of the existential graphs in Peirce's late work: not only do the graphs take propositions as their objects, but their technique is devised to capture their abstract structure. Indifferently "symbol" or "proposition," this is the mystery to which semiotic is required to provide the key. Thus does Peirce revert to the semiotic of the "New List." Finding the key to this mystery is the telos of Peirce's grand design for Pragmatism. Yet for all practical purposes, Peirce no longer needs the symbol in his system: all its functions are performed otherwise—its conventionality, by the type; the general and consensual nature of its relation with its object, by the term; talk, by the assertion.

As Skagestad remarks, mind remains a part of Peirce's system to the extent that he must include within it the power he calls "self-control." Only by reflecting on the constitution of any sign that comes before it, can a symbol generate arguments and judge them to be true or false. Yet it is precisely at this point that the symbol is indistinguishable from the assertion and the argument. It seems to be the case, then, that the specificity of the symbol as a class has all but dissolved; as a result, the symbol retrieves the quasi-transcendental function of representing the general form of knowledge, at the same time as it loses its specificity as a kind of sign. Although it started life as the technical issue of semiotic, the symbol has effectively been resolved on the one hand into the icons and the indices, the types and the tokens that are the constituents of its formation and the instruments of its powers, and on the other, into the grammar of assertion and the rules of inference. Yet the late analyses have it represent the place of the proposition. As such, it guarantees the place of thought within the system, ensuring by that very fact that the system remains within the space of thought, which is Philosophy. What is the symbol under the pragmatized semiotic that is spelled out by the second classification and its descendants? It is a point of relay, converting the instruments of semiosis into its processes and effects. In the logic of Peirce's argument for pragmatism, however, it is the form in which human reason grasps the reason of the universe. Hence the difficulties surrounding the issue of the end of semiosis. The symbol plays no part in the machinery of talk. It greets the neighbors; it discusses signs; it is talk, period.

Epilogue

Of all the professional relationships—let us call them conversations—that Peirce entered into and sometimes left during his lifetime, the one we know most about is the conversation with Welby.[1] This is because it was maintained entirely by correspondence, the collection of which has been published in full. It is a wonderful correspondence in many ways—warm, wide-ranging, alert, intelligent—each of the participants taking advantage of it to develop ideas and to discuss them with one another. It is, moreover, a fine example of a relationship fostered by technical means: printing, the international book trade and the circulation of learned journals, literacy, the international dating system, photography, the postcard, shipping, the postal and telegraph services, typewriters, pens, and paper.

My dear Mr. Peirce
I am very sorry that you did not send me that other letter that weighs 5 oz.! (WP June 29, 1904)

Dear Mr Peirce
I hope my cablegram—the first I ever sent—arrived all right and was clear. (WP December 13, 1904, p. 44)

My dear Lady Welby:
I will not let a steamer go without writing to you. (PW May 14, 1905)

My dear Lady Welby:
Please excuse my writing on this paper, as I find to my surprise that I have run out

of everything else except such as is still less fit for writing to you; and it is 3:1/2 A.M. and I am 5 or 6 miles from a stationer's.

I cannot tell you how delighted I was on Saturday last to see your handwriting on the envelope. (PW December 14, 1908, p. 66)

My dear Mrs Peirce
Though, alas, I cannot emulate the delicacy of your dainty handwriting, my grateful and affectionate thanks are due to you. (WP October 19, 1909, p. 135)

My dear Mr. Peirce,
I find I am typing the wrong letters so only add eager response of [my] grandson to ideas still unmeaning.[2]

These exosomatic agencies and devices are moreover complemented by other persons—Mrs. Peirce, the grandson as we have seen, Welby's daughter-in-law, as well as the Peirces' neighbor who collected their mail. Welby herself was in the habit of acting as intermediary to effect the contact of other people of her acquaintance, often including transcriptions of letters that she received. A nice example is her attempt to reconcile Peirce to Russell and his views (WP November 20, 1904, and WP January 7, 1905). On another occasion, she is keen to tell him the news that she has recruited a disciple for his own work—that disciple being, as it happens, C. K. Ogden, who made known a simplified version of Peirce's semiotic by including it as an appendix to *The Meaning of Meaning*, coauthored with I. A. Richards (WP May 2, 1911, pp. 138–39). The book was reviewed by Frank Ramsey, who made special mention of the interest of this appendix, and it is Ramsey who is speculatively credited with bringing the type/token distinction into circulation in mainstream British logic.[3] Note that in all these instances of mediation, semiosis is effected by specific genres, each of which relies crucially on the deployment of particular technologies, whether these be "hard" or "soft," the former including anything from a steamer to typewriting, the latter including rhetorical decorum and strategies adopted and adapted to the local requirements of urbane and professional intercourse.

Without question, however, the most prominent of the "instruments of thought" is the body itself, a perennial preoccupation of these two frail and aging intellectuals as they struggle against the odds to complete their work. "I had the other day a sharp reminder that time is daily more precious; and the worst is that as one ages one tires sooner" (WP November 8, 1906). We have seen Welby having difficulties typing; so, too, Peirce recounts impediments to writing resulting from injuries to his brain and to his hand (PW December 16, 1904, p. 45). More gravely, Welby, who "had great trouble a fortnight ago with aphasia & loss of power in the right hand" loses the power of her very voice to the extent that "it is not always easy to catch what she says" but who, even then, has expressed anxiety that "I should write & thank you" (Maria Welby, February 25, 1912, p. 153). Agency depends on physical competence, just as subjectivity is built up over the years by technical and active experience of the variety of semiotic practices. The poignancy of the closing letters of the correspondence results from the fact that the two writers can no longer command the means of semiosis. Theory, we might say, has definitively separated from practice.

Even before this, however, and almost from the outset, they both display the anxiety of interruption or delay. Financial difficulties on Peirce's side, the extraordinary range of activities on Welby's, accidents and fatigue, or simply the intrusive demands of "chores" or piles of mail—even on one occasion an unexplained visit to a magistrate—all threaten to interrupt the correspondence, and all provide matter for the openings of letters, as if—like fences, like their relationships with others, and like their professional writing—such things are both the obstacles to conversation and the means to mediate its pursuit. I haven't written, Peirce frequently tells Welby, because I was trying to get my book done. Later, this is the reason for not being able to deliver the essay she has asked him for. Which is interruption to which, one might ask, when we read in PW June 20, 1911, that it is this book that he has interrupted in order to write for hers. In any case, Peirce rarely fails to use a letter to expound a part of the argument, and it is progressively less clear whether he is referring to the book or to the article. What he "wanted to write" was "an abstract of my entire system of logic," but the first part will have to do, because of "the limits of space and time" as well as considerations on readability (PW July 25, 1911). "It would be a joy to hear and a double joy to find that the promised Essay was on its way" she finally writes (December 31, 1911, p. 153). The letters *represent* the book, the essay, promising them, telling them in advance to their chosen reader, projecting them into a would-be that would not be.

Welby, likewise, tells Peirce that she is "hoping to gather strength for the most important of my books (so far as!) giving both witness to and universal application of Significs" (WP December 31, 1911), but the parallels between the two writers are not exact. After all, Welby was capable of completing an article between 5 and 6 A.M. (WP October 8, 1909), and it is she, not Peirce, for whom the anxiety of delay translates into a practical issue: encouraging Peirce to "get [his book] written and published as soon as [he] can," she tells him that hers is nearly ready. "You must remember that we cannot get on without work like yours" (WP May 2, 1911). Expressing this anxiety as a theoretical issue, and explaining the point of significs as the "question of *sense*," her concern being "the caprices or inconsistencies or technicalities of Sense," Welby goes on to deplore "the present state of language" which fosters "inconclusive argument" (January 21, 1909, p. 87):

Our sense both of fitness and of consequence—not merely what *follows* but what *leads*, is more maimed than we know by the present lack betrayed by our helpless toleration of the unrecognized confusion of imposed usage in which the conventions of expression for most of us remain. (WP January 21, 1909, p. 88)

Peirce's solution to this, expounded in his response, is translation into the precision of the Existential Graphs; Welby's is a desire to police usage, a desire expressed in this letter in an aside:

The French *sens* means here *direction*, and it seems a pity we cannot adopt that expressive French idiom and ask, "In what direction are you thinking?" (WP January 21, 1909, p. 87)

Yet despite this desire, these letters, being conversational in the strict sense, are frequently digressive, and herein lies much of their charm. This fact too seems sometimes to trouble the writers, as if digression were itself an interruption, a deferral of the end of semiosis. Welby objects to Peirce's use of the term *play*, "which we so often connect . . . with . . . mere random wandering" (WP December 4, 1908); Peirce defends it, on the authority of Schiller's *Aesthetische Briefe* (PW December 33, 1908, p. 77). For him, digression is the mind in action, its "power to establish relations between objects" (p. 69). "But I wanted to write to you about signs," he writes at the start of the most succinct and elegant exposition of the theory that subsists from his pen (PW October 12, 1904). It is as if he has strayed from the "direction" and had just returned to it. Again, in response to Welby, he protests: "I smiled at your speaking of my being 'kindly *interested*' in your work, as if it were a divergence—I should say a *deviation*, from my ordinary line of attention," whereas all topics are in some way or another "semeiotic" (PW December 23, 1908, pp. 85–86). *All* topics: but then, "in what direction are you thinking?"

Is the road of inquiry straight, and is it narrow? The original editors of the *Collected Papers* consider that digression is the sign of private, indeed monologic, writing, and one senses that it is for this reason that they adopted the somewhat aggressive editing policy that characterizes those volumes:

If the . . . merely private or preliminary nature [of some of the manuscript writings] is at all betrayed, this is because in them Peirce allows himself to follow out the ramifications of his topic, so that digressions appear which are inadmissible in print, but which show vividly the interconnectedness of his thought and the unsystematic character of his writings. (introduction, CP vol. 1)

More recent commentators have also taken Peirce to task for the digressive structure of his writing, taking that structure as a justification for overlooking Peirce's text as text. Yet all exemplification is potentially digressive; I would have had little matter had I done likewise. James Liszka has his doubts about the value both of digression and of exemplification, short-circuiting the former and preferring "illustration" to the latter:

Let's be frank. Peirce's writing is terse and convoluted, without much wit or grace. . . . His examples are obscure and exotic, and so they confuse rather than help. He has a tendency toward digression. As a result, I don't quote Peirce as much as I should, although I reference the relevant passages profusely. Where Peirce's own examples are enlightening, I use them; otherwise I devise ones I believe convey the same illustration.[4]

I believe Liszka gives too much credit to Peirce's own lamentations concerning the difficulties of writing. These lamentations abound in the late manuscripts, but in his active career, both as a professional scientist and as a logician, Peirce was very productive, writing and publishing several papers and reports every year, in admirably lucid prose.[5] Welby evidently found some of the letters difficult, but she also found his letters "living" (WP January 21, 1909, p. 86) and discerned in them a "commanding power of thought and exposition" (WP April 1909, p. 130). It is simply not true that writing was a problem for him until the period when, retired from active scientific work, he embarked on attempts to write out his philosophical system. The difficulties of this period were material, but more to the point, they were rhetorical: he no longer formed part of a community of fellow workers whom he could address in a shared language. Increasingly, Peirce came to fear that he had no audience, and to accept speaking engagements with a kind of desperation in which he attempted to do everything at once. Doing everything at once, I note, is collecting everything he knows, every hard argument he wants to make in every field, every example drawn from the full breadth of his reading, and spelling out every presupposition, into a single genre, an "abstract of his entire system." It is not possible. Frequently in the manuscripts we find him acknowledging his failure. This is a typical passage:

> One of the most extreme and most lamentable of my incapacities is my incapacity for linguistic expression. . . . I have suffered grievously from it since childhood; and I cannot tell you how assiduously I have laboured to overcome it. I myself am conscious of the badness of my style, although I am probably not fully conscious of it. I can imagine one of my readers saying to another "Why can he not express himself naturally?" I can supply the answer to that. It is because no linguistic expression is natural to him. He never thinks in words, but always in some kind of diagrams. He is always struggling with a foreign language; for him, every language is foreign. (MS 632, 5–7)

I must agree, but I would not attribute the point to a personal incapacity. Conversing with neighbors is always a matter of speaking a foreign language and teaching them to speak one's own. This is what Peirce and Welby achieve. Perhaps it is chiefly that written form of conversation that results in a correspondence that can do so. Its forms of composition admit the vagabondage across fields and topics, the asides, the examples, the passage from logic to autobiography, debate to interpersonal concern. Conversation in this sense is transgeneric, and it is for this reason—its rhetorical powers to allude to and appropriate a range of other genres—that the term *conversation* is frequently used in philosophical discourse to refer to an undifferentiated class of human semiosic practices. But conversation strictly so called is a particular genre, deploying a range of particular rhetorical powers that enable it to wander among a variable collection of other genres. It does not include them so much as refer to them and use them for its own purposes. One of these purposes is to bring into contact genres that are held separate under other circumstances.

The benchmark for good style in Peirce's lifelong experience was the James family. Well, yes, it must have been hard. . . . At best, Peirce's writing is a kind of no-nonsense plain style; at worst, it is crabbed and compositionally inept. But he could turn a joke and tell a story, and when he expounds a technical argument, whether in logic or in a scientific report, the writing is limpid, if uncompromising. There is a tendency in the scholarship to elide the issue of style with Peirce's own sense of failure at the end of his career; I prefer to interpret the fact that he did not publish a philosophical treatise as a technical issue of rhetorical practice. I propose two ways of considering it in this light: the first derives from an argument expounded by Chaïm Perelman concerning the argumentative strategies of two styles of metaphysics,[6] and the second extrapolates from this to an explanation in terms of genre.

Perelman establishes a distinction between what he terms *first philosophies* and what he terms *regressive philosophies*, meaning by the former those that rest on an absolute and necessary a priori principle, and by the latter those that rest on first principles that derive from matters of fact (p. 157). Where first philosophies posit an eternal and immutable foundation that stands independently of all further research, regressive philosophies consider such principles as provisional (pp. 159–63). Insofar as such principles count as a limit, that limit is a horizon subject to further research (hence the term *regressive*). While first philosophies seek the completion of their system, regressive philosophies accept that any system erected on such bases is subject to revision and correction. Perelman does not mention Peirce; nevertheless, his description of regressive philosophies seems to apply precisely to pragmatism as he developed it, a "truly scientific philosophy." This impression is confirmed when he goes on to detail a further characteristic of regressive philosophies: this he calls the principle of responsibility, which holds that it is human judgment, not any transcendental criterion external to the system itself, that is responsible for the choices made within the system (p. 165). This implies, Perelman argues, a place for rhetoric, for it is rhetoric that deals with the business of *preferring* one method, or one outcome, or one line of research, over another. In Peirce's work, there is a principle for making such choices: it is the pragmatic maxim and its corollaries. A *maxim*: unprovable, eminently human, customary, and not divine.

By means of this distinction, it is possible to analyze Peirce's difficulties as follows. His philosophy is "regressive" in Perelman's sense: it rests on the *indubitable in fact*; it is in principle imperfect, always subject to revision; and, in its 1903 version in the Harvard Lectures, it gives an explicit place to ethics, to responsibility, and to choice. Choice is a pragmatic business, and Peirce's concern was to make it principled: any choice we make must have practical consequences, and it must do the job better than some option we discard, where "better"—the issue of preferences—is handled by ethics and aesthetics. At the end of his life, Peirce sought a proof of pragmatism, but he was not seeking the kind of foundation sought by a first philosophy. Never would he accept that the first principle of his system would stand, as Perelman puts it, outside the "concrete conditions of verification" (p. 158). Accordingly, we find him hesitating between two starting points: one, the indubitable observations of everyday experience, that is, phenomenology; the other, the indubitable formal axioms of logic. In both cases, they are tested by their consequences, not founded. What would it be beyond this, to prove either of them? As Perelman puts it again, absolute first principles that stand outside conditions of verification rest on "intuition" (p. 158), what Peirce scoffs at as "feeling." In place of such psychological hypotheses, Peirce posits *signs.* Signs are just there; but they are there as a matter of fact.

When toward the end of his working life Peirce attempted to provide a proof for taking signs as his starting point, he sought to do so by means of the existential graphs. They would demonstrate, he thought, the truth of the propositions upon which his system depended. However, this demonstration could not rest on intuition: the graphs had to be shown to work in practice. So Peirce was inclined to start his drafts for his books with the rationale for the graphs, and with an exposition of them. But they, like all signs, are instruments; they do not admit of proof so much as testing. Peirce was therefore defeated by his own *dada,* the device for the translation of thought, the existential graphs. This device was needed as an analytical instrument in the arguments for the system, but the system was needed for the rationale of the graphs.

Perelman's analysis of the two styles of metaphysics suggests that Peirce was, as it were, caught between them. His model for a systematic metaphysics is drawn from the great first philosophies with which he had always taken issue—Descartes, for instance, or Hume—and above all from Kant, from whom he had always drawn his inspiration. His own philosophical work conflicted with this model. It had led him to two major principles concerning starting points: we start, he had written, from where we are, revising it if, and only if, we have grounds for doubting it, and we can start only by using sound instruments of thought, which it is our obligation to design for the particular tasks at hand. These are the working principles of pragmatism: they undermine in practice as well as in theory the principles of a first philosophy.

This does not mean, of course, that Peirce could not write philosophy: he did so, persuasively, for decades. Nor a fortiori does it mean that he could not write. What he wrote, frequently with great clarity, and again, most persuasively, were expositions of the instruments of thought—logic, probability theory, metrology—and arguments concerning what it was for philosophy to adopt not merely the findings, but notably the principles of scientific practice. What do we mean in practice, he asked, by coming to a conclusion concerning matters of fact? What do we mean by "reasonable doubt"?

New modern science does not write treatises; it writes papers on specific problems, on methods, on findings, casting doubt on or confirming those of previous workers. Peirce's work lies on the cusp of modernism in this technical sense: as Louis Menand sums up the situation, Peirce

regarded his work as an amplification and extension of what his father had done. This essentially meant adapting the worldview of science before Darwin to post-Darwinian thought—adapting, that is, a view predicated on the conviction that there is certainty in the universe to views predicated on the presumption that there is not. The task was impossible . . . [Peirce's] failure was of a singular and spectacular kind.[7]

Menand's account is a history of ideas played out across a generational cusp; mine translates this history into the problem of what it would be to write at this cusp. A treatise is a premodern genre suited to the disciplines that do not adopt the methods of scientific research, and Peirce's desire to write one conflicts directly with his espousal of the methods of science in philosophy. Tools, rhetorical tools like any others, are devised for particular purposes; they have their limits.

The pity of it is that so many of Peirce's commentators have understood the problem as one concerning the systematicity of Peirce's *thought*. There is no contradiction in his thought on this issue: he tried to write a systematic philosophy on pragmatic principles, and at all stages in his search, he approached the question as the philosophical problem of the starting point. The problem as I see it is a conflict between the rhetorical tools available to him and the task he needed them to perform. Accordingly, his commentators have sometimes sought to reconstitute a "system" from writings that were never devised to make a treatise, and James Liszka notably has found the model for this treatise in the "ladders of the sciences." Liszka's is a meticulous introduction to Peirce's terminology; it is a plain-style translation that contains the semiotic within a region, in the sense that it treats it as if it were a discipline whose language was a nomenclature and whose logic was given by its place in an ordered hierarchy. Liszka proceeds by reading down the ladders of the sciences, placing the semiotic carefully within the architectonic. The metaphysical categories then give the rule for reading the classifications. However, if this logic orders the disciplines according to a hierarchy of more to less abstract, the reverse logic reads the relations among the sciences according to the uses they can make of one another's findings. Indeed, if we are philosophers, or more modestly, semioticians, Peirce instructs us to work *upward*, since the special sciences furnish material to the general ones such as logic, phenomenology, and metaphysics (CP 7.52). This is how Peirce himself works; it is a systematic practice of interdisciplinarity.

To illustrate this point, let me return to the description of the physicochemical properties of protoplasm (CP 1.392–94). It is misleading to read such a passage as if it conformed—or should conform—to the rhetorical taxis that subordinates example and analogy to a general point made independently. This subordination is frequently reversed in Peirce. The example, or the analogy, provides the premiss for an argument designed to reinterpret the terms of a general problem. An example is always cited from its home genre, and it brings with it the presuppositions of that genre. In this sense, one genre or discipline comes to disturb the presuppositions of its host. In this sense, too, most of Peirce's writing is a display of a methodology and an argument for that methodology. This method must, of necessity, digress, as exemplification always defers the pursuit of argument. If we do not read that methodology—and for Peirce, "rhetoric" *is* method—we simply, I believe, do not read Peirce.

For this reason, we must acknowledge that although Welby may count as the dream reader for her correspondent, returning to him the image of what he wanted to be, she is not in fact the exemplary, or even the ideal reader of his work. Indeed, she is the first in line of a series of readers who have sought in his writing exactly what he could not provide: a conclusion. Between the difficulty of the "starting point" and the impossibility of concluding, Peirce was no doubt, though unwittingly, a "loiterly" writer.[8] All of Peirce's writing "deviates"; very little of it pursues its direction without stopping to reflect on the individua of strange mien that it encounters on its way.

> . . . some effects of cuckoos. . . . (CP 8.119)

On one remarkable occasion in his correspondence with Welby, Peirce apologizes for not replying promptly to a cable from her and presents as his excuse "a curious event" at his house that prevented him from looking at his mail.[9] This curious event was a visit. There was a "for sale" notice outside Peirce's property, and the visitor had presented himself on the excuse that he was responding to it. But he was not. The Peirces found him to be an altogether attractive guest, and Charles enjoyed his conversation with him. Only when he had begun to see "that there was a mystery in him" and that he "hadn't a dollar" did it come to light that his guest was a refugee from an insane asylum. Neighborhood gossip prevailed, and the man was returned to confinement at the hands of rational order.

The letter is a digression, a diversion, so entertaining that it takes on independent status, entirely supplanting the topics of common interest to the correspondents, the story it tells remaining without acknowledgment or response. Let us offer it some hospitality by turning to the text of the letter and to the letter of the text.

Milford, Pa.
1911 June 3

My dear Lady Welby:

Your word of cheer by cable which would have made you really "dear" to our hearts if you had not already been so, did me particularly ever so much good; not that Juliette was not fully as much touched by it as I. Only she was not herself, I think, so despondent as I, and certainly had no suspicion of the state of my feeling, since I knew she had enough to bear on her own score,—and far more than she ought,—without worrying about me.

A curious event that was taking place in our household prevented my looking at my mail; so that I did not see your dispatch until it was too late to acknowledge it that day. I will tell you what happened. You know, or rather you don't know, that along sometime since the middle ages, I was for a year or two in charge of the Coast Survey Office, and that circumstance made me well acquainted with all the particularly clever instrument-makers in the country. (Besides, among the various operations for the proper conduct of which I was responsible was an Instrument Shop where new kinds of instruments of geodesy, astronomy, & micrometry had to be built. So you will easily understand that I came to have a tolerably thorough acquaintance with the nature of the species so many individuals of which I had to deal with as instrument mechanics.) Well, day before yesterday, Juliette being away, a man in one of those long grey linen coats they call "dusters" and a hat that looked as if it had lain on a dust heap several years made his appearance and wished to view the house & the place. For there is a board out directing people to inquire within about buying. I took him over the house with which he was frankly delighted; and his remarks indicated a positiveness & a kind of taste that is by no means usual. But I could not show him over the grounds &

so invited him to sit down and wait for Mrs. Peirce. So he began to talk & I saw at once that he was so skilled an instrument maker that I must have known him, for he was about my age. I was much attracted to him & so was Juliette when she got home. But I had seen that there was a mystery about him & felt pretty sure he hadn't a dollar. He was such a sympathetic person that one hated to be any ruder to him than was necessary, yet Juliette became timid when it turned out he had escaped from the state Insane Asylum at Middletown, N.Y. and though we are in a sovereign state, Pennsylvania, so that no N.Y. official would dare arrest him here yet he was evidently terrified at the idea of leaving until it was quite dark. In the morning he was the first object we saw yesterday, he took breakfast with us, showed better than ordinary good manners,—really delicate manners,—and a little later his son appeared with the hostess of a little inn where the father had passed the night before I saw him, & after a very touching but long discussion carried him off to New York City. That is why I could not write until today. For they did not get away until the mail had gone; and then we were quite done up.

So your cable came at a moment to do us both even more good, perhaps, than it would if we had been quite in our "assiettes." It was so very good of you, dear Lady Welby.

C. S. Peirce

Peirce is responding to a cable from Lady Welby, which in turn is a response to a previous letter. Not, I think, the one immediately preceding this one, but the one before that; these are still the days in which letters between England and the United States were carried by sea, and the letters between Peirce and Welby frequently crossed. In that previous letter (dated May 20, 1911), Peirce had detailed some of the material difficulties he was then facing. He had been invited to contribute to a volume of essays edited by a colleague of Welby's, but his letter opens by casting doubt on his capacity to do so: "I have put off answering your last letter as well as one from Mr. Slaughter, because I could not bear to say it was impossible for me to write for the book, and yet I do not see how I can." He goes on to tell Lady Welby that his writing is contingent upon finding a solution to his financial problems, to which end, he tells her, "We have been advertising the place for sale. . . . I must sketch my whole situation to you," he writes, with some embarrassment; "I don't see any issue to it." He is so ill, and so emotional, that he can "hardly hold a pen"; his wife also is ill; they live, he writes, in "ultimate penury," without a servant, unable to heed the doctor's instructions, and we know from other sources that when he writes that his wife "could not survive another winter in this house," he means that he cannot afford to heat it. But the letter is followed by a long post-script in which Peirce acknowledges that "the word 'penury' is probably an exaggeration" and registers his "fear that, in [his] eagerness" to make it en-tirely clear to Welby how very much he did indeed want to write for the volume (which was planned in her honor), "the letter might have the air of soliciting some aid." He and his wife are able to sustain life without run-ning into debt.[10] His letter is not, he assures her, this kind of discursive act.

A certain genre has thus been evoked and canceled. Accordingly, Welby responds not with an offer of "aid," but with what Peirce calls, on June 3, a "word of cheer by cable." "It was so very good of you, dear Lady Welby." Peirce's uptake is a simple act of acknowledgment and thanks. But a fortnight later, he writes again, fretfully: "Your cablegram . . . promised a letter. / I replied warmly to it. / No letter from you has since been received by me." Evidently wanting to allay the doubt on his contribution that he has cast, perhaps fearing to have offended Welby, or rejecting the image of failure that he has given of himself, he adds that "The piece for your book is getting written," but the reassurance is curt and ungracious. There is no allusion in Welby's further correspondence to this note. It must have crossed with the next letter, dated June 27. She explains that she too has been ill, encourages him to optimism concerning his situation in general and urges him to write the piece, which will be "very important." In a later letter (July 25) Peirce acknowledges that he "disappointed [Welby] and [himself] about the essay for the book or else held out hopes which I had no right to be confident that I could fulfil," thus closing this sequence of uptakes, and the correspondence tails off in the following six months, end-ing with the death of Welby.

The sequence contains a number of discursive acts—promises and the failure to fulfill them, apologies, explanations—and it is of some in-terest to note the extent to which both the failure and the possibility of up-take depends on material circumstances. Perhaps it is wise not to conflate this category entirely with "technology," but in fact many of those material circumstances are technological, not least of these being the carriage of mail across the seas, and the concomitant delay between act and uptake that this causes. Hence the crossed letters, and the misunderstandings and anxieties that accompany them. The cable overcomes this delay, but Peirce responds by letter, disturbing the material, temporal rhythm of responses. Had he not done so, he would not have told his story. I also note this de-tail: Peirce's material circumstances make him unable to hold a pen. Not being able to hold his pen is technically equivalent to not being able to tap into his brain. Sign production is the act of a body wielding tools. The technologies of writing are not incidental to writing; they are the conditions of its possibility.

Let me also note this poignant and eloquent fact. Peirce laments his lack of access to recent scholarly publications and adverts to this on several occasions. He no longer has access to a professional library (PW October 11, 1909, p. 134), and it is years since he has seen a new book in the areas that are germane to his endeavors (PW May 20, 1911). This is not an empty excuse, it is not special pleading. Scholarly writing is always the uptake of previous work. Indeed, this is primarily what Peirce means by "semiosis." Cut off from current debates, Peirce cannot participate in them. As Peirce himself insists, all thought is in signs, and the condition of possibility of inquiry is a scholarly community. That community is in part the material effect of the publication and circulation of books and journals, and, to a lesser extent, of access to a public transport system that would take an isolated scholar to a conference. Printing, bookselling, and the railway. Left only with the postage system, his body no longer a reliable instrument, Peirce was effectively—and he knew it—no longer an active thinker.[11]

Now when, on June 3, Peirce gives an excuse for not responding to the cable as promptly as he should have done, he recounts the visit of an instrument maker. Outside Peirce's property, there had been set a board "directing people to inquire within about buying." Accordingly, Peirce's visitor inquired within, and looked over the house, which he appears to have appreciated, showing a "positiveness & a kind of taste that is by no means usual." But Peirce "could not show him over the grounds," so he "invited him to sit down and wait for Mrs. Peirce." It is at this point that the pragmatics of the conversation changes. "So he began to talk." And Peirce accepts the change, his courtesy, perhaps also his solitude, inciting him to take up his end of the conversation. In it, he discovers the man's professional identity and reveals some of his own. He was an attractive and sympathetic personality, Peirce tells us, but there was a mystery about him, and when the nature of this mystery is revealed, Juliette "became timid." Peirce mentions the possibility of "rudeness," but the visitor himself had "really delicate manners." The issue of uptake here is clearly about etiquette, and each change in genre requires an adjustment. One of these changes occurs as the result of the arrival of a new participant in the conversation. We can only guess at the negotiation between Juliette and Charles, which led to a kind, but no longer a warm, solution: they allowed the man to take refuge overnight and breakfast next morning, but they did not invite him to stay as a guest. Charles appears, too, to have given him advice as to the legal reach of the state authorities—this is his uptake of the man's evident terror—but to have desisted from hiding him from his son and the interfering neighbor when they arrived to take him back into custody.

Peirce's story is offered as an excuse for not responding to Welby's communication; it explains his delaying two days, and it also explains why the cable did the Peirce household "more good, perhaps, than it would if we had been quite in our 'assiettes.'" Yet there is no sense in the course of the narrative that Peirce was "out of his *assiette*"; on the contrary, he seems to have enjoyed the visit. Unless he means by his *assiette* a set of habits, which he may well have done. If so, then, out of his *assiette*, out of his habitual forms of communication, he sends Welby a story. It is the first and the only time. In his *assiette*, he would have responded to Welby's cable promptly. Now the function of the storytelling is already double: it is an excuse, which registers a failure of uptake; and it gives a context within which Welby's attentiveness is particularly welcome. This second function allows Peirce to return to his habits; the very last paragraph of the letter is the response to the cable; and in this function, it is the expected uptake. The failure has now been repaired.

The visitor, too, has used an excuse, or better, a pretext. Needing shelter, this poor, dippy old man has used the "for sale" sign to give him an excuse for knocking at the door. It is not his initiative, this interchange with Peirce; it is Peirce's. The "for sale" sign is an invitation to passersby that he has taken up: inquiries welcome, it might have said. The visitor was not up to inquiry in the strong Peircean sense: *welcome* is the word that mattered to him. Still, he inquired, and semiosis ensued. He has taken the opportunity afforded by Peirce's invitation, and in response, Peirce takes advantage of his visit to enjoy a chat. Throughout the episode, semiosis is seen to be opportunistic. In its two moments, there is a generic structure provided—a sequence of act and uptake—to which first, a ploy for refuge, and second, a diverting conversation, have been grafted. We could extend this analysis to Peirce's letter to Welby: the response to the cable gives Peirce an opportunity to divert his correspondent, but at the same time, the diverting narrative gives him a way of repairing some pragmatic damage. But we may also speculate that Welby's uptake must have been embarrassing to Peirce; he read in it an image of himself that he had tried to dispel in the postscript to his previous letter. Peirce did not know how to respond to Welby's cable. His problem was solved when he found a way of avoiding the content to which the cable referred, telling a story in which he could displace the role of beggar on to his visitor and take for himself a role in which he retrieved his capacity to display his generosity, his knowledge of the law, his cultural and social authority, his dignity.

I think we should bear this in mind when we think about the pragmatics of semiosis. A genre can take advantage of the legitimating structure provided by another to achieve quite different ends. Sometimes these ends are not goal oriented. It may be misleading to think of writing, or any other semiotic practice for that matter, as working toward simple ends and singular outcomes, or as always standardized and habitual, as remaining firmly in its *assiette*. Nor is it particularly interesting to think of creativity as simply the "breaking" of habits, or the violation of conventions. What seems to happen—and we see it happen in this case—is that the habits are taken advantage of. Some genres, narrative for example, have the habits of cuckoos; they take up residence in other people's houses.[12]

Peirce's visitor talks his way in, and for a while, he makes a pretty good fist of convincing the owner of his bona fides. The house, called "Arisbe," itself has allegorical status in Peirce studies. Peirce constructed it as he attempted to construct his system, but he kept adding to it, one wing here, a further story there, a conservatory and a music room, many entrances and exits. It was his folly. It is easy to see how seduced he must have been by a visitor who was "frankly delighted" at it, who appeared to share his taste and who might have paid him for the privilege of living in it. Yet what happens is that once he has invited him to wait for Mrs. Peirce, the pragmatics of the conversation have already been diverted. This is no longer the uptake of the "board outside directing people to inquire within about buying." "Buying" has dropped entirely out of the picture. The visitor "inquired within," and, like Beckett's tramps, he and his host got talking to while away the time. That talk turns toward what Peirce and his visitor really do share: not the house or the system it represents, but an interest in, and a common experience of, technical instrumentation.

Peirce sets his reader up for this topic by reminding her of a feature of his professional biography:

You know, or rather, you don't know, that along sometime [*sic*] since the middle ages, I was for a year or two in charge of the Coast Survey Office, and that circumstance made me well acquainted with all the particularly clever instrument-makers in the country.

"You know, or rather you don't know." Peirce has been corresponding with Welby since 1903; this is 1911, and he has to remind himself that he has never told her before that he was a working scientist with an official position of this sort. This is a most interesting fact. He has an interest in instruments, he tells her, not just in representation, but in its technologies.

Peirce's visitor reminds him of his past, and reminds him to remind Welby, that instruments are in the background, somewhere, of his work. Semiotics is not the study of pure rationality. Signs are a craft of *homo faber*. Without them, there is no sign. And note, now that we are talking about rationality, that there is a sort of struggle going on in this text as to whether the visitor really was mad or not. There is no evidence that Peirce thought so, despite the opinion of the state authorities and of the worried son. On the contrary, Peirce enjoys his conversation, and one suspects that he identifies in his visitor some version of himself, finding in the man's conversation an image of his own technical authority and returning to his interlocutor the image of his skills and of their scientific dignity. Is technology the madness of signs, in that it has nothing to do with the reason of pure reason? Or does it, as I believe Peirce thought, have its own rationality, which is the reason of practice? What exactly is the nature of the bond, between philosophy and the design and manufacture of tools? This question has very deeply to do with the nature of Peirce's pragmatism.

The identification between host and guest is not entirely fanciful. Peirce, too, had had to flee the reach of the law by escaping across state boundaries, taking shelter with friends in New York and entertaining them with his stories. This is called singing for one's supper. It is the way of the parasite, the guest who cannot earn his keep in any other way.[13]

Here I invoke Michel Serres, as well as Charles Peirce. For Serres, who makes much of the lexical identity of host and guest in French, the parasite is any element that both enables a communication and by its very powers to do so, can also disable it.[14] It is the guest who oils the wheels of a dinner conversation and takes over that conversation; it is also the machine without which there would be no contact between two terms, the machine, therefore, that must be sacrificed in the binary relation and at the same time is there to guarantee that relation. It is the *tertium quid*, the mediator, and Peirce would say, therefore, that it is the sign, the interpretant, the devices and contrivances of knowledge. It is the fence, across which neighbors do their business. Peirce's guest interrupts his conversation with Welby, but he also contributes to it. He is the reminder of the technical condition of semiosis. It is important for us, reading Peirce, to bear firmly in mind, that such things as microscopes and pendula, clocks and formal notations, telegraphy and the telephone, diagrams and maps are signs; they are *not like* signs, they *are* signs; like quotation and transcription, like book reviews and storytelling, they are instruments that construct representations and bring them into talk. Peirce insists that all signs do this, each in its own way according to its local protocols. Hence, on another occasion, Peirce writes to Welby that a certain class of signs is equally well exemplified by "a barometer or a written narrative of any series of events" (PW December 23, 1908, p. 85).

The issue of the technical or technological bases of representation has been at the center of concerns in recent poststructuralist philosophy. I mention Michel Serres, but also the significant work of Philippe Lacoue-Labarthe on Plato's account of mimesis, and Jacques Derrida's account of the *tekhnè* throughout his opus, but most particularly in *Mal d'archive*.[15] The technical is not merely a material support for signhood conceived as the product of pure cerebration but is the condition sine qua non of all semiosis. However, it is important to recall that the tradition of structuralist semiotics does not take this for granted. Saussure's account of the sign is determined to idealize all its dimensions, so that at the level of *langue*, the signified is a "concept" and the signifier is also a concept, the "mental image," merely, of a materiality. The result is that only at the level of *parole* can we locate material practices.

Peirce's account of this issue is more complex than this: the token is the sign of its type, and Peirce's account of the relation between the type and its tokens makes of the type a projected object like that of any icon, and hence dependent for its positing on the technical apparatus of its representation. Indeed, the very idea of the type is derived from printing, or, in antiquity, from the canon of tradition. If a technical apparatus is in principle the condition of possibility for any sign, this displaces the locus of activity from cerebration, from concepts, from the universal scope of the theory of knowledge in general, on to local contrivances, with their constraints, their limited and specific capacities, and their local applicability. The visit of the instrument maker is the story of a tension as well as of a bond, where, under the pressure of a certain tradition in philosophy, reason may treat technology as its other. Peirce's enchantment with his guest gives way to his guest's return under duress to the institutions of reason. But this is not the end of the story, because while the man in the shabby duster and crumpled hat disappears, he returns in Peirce's narrative, where he writes to Welby, "you know, or rather you don't know" that *homo faber* is an irrepressible part of our intercourse.

Peirce's visitor is a parasite in all of these senses. But I note besides that Peirce's story is parasitic of the pragmatic structures of his conversation with Welby, in just the same way as the conversation with the instrument maker is parasitic of the apparent structure provided by the inquiry concerning purchase of the house. This fact can provide a way of thinking about generic mixity. Because mixity is not soup, texts don't consist simply of bits and pieces stirred together. On the evidence of this example, one generic form that has no place in a situation takes advantage of a form that does have a place there, to achieve an outcome that is heterogeneous to that situation. It may, or it may not, undermine the intentions of that situation, and we have an example of each of these possibilities. Peirce's storytelling mediates his relation with Welby and repairs the pragmatic failure, thus potentially enabling the correspondence to get back on track.

But the visit is another matter. When the shabby old man comes to the door, he mimics the genre which has given him his opportunity. He did not have to undertake to buy the house in order to carry off his performance; he could simply have concluded the inspection of the property by saying, "Look, Mr. Peirce, I'm very taken with your house, but it's not quite what I'm after at the moment," and gone on his way. But the genre aborts when he can bring it to neither of these conclusions. Conclusion is not what he wants. He wants to stay. He needs the welcome of the house and the householder. To achieve this aim, he must divert the structure of the genre he has used before its usual sequence of uptakes comes to closure; to do so, he sings for his supper. Then Peirce offers hospitality, and he becomes a guest: their roles have changed, as has the genre of their interchange. In both these cases, the conversation, and the letter, we have generic mixity; in both, the opportunistic genre takes advantage of a host, but where in the case of the letter, the apologetic acknowledgment, the excuse itself, is maintained, in the case of the conversation, the parasite takes over; it is taken over in turn by a third genre, in which, notwithstanding his evident sympathy, wittingly or unwittingly, willingly or not, Peirce mediates the man's recapture. The story of Peirce's visitor is a story of the play of power: the parasite is more powerful than its host, as it appears, but is in turn overpowered by the forces of law and order. Notice that this story is one in which staying in one's assigned place is the rule. This is also the rule of pure genre.[16] But the law of genre is reasserted only in the face of its flouting; its function is to account for mixity, not to prevent it.[17]

Peirce's writing is largely generically simple until the last decade of the nineteenth century, at least to the extent that both the technical logic and the scientific reports are quite distinct from the writing of other philosophical projects. I have argued that by the time of the Schröder reviews, the generic separation of formal logic from philosophy is no longer acceptable for reasons arising from pragmatism. Logic must serve this project, and thus must subordinate its protocols—indeed, its very language—to the aim of dealing with positive contents. From then, generic mixity is the rule, and we have traced in the great writings of 1903 both the tensions subsisting from this mixity and its fruitful outcomes. But thereafter, mixity gets out of hand, in such a way as to prevent Peirce from finding a form of composition that could handle the "entire system." Has pragmatism occupied the project of logic, or is it the other way about? Peirce would answer that semiotic is the key to the unity of the system, and the draft introductions put this answer in various ways. This is a story of parasitism. Where semiotic had been an instrument in the critique of consciousness, and likewise—the second duty of the logician—an instrument for describing a notation, gradually it came to take on greater significance, and both the logic and the philosophy take on instrumental status in its invention. Add this to the need to provide a semiotic rationale for the existential graphs and a philosophical rationale for semiotic: we have a toolmaker's paradise and a philosopher's purgatory.

The story of the instrument maker's visit recurs in a draft introduction for one of Peirce's unwritten books, but it is somewhat transformed, again to a different end. There the visitor is "an elegant stranger," and the householder is seeking to let the house for rent; it is not for sale:

If one wishes to rent his house, and an elegant stranger appears at the door and expresses a desire to look it over, commonsense will stimulate the [owner] to explain all the conveniences of the dwelling that need any explanation, and to display its chief elegances without concealing any trifling faults that it may have, since it will be a contented tenant that he seeks, and not an incessant fault-finder. . . . Just so, supposing that he who is casting his eye over these lines has just taken up the volume from a book-seller's counter to see what it may contain, the writer is eager to explain what benefit he may gain from the perusal of it, as well as what he must not expect from it. (MS 678, alt. p. 14)

In this place, the story serves as a self-reflexive analogy, where the implied "for rent" sign and the owner's "explanation" perform the writer's desire, and the prospective tenant's inquiry, the reader's. Peirce's anxious desire for a reader is manifest in these late manuscripts, where his increasing, and increasingly painful, incapacity to write motivates a string of introductions, all attempting to give a foretaste of the content of the impossible book, and some spelling out "the kind of readers whom the writer would most welcome . . . such tenants as the house would suit best" (MS 678, alt. p. 14).

The instrument maker did not stay, but he was—as far as we know—the only person to come off the road and evince a desire to do so. Many Peirce scholars have sought to inhabit his dwelling, and many have gone so far as to reconstruct its architecture. I mimic Peirce scholarship, but I do so to parasite it to my own ends. These are to reflect upon genre, upon the genres of semiotics, and upon the technological condition of signhood; thus the cuckoo.

The story of the instrument maker could serve to illustrate all my themes. The man is a tramp, to all intents and purposes, appearing opportunely to remind us of the ways and means of semiosis—the language, the notice on the fence, the message for those who come after. Indexicality is of the essence in providing the conditions under which, staying awhile, he and his host converse. The board outside "directs" people to inquire "within," and he must have knocked on the door. Keen observer that he was, Peirce records a number of indices: the man's hat "looked as if it had lain on a dust heap several years"; "I saw at once that he was so skilled an instrument maker that I must have known him, for he was about my age"; "I had seen that there was a mystery about him"; "he was evidently terrified." Keen observer that she was, the hostess of the inn was able to direct the man's son to find him and thus, with Mrs Peirce's prior intervention, to thwart the conversation. Hence, the conversation comes to an end for contingent reasons, it does not conclude, and indeed, it furnishes the matter for further semiosis with a different interlocutor, reinterpreted to pursue a different end. Unpredictably for Peirce, it has served me beyond that.

We do not know how Welby would have read it. Would she have added the instrument maker to the list of New England intellectuals among whom Peirce was raised (PW March 14, 1909, p. 113 ff.), and his work in the instrument shop to his training by his father in chess and mathematics? Would she have connected this episode with the story of his discovery of logic and the list of things that are comprised within the study of signs? (PW December 23, 1908, pp. 85–86). Maybe she did not read it, not in the active sense of "read." But it is readable, and there *is* a connection in the final item of the list: metrology, the technologies of measurement, the very business of the instrument makers with whom Peirce worked. This list, which ranges from metaphysics and ethics to whist, wine, and "men and women," brings together under "semiotic" those fields which elsewhere Peirce separates as "theoretical" and "practical."

This is one of Peirce's most sharply drawn distinctions, and it is strictly generic, both on grounds of subject matter and of procedure. It develops within his project to classify the sciences, which itself dates from the two decades preceding his death. The classifications display considerable variation. At times (for example, EP 2:18, pp. 258 ff. [CP 1.180 ff.], Peirce divides the sciences into three branches: the sciences of discovery, the sciences of review, and the practical sciences. Within the sciences of discovery, mathematics and logic constitute one branch, philosophy the second, and idioscopy (that is, here, all the physical sciences) the third. The practical sciences are not outlined but can be understood to be anything not included in the sciences of review or of discovery. This is recast elsewhere:

I recognize two branches of science: Theoretical, whose purpose is simply and solely knowledge of God's truth; and Practical, for the uses of life. In Branch I, I recognize two subbranches, of which, at present, I consider only the first, [the sciences of discovery]. Among the theoretical sciences [of discovery], I distinguish three classes, all resting upon observation, but being observational in very different senses. (CP 1.239)

In this scheme, mathematics, philosophy, and idioscopy are all comprised within the theoretical branch. Elsewhere, "there are but five theoretical sciences," of which one is logic (CP 2.120). Following this passage, we read

I still persist in leaving unnoticed a certain subbranch of theoretical science [the sciences of review]; and as for the practical sciences, I shall merely mention a few of them, just to give an idea of what I refer to under that name. I mean, then, all such well-recognized sciences now *in actu*, as pedagogics, gold-beating, etiquette, pigeon-fancying, vulgar arithmetic, horology, surveying, navigation, telegraphy, printing, bookbinding, paper-making, deciphering, ink-making, librarian's work, engraving, etc. In short, this is by far the more various of the two branches of science. I must confess to being utterly bewildered by its motley crowd, but fortunately the natural classification of this branch will not concern us in logic—at least, will not do so as far as I can perceive. (CP 1.243)

Notice that the ingredients of ink, indeed of paper, figure in this list, as do many of the other "technologies of intellect"[18] we have come to notice as germane to the business of signs.

According to this distinction, in the conversation between Peirce and his visitor, Peirce might stand for "theory" to the instrument maker's "practice." Yet binary oppositions are uncharacteristic in his work. We must acknowledge, furthermore, that both the distinction between theory and practice, and Peirce's claim to the theoretical side of it, are late developments. His retirement from the Coast Survey in 1891 marked in effect his retirement from practical science; equally, his renewed interest in pragmatism, dating from the same period, staked his claim to "philosophy."[19] His attempts to theorize the bases of pragmatism can therefore be read as a claim to the dignity of theoretical generality as against the locally effective practical upshots of the daily grind.

It is this distinction that underpins the heated debate he entered into with William James. To understand that debate, we must also acknowledge that the word *practical* is among the most contested of Peirce's vocabulary: its range is such that it cannot be made to stay on its own side of the binary Peirce has drawn. "Practical consequence" is the key concept in the Pragmatic Maxim:

In order to ascertain the meaning of an intellectual conception one should consider what practical consequences might conceivably result by necessity from the truth of that conception; and the sum of these consequences will constitute the entire meaning of the conception. (CP 5.9)

Pragmatism is the principle that every theoretical judgment expressible in a sentence in the indicative mood is a confused form of thought whose only meaning, if it has any, lies in its tendency to enforce a corresponding practical maxim expressible as a conditional sentence having its apodosis in the imperative mood. (EP 2:10, p. 134 [CP 5.18])

For the maxim of pragmatism is that a conception can have no logical effect or import differing from that of a second conception except so far as, taken in connection with other conceptions and intentions, it might conceivably modify our practical conduct differently from that second conception. (EP 2:16, p. 234 [CP 5.196])

James and the "younger pragmatists" had taken up this maxim, and Peirce disapproved of their uptake. It was too close to the ordinary business of life, he thought, too far from the ideals of inquiry. In an attempt to rationalize his displeasure, he wrote this sort of thing:

Thus, pure theoretical knowledge, or science, has nothing directly to say concerning practical matters, and nothing even applicable at all to vital crises. Theory is applicable to minor practical affairs; but matters of vital importance must be left to sentiment, that is, to instinct. (EP 2:4, p. 33 [CP 1.637])

A similar view is expressed to Welby:

Reason blunders so very frequently that in practical matters we must rely on instinct & subconscious operations of the mind, as much as possible, in order to succeed. Thus, in my logic there is a great gulf between the methods proper to practical and to theoretical question [*sic*], in which latter I will not allow instinct, "natural" reason, etc. to have any voice at all. (PW May 7, 1904)

The "gulf" is now supported by a second binary, this one between two methods, "instinct" and "logic." Welby responds by rebuking him:

"Never confound, never divide" is in these matters my motto. And I had gathered, I hope not quite mistakenly, that you also saw the disastrous result of digging gulfs to *separate* when it was really a question of *distinction,*—as sharp and clear as you like. (WP June 29, 1904)

Even the distinction is hard to maintain once Peirce's predilection for three-way divisions is reasserted. In the following passage, there are "three classes" of men, and in order to make this good, Peirce introduces "art":

If we endeavor to form our conceptions upon history and life, we remark three classes of men. The first consists of those for whom the chief thing is the qualities of feelings. These men create art. The second consists of the practical men, who carry on the business of the world. They respect nothing but power, and respect power only so far as it [is] exercized. The third class consists of men to whom nothing seems great but reason. (CP 1.43)

This is a relatively straightforward version of the three categories, used here to differentiate true inquiry from its others. The first of the three categories introduces iconicity, and we should recall the significance this has in the formation of hypotheses. Peirce will find it hard to locate himself in one of these classes:

For men of the first class, nature is a picture; for men of the second class, it is an opportunity; for men of the third class, it is a cosmos, so admirable, that to penetrate to its ways seems to them the only thing that makes life worth living. These are the men whom we see possessed by a passion to learn, just as other men have a passion to teach and to disseminate their influence. (CP 1.43)

Furthermore, the analogy he introduces disturbs the opposition between theory and practice, for if the third class, the men of reason, have a "passion to learn," they are compared, here, with those who have a passion to teach. Yet "pedagogics," as we have seen, is a practical science.

The distinction is further disturbed by discovering that "natural reason" is not the opposite of Reason:

every science must develop its own method out of the natural reason of man; and that is the very way in which this method has been developed. Balancing reasons *pro* and *con* is the natural procedure of every man. No man can avoid doing so continually; and if he could, he would only have trained himself to the observance of rules having no foundation in reason. For reason is nothing but man's natural way of thinking, carefully and consistently observed. (EP 2:8, p. 78 [CP 7.172])

This, in turn, will disturb a further binary. A predictable, though predictably hidden, assumption in Peirce's opposition between instinct and reason is that the former is feminine to the latter's masculine.[20] Women, he writes to Welby, "are less likely to be influenced by theories of logic, and . . . their instincts . . . are better than men's" (PW December 14, 1908). Gender operates the "gulf," the "divide" on which Peirce relies to make his classification work. Women are practical, and their instincts fit them better for practical affairs than all the logical training of men, which too frequently results in blunders. This aligns them with the sea captain, whose "stout belief" is worth a great deal more in avoiding shipwreck than the soundest logical maxim of science (EP 2:12, p. 156 [CP 5.60–61]). He too is "practice" as opposed to "philosophy," just as it is in matters of belief that the instincts of "sensible women" are more reliable than the theories of men (PW December 14, 1908). But the difference between "instinct" and reason is at bottom only the difference between fast and slow, between "unconscious" and "conscious" reasoning. The following passage appears to take the difference as absolute, but its upshot is to give the rationale for logic. This is to spell out the processes whereby "stout belief," instinctive judgments, are reached, and then to submit them to "critic."

Reasoning unconsciously can hardly be called reasoning at all. As long as I simply find myself seized with a belief without being able to give any account of how I came by it, logic has nothing to say except to warn me of the extreme danger of my being in error. (MS 736, p. 4)

If Peirce believed stoutly in anything, it was that his work should investigate both the practice of reason and the reason of practice, hence his interest in method, all methods, those of practical affairs and the manual arts as well as those of science and philosophy. Practice it is that bridges the "gulf" between instinct and reason. Perhaps, too, it bridges the gulf between men and women, for the stout belief in this difference is a topic for semiotic and must not stand without scrutiny of its credentials as a representation. When Peirce writes to Welby about the visit of the instrument maker, he is—among other things—eliciting her interest in the work, the instrumental status, of signs, and hence in the nonsense that would ensue, were we to place semiotic on one side or the other of the divide between theory and practice.

"Pure theory" is not what concerns Peirce. The distinction between "theory" and "practice" is unsustainable for a pragmatist, and he knew it. The pragmatic maxim has its source in his practical scientific work, as an account of the relation between method, conceptual tools, and practical results. Hence the distinction between "metaphysical" truth and the truths of science. His later work is an attempt to transform this methodological principle into a systematic philosophy, and the distinction between "theoretical" and "practical" sciences serves to underpin the claim to do so. His philosophy is not to be a rationale for practical outcomes in the day-to-day conduct of life; far less is it the rationale for the calculations of power. He wants it to be an account of the search for truth, and the notion of practical consequences is therefore subordinated to this aim. But Peirce never reneges on the notion of practical consequences, and seeks to exclude from it only the kind of punctual action that is "other than" "such action as tends toward regularization." Explaining himself in a late letter to William James, he makes it quite clear that the only *practical* distinction between the two is between the short and the long term, secondness and habit:

That everything is to be tested by its practical results was the great text of my early papers; so, as far as I get your general aim in so much of the book as I have looked at, I am quite with you in the main. In my later papers, I have seen more thoroughly than I used to do that it is not mere action as brute exercise of strength that is the purpose of all, but say generalization, such action as tends toward regularization, and the actualization of the thought which without action remains unthought. (CP 8. 250)

Using the categories to make the distinction which he thought he needed to combat James, Peirce—it seems to me—undermined his own account of pragmatism. James, and many other people since, have taken the late Peirce as reverting to a metaphysical conception of truth over the practical consequences account for which his work is famous. I do not believe he was doing so, but the distinction between theory and practice made his position very difficult to sustain.

On the evidence of the manuscript writings, Peirce seems to have relaxed about the distinction between theory and practice following James' death. The drafts for the book Peirce reports on so regularly to Lady Welby can be found among the manuscripts of 1910 and 1911; many of these manuscripts are linked, or alternative drafts of one another. In one of these (MS 677), Peirce returns to the distinction between the practical sciences and the other branches. However, here the term *theoretical* is not the name of a branch; instead, the major structuring distinction is between the "arts" and the "sciences." The text lists as the branches of the sciences "heuretic" (that is, discovery) and "tagmatic" (that is, classificatory) alongside "practic," defining this last as "all research which has some inseparable purpose other than informing men of truth" (p. 3). The opening defines "art":

An *art* is, in one sense the practice, and in another, the theory or doctrine of the practice, of any kind of work that is so difficult as to require, for any distinction in it, the devotion of a person's best energies to it for many years. (p. 1)

Theory, here, has retreated to its proper place: it is reflection on, analysis of, practice, it is not its opposite, and the two work together. An "art" is distinguished from a "science." However,

It is to be remarked that the heuretic sciences are, one and all, arts, according to the above definition. Those that require the use of instruments are clearly so; and those that do not use instruments are the most artistic of all. Linguistics, for example, does not yet use material instruments; but it requires one to perform upon various languages. (MS 677, p. 4)

The title of the book, we learn from the following manuscript, MS 678, was to be "The Art of Reasoning Elucidated." Logic is the theory and the practice of reasoning, an explicit account of what is involved in avoiding shipwreck.

Only by understanding the deep solidarity of theory and practice do we understand what Peirce was about as he sought a satisfactory account of pragmatism. Only by understanding this do we see the significance of the term *art* in his very late work; though late, it captures an insight that pervades a lifetime of work.[21] And only by understanding that thought is nothing without its instruments do we understand his conception of semiotic. This, I believe, is what Peirce remembered in his conversation with the instrument maker, and this is what he remembered to tell Welby in this diversion, this digression from the system, enlisting her complicity with the arts of the sign and challenging her challenge to their errancy. It is a long lane, she replied, that has no turning (WP June 27, 1911). I hope to use it widely (WP November 20, 1904).

Notes

PREFACE

1. Anne Freadman, "Structuralist Uses of Peirce: Jakobson, Metz et al.,"
Sydney Studies in Society and Culture 3 (1986): 93–124.

INTRODUCTION

1. We can find the beginnings of this topos in the very first accounts of
Peirce's philosophy, written in the memorial volume dedicated to him of the *Journal of Philosophy, Psychology, and Scientific Methods* 13, no. 26 (1916) (the whole volume is devoted to Peirce). Royce, describing the manuscripts (and not only, we suspect, their material aspect), notes: "The papers are in many ways fragmentary" (p. 703), and of Peirce's contribution to psychology, he writes of his "fragmentary way" (p. 702). Dewey's reading of his pragmatism allows it considerable cogency, but Ladd-Franklin's account of his lectures at Johns Hopkins University describes them as "devious and unpredictable" (p. 717). All the writers in this volume refer to the difficulty, even the inaccessibility, of Peirce's work, Royce taking it as a deliberate strategy and Ladd-Franklin predicting that in the interpretive exercise offered by it to future students it may "remain forever indecipherable" for them (p. 720).

2. Christopher Hookway, *Peirce* (London: Routledge & Kegan Paul, 1985), p. ix. Further references will be given in the text.

3. Carl Hausman's is a recent proposal for a unified Peirce, read so as to reconstruct the architectonic. Such attempts are deliberately set against the tendency in so-called neopragmatism to give up on foundationalist systems. Carl R. Hausman, *Charles S. Peirce's Evolutionary Philosophy* (1993; reprint, Cambridge: Cambridge University Press, 1997).

4. Murray Murphey, *The Development of Peirce's Philosophy* (Cambridge, Mass.: Harvard University Press, 1961).

5. Manley Thompson, *The Pragmatic Philosophy of C. S. Peirce* (Chicago: University of Chicago Press, 1953). Thompson's strategy is to override the fragmented arrangement of the *Collected Papers* by retrieving the sets of papers published and delivered by Peirce—a strategy that contrasts with the genetic reading of Murphey and with the "collage effect" of some work on Peirce.

6. Joseph Morton Ransdell, "Charles Peirce: The Idea of Representation" (Ph.D. diss., Columbia University, 1966).

7. Max H. Fisch, "Peirce's Progress from Nominalism Toward Realism," *Monist* 51 (1967): 159–78. The argument of this paper is summarized in *Writings*, vol. 2, introduction, p. xxvii, and passim.

8. See Max H. Fisch, ed., *Writings of Charles S. Peirce: A Chronological Edition* (Bloomington: Indiana University Press, 1982), 1:xxviii. He adds that the backward reference is based on the individual apprehension, where the forward reference is collectively based.

9. Cf. Israel Scheffler, *Four Pragmatists: A Critical Introduction to Peirce, James, Mead, and Dewey* (1976; reprint, London: Routledge & Kegan Paul, 1986). Scheffler concludes an illuminating discussion of the papers against Cartesian philosophy with some comments concerning the historical importance of the cable metaphor: "the 1868 papers are very important. They express, in pioneering manner, a clearly modern philosophy, one that proposes fundamentally new ways of thinking about knowledge, based upon deep reflection on the import of modern empirical science" (p. 55). Peirce's "cable" is the first in a series of metaphors that Scheffler finds in Wittgenstein, Russell, Popper, and Neurath that "purport to capture that elusive, yet profoundly important capacity of science to construct, without certain foundations or indubitable beginnings, a firm habitation for man's knowledge, capable, moreover, of continuous use and continuous repair. It is Peirce's merit to have offered the earliest of such figures, but more significantly, to have appreciated the need for philosophy to rethink its conceptions of knowledge in the light of a new understanding of scientific thought" (p. 57).

10. The full set of the anti-Cartesian papers ("Questions Concerning Certain Faculties Claimed for Man," W 2:21, pp. 193–211 [CP 5.213–63]; "Some Consequences of Four Incapacities," W 2:22, pp. 211–42 [CP 5.264–317]; and "Grounds of Validity of the Laws of Logic: Further Consequences of Four Incapacities," W 2:23, pp. 242–72 [CP 5.318–57]) is concerned with arguing this position and its implications.

11. When Peirce writes that "every endless series must logically have a limit" (e.g., EP 2:22, p. 323), he means this in the technical sense of the calculus. This applies to the interpretant of "nothing" that "hovers" "*ad infinitum*" between vagueness and determinacy and a fortiori of any other sign, for semiosis seeks to determine that which is vague: "A symbol is essentially a purpose, that is to say, is a representation that seeks to make itself definite, or seeks to produce an interpretant more definite than itself" (EP 2:22, p. 323). I think it is a serious misinterpretation to take it as implying that semiosis must end.

12. The text of these lectures has been published in a variorum edition by Patricia Turrisi, to which I shall refer on occasion. For the sake of consistency, all textual references are to *The Essential Peirce*, vol. 2. The 1903 work has attracted particular attention in several recent studies of Peirce's semiotic; see, for example, T. L. Short, "Life Among Legisigns," *Transactions of the Charles S. Peirce Society* 18, no. 4 (1982): 285–310; and Priscila Farias and Joao Queiroz, "Notes for a Dy-

namic Diagram of Charles Peirce's Classifications of Signs," *Semiotica* 131, no. 1/2 (2000): 19–44.

13. For an elaboration of these claims, see Anne Freadman, "Peirce's Second Classification of Signs," in *Peirce's Doctrine of Signs: Theory, Applications, and Connections*, ed. Vincent Colapietro and Thomas Olshewsky (Berlin: Mouton de Gruyter, 1996), 143–60. Some of the arguments presented in this article will be restated in Chapter 3.

14. A detailed account of the professional interactions of Peirce and James in 1897–98 is given by Kenneth Laine Ketner and Hilary Putnam, in their introduction to the volume published as Charles Sanders Peirce, *Reasoning and the Logic of Things: The Cambridge Conferences — Lectures of 1898* (Cambridge, Mass.: Harvard University Press, 1992).

15. Karl-Otto Apel's view is that the two strands of "pragmatism" are present in Peirce's own work from the outset; hence, the difference between them does not depend on James' uptake. Karl-Otto Apel, *Charles S. Peirce: From Pragmatism to Pragmaticism*, trans. John Michael Krois (Amherst: University of Massachusetts Press, 1981).

16. See Richard Robin, "Classical Pragmatism and Pragmatism's Proof," in *The Rule of Reason: The Philosophy of Charles Sanders Peirce*, ed. Jacqueline Brunning and Paul Forster (Toronto: University of Toronto Press, 1997), 139–52.

17. Susan Haack, *Confessions of a Passionate Moderate* (Chicago: University of Chicago Press, 1998), pp. 125, 133 n. 66. For Peirce's review of Welby, see Charles S. Hardwick, ed., *Semiotic and Significs: The Correspondence Between Charles S. Peirce and Victoria Lady Welby* (Bloomington: Indiana University Press, 1977), appx. A. The review is also printed at CP 8.171–85.

18. Peirce did, to be sure, move from the propositional logic that sustains "On a New List of Categories" to the genre called variously "algebraic," "mathematical," and then "symbolic logic" through the 1870s; this is certainly a "biographical" fact, and the order in time of the two papers is certainly not negligible. But it does not gainsay my point, because this move itself corresponds to a generic shift.

19. Jean-François Lyotard, *The Differend: Phrases in Dispute*, trans. Georges van den Abbeele (Minneapolis: University of Minnesota Press, 1988).

20. Further, as I have written elsewhere, any *theory* of genre is itself conditioned by the genre that requires it for some purpose.

21. I have written at greater length on this problem in "The Sign Hypothesis," *Versus* 85–86–87 (2002): 359–402.

22. Ross Chambers, *Loiterature* (Lincoln: University of Nebraska Press, 1999), p. 115.

23. John J. Fitzgerald, *Peirce's Theory of Signs as Foundation for Pragmatism* (The Hague: Mouton, 1966).

24. Cf. Vincent M. Colapietro, who asks whether "communication" is derivative or explanatory. "Immediacy, Opposition, and Mediation: Peirce on Irreducible Aspects of the Communicative Process," in *Recovering Pragmatism's Voice:*

The Classical Tradition, Rorty, and the Philosophy of Communication, ed. Lenore Langsdorf and Andrew R. Smith (New York: SUNY Press, 1995), 23–48.

25. When Peirce gives up the algebraic "style" of logic, he gives up the questions that only this style is equipped to ask, substituting for it the existential graphs, a notational system based on topology designed to investigate the properties of propositions. Do we count, then, two distinct genres of formal logic? Peirce's views on this matter changed, so that where "logic" is contrasted with metaphysics in the work up to around 1890, following this, "mathematical logic" is contrasted with "logic viewed as semiotic." Peirce's view of the latter, however, was such that it required a formal part, for which he designed the existential graphs. For my purposes, one genre—"formal logic"—will do, because certain issues concerning signs arise as part of Peirce's metadescription of both the algebraic and the topological notations that do not arise when he discusses the natural language devices of metaphysics, which interest him only for their representational content. For further discussion of this question, see Chapter 2 and the Conclusion.

26. In a remarkable text from 1904, "Ideas, Stray or Stolen, about Scientific Writing" (EP 2:23), Peirce raises the issue of genre and identifies this very provocation: "to talk about the style of a scientific communication [is] somewhat like talking of the moral character of a fish" (p. 325). However, "our conception of rhetoric has got to be generalized" because "a proposition of geometry, a definition of a botanical species, a description of a crystal or of a telescopic nebula is subject to a mandatory form of statement that is artificial in the extreme" (p. 326).

CHAPTER 1

1. The question of whether Peirce's semiotic is transcendental or empirical is considered in an illuminating article by Klaus Oehler, "Is a Transcendental Foundation of Semiotics Possible? A Peircean Consideration," *Transactions of the Charles S. Peirce Society* 23, no. 1 (1986): 45–63. Oehler's is a concerted dismantling of Apel's position and of Habermas' early work, with a view to answering his question in the negative and to reading Peirce's semiotic as empirical and based on a formal foundation, rather than a transcendental one. My reading will support this view, but I shall also argue that there are problem points in Peirce's work where traces of transcendentalism are in evidence.

2. Immanuel Kant, *Critique of Pure Reason*, trans. Norman Kemp Smith (1929; reprint, London: Macmillan, 1982), p. 7. This sentence has no counterpart in the preface to the second edition.

3. For an analysis of the language of Greek philosophy, see Emile Benveniste, "Categories of Thought and Language," chap. 6. in *Problems in General Linguistics*, trans. Mary Elizabeth Meek (Coral Gables: University of Miami Press, 1971); and for a reading of this piece, see Jacques Derrida, "The Supplement of Copula: Philosophy Before Linguistics," in *Margins of Philosophy*, trans. Alan Bass, pp. 175–206 (Chicago: University of Chicago Press, 1982).

4. John Frow, *Marxism and Literary History* (Cambridge, Mass.: Harvard University Press, 1986), chap. 3.

5. Karl-Otto Apel, *Charles S. Peirce: From Pragmatism to Pragmaticism*, trans. John Michael Krois (Amherst, Mass.: University of Massachusetts Press, 1981).

6. Apel, *Charles S. Peirce*, pp. 34–36.

7. Apel, *Charles S. Peirce*, p. 38.

8. The "theory already established" is a citation to the very first paragraph of Kant's *Critique of Pure Reason*: "There can be no doubt that all our knowledge begins with experience. For how should our faculty of knowledge be awakened into action did not objects affecting our senses partly of themselves produce representations, partly arouse the activity of our understanding to compare these representations, and, by combining or separating them, work up the raw material of the sensible impressions into that knowledge of objects which is entitled experience?" (p. 41, B1).

9. Max Fisch, introduction to *Writings of Charles S. Peirce: A Chronological Edition* (Bloomington: Indiana University Press, 1982).

10. Gilles Deleuze, *Difference and Repetition*, trans. Paul Patton (London: Athlone Press, 1994).

11. Christopher Hookway, *Peirce* (London: Routledge, 1985), p. 17. Thus, continues Hookway, Peirce's logic is restricted "to a particular set of facts about representations—those involved with the reference of words and predicates, the truth conditions of sentences and the validity of arguments."

12. Some helpful comments on this question are to be found in T. L. Short, "Life Among the Legisigns," *Transactions of the Charles S. Peirce Society* 18, no. 4 (1982): 285–310: "Something is a sign in virtue of a *ground*—or relation of sign to object—that would justify a particular interpretation of it" (p. 285).

13. Peirce frequently argues from the relative logic that the appearance of a four-term relation is resolved into two triads; this is the case of one sign that is interpreted in a subsequent sign. See *Reasoning and the Logic of Things: The Cambridge Conferences—Lectures of 1898*, edited by Kenneth Laine Ketner and Hilary Putnam (Cambridge, Mass.: Harvard University Press, 1992), Lecture 3.

14. Peirce took pains to distance his later work from Hegel, but the "New List" was first published in the leading neo-Hegelian journal of its day.

15. An alternative reading of the ground as the foundation of meaning in the real is given by Hausman: "Every sign is caught up in an interpretive web. At the same time, however, interpretation is itself grounded in something that prevents interpretation from being arbitrary. One reason for the resistance to arbitrariness has been overlooked by some commentators who believe themselves to be adopting Peirce's theory of signs. The reason lies in what Peirce says about the way a sign stands for something *in some respect*. The respect is the *ground* of the sign or representamen. . . . Meaning is grounded in a real, a condition that functions in part independently of any particular sign and any particular interpretation." Carl Hausman, *Charles S. Peirce's Evolutionary Philosophy* (Cambridge: Cambridge University Press, 1993), p. 9. I think my reasons for rejecting this account are plain. Just as we require extra features to describe subclasses of any class, so do we require extra features to account for the regulation of meaning under specific empirical

conditions. Hausman's mistake, it seems to me, lies in his requirement that the basic structure of semiosis correspond with the regulatory protocols of a pragmatic account of inquiry. It also presupposes a metaphysics in the logic. Consistently with his position on these issues, Hausman also questions "whether nongeneral terms can be meaningful," limiting his account of pragmatism effectively to symbols and including icons and indices only when they are integrated into propositions (p. 7 and passim). The present chapter is my discussion of why this position, while perhaps adequate to deal with "inquiry," is unnecessarily narrow in respect of the sign hypothesis in general.

16. Robert Innis, *Consciousness and the Play of Signs* (Bloomington: Indiana University Press, 1994).

17. cf. Umberto Eco and Thomas A. Sebeok, *The Sign of Three: Dupin, Holmes, Peirce* (Bloomington: Indiana University Press, 1988).

18. Compare Oehler's denunciation of "German idealism" and "the age-old German longing for the Blue Flower of ultimate foundations" with Peirce's attribution of Royce's error to "German metaphysics." This review gives textual justification, if it is needed, to Oehler's claim that "Peirce manages without a transcendental model of any kind, and is as far as can be from invoking one" ("Transcendental Foundation," p. 54).

19. Royce later was won over to a kind of idealist pragmatism, for which he declared himself indebted to Peirce. I discuss this briefly in Chapter 4.

20. C. J. Misak, *Truth and the End of Inquiry: A Peircean Account of Truth* (Oxford: Clarendon Press, 1991), p. 83.

21. It is of some interest to note that Peirce conducts his polemic against Hegelian idealism in almost exactly parallel terms to the way he conducts his polemic against nominalism. Here, the diagnosis that "the capital error of Hegel which permeates his whole system, in every part of it is that he almost altogether ignores the Outward Clash" can be translated into the categorial scheme by saying that Hegel leaves out experience of brute existence—i.e., secondness; the polemic against nominalism takes the form of diagnosing the absence of thirdness: "I see a great many thinkers who are trying to construct a system without putting any thirdness into it. Among them are some of my best friends who acknowledge themselves indebted to me for ideas but have never learned the principal lesson" (PW, October 12, 1904, pp. 28–29). The struggle against nominalism became far more dominant in the last decades of Peirce's life, when the issue of idealism had receded, partly because, one supposes, Royce himself, the leading Hegelian of his day, appears to have taken some account of Peirce's views as expressed in this review.

22. Mitchell's work was independent of Frege's and almost exactly contemporaneous with it. Frege's system became canonical as a result of Russell's use of it. See J. Jay Zeman, "Peirce's Philosophy of Logic," *Transactions of the Charles S. Peirce Society* 22, no. 1 (1986): 1–22.

23. In a valuable assessment, John Fitzgerald considers some of the apparent ambiguities in Peirce's account of the symbol; notably, he writes, "it is the fact

that law serves as the basis for the relation of sign to object that constitutes a Symbol as such" (p. 164). We might labor the point by adding "the only basis." See John Fitzgerald, "Peirce's Doctrine of Symbol," in Vincent Colapietro and Thomas Olshewsky, eds., *Peirce's Doctrine of Signs: Theory, Applications, and Connections* (Berlin: Mouton de Gruyter, 1996), pp. 161–72.

24. George Boole, *An Investigation of the Laws of Thought* (1854; reprint, New York: Dover, 1951). Subsequent references to this text are cited parenthetically.

25. The history of this claim is the subject of Umberto Eco's *The Search for the Perfect Language* (Oxford: Blackwell, 1995).

26. This becomes a significant polemical issue for Peirce at the time when he comes to the end of his active contribution to algebraic methods in logic. His reviews of Schröder (CP 3.425–55; CP 7.456–552) spell out this issue in some detail and are considered below, in Chapter 2.

27. I allude to Jacques Derrida's remarks concerning the importance of formal systems of notation in his deconstruction of the sign as modeled on "speech." See *Of Grammatology*, trans. Gayatri Chakravorty Spivak (Baltimore: Johns Hopkins University Press, 1976); *Speech and Phenomena, and Other Essays on Husserl's Theory of Signs*, trans. David B. Allison (Evanston: Northwestern University Press, 1973); and *Positions*, trans. Alan Bass (London: Athlone Press, 1981). I quote from this last: "It is clear that the reticence, that is, the resistance to logical-mathematical notation has always been the signature of logocentrism and phonologism in the event to which they have dominated metaphysics and the classical semiological and linguistic projects. . . . Everything that has always linked *logos* to *phonè* has been limited by mathematics, whose progress is in absolute solidarity with the practice of a nonphonetic inscription. . . . But the extension of mathematical notation, and in general the formalization of writing, must be very slow and very prudent, at least if one wishes it to take over *effectively* the domains from which it has been excluded so far. . . . We must also be wary of the 'naïve' side of formalism and mathematism, one of whose secondary functions in metaphysics, let us not forget, has been to complete and confirm the logocentric theology which they otherwise could contest. . . . The effective progress of mathematical notation . . . goes along with the deconstruction of metaphysics, with the profound renewal of mathematics itself, and the concept of science for which mathematics has always been the model" (pp. 34–35). I do not claim that Peirce's work on formal notations has the deconstructive effects that Derrida envisages, nor indeed, on the other hand, that it was "naive" in Derrida's sense. Rather, the problems that Peirce raises concerning signs in this work demonstrate how formal languages unsettle certain presuppositions concerning "language." However, when formal languages are conceived to do nothing more than to represent "natural" languages, they are restrained from having these effects. My contention in this part of my argument is just that technical logicians may say that that is what their formal languages do, but the work they do on those formal languages cannot, by its very project, be confined to or by that representational function. Peirce's late work, on the existen-

tial graphs, is explicitly a project to constrain a (topological) notation back to its secondary role in the representation of "ordinary language"; yet even here, as he works on its technical instrumentality, other questions arise.

28. See Philip P. Wiener, *Evolution and the Founders of Pragmatism* (Cambridge, Mass.: Harvard University Press, 1949).

29. I discuss the ambiguities of Peirce's analyses of the symbol in the Conclusion.

30. Vincent Colapietro, "Two Rival Conceptions of the Semiological Ideal: Peirce Versus Saussure," *FACE* 1 (August 1991): 135–58.

31. Consistently in his ladders of the sciences, Peirce treats logic as one of the fundamental general sciences, in the sense that it is used by all the others; nevertheless, the technical work that advances it as a science is evidently highly specialized, and it is in this sense that I intend what might otherwise count as a contentious claim. The same will be true of semiotic, for although "the whole world is perfused with signs" and "logic viewed as semiotic" is a fundamental general science, when Peirce elaborates his theses concerning the sign hypothesis, the classes of signs, and their modes of acting, semiotic is classificatory and descriptive in exactly the ways that pertain for others of the special sciences.

CHAPTER 2

1. "The Regenerated Logic," *Monist* 7 (1896): 19–40; and "The Logic of Relatives," *Monist* 7 (1897): 161–217.

2. Max H. Fisch, ed., introduction to *Writings of Charles S. Peirce: A Chronological Edition* (Bloomington: Indiana University Press, 1982), 2:xxviii.

3. See *Writings*, vol. 3, introduction, for a detailed account of this work and of the celebrated discussions of the Cambridge Metaphysical Club from which it emerged. It is in the series of papers entitled "Illustrations of the Logic of Science" that the pragmatic maxim first makes its appearance, and it is the informal paper read to the Metaphysical Club that is presumed to lie at the source of the published series to which William James referred in 1898, when he attributed the doctrine of pragmatism to Peirce. For a more detailed account of these issues, see Louis Menand, *The Metaphysical Club: A Story of Ideas in America* (New York: Farrar, Straus & Giroux, 2001); see especially chap. 9.

4. Ian Hacking, *Why Does Language Matter to Philosophy?* (Cambridge: Cambridge University Press, 1975). Hacking uses this move to trace the major shifts in the history of philosophy from the seventeenth century, from "ideas" to "meanings" and finally to "sentences." Peirce's focus on "assertion" and "conversation" stresses the public dimension of "sentences."

5. The anti-Cartesian papers, also known as the cognition series, were published shortly after the "New List," in 1867–68; W 2:21, 22, 23.

6. Jarret Brock, "An Introduction to Peirce's Theory of Speech Acts," *Transactions of the Charles S. Peirce Society* 17 (1981): 319–26.

7. I allude to my "Peirce's Barrister: An Exemplary Story of an Example in

the Theory of Signs," *History of the Human Sciences* 4, no. 1 (1991): 93–106. The barrister example is first used in "On a New List of Categories," W 2:4, p. 54. It is discussed at greater length in Chapter 6.

8. The model is again Descartes, and the deductive chain of the *prima philosophia* is modeled on the expository techniques of geometry.

9. Discussing Peirce's critique of Descartes, Israel Scheffler writes: "Peirce argues against the mathematical method of 'linear' deduction, at least as applied in philosophy. Philosophy, he insists, ought rather to take the successful sciences as a whole, inclusive of the empirical sciences, as a model for its reasonings. It ought 'to trust rather to the multitude and variety of its arguments than to the conclusiveness of any one' (W 2:22; p. 213). The notion of a deductive chain of inference anchored to fixed and certain premises, and capable only of transmitting what is already contained in those premises, must be surrendered as a model of philosophical reasoning. Such reasoning should not be construed to 'form a chain which is no stronger than its weakest link, but a cable whose fibers may be ever so slender, provided they are sufficiently numerous and intimately connected' (W 2:22; p. 213). . . . Scientific reasoning is circumstantial, multiform, hypothetical, explanatory. Though it builds only on modestly firm data, the web it forms is extremely powerful." Israel Scheffler, *Four Pragmatists: A Critical Introduction to Peirce, James, Mead and Dewey* (1974; reprint, London: Routledge & Kegan Paul, 1986), p. 54.

10. Austin and the later Wittgenstein, he writes, "establish their sense that the voice has become lost in thought. It has become lost methodically, in philosophy's chronic distrust of ordinary language, arriving at some final crisis in analytical philosophy's unfavorable . . . comparison of ordinary language with logical construction; and lost theoretically, in the conclusions of modern skepticism" in, e.g., Descartes' astonished discovery of "his impotence to prove his existence." Stanley Cavell, *A Pitch of Philosophy* (Cambridge: Harvard University Press, 1994), 58–59.

11. See Richard Rorty, ed., *The Linguistic Turn: Recent Essays in Philosophical Method* (1970; reprint, Chicago: University of Chicago Press, 1981).

12. This range is theoretically innumerable, despite attempts to close the set and classify its kinds. Cf. Ludwig Wittgenstein, *Philosophical Investigations*, trans. G. E. M. Anscombe (1953; reprint, Oxford: Blackwell, 1989), §23.

13. A fruitful way of reading Benveniste's project to establish a linguistics of discourse would be to show, first, that his theoretical premises assume the irreducible separation of the assumptions of these two traditions, and second, that the drive of his work is to articulate them into a complementary structure. See Emile Benveniste, *Problems in General Linguistics*, trans. Mary Elizabeth Meek (Coral Gables: University of Miami Press, 1971). In various ways, this description holds of the whole field of discourse linguistics and can be held to account for its theoretical impasses.

14. "Language exists in the form of a sum of impressions deposited in the brain of each member of a community, almost like a dictionary of which identical

copies have been distributed to each individual." Ferdinand de Saussure, *Course in General Linguistics*, ed. Charles Bally and Albert Sechehaye in collaboration with Albert Reidlinger, trans. Wade Baskin (Glasgow: Fontana/Collins, 1974), p. 19.

15. For a linguist, the "dictionary" contains not only "words" with their representational definitions, but signs with their full grammatical specifications. Given (1) Saussure's strictures against construing "sign" as "word," (2) his strictures against the name/thing construal of sign, and (3) his insistence that the systemic value of a sign is specified by its paradigmatic and its syntagmatic relations, Saussure's own analogy does not partake of the same naiveté as the derivative accounts.

16. I have no doubt that one of the key episodes in this history is the appropriation of what is called "structural linguistics" by exercises of literary analysis. One of the key players is the early A. J. Greimas (who had been a lexicographer). See in particular his *Structural Semantics: An Attempt at a Method*, trans. Daniele McDowell, Ronald Schleifer, and Alan Velie (Lincoln: University of Nebraska Press, 1983); and his reworking of the Lévi-Straussian method in *Essais de sémiotique poétique* (Paris: Larousse, 1972).

17. See Walter Ong, *Ramus, Method and the Decay of Dialogue: From the Art of Discourse to the Art of Reason* (Cambridge, Mass.: Harvard University Press, 1958).

18. Standard exegeses of Saussure's "theory of the sign" (cf. note 16) are content to gloss the account given in part 1, chap. 1, where Saussure transforms the "name/thing" pair, first into "sound image/concept," then into "signifier/signified," and formulates the principle of arbitrariness. It is not until part 2, chap. 4, that he reworks the notion of the system by means of that of value that the theory of the sign is fully developed. The text of the *Course* makes it perfectly clear that the "signifier/signified" pair is a first approximation (p. 162).

19. Wittgenstein, *Philosophical Investigations*, §1–7, etc.

20. Wittgenstein, *Philosophical Investigations*, §21–27, etc.

21. Peirce's is not a unique example in philosophy of the use of the term *grammar* to describe the "structure" or "necessary features" of a concept. Cf. Ludwig Wittgenstein, *Philosophical Grammar*, ed. Rush Rhees (Oxford: Blackwell, 1974). Linguists tend to regard this usage as metaphorical. For Derrida, the project of a grammar that forgets its condition in *gramme* is symptomatic of the systematic marginalization of "writing" in the philosophical project in general. See Jacques Derrida, *Of Grammatology*, trans. Gayatri Chakravorty Spivak (Baltimore: Johns Hopkins University Press, 1976).

22. It should also be remembered, however, that for Peirce, thoughts are equivalent to, and the same sort of thing as, utterances of public communication. See Christopher Hookway, *Peirce* (London: Routledge & Kegan Paul, 1985), pp. 119–20.

23. Cf. Jacques Derrida, *Of Grammatology*; and Jacques Derrida, *Writing and Difference*, trans. Alan Bass (Chicago: University of Chicago Press, 1978).

24. Cf. Jacques Derrida, "Signature Event Context," in *Margins of Philosophy*, trans. Alan Bass (Chicago: University of Chicago Press, 1982).

25. For a more nuanced account of this purported opposition, see Ross Chambers, *Loiterature* (Lincoln: University of Nebraska Press, 1999), chap. 5: "the most haphazard of rambles show some degree of *suite dans les idées* . . . while the most logical of meditative progressions can have moments of (acknowledged or unacknowledged) *de fil en aiguille* looseness" (p. 127).

26. G. W. F. Hegel, *Phenomenology of Spirit*, trans. A. V. Miller, analysis and foreword by J. N. Findlay (Oxford: Oxford University Press, 1977), p. 61.

27. Vincent Colapietro, *Peirce's Approach to the Self: A Semiotic Perspective on Human Subjectivity* (Albany: State University of New York Press, 1989).

28. Wittgenstein, *Philosophical Investigations*, §19.

29. I borrow this notion from Arthur Danto, *The Transfiguration of the Commonplace* (Cambridge, Mass.: Harvard University Press, 1981).

30. Cf. MSS 454–55; 611; 654; 670; etc.

31. The distinction between "use" and "mention" corresponds in some respects to the medieval logicians' distinction between first and second intentions, frequently invoked by Peirce, with various attempts at formalization. A useful, if brief, account of its importance in formal logic is given in W. V. O. Quine, *Quiddities: An Intermittently Philosophical Dictionary* (1987; reprint, London: Penguin, 1990), 231–35. While its technical importance in formal logic is not here contested, it is apt to be reified and is misleading except in these contexts. Wittgenstein, *Philosophical Investigations*, shows the relative uselessness of the distinction in ordinary language (§16); it is open to deconstruction by "citationality" as developed by Derrida ("Signature Event Context"). Peirce himself points out that a sign is not sign unless it be *taken as* sign, an argument that would have the same effect if taken to its implications. The use/mention distinction is perhaps the same as Descartes' distinction between actors and spectators. But once you are on the road, it's almost impossible not to get involved.

CHAPTER 3

1. There are now three editions of the Harvard Lectures, the first in the *Collected Papers* (5.14–212), the second a variorum edition that publishes material from the several existing drafts of the lectures (Patricia Turrisi, ed., *Pragmatism as a Principle and Method of Right Thinking: The 1903 Harvard Lectures on Pragmatism* [New York: State University of New York Press, 1997]), and the third published in vol. 2 of *The Essential Peirce: Selected Philosophical Writings*, ed. Nathan Houser and Christian Kloesel (Bloomington: Indiana University Press, 1998). Because the *Essential Peirce* draws on the work in preparation for the Chronological Edition of the *Writings*, the version of the Lectures it publishes will become the standard version. In my analysis of the Lectures, I have worked from the *Essential Peirce*, including in brackets paragraph references to the *Collected Papers* where there is correlation between the two texts. Where appropriate, variants published by Turrisi will also be referred to. Note that the new scholarly editions do not use Peirce's coinage *pragmaticism* but instead use the standard *pragmatism* throughout. I shall follow them in this usage.

2. See my "Peirce's Second Classification of Signs," in *Peirce's Doctrine of Signs: Theory, Applications, and Connections*, ed. Vincent Colapietro and Thomas Olshewsky (Berlin: Mouton de Gruyter, 1996), pp. 143–60. Part of that article provides the basis for the argument I make below.

3. The integral edition of these 1898 lectures has been published under the title *Reasoning and the Logic of Things: The Cambridge Conferences—Lectures of 1898*, ed. Kenneth Laine Ketner and Hilary Putnam (Cambridge, Mass.: Harvard University Press, 1992). I shall refer to these by lecture number and page number where necessary.

4. Peirce, *Reasoning and the Logic of Things*, Lecture 3, p. 146.

5. Karl-Otto Apel, *Charles S. Peirce: From Pragmatism to Pragmaticism*, trans. John Michael Krois (Amherst: University of Massachusetts Press, 1981).

6. Turrisi, ed., introduction to *Pragmatism*.

7. Joseph Brent, *Charles Sanders Peirce: A Life* (Bloomington: Indiana University Press, 1993), p. 280.

8. Turrisi, ed., *Pragmatism*, p. 8.

9. Apel writes that the new role as "founder of Pragmatism," forced on him by James, "forced Peirce to return to an approach that he himself had always regarded as a maxim in the larger context of the logic of inquiry, not as the positive foundation and *ratio sufficiens* of a philosophy or even of a world view" (*Charles S. Peirce*, p. 81).

10. Klaus Oehler, "Is a Transcendental Foundation of Semiotics Possible? A Peircean Consideration," *Transactions of the Charles S. Peirce Society* 23, no. 1 (1986): 59.

11. Oehler, "Transcendental Foundation," p. 56.

12. Apel, *Charles S. Peirce*, p. 104.

13. Apel, *Charles S. Peirce*, p. 96.

14. Cf. J. Jay Zeman, "Peirce's Philosophy of Logic," *Transactions of the Charles S. Peirce Society* 22, no. 1 (1986): 1–22.

15. There exists one way of salvaging the foundational account of iconicity. This would consist in arguing for an "iconic faculty" along the lines of the "mimetic faculty" proposed by Walter Benjamin, "On the Mimetic Faculty," in *Reflections: Essays, Aphorisms, Autobiographical Writings*, trans. Edmund Jephcott, ed. Peter Demetz (New York: Schocken Books, 1986); and explored by Michael Taussig, "The Beach (A Fantasy)," *Critical Inquiry* 26, no. 2 (2000): 249–77. In Taussig's development, this argument goes precisely in the direction sought by Apel in that it argues for a continuity between the forms of mimesis found in nature (fossils, for instance) and human art. It is an open question whether this solution is compatible with Peirce's thinking on this issue. The concept of the Kantian faculties is barely alluded to in his work. This can be read in two ways: on the one hand, Peirce may have found the separation of the faculties incompatible with the totalizing continuity he envisaged, but on the other, it is most unlikely that he would base this thoroughgoing continuity on the generalization of a "faculty,"

which is human *ex hypothesis*, and located in what he would have thought of as "psychology." The issue of whether mathematics or phenomenology is the basis of the system has a parallel with the issue of whether semiosis can be theorized independently of human subjectivity, or whether it must rest on a subjective basis. This will be discussed in Chapter 6 and in the Conclusion.

16. It should be noted that mathematics can intervene at (potentially) any point of the process, again confirming its procedural, rather than transcendental, status.

17. Jarrett Brock, "Peirce and Searle on Assertion," in *Proceedings of the C. S. Peirce Bicentennial International Congress*, ed. K. L. Ketner et al. (Lubbock: Graduate School, Texas Technical University, 1981), pp. 281–87.

18. Moral goodness may be possessed by a proposition or by an argument but cannot be possessed by a rhema. Logical truth is the property of arguments. See Turrisi, ed., *Pragmatism*, 216–17. This claim concerning logical truth is accompanied by an argument to the effect that Peirce rejects the distinction between material and logical truth, or between the truth of a proposition (material) and the soundness or validity of an argument. His argument rests on this: "the only difference between material truth and the logical correctness of argumentation is that the *latter* refers to a single line of argument and the *former* to all the arguments which could have a given proposition or its denial as their conclusion."

19. The materiality of the book is of particular interest to Peirce during this period. As J. Jay Zeman points out, "in CP 4.510ff., he discusses a graphical system which will have not just one, but a *book* of sheets of assertion; each of these will represent a different possible universe of discourse"; this counts as a serious anticipation of possible world semantics ("Peirce's Philosophy of Logic," p. 9).

20. Michel de Montaigne, "Of Giving the Lie," in *Montaigne: Selected Essays*, trans. Charles Cotton and W. C. Hazlitt, rev. and ed. Blanchard Bates (New York: Modern Library, 1949), p. 227. I owe the remarking of this quote to Bill Everdell, who sent it to the Peirce-List, and whom I thank. The link I make between the Montaigne and the Peirce relies on understanding *moeurs* as being translatable both as "manners" and as "morals."

21. It goes without saying that Peirce has always attended to, and displayed his deep knowledge of, the history of philosophy and the history of science. I claim only that these examples—the Bunker Hill Monument and Patrick Henry's call—are symptomatic of a more self-conscious attention to historical time as the empirical condition of events, rather than as mere sequence, and that this kind of attention is intimately connected with the imperatives of pragmatism.

22. cf. George Benedict, "What Are Representamens?", *Transactions of the Charles S. Peirce Society* 21, no. 2 (1985): 241–70. Benedict inquires into the use of the term *representamen* in relation with "representation" and with "sign," asking whether it is to receive a technical construal and why Peirce seems to have abandoned it. He argues that the term must be retained because semiotic cannot do without a distinction between the sign taken as one term of the semiotic relation,

and the relation itself. My argument against this conclusion is that this distinction lapses when Peirce comes to distinguish the first trichotomy as a means of identifying the thinghood and the eventhood of a sign.

23. In one respect, my assertion that "he cannot" study the effects of the proverb is circular: he cannot study it until and unless he studies its enunciation in a particular context and scrutinizes what follows from that. The need to do so is precisely what is at issue in the introduction of the replica.

24. There is an obvious connection to be made between the author(iz)ing function of the grapheus and the ultimate authorities for the fictions, hypotheses, and professions of faith Peirce uses in the Harvard Lectures. Here, however, the chain of authority is itself avowedly a fiction.

25. PW January 31, 1909, p. 96.

26. Note that the terminology that is most familiar for the first trichotomy, "tone," "token," and "type," was introduced by Peirce some years after this first attempt at a combinatorial scheme.

27. For a careful gloss of the classes distinguished in Figure 3.4, see James Jakob Liszka, *A General Introduction to the Semeiotic of Charles Sanders Peirce* (Bloomington: Indiana University Press, 1996), chap. 2.

28. Irwin Lieb, in Charles S. Hardwick, ed., *Semiotic and Significs: The Correspondence Between Charles S. Peirce and Victoria Lady Welby* (Bloomington: Indiana University Press, 1976), appx. B.

29. Note that the first classification says of the line of identity and the proposition that they have the same structure, and may effectively be the same (kind of) sign. It is not clear that this would be the case under the second classification.

30. Priscila Farias and Joao Queiroz, "Notes for a Dynamic Diagram of Charles Peirce's Classifications of Signs," *Semiotica* 131, no. 1/2 (2000): 19–44.

31. Cf. Arthur Burks and Paul Weiss, "Peirce's Sixty-six Signs," *Journal of Philosophy* 46 (1945): 383–88; Lieb, in Hardwick, appx. B; Gary Sanders, "Peirce's Sixty-six Signs?", *Transactions of the Charles S. Peirce Society* 6 (1970): 3–16.

32. Cf. Douglas Greenlee, *Peirce's Concept of Sign* (The Hague: Mouton, 1973); T. L. Short, "Life Among Legisigns," *Transactions of the Charles S. Peirce Society* 18, no. 4 (1982): 285–310.

33. Priscila Farias and Joao Queiroz, "Notes for a Dynamic Diagram of Charles Peirce's Classifications of Signs," *Semiotica* 131, no. 1/2 (2000): 19–44.

34. See John J. Fitzgerald, "Peirce's Doctrine of Symbol," pp. 161–72 in Colapietro and Olshewsky, ed., *Peirce's Doctrine of Signs*, for a helpful exegesis of the twin notions of "genuine" and "degenerate" in Peirce's usage.

35. In a marginal note printed with CP 4.395, dated 1910, Peirce writes: "I abandon this inappropriate term, replica, Mr. Kempe having already ('Memoir on the Theory of Mathematical Form' [*Philosophical Transactions*, Royal Society (1886)], §170) given it another meaning. I now call it an instance."

36. Cf. Short, "Life Among Legisigns."

37. André de Tienne, personal communication, May 4, 1998.

38. George Benedict, worrying about the demise of the word "representa-men," considers 1903 to have been "A BIG Year" ("What Are Representamens?"); he is clearly right.

39. The example of "Hi!" recurs from time to time in the manuscript sources. A published instance of it, here uttered by "a driver," is to be found in Peirce, *Reasoning and the Logic of Things: The Cambridge Conferences—Lectures of 1898*, edited by Kenneth Laine Ketner and Hilary Putnam (Cambridge, Mass.: Harvard University Press, 1992), Lecture 2, p. 129.

CHAPTER 4

A version of part of the argument for this chapter was first read to a conference on genre held at Colgate University in September 1998. I thank the organizers of that conference for the opportunity to develop this material for that occasion. Another part, under the title "Peirce on Indexicality," was read to a seminar at the Department of Philosophy of the University of Queensland in October 1998. I thank the participants for their interesting discussion of the issues, in particular William Grey, Graham Priest, and Byeong-uk Yi for points they raised to which I have attempted to respond, and Roger Lamb and Gary Malinas for helpful discussions of the material on a previous occasion.

1. Peirce writes that the reality of experience is *esse in praeterito*, whereas the reality of a law is *esse in futuro* (CP 2.87).

2. In the case of proper names, Peirce stresses that they are only restrictively indexical, that is, on the first occasion of use; thereafter, they acquire the characters of symbols because their representations are habitual (CP 2.329).

3. Cf. John Perry, "The Problem of the Essential Indexical," *Nous* 13 (1979): 3–21; Geoffrey Nunberg, "Indexicality and Deixis," *Linguistics and Philosophy* 16, no. 1 (1993): 1–43.

4. This objection was put to me by Graham Priest in discussion.

5. This group forms the basis of Sebeok's account of indexicality. Sebeok uses this group to sustain his argument for a biological basis for all sign behavior. See Thomas A. Sebeok, "Indexicality," in *Peirce and Contemporary Thought: Philosophical Enquiries*, ed. Kenneth L. Ketner (New York: Fordham University Press, 1995).

6. As Ian Hacking remarks, Peirce "finished almost nothing, but he began almost everything." His inclusion of the technical instruments of science in the broad class of signs is a clear example of this dictum: it points the way toward, but does not complete, Hacking's own argument concerning the way in which scientific procedures, and the invention and operation of instruments for their implementation, "intervene" in the business of representation. "Often," writes Hacking, "the experimental task . . . is less to observe and report, than to get some bit of equipment to exhibit phenomena in a reliable way"; and again, "experimenting is

not stating or reporting, but doing—and not doing things with words." Peirce would write "mediate" in place of "intervene" and would balk at the idea of "creating" phenomena, but the point is similar: neither is observation direct nor the data raw for these philosophers, both of whom are arguing specifically against positivist accounts of observation. See Ian Hacking, *Representing and Intervening* (Cambridge: Cambridge University Press, 1983), pp. 61, 167, 173.

7. Umberto Eco, *A Theory of Semiotics* (1976; reprint, Bloomington: Indiana University Press, 1979).

8. This claim may be too strong. On the argument of some scholars of the later classifications, the relations among the ten classes are ordered such that only signs of a higher order can interpret those of lower orders, where the orders are defined both by the trichotomies and by the categories. For a helpful survey of these arguments, see Priscila Farias and Joao Queiroz, "Notes for a Dynamic Diagram of Charles Peirce's Classifications of Signs," *Semiotica* 131, no. 1/2 (2000): 19–44. The properties of the diagram proposed by Farias and Queiroz are such as not to require linear ordering of this kind, and my own feeling is that it is both wiser and more accurate not to constrain the model in any way that could imply a teleology.

9. In Chapter 6, I consider an issue that I gloss over here, namely, the difference it makes to Peirce's view of semiosis whether we limit semiosis to communication and to its acts, or whether we allow it to extend beyond this range.

10. Peirce is dealing here with a complex symbol, so we should expect that its components are drawn from the one trichotomy and that the sign of the idea is therefore an icon; on the other hand, given that the case is an assertion, the sign of the idea might be better construed as a term. The difference is of no moment, pointing again to the reduction of the classes under certain analytical circumstances. More interesting is the fact that Peirce's analysis is mixed over two protocols: the classifications of signs and the branches of semiotic. He draws from both as they serve his purposes, without being bound by their constitutive rules.

11. For a fine argument construing Peirce's "rhetoric" in terms of the twentieth-century problematic of "communication," see Mats Bergman, "Reflections on the Role of the Communicative Sign in Semiotic," *Proceedings of the Charles S. Peirce Society* 36, no. 2 (spring 2000): 225–54. The implication of this construal is that the understanding of "rhetoric" is advanced through the insights of a more contemporary problematic. Although some of Bergman's insights are indeed illuminating, I prefer to retain the term *rhetoric* because this word carries with it the long tradition of investigating the effectivity of public discourse without the romantic baggage that comes with the word *communication* (this latter often being modeled on personal interaction with the emotional and even psychological presuppositions that this brings with it), and because the basic presupposition of rhetoric is generic variety.

12. For example, contrast the example in which two travelers meet on a country road, where their relationship is socially minimal, with the example of two

scientists exchanging information concerning techniques of measurement at a conference, or by E-mail.

13. For example, while we may be friends with the colleagues we meet at conferences, we are normally careful to respect the decorum that demands the strict separation of the genres in which we exchange professional and personal information. The subject line in E-mails has the function of a generic separator in this sense.

14. Peirce's very explicit instructions on the conduct of the card trick provide a clear illustration of these elements.

15. This criterion is elaborated by Lyotard in *The Differend: Phrases in Dispute*, trans. Georges van den Abbeele (Minneapolis: University of Minnesota Press, 1988), where the difference between protocols of evidence and proof, in history, in the law courts, and in science is the central problem considered.

16. I have elaborated on this topic in my "Uptake," in *The Rhetoric and Ideology of Genre: Strategies for Stability and Change*, ed. Richard Coe, Lorelei Lingard, and Tatiana Teslenko (Cresskill, N.J.: Hampton Press, forthcoming). The argument of this is inspired by Peirce's development of the interpretant.

17. The analogy of games with genres is extrapolated from Wittgenstein's analogy for speech acts, "language games." See my "Untitled (On Genre)," *Cultural Studies* 2, no. 4 (1988): 67–99. If speech acts are continuous with genres, as Wittgenstein suggests, then Lyotard's hypothesis also extends across the scale of "small" to "large" language games. This is clearly consistent with the fact that his argument derives directly from an adaptation of Wittgenstein's work in this area in the first place.

18. Peter Read, *Returning to Nothing: The Meaning of Lost Places* (Cambridge: Cambridge University Press, 1996), pp. 68–69.

19. Yet another shocking fact about this object is that the stones have been set in concrete. This is not impertinent to the concerns of this chapter.

20. I have made the argument in several places that cultural knowledge is effectively coextensive with generic knowledge; some genres are shared across language boundaries, national boundaries, and other forms of delimitation; others are not, and there is no congruence, for example, between the spread of a genre and the spread of any of these other factors. See Anne Freadman, "The Culture Peddlers," *Postcolonial Studies* 4, no. 3 (2001): 275–95; Anne Freadman, "The Vagabond Arts," in *In the Place of French: Essays in and Around French Studies in Honour of Michael Spencer*, ed. Peter Cryle, Anne Freadman, and Jean-Claude Lacherez (Brisbane: University of Queensland, 1992); and Anne Freadman, *Models of Genre for Language Teaching*, the 1994 Sonia Marks Memorial Lecture (Sydney: University of Sydney, 1994).

21. Bruce Chatwin's *The Songlines* (London: Cape, 1987) gives a fine account of these practices for the area northwest of Alice Springs.

22. In the available information concerning the design of the Bunker Hill

Monument, Greenough is not mentioned. Loammi Baldwin is credited with the design. Peirce may have misremembered his source.

23. See http://charlestown.ma.us/monument.html (accessed October 23, 2003).

24. Evidently, I could expect an objection at this juncture to the effect that my analysis relies on a concept of original meaning at odds with the argument that all signs are subject to the rule of citationality. I do not deny that these signs acquire a different force as a result of their displacement, any more than I could deny the same proposition for the case of examples. However, the rule of citationality is trivial if it is not accompanied by an account of temporary stopping places. To provide that account is the point of Peirce's category of the index, and of my investigation of the rhetorical conditions of indexicality.

25. Mikhail Bakhtin, *Speech Genres and Other Late Essays*, ed. Caryl Emerson and Michael Holquist, trans. Vern McGee (Austin: University of Texas Press, 1986); Wittgenstein, *Philosophical Investigations*, trans. G. E. M. Anscombe (Oxford: Blackwell, 1989).

26. The Harvard Lectures of 1903 demonstrate how thoroughly performative Peirce's thinking had become. See EP 2, no. 10, p. 140 (CP 5.30–31), in which an assertion is explicated first in terms of "making an affidavit," and second, in terms of "laying a wager," under both of which circumstances, the speaker takes explicit responsibility for the consequences of the truth or falsity of the assertion.

27. My preference for the term *genre* over *speech act* is in line with my choice of rhetoric rather than communication as my general framework. See note 11.

28. Jacques Derrida, "Signature, Event, Context," in *Margins of Philosophy*, trans. Alan Bass (Chicago: University of Chicago Press, 1982).

29. I am aware that the Derridean argument, in *Of Grammatology*, trans. Gayatri Chakravorty Spivak (Baltimore: Johns Hopkins University Press, 1976); and in *Limited Inc.* (Evanston, Ill.: Northwestern University Press, 1988), obviates the need to state this argument, which is necessary only as long as one supposes that face-to-face communication, "speech," or *parole* is the paradigm case of language use. This supposition is shared by Peirce in the main, hence my use of it. It is not part of Derrida's argument, however, that face-to-face communication does not have its own specificity. See Derrida, "Signature Event Context," p. 327. In this sense, my conclusion—that it is a genre among others—is not in conflict with Derrida's deconstruction of the speech-act hypothesis. Were I to pursue a Derridean analysis of the problem of "the interface of my uptake of Peirce's work, and yours of mine," it would go something like this: the generic mixity of my "reading" (of any reading, taken as a genre?) displays explicitly the structural moment of *différance* that implies that no sequence of sign and interpretant is synchronic with itself. This conclusion is entirely consonant with Peirce's account of the temporality of the interpretant.

30. Note that in the case of formal notations, "left" and "right" refer to the material page in relation to the reading position; it is difficult (never impossible) to use them in written verbal discourse, where the spatiality of the page is rarely at

issue (again, not "never"), and where the temporal dimension is translated into "above" and "below."

31. Leonard Linsky came to the same conclusion: "In speaking about movies, plays, novels, dreams, legends, superstition, make-believe, etc., our words may be thought of as occurring within the scope of special 'operators.'" Leonard Linsky, "Reference and Reference," in *Semantics: An Interdisciplinary Reader in Philosophy, Linguistics and Psychology,* ed. Danny D. Steinberg and Leon Jakobovits (Cambridge: Cambridge University Press, 1971); from Leonard Linsky, *Referring* (London: Routledge & Kegan Paul, 1967).

CHAPTER 5

1. I rely here on Paul Chipchase, "Some Account of the Literary Production of Lady Welby and Her Family," in *Essays on Significs,* ed. H. Walter Schmitz (Amsterdam: Benjamins, 1990), 17–62; "Her books and letters are full of brilliant disconnected flashes and high endeavour and ingenious disintegrative criticism, but they are without architecture" (p. 27).

2. William James, to whom Peirce wrote several letters on semiotic, died in 1910. Precious few of Peirce's correspondents took an active interest in the topic; Josiah Royce, who did in a limited way, extrapolated from it in his *The Problem of Christianity* (1913; reprint, Chicago: University of Chicago Press, 1968). Royce sent this work to Peirce, who is said to have approved the use of semiotic expounded in it. See James Liszka, *A General Introduction to the Semeiotic of Charles Sanders Peirce* (Bloomington: Indiana University Press, 1996), p. 85 ff. and notes 9 and 11.

3. Editor's note, EP 2:22, p. 300.

4. Editor's note, EP 2:22, p. 300.

5. "Logic viewed as semiotic" comprises all three, so the class of signs it can consider is effectively coextensive with the class of all objects that can operate as a sign. The extension of the term thus coincides with that of "grammar."

6. The "Ideas, Stray or Stolen, on Scientific Writing" consist only of a preface to an exposition of rhetoric and contribute no work to the classifications. This text will not command my attention in this chapter except in passing.

7. The full classification, using the ten trichotomies yielding sixty-six classes, is outlined by Irwin Lieb. His article is reprinted as appx. B of the Hardwick edition of the Peirce–Welby correspondence; Charles S. Hardwick ed., *Semiotic and Significs: The Correspondence Between Charles S. Peirce and Victoria Lady Welby* (Bloomington: Indiana University Press, 1976).

8. Briefly, in the letter of 1909, Peirce discusses the arithmetic of the combinatory, and there is a projected tabular array of ten classes given at CP 8.376.

9. See, for example, Roman Jakobson, "Quest for the Essence of Language," in *Selected Writings,* vol. 2 (The Hague: Mouton, 1971), 2:345–59; Umberto Eco, "Unlimited Semiosis and Drift," in *The Limits of Interpretation* (Bloomington: Indiana University Press, 1990), p. 37 ff. For a more recent version of this argument, see Jørgen Dines Johansen, "Let Sleeping Signs Lie: On Signs, Objects,

and Communication," *Semiotica* 97, no. 3/4 (1993): 271–95. Johansen does not use the structuralist terminology, preferring to read Peirce in terms of the Kantian distinction between the *Ding an sich* and the *Ding für uns*.

10. The editor of the correspondence remarks of this list that it does not correspond with the summary given in the letter, where "Peirce provides conceptions for ten trichotomies, and hence sixty-six classes of signs" (note 23, p. 36). That he does argue for ten trichotomies elsewhere in his work is not in doubt.

11. Gérard Deledalle, "Victoria Lady Welby and Charles Sanders Peirce: Meaning and Signification," in *Essays on Significs*, ed. Schmitz, pp. 133–50 (p. 141 and passim).

12. It is well to bear in mind that "by 'determines' Peirce means 'delimits the possible' rather than 'causes' (CP 8.177)" (p. 290). T. L. Short, "Life Among the Legisigns," *Transactions of the Charles S. Peirce Society* 18, no. 4 (1982): 285–310.

13. In the case of a proper name, it might be thought that this class is a class of one; but this applies only to the object. Peirce makes it clear that a proper name becomes a term or rheme through the multiple occasions of its use. Thus, the class of usage is plural in the same way as for any rheme.

14. Teresa de Lauretis, *Alice Doesn't: Feminism, Semiotics, Cinema* (London: Macmillan, 1984), chap. 6.

15. No further paper in the series was published, although manuscript notes for the continuation do exist.

16. This problem is discussed in some depth by Jürgen Habermas in his "Peirce and Communication," in *Peirce and Contemporary Thought: Philosophical Inquiries*, ed. Kenneth Laine Ketner (New York: Fordham University Press, 1995), chap. 14; see in particular pp. 251–60. I shall discuss Habermas' debate with Peirce's account of semiosis in the Conclusion.

17. I think that there is a confusion here. The "two parts" of the dicisign—the subject and the predicate—do not correspond with the two tasks assigned to the interpretant: its requirement to represent the object, and its requirement to represent the representation. This latter distinction corresponds rather to the distinction between first and second intentions. This confusion is symptomatic of the more pervasive problem in the letters, which I shall discuss below.

18. See C. J. Misak, *Truth and the End of Inquiry: A Peircean Account of Truth* (Oxford: Clarendon Press, 1991). See also Karl-Otto Apel, *Charles S. Peirce: From Pragmatism to Pragmaticism*, trans. John Michael Krois (Amherst: University of Massachusetts Press, 1981).

19. Cf. Short: "The *immediate interpretant* is the potential interpretant that constitutes the grounded interpretability . . . of the sign" ("Life Among the Legisigns," p. 286).

20. The distinction entered mainstream logical vocabulary through Frank Ramsey, who borrowed it from Peirce in his review of Wittgenstein's *Tractatus*. See Deledalle, "Victoria Lady Welby," p. 134. W. V. O. Quine gives a convenient ac-

count of the logical difficulties associated with the standard definition of the type as the "class of all its tokens" in *Quiddities: An Intermittently Philosophical Dictionary* (1987; reprint, London: Penguin Books, 1990). The difficulty Quine points to in formal logic turns on the distinction between "single signs" and "strings of signs" and is thus parallel to the difficulties that attend the *langue/parole* distinction, which cannot handle "sentences." Peirce's formulation in this paper dissolves the difficulty by construing the relation between type and token as a relation of representation, rather than as a relation of class membership. Note that Peirce treats occurrences as tokens, whereas Quine disallows this.

21. For example, Peirce insists that the existential graphs are not a calculus but a means of fine analysis of the properties of propositions and hence of the way they collocate in arguments.

22. For example, Philippe Lacoue-Labarthe, "Typography," in *Typography: Mimesis, Philosophy, Politics*, ed. Christopher Fynsk, introduction by Jacques Derrida (Stanford: Stanford University Press, 1998), chap. 1; Jacques Derrida, *Archive Fever: A Freudian Impression*, trans. Eric Prenowitz (Chicago: University of Chicago Press, 1996).

23. Peirce always avoids recourse to grammatical categories, but there is really very little difference between "descriptive, designative, and copulant" on the one hand, and the traditional grammatical distinction between adjectives, nouns, and simple predicative sentences on the other. It seems that the wholesale application of the categories has favored a second translation, in which classes of words (which are devices of a sort, though local to language groups) are represented as kinds of meaning, which in turn are supposed to be universal.

24. Johansen, "Let Sleeping Signs Lie," p. 283 ff.

25. Peirce writes here that the icon "does not profess to represent anything" and goes on to explain why. This is evidently inconsistent with the claim that an icon is a sign and has the same general form as the problem of fiction, discussed in relation with the Harvard Lectures (I/2). There is no need to reiterate this discussion here.

26. Chipchase, "Some Account," p. 21.

27. As logician, Peirce distinguishes sharply between logical and metaphysical truth (see, e.g., CP 5.572). This distinction seems to be lost from his discussions with Welby, as from certain other philosophical writings from the same period. This problem leads to the ambiguities attaching to the "final interpretant." See Chapter 6 for my discussion of this issue.

28. Johansen provides an interesting discussion of "fusion" as a solution to the issue of imperfect communication in "Let Sleeping Signs Lie," p. 278 ff. My reading of the Peirce–Welby correspondence, however, leads to the opposite conclusion: fusion may on occasion disguise a deep misunderstanding.

29. Short, "Life Among the Legisigns," p. 285 and passim.

30. "Which is not always the same thing as determining what their interpretation is." Short, "Life Among the Legisigns," p. 289.

CHAPTER 6

1. Arthur C. Danto, *The Transfiguration of the Commonplace: A Philosophy of Art* (Cambridge, Mass.: Harvard University Press, 1981).

2. I. A. Richards, *The Philosophy of Rhetoric* (1936; reprint, Oxford: Oxford University Press, 1981), p. 12.

3. It is not without interest to note that the sign is a question. In some respect, all signs must be, or must imply, questions under the assumptions of the theory of inquiry, if only because Peirce assumes that any actual sign represents an imperfect state of knowledge, expressible as its probability. Any sign thus has more or less low modality, so that there is little logical difference between a question and an assertion except insofar as the rhetoric of an assertion makes a claim to higher modality, or greater probability, whereas the rhetoric of a question makes no such claim. This assumption is another reason for which it is difficult to understand the idea of the final interpretant, which is an answer that claims 100 percent certainty and thus implies no further question. In fact, we will find that Peirce is appropriately cautious about this issue. Any particular "final interpretant" is not deemed to have excluded all *possible* doubt, merely all *reasonable* doubt.

4. Note that Peirce uses Welby's vocabulary here. Much of the letter is taken up with translating Welby's theory of meaning into his own theory of interpretation and serves to specify the differences between them. The issues raised by Peirce are the same as those he raises directly with Welby, and they have been discussed above. The date of this letter to James is March 14, 1909, the same day as the comparable letter to Welby.

5. Carl R. Hausman suggested this notion to me in a personal communication in response to an unpublished paper in which I argued, on the basis of the implications of the onion, that a Peircean semiotic could not consistently provide a theory of metaphor because any such theory requires an account of literal meaning. Hausman's account of metaphor can be found in his book devoted to that subject: Carl R. Hausman, *Metaphor and Art: Interactionism and Reference in the Verbal and Nonverbal Arts* (Cambridge: Cambridge University Press, 1989). His account of a Peircean theory of metaphor can be found in the C. S. Peirce online encyclopedia, available at http://www.digitalpeirce.org/ (accessed October 23, 2003). Because my topic here is not metaphor as such, my response to Hausman here will focus on the general issue underlying our debate—namely, the nature of finality implied by the postulate of "the final interpretant."

6. Hausman, *Charles S. Peirce's Evolutionary Philosophy* (Cambridge: Cambridge Univesrity Press, 1993), p. 201 ff.

7. Richard Rorty, *Objectivity, Relativism, and Truth* (Cambridge: Cambridge University Press, 1991), p. 131.

8. Hausman, *Charles S. Peirce's Evolutionary Philosophy*, p. 217.

9. The reason for this is that "mind" is a hypothesis inferred from the distinction between error and its opposite. To err is human, so "reason" is a human

attribute, not a divine one. See Joseph Morton Ransdell, "Charles Peirce: The Idea of Representation" (Ph.D. diss., Columbia University, 1966), p. 53 ff., for an elaboration of this argument.

10. There is a further question in connection with Peirce's account of truth to which I have not attended. This is the issue of "convergence," whether construed globally (the convergence of all inquiry in a universal and totally coherent account of reality) or locally for particular theories. Quine's objection to Peirce's position on this point seems to be definitive: W. V. O. Quine, *Word and Object* (Cambridge, Mass.: Technology Press of the Massachusetts Institute of Technology, 1960). Hausman accepts it (*Charles S. Peirce*, pp. 215 and passim); and so does Israel Scheffler, in "A Plea for Pluralism," *Transactions of the Charles S. Peirce Society* 35, no. 3 (1999): 425–36. This point is still open to the objection made by Quine, who finds in Peirce "a faulty use of numerical analogy in speaking of a limit of theories, since the notion of 'limit' depends on that of 'nearer than,' which is defined for numbers but not for theories." Quoted in Hausman, *Charles S. Peirce*, p. 203. C. J. Misak has also discussed Quine's objection, which in her view rests on a faulty interpretation of the argument. See C. J. Misak, *Truth and the End of Inquiry: A Peircean Account of Truth* (Oxford: Clarendon Press, 1991), p. 120 ff.

11. Misak, *Truth*.

12. Note that this is not the same—although it is equally pragmatic—as to argue solely in terms of semiosis, as if there were nothing but the free play of interpretation; for it is difficult to see what interpretation is interpretation of if the argument for it does not include some account of the sign. Arguments of this sort are usually devised to counter *binary* accounts of the sign (signifier/signified), in particular to counter the hypothesis that there is a "signified." For this reason, their use of the term *semiosis* to name interpretation is misleading.

13. Naomi Cumming, "Musical Signs and Subjectivity: Peircean Reflections," *Transactions of the Charles S. Peirce Society* 35, no. 3 (summer 1999): 437–74 (p. 447).

14. "Rhetoric," in W. V. Quine, *Quiddities: An Intermittently Philosophical Dictionary* (1987; reprint, London: Penguin Books, 1990), p. 183.

15. Umberto Eco, introduction to *A Theory of Semiotics* (Bloomington: Indiana University Press, 1979).

16. Susan Haack, *Confessions of a Passionate Moderate* (Chicago: Chicago University Press, 1998), pp. 1, 8. Page references will be included parenthetically in the text.

17. Note that Peirce's usage records the shift in general American usage, from "barrister" to "attorney" attendant on the abolition of the formal distinction between attorneys (or solicitors), who are not admitted to plead at the bar (except in petty sessions), and barristers, whose specific role this is. The term *barrister* is still used in jurisdictions where the distinction obtains.

18. I refer particularly to Lyotard, *The Differend: Phrases in Dispute*, trans. Georges van den Abbeele (Minneapolis: University of Minnesota Press, 1988), the

work in which Lyotard brings together the strands of work represented in *Just Gaming*, trans. Wlad Godzich (Minneapolis: University of Minnesota Press, 1985); *The Postmodern Condition: A Report on Knowledge*, trans. Geoff Bennington and Brian Massumi (Minneapolis: University of Minnesota Press, 1985); "Judiciousness in Dispute, or Kant After Marx," trans. Cecile Lindsay, in *The Lyotard Reader*, ed. Andrew Benjamin (Oxford: Basil Blackwell, 1989); and "Lessons in Paganism," trans. David Macey, in *The Lyotard Reader*. A helpful overview of this work, with an acute discussion of the problems it raises, is to be found in Fançois Guibal, "Penser (avec Jean-François Lyotard): Le temps du risque," in *Témoigner du différend: Quand phraser ne se peut*, introduction by Pierre-Jean Labarrière (Paris: Editions Osiris, 1989), pp. 11–58.

19. Peirce writes to Welby on one occasion that the great advantage of not publishing in philosophy is that it is only in oral exchange that "there is opportunity to object & cross-question" (PW December 2, 1904, p. 44).

20. W 3, introduction, passim.

21. One could add that they are involved in an elementary agonistics of the "might is right" variety, but this would not be true of all indices, or even of all imperatives or of all exclamations.

22. Roman Jakobson, "On Linguistic Aspects of Translation," in *Selected Writings*, vol. 2 (The Hague: Mouton, 1962).

23. Mats Bergman, "Reflections on the Role of the Communicative Sign in Semiotic," *Transactions of the Charles S. Peirce Society* 36, no. 2 (spring 2000): 225–54 (p. 232). Richard J. Parmentier, "Signs' Place in Medias Res: Peirce's Concept of Semiotic Mediation," in *Semiotic Mediation: Sociocultural and Psychological Perspectives*, ed. Elizabeth Mertz and Richard Parmentier (Orlando: Academic Press, 1985).

24. The process is spelled out clearly in this passage from the Harvard Lectures of 1903: "All necessary reasoning without exception is diagrammatic. That is, we construct an icon of our hypothetical state of things and proceed to observe it. This observation leads us to suspect that something is true, which we may or may not be able to formulate with precision, and we proceed to inquire whether it is true or not. For this purpose it is necessary to form a plan of investigation and this is the most difficult part of the whole operation. We not only have to select the features of the diagram which it will be pertinent to pay attention to, but it is also of great importance to return again and again to certain features. Otherwise, although our conclusions may be correct, they will not be the particular conclusions at which we are aiming. But the greatest point of the art consists in the introduction of suitable *abstractions*. By this I mean such a transformation of our diagrams that characters of one diagram may appear in another as things. A familiar example is where in analysis we treat operations as themselves the subjects of operations." EP 2:15, pp. 212–13 (CP 5.162).

25. Ransdell, "Charles Peirce," chap. 3, p. 63 ff.; and chap. 5.

26. Ransdell, "Charles Peirce," p. 128.

27. Ransdell, "Charles Peirce," p. 133.

28. Ransdell, "Charles Peirce," p. 58.

29. Ransdell, "Charles Peirce," p. 59. It should be understood that Ransdell uses the term *formal* to mean something a little different from my usage: *formal* means the element of a proposition that is isolated when, under the protocols of a certain analytical technique, the predicate is emptied of all material content. I am using *formal* to refer to what Peirce means by the "mathematical point of view" in the analysis of the properties of formal notations.

30. Ransdell, "Charles Peirce," pp. 62–63.

31. Jørgen Dines Johansen, "Let Sleeping Signs Lie: On Signs, Objects, and Communication," *Semiotica* 97, no. 3/4 (1993): 271–95; page references will be given parenthetically in the text.

32. Thomas L. Short, "Life Among the Legisigns," *Transactions of the Charles S. Peirce Society* 18, no. 4 (1982): 285–310.

33. Gregory Bateson, "A Theory of Play and Fantasy," in *Semiotics: An Introductory Anthology*, ed. Robert E. Innis (Bloomington: Indiana University Press, 1985), pp. 131–44.

34. Gale L. McLachlan and Ian Reid, *Framing and Interpretation* (Carlton, Australia: Melbourne University Press, 1994).

35. Part of the difficulty in Johansen's account stems from his pluralizing of "semiosis"—"semioses." This is not a usage we find in Peirce, and the plural suggests that "semiosis"—the process—is cut up into discrete sequences. These latter correspond with "signs," and the usage is effectively redundant. Furthermore, this entrains a loss, which is precisely the conception of semiosis as continuous. There are signs, and there is semiosis, which is the process in which signs are taken up in other signs.

36. This is not to gainsay the significance I have argued for in the first trichotomy, which, inter alia, clarifies some key issues in the analysis of the second trichotomy. The preeminence—acknowledged by Peirce—may be due simply to familiarity and to the amount of work these three have received, both in Peirce's writing and in the commentaries. My suggestion would give it a second rationale.

CONCLUSION

1. Max Fisch, *Peirce, Semeiotic, and Pragmatism* (Bloomington: Indiana University Press, 1986); Vincent Colapietro, *Peirce's Approach to the Self: A Semiotic Perspective on Human Subjectivity* (New York: State University of New York Press, 1989), p. 38.

2. Klaus Oehler, "Response to Habermas," in *Peirce and Contemporary Thought*, ed. K. L. Ketner (New York: Fordham University Press, 1995), 267–71. Oehler uses Habermas' term *communication*, but I take it that the issues are broadly the same.

3. Cf. Vincent M. Colapietro, "Immediacy, Opposition, and Mediation: Peirce on Irreducible Aspects of the Communicative Process," in *Recovering Prag-*

matism's Voice: The Classical Tradition, Rorty, and the Philosophy of Communication, ed. Lenore Langsdorf and Andrew R. Smith (New York: SUNY Press, 1995), chap. 2. Colapietro notes the ambiguity in Peirce on this question, but he opts to read Peirce as offering an explanation of communication on the basis of the sign (p. 34 ff.).

4. Jürgen Habermas, "Peirce and Communication," in *Peirce and Contemporary Thought: Philosophical Inquiries*, ed. Kenneth Laine Ketner (New York: Fordham University Press, 1995), p. 247.

5. Habermas argues for the closure of semiosis: intersubjectivity has the task of accounting both for the "initial understanding" and for the "final object" represented in the "ideal consensus." This closure is guaranteed by the construal of the dynamical object as external to the sign ("Peirce and Communication," pp. 256–59 and passim).

6. Clearly, if what Habermas is seeking in Peirce is a theory of society, then he will not find it. My argument seeks simply to counter Habermas' charge that Peirce's position is inconsistent.

7. Jørgen Johansen, "Let Sleeping Signs Lie: On Signs, Objects, and Communication," *Semiotica* 97, no. 3/4 (1993): 271–95.

8. See "The Fixation of Belief," W 3:60, pp. 242–57; and A. J. Ayer, *The Origins of Pragmatism* (London: Macmillan, 1968), pp. 27–35, for a close discussion of the arguments of this paper. Some of Ayer's remarks pertain to Peirce's rhetoric: he notes his "largely ironic" defense of the methods of which he disapproves, and concludes "that the method of science is victor"—later "judge"—in its own cause (pp. 34, 38). The major difficulty Ayer discerns in Peirce's position is precisely the function rhetoric might have in the "fixation of belief": the *method* of science requires not only a test of conformity to the properties of physical objects, but also conformity to collective interpretation of the experiences that make such properties available to judgment. Collective interpretations are exactly the issue.

9. Arguing against the "formalism" of the "Cartesian criterion," Peirce writes: "If I were really convinced, I should have done with reasoning and should require no test of certainty. But thus to make single individuals absolute judges of truth is most pernicious. The result is that metaphysicians will all agree that metaphysics has reached a pitch of certainty far beyond that of the physical sciences;— only they can agree upon nothing else" (W 2:22, p. 212).

10. See H. S. Thayer, *Meaning and Action: A Critical History of Pragmatism* (New York: Bobbs-Merrill, 1968), part 3, chaps. 3 and 4. "The better part of human thought is not to be found in logic, and the best use of language is not to serve thought but the will. Persuasion, as an art whereby the will is able to exert power over men, especially interested Prezzolini. The beauty of language in creating an effective parable and the power of rhetoric is of greater human importance than a valid syllogism" (p. 332). Prezzolini's "manual for liars," as Vailati dubbed it, is no mere treatise on rhetoric, but a rationale for political propaganda. The annexation of something called "pragmatism" by the Italian fascists was one of the

most unfortunate consequences of the movement. William James, too, would have been appalled by this turn of events; his encouragement of Papini, and the adulation of James expressed by the group surrounding Papini, cannot be held responsible, as Thayer shows; but their taking of James' writings as doctrine—indeed, dogma—quite in isolation from the robust debates characteristic of the first generation of pragmatism is certainly part of the story. Another part, also shown by Thayer, is the curious connection between the writing of the socialist Georges Sorel and some "pragmatic" slogans adopted by Mussolini.

11. Quoted in Colapietro, *Peirce's Approach to the Self,* p. 65.

12. Notice how important this construal is for understanding Peirce's dual principle that, as the self is defined in relation to its communities, so does the person possess the form of a community; see Colapietro, *Peirce's Approach to the Self,* chap. 2. Without this construal, Habermas' fears concerning "fusion" are entirely realized: "To the extent that the dimension of possible contradiction and difference would close, linguistic communication would contract into a type of communion that no longer needs language as the means of reaching initial understanding." Habermas, "Peirce and Communication," p. 264.

13. Compare this description of "The Association of Ideas": "In the absence of external impressions, thoughts chase one another through the mind in a sort of Bacchic train. Each suggests another. After a while, the clear train of thought is broken, the ideas remain scattered for a time, and then reconcentrate in another train" (MS 736, p. 3).

14. See Robert S. Corrington, *An Introduction to C. S. Peirce: Philosopher, Semiotician, and Ecstatic Naturalist* (Maryland: Rowman & Littlefield, 1993), for a reading of Peirce's "conception of the universe" as "anthropocentric and anthropomorphic" (p. 75).

15. Colapietro, *Peirce's Approach to the Self,* p. 28.

16. Ian Hacking, *Why Does Language Matter to Philosophy?* (Cambridge: Cambridge University Press, 1975).

17. Hacking, *Why Does Language Matter to Philosophy?,* chap. 13, p. 168 ff.

18. Hacking *Why Does Language Matter to Philosophy?,* p. 184 and passim. At the end of his discussion, Hacking gestures to Karl Popper's proposal for an "epistemology without a knowing subject" that is indebted to Hegel's concept of a "process without a subject." Peirce, too, was deeply indebted to his early reading of Hegel.

19. Peter Skagestad, "Peirce's Inkstand as an External Embodiment of Mind," *Transactions of the Charles S. Peirce Society* 25, no. 3 (summer 1999): 551–61.

20. See Habermas, "Peirce and Communication": "Within this traditional paradigm of representative [*sic*] thinking, the objective world is conceived as the totality of mentally representable objects, while the subjective world is conceived as the sphere of our mental representations of possible objects. . . . Peirce undermined this architectonic by giving a semeiotic reinterpretation to the fundamental concept of 'representation': the two-placed relation of mental representation

(*Vorstellung*) is made into the three-placed relation of symbolic representation (*Darstellung*)" (p. 249). This latter is "representation of . . . to . . . ," where "representation to" locates the "pragmatic turn": "in the new paradigm the role of the subject is assumed not by language *per se*, but by communication among those who demand explanations from each other in order to reach reasonable agreement about something in the world. The place of intersubjectivity is taken over by an intersubjective practice of reaching initial understanding" (p. 250).

21. Interest in the suppressed technological premises of classical philosophy has been sustained of recent years; I note in particular Philippe Lacoue-Labarthe, "Typography," in *Typography: Mimesis, Philosophy, Politics* (Stanford: Stanford University Press, 1998) on Plato's account of mimesis; and Jacques Derrida, *Archive Fever: A Freudian Impression*, trans. Eric Prenowitz (Chicago: University of Chicago Press, 1996), on the technologies of memory. The *locus classicus* is Martin Heidegger, "The Question of Technology," in *The Question Concerning Technology and Other Essays*, trans. William Lovitt (New York: Harper and Rowe, 1977), pp. 3–35.

22. Section II of the "New List" reads as follows (W 2:4; pp. 54–55; emphasis added): "the *five* conceptions thus obtained, for reasons which will be sufficiently obvious, may be termed *categories*. That is,

> BEING
> Quality (Reference to a Ground)
> Relation (Reference to a Correlate),
> Representation (Reference to an Interpretant),
> SUBSTANCE The *three intermediate* conceptions may be termed accidents.

23. John J. Fitzgerald, *Peirce's Theory of Signs as Foundation for Pragmatism* (The Hague: Mouton, 1966), p. 10. Further references will be given parenthetically in the text.

24. Notice the similarity between this view and the distinction between "semantics" and "pragmatics" in Charles Morris' work, *Writings in the General Theory of Signs* (The Hague: Mouton, 1971). The same distinction is central to John Searle's account of speech acts: *Speech Acts* (Cambridge: Cambridge University Press, 1978).

25. Habermas' account of the need for intersubjectivity within the theory of signs is therefore right for the special case of the symbol in the late work.

26. It is also this that confirms that the "infinite long run" has the status of a counterfactual needed for definitional purposes only.

27. For this reason, as well as its similarity to parts of the early chapters of the Syllabus, I am inclined to doubt its dating of 1904. At the same time, however, I recognize that my temptation to that doubt is a way of avoiding the discomfort occasioned by what must otherwise count as an inconsistency.

28. "The distinction between an assertion and an interrogatory sentence is

of secondary importance. An assertion has its modality, or measure of assurance, and a question generally involves as part of it an assertion of emphatically low modality. In addition to that, it is intended to stimulate the hearer to make an answer. This is a rhetorical function which needs no special grammatical form. If in wandering about the country, I wish to inquire the way to town, I can perfectly do so by assertion, without drawing upon the interrogative form of syntax" (CP 4.57).

EPILOGUE

1. All references to the correspondence are to the Hardwick edition: Charles S. Hardwick, ed., *Semiotic and Significs: The Correspondence of Charles S. Peirce and Victoria Lady Welby* (Bloomington: Indiana University Press, 1976). Note the convention I have adopted: for letters from Peirce to Welby, the texts are referenced "PW," whereas for letters from Welby to Peirce, I use "WP." The dates are quoted as in the text of each writer, rather than standardized.

2. The editor of the correspondence adds this note: "This letter has been reconstructed from a draft in Lady Welby's correspondence. As is the case with many drafts in Lady Welby's correspondence, it is partially in a typewritten 'shorthand'" (p. 61).

3. See Hardwick, ed., *Semiotic and Significs*, introduction.

4. James Jakób Liszka, *A General Introduction to the Semeiotic of Charles Sanders Peirce* (Bloomington: Indiana University Press, 1996), preface.

5. See the introduction to *Writings of Charles S. Peirce: A Chronological Edition*, ed. Max H. Fisch, vol. 1, for details of Peirce's publishing activity.

6. Chaïm Perelman, *Rhétoriques* (Brussels: Editions de l'Université de Bruxelles, 1989), part 3, chap. 1. Further references will be given parenthetically in the text.

7. Louis Menand, *The Metaphysical Club: A Story of Ideas in America* (New York: Farrar, Straus & Giroux, 2001), p. 152.

8. Ross Chambers, *Loiterature* (Lincoln: University of Nebraska Press, 1999). See in particular Chambers' remarks concerning the economy of digressivity and the tendency for digressive narrative to become "all middle" (chap. 1).

9. This reading of the letter is quoted from a longer exposition: Anne Freadman, "The Visit of the Instrument Maker," in *The Semiotics of Writing: Transdisciplinary Perspectives on the Technology of Writing*, ed. Patrick Coppock, pp. 185–236 (Bologna: Bepols, 2001). For information concerning Peirce's life, I rely on Joseph Brent, *Charles Sanders Peirce: A Life* (Bloomington: Indiana University Press, 1993).

10. In fact, they had already been living for some time on disguised charity, and in 1907, William James organized a subscription among Peirce's old friends and colleagues to be paid "yearly . . . for as long as not too inconvenient." "The time has come," James wrote to Henry Bowditch, "to recognize that he can't make his living . . . he must be kept going by friends & relatives." See Brent, *Charles Sanders Peirce*, chap. 5, for details of the whole period; and see p. 303 ff. for James'

part in Peirce's support and the associated correspondence, from which this quotation is drawn.

11. Cf. a note to himself, to be found in the alternative pages of MS 632 (1909), in which Peirce counts thought as contingent on muscular control as well as on satisfactory writing equipment: "This page amounts to nothing anyway. I haven't sufficient comman[d] over my muscles today to judge very well. But all three pens are satisfactory; this, I think, is the best. If I had a decent writing table, it would be better."

12. This analysis follows suggestions made by Ross Chambers in his work in progress on witnessing narratives. Chambers presents an argument concerning the formation of new genres, where untellable stories come to be told by borrowing the forms and strategies of familiar genres and turning them to other purposes. The kind of local, tactical opportunism that is operative in Peirce's letter does not result in wholesale invention of this order, because the other requisite conditions are not in place.

13. Ross Chambers, *Story and Situation: Narrative Seduction and the Power of Fiction* (Minneapolis: University of Minnesota Press, 1984), chap. 8.

14. Michel Serres, *The Parasite*, trans. Lawrence R. Schehr (Baltimore: Johns Hopkins University Press, 1982); see in particular part 2.

15. Philippe Lacoue-Labarthe, *Typography: Mimesis, Philosophy, Politics*, ed. Christopher Fynsk (Cambridge, Mass.: Harvard University Press, 1989); Jacques Derrida, *Archive Fever: A Freudian Impression*, trans. Eric Prenowitz (Chicago: University of Chicago Press, 1996).

16. "Everything must keep the appropriate place to which it was allotted." Horace, *The Art of Poetry*, §90; quoted from *Classical Literary Criticism*, ed. D. A. Russell and M. Winterbottom (Oxford: Oxford University Press, 1989). Notwithstanding his strictures against the mixing of genres, Horace's main concern is with "simplicity and unity," and he warns us that "most of us . . . are deceived by appearances of correctness."

17. Rosalie Colie, *The Resources of Kind: Genre Theory in the Renaissance*, ed. Barbara Lewalski (Berkeley: University of California Press, 1973).

18. The phrase is cited from Jack Goody, *The Interface Between the Written and the Oral* (Cambridge: Cambridge University Press, 1987).

19. See Murray Murphey, *The Development of Peirce's Philosophy* (1961; reprint, Indianapolis: Hackett, 1993), part 4, and particularly chap. 17.

20. Genevieve Lloyd, *The Man of Reason: "Male" and "Female" in Western Philosophy* (London: Methuen, 1984).

21. The usage is in fact attested in some of the early drafts for a book on practical logic; cf. W 2:34, 35, 36, 37. Likewise, Peirce regularly refers to algebra as an "art": e.g., W 5:30, p. 223.

Index

There are certain important words that appear throughout the text that are not included in the index simply because they appear so often indexing would be pointless. Clearly the terms "semiosis" and "semiotic(s)" fall into this category, since the book is largely concerned with them, along with the words "sign" and "genre," although it has been necessary to index particular aspects of "sign" and "semiosis."

Other words not indexed individually because of their frequency of use are "icon," "index," and "symbol," unless they are referred to as a group as "second trichotomy," which is indexed. However, for an analysis of the terms readers are referred to Chapter 1, for a discussion of "icon" readers are referred to Chapters 3 and 6, for "index" to Chapter 4, and for "symbol" to the Conclusion. Also see entries "iconicity" and "indexicality."

The terms "interpretant" and "representamen" are not indexed unless other than general. Other words that appear often, forming too large a category alone for easy comprehension, have been divided into specific subheadings—including "classification," "existential graphs," "Harvard Lectures," "inquiry," "New List," "Pragmatism," "reference," and "trichotomies."

There are several instances of allegory, analogy, metaphor and story in the text—these have all been grouped under the heading "examples," for ease of location.

Aboriginal, *see* marker stones

Algebra of Logic, xxix, 18, 22f, 30f, 69, 79ff, 83, 85

algebraic paradigm, xxvi

algebraic signs, 99

anti-Cartesian, xxiv, xxv, 9, 33f, 47

Apel, Karl-Otto, 7, 67f

Aristotle (or Aristotelian), xxxv, 7, 15, 51f, 83, 96, 98, 195, 200

art (definition of), 273

assertion, 18, 75, 89, 99, 129, 235–39 *passim*, 246

Bakhtin, Mikhail, 129

Baldwin, Loammi, 292n22

Baldwin's Dictionary, 189, 194, 196

Barthes, Roland, 176

Benjamin, Walter, 286n15

Benveniste, Emile, 129

Bergman, Mats, 201

Berkeley, George, 9

binarism, 52, 163, 186f, 269, 271

Boole, George, 19–22 *passim*, 26f, 87, 89, 133

Boston, 127f, *see also* Bunker Hill

boundaries, 13f, 22, 66, 75, 224ff
branches of science, 41, 268
Brent, Joseph, 303n9
Bunker Hill, *see* examples

Cambridge Conferences, 66
Canberra, 128
Cartesian tradition, xxv, 7, 41, 53, 55,
    222, 227f, *see also* anti-Cartesian
Carnegie Institute, 67
Cavell, Stanley, 44
Category the First, 69, 95, 270; the
    Second, 69, 84; the Third, 69, 93, 170
centaur, *see* examples
Century Dictionary, 180
Chambers, Ross, 304n12
chronology, 101
Cicero, 186, 198
class, xxxiii, 65, 124, 197f
classes of sign, 10, 12, 22, 68, 75, 84f,
    109f, 119
classification, xxvi, xxix, xxxv, 28, 94,
    134, 138, 161, 168, 243, 268; standard,
    91; hierarchical, 96, 98
—first, 92, 238
—second, xxxii, 60, 65, 91ff, 98–102
    passim, 138, 141, 167, 213, 240, 243
cognition series, *see* anti-Cartesian
Colapietro, Vincent, 29, 215, 227ff,
    301n12
Collected Papers, 74, 79, 94, 101, 250
common ground, 217, 220–22 *passim*
communication, 131f, 216
conversation, xxii-xxviii *passim*, xxxv,
    33–37 *passim*, 61, 78, 215–24 *passim*,
    232
coreference, 221
cosmology, 217, 219
Cummings, Naomi, 184

Danto, Arthur, 172
Darwin, Charles (or Darwinian), xiii, 24
de Lauretis, Teresa, 145

De Morgan, Augustus, 13
de Tienne, André, 103
degeneracy, 23, 73, 110, 117, 141, 236f, 242
Deledalle, Gérard, 143
Deleuze, Gilles, xxx, 10
Derrida, Jacques, 130, 264, 284n21,
    285n31
Descartes, René, xxiv, 34, 55, 176f, 254,
    285n31
Dewey, John, 223, 275n1
diagrams, *see* geometric diagrams
diagrammatization, 47
dicent sign, 96
dichotomy, 65, 142
dicisign, 149
dictionary, 11, 156; extracts, 39–41
Differend (The), xxx
doubt and belief, 183, 187, 213, 254
dualism, 9, 32, 240, 243
dyadic relations, 96, 98
Dynamoid Object, 161

Eco, Umberto, 112, 186, 227f
end of inquiry, 16, 180, 188
Enlightenment, 216
Essential Peirce, 139
Euclidean model, 137
examples
—Aboriginal, 123
—barrister, 185–91 *passim*, 196–99
    passim, 225
—bullet-hole, 110
—Bunker Hill, 73, 125, 127, 134
—cars for sale, 212f
—centaur, 70–75 *passim*, 99
—clothes, 173
—cuckoo, 6, 15, 256, 262, 267
—fence, 60, 224
—greeting, 102, 128f, 196f
—Henry, Patrick, 78, 82, 87, 197
—house on fire, 177, 220f
—judge and jury, *see* barrister
—landmark, 73f, 125, 127

—line of identity, 79f, 85, 91f, 101f, 197
—monuments, 125–28 *passim, see also*
   Bunker Hill
—murderer, (or murder), 8, 14, 24
—onion, 172–76 *passim*, 184, 203, 208,
   243
—painting, (or picture), 26f, 58
—playing cards, 108, 122, 124
—protoplasm, 225, 256
—proverb, 77ff, 86
—robin, 211
—Scherherazade, 71–75 *passim*
—simpleton, 132
—thunderclap etc, 113
—toolkit, 229, 232
—tramp, 38, 51, 54–59 *passim*, 105ff, 125,
   197, 221
—type, 157
—veil of truth, 172–76 *passim*, 183
—visitor, xxxvii, 256–67, 271, 273
—weathercock, 14f, 24f, 31, 44, 73, 111f,
   117, 186, 197
existential graphs, 83, 86–91 *passim*, 100,
   102, 146–53 *passim*, 165, 218, 226, 245,
   250, 254
—development, 33, 79
—and language, 42, 47, 60, 137
Existential System, 83

fiction, 70ff, 79
Fillmore, Charles, 129
financial difficulties, 67, 249, 303n10
Fisch, Max, xxiv, 9, 32, 102, 139, 192, 215
Fitzgerald, John, 237–40 *passim*
formalism, 88
Fregean pair, 141
Frow, John, 6
functions of index, 105ff

gender distinctions, xxvii, xxviii, 271
geometric diagrams, 25, 30
Goudge, xxii

graphs logical, 97, *see also* existential
   graphs
Green, Nicholas St. John, 192
Greenough, Horatio, 127
Greimas, A.J., 284n16
Grice, H. P., 123
Guibal, François, 190

Haack, Susan, xxvii, 188–90 *passim*,
   193–96 *passim*
Habermas, Jürgen, xxx, 216–22 *passim*,
   225–29 *passim*, 232, 234, 236, 301n12
habit, 153, 205, 211f, 226
Hacking, Ian, 33, 227f
Harvard Lectures, 65–69 *passim*, 91f,
   101f, 118, 139, 146f, 151, 198, 243
—categories, 34, 82, 84, 200, 253
—and Pragmatism, xxvi, 65, 67, 78, 86,
   88, 146f, 166, 178
Hausman, Carl, 177, 180, 183, 279n15
Hegel, George Wilhelm Friedrich, xxii,
   xxiv, 9, 12, 16, 18, 38, 55, 68, 301n18
Heidegger, Martin, 302n21
Henry, Patrick, *see* examples
Hodgkins, *see* example Aboriginal
Holmes, Oliver Wendell, Jr., 192
homely thinker, 37ff, 47, 53–56 *passim*
homogeneity, xxxiv
Hookway, Christopher, xxii, xxiii
Hume, David, 7, 254

icon, mathematical and
   phenomenological, 72
iconicity, 15, 22, 25, 27, 48, 68, 208, 241,
   270
"Ideas Stray or Stolen," 137
idealism, 53, 88, 141
identity, construction of, 126f
indexicality, 14, 22, 28ff, 81, 106–16
   passim, 120–34 *passim*, 176, 211, 221,
   225, 241
indexicals, 129f
individualism, xxiv, 222

Innis, Robert, 13
inquiry, 20, 180 -190 *passim*, 193ff, 209,
    216, 232–40 *passim*, 244f
—process of, 77, 89, 212, 219, 223; *see
    also* road of inquiry; end of inquiry
—and truth, 33, 172ff
instrument maker, *see* examples visitor
instruments, 111, 229ff, 247ff, 264;
    scientific, 128
Instruments of Logic, 16
intention, first, 110, 112, 119, 154, 209;
    second, 109–13 *passim*, 116f, 120, 154,
    209, 213, 245
interpretant, dynamic 144f, 162, 239;
    signified, 144f
intersubjectivity, xxxv, 216–20 *passim*,
    227ff

Jakobson, Roman, 129f, 199
James, William, xxvii, xxx, 66, 77, 155,
    166, 174, 252, 269, 272, 301n10,
    303n10
Johansen, Jørgen, 162, 209–13 *passim*,
    220, 229, 293n9
Johns Hopkins University, 275n1

Kant, Immanuel (and Kantian), xxx, 5ff,
    18, 20f, 29, 162f, 188, 254, 286n15
Kempe, A. B., 88

Lacoue-Labarthe, Phillipe, 264, 302n21
Ladd-Franklin, Christine, 275n1
landmark, *see* examples
language, 19–22 *passim*, 27–34 *passim*,
    42f, 47–54 *passim*, 60, 78, 129; *see also*
    syntax
legisign, 95f, 99ff, 130, 159
letters, of geometry, 112
Lieb, Irwin, 293n7
Line of identity, *see* examples
Linsky, Leonard, 293n31
Liszka, James, 251, 255

Locke, John, 11
Logic Notebook, 94
logical criteria, 139
Logical Tracts no.2, 101ff, 147
Lowell Lectures, xxvi, xxviii, xxix, 65,
    69, 93, 103, 146
Lyotard, Jean-François, xxx, xxxvii, 190,
    197, 291n17

machinery of talk, 42, 216–46
map, 79, 106, 181
marker stones, 126ff
mathematical consequences, 16
mathematics/logic distinction, 37, 42
mediation, 11, 20
men/machines paradigm, 231
Menand, Louis, 255, 282n3
Mendeleef, D.I., 98
mentalism, 220, 233–36 *passim*
metaphor, *see* examples onion; veil of
    truth
Metaphysical Club, 192
mind/symbol, 233–36 *passim*, 240
Misak, Cheryl, 150, 183, 297n10
Mitchell, O. H., 18
Monist series, xxxii, 137, 147, 155, 160, 165
Montaigne, Michel de, 78
Monuments, *see* examples
Murphey, Murray, xxiii

neighbor, 60, 221–25 *passim*
neighborhood, 223–26 *passim*
"New Elements," 137–40 *passim*, 167,
    223ff, 242f
New List, xxiii, xxiv, 5–10 *passim*, 111,
    147, 159f, 185, 198f, 207, 245
—and classification, 13f, 75, 118, 194,
    232ff, 240
—modifications to, 16, 18, 23–27 *passim*,
    67, 109, 170f, 219, 242
nominalism, xxiii, xxiv, 9f, 20, 32, 107,
    141, 226, 232, 234, 240, 243f

notation, 18f, 23, 42, 60f
—algebraic, xxxv, 31, 47, 73, 79, 89, 113, 154
—formal, xxxii, 18, 28f, 32, 83, 86, 132, 240
—geometrical, 73
—logical, 14, 66, 157f
—topological, xxix, xxxiii, xxxv, 47

obituary, *see* Green
object, division of, 29, 51, 142, 165, 168, 210, 241
Oehler, Klaus, 67f, 215ff, 229
Ogden, C. K., 248
"On a New List of Categories," *see* New List
"On the Algebra of Logic," *see* Algebra of Logic

Parmentier, Richard, 201
Peirce Edition Project, 101
Perelman, Chaim, 253f
periodic table, 98
phenomena subsets, 215f
phenomenology, xxxv, 6, 9, 21, 33, 67–72 *passim*, 79, 143, 254, 256
philosophy, xxii, 48, 118
Plato (or Platonic), xxxv, 28, 37, 52, 88, 156, 191, 264
Popper, Karl, 230, 301n18
pragmatic maxim, 77, 117, 269
Pragmatism, 54, 57, 70, 77ff, 107, 161, 164, 174, 204f, 223, 245, 266; *see also* Harvard Lectures
—debate on, 219, 237–41 *passim*, 253
—definition, 75, 116, 188, 194, 215, 235, 254, 263, 273
—formulation, xxv, 33, 137, 182
"Pragmatism" Manuscript, (283) 203
pragmatization, xxxiii, 138, 217, 237
Prezzolini, 223
probability theory, 42
proposition/argument, 144

proverb, *see* examples

qualisign, 96, 100, 121, 141, 168
Quine, W. V. O., 180, 185, 285n31, 294n20, 297n10
Quintilian, xxx, xxxvi, 191

Ramism, 51f, 58
Ramsey, Frank, 248
Ransdell, Joseph, xxiii, 196, 206ff
realism, xxiii, xxiv, 10, 20, 219
reductiveness, xxxiv
reference, xxxiii, 11, 17, 71, 141, 159ff, 172, 207, 212, 244
—backward and forward, xxiv, 32, 207, 276n8, 282n2
—definitions, 28f, 108ff, 123ff, 131,133
—problems of, xxxi, 9, 177, 244, 279n11
referent, 95, 141ff
relation, three term, 116ff
relationship, logic/metaphysics, xxxv, xxxvi, xxxvii
replicas, 95, 99f, 242ff
Representation, 8, 10, 20–23 *passim*, 118, 170
reviews, *see* Berkeley, Royce, Schröder, Welby
rhetoric, 123, 139, 149; Speculative, 93f
road of inquiry, 37f, 53, 177ff, 183, 250
Robin, Richard, 97, 102
Rorty, Richard, xxii, 180, 183, 194f
Royce, Josiah, 16ff, 29, 33, 38, 54, 66, 79, 88, 163–66 *passim*, 239, 280n20
Russell, Bertrand, xxvii, xxviii, 248
Sartre, Jean-Paul, 50
Saussure, Ferdinand de (and Saussurean), xxxi, 19, 22, 29, 51, 81, 151–54 *passim*, 264, 284n15
Scherherazade story, *see* examples
Schiller, F. C. S., 250
Schröder, Ernst, xvii, 32–38 *passim*, 43–49 *passim*, 53, 56–60 *passim*, 88, 266

Searle, John, 302n24
Sebeok, T. A., 110, 211
selfhood, *see* subjectivity
semiology, xxx
semiosis, infinite, xxxiv, 177, 182f, 211
Serres, Michel, 263f
shared experience, 132f
Short, T. L., 13, 167, 211
sign hypothesis, xxii-xxxiii *passim*, 15
Sigwart, Christoph, 56
sinsign, 96, 99ff, 130
Skagestad, Peter, 216, 229–32 *passim*, 246
spatial contiguity, 28
struggle, 84
subjectivity, 211, 226–31 *passim*
Syllabus (The), 65f, 82, 84, 91–96, 101ff,
    118, 139ff, 167ff, 217, 244
syntax of signs, 23, 30, 57f, 185

Taussig, Michael, 286n15
technical aids, *see* instruments
theory, global, 166;
theory/practice, 217f, 272f
Thompson, Manley, xxiii
token, *see* type/token distinction
tools, *see* instruments
tramp, *see* examples
translation and translators, 9, 143, 200ff,
    207ff, 212, 222, 231
travelers on the road, *see* examples tramp
triad, 66, 75, 92, 96, 161, 241
triadic relations, 96ff, 119
trichotomic table, 141

trichotomies, xxvi, 69, 91–97 *passim*, 103,
    138–42 *passim*, 147, 159, 167, 213
—First, 82, 95–101 *passim*, 120, 146, 160f,
    210, 243
—development, xxxiv, 60f, 151–54
    passim, 167f, 198–201 *passim*
—Second, 61, 94, 143–46 *passim*, 243
—Third, 94f, 153, 242
Turrisi, Patricia, 67
type/token distinction, xxxiii, xxxiv, 29,
    119, 151–58 *passim*

ultimate, 179f, 218, 241
unitary system, 67
Unity, 8
University of Queensland, 126, 128

vagabond, *see* Chapter 2, 252, *see also*
    examples tramp
vocabulary, *see* syntax of signs

weathercock, *see* examples
Welby, Victoria Lady, xxvii, xxviii, 143,
    160–67 *passim*, 196
—correspondence, xxxii, 9, 137–51
    passim, 156–62 *passim*, 165, 193, 222,
    247–52 *passim*, 258–73 *passim*
whole theory, 138, 146, 150, 159f
Wittgenstein, Ludwig, xxxvi, 52, 109,
    129, 197f, 291n17
women, *see* gender distinction
worlds (outer and inner), 141
writing/thinking, 260

Cultural Memory | *in the Present*

Anne Freadman, *The Machinery of Talk: Charles Peirce and the Sign Hypothesis*

Stanley Cavell, *Emerson's Transcendental Etudes*

Stuart McLean, *The Event and its Terrors: Ireland, Famine, Modernity*

Beate Rössler, ed., *Privacies: Philosophical Evaluations*

Bernard Faure, *Double Exposure: Cutting Across Buddhist and Western Discourses*

Alessia Ricciardi, *The Ends Of Mourning: Psychoanalysis, Literature, Film*

Alain Badiou, *Saint Paul: The Foundation of Universalism*

Gil Anidjar, *The Jew, The Arab: A History of the Enemy*

Jonathan Culler and Kevin Lamb, eds., *Just Being Difficult? Academic Writing in the Public Arena*

Jean-Luc Nancy, *A Finite Thinking*, edited by Simon Sparks

Theodor W. Adorno, *Can One Live after Auschwitz? A Philosophical Reader*, edited by Rolf Tiedemann

Patricia Pisters, *The Matrix of Visual Culture: Working with Deleuze in Film Theory*

Andreas Huyssen, *Present Pasts: Urban Palimpsests and the Politics of Memory*

Talal Asad, *Formations of the Secular: Christianity, Islam, Modernity*

Dorothea von Mücke, *The Rise of the Fantastic Tale*

Marc Redfield, *The Politics of Aesthetics: Nationalism, Gender, Romanticism*

Emmanuel Levinas, *On Escape*

Dan Zahavi, *Husserl's Phenomenology*

Rodolphe Gasché, *The Idea of Form: Rethinking Kant's Aesthetics*

Michael Naas, *Taking on the Tradition: Jacques Derrida and the Legacies of Deconstruction*

Herlinde Pauer-Studer, ed., *Constructions of Practical Reason: Interviews on Moral and Political Philosophy*

Jean-Luc Marion, *Being Given: Toward a Phenomenology of Givenness*

Theodor W. Adorno and Max Horkheimer, *Dialectic of Enlightenment*

Ian Balfour, *The Rhetoric of Romantic Prophecy*

Martin Stokhof, *World and Life as One: Ethics and Ontology in Wittgenstein's Early Thought*

Gianni Vattimo, *Nietzsche: An Introduction*

Jacques Derrida, *Negotiations: Interventions and Interviews, 1971–1998*, ed. Elizabeth Rottenberg

Brett Levinson, *The Ends of Literature: Post-transition and Neoliberalism in the Wake of the "Boom"*

Timothy J. Reiss, *Against Autonomy: Global Dialectics of Cultural Exchange*

Hent de Vries and Samuel Weber, eds., *Religion and Media*

Niklas Luhmann, *Theories of Distinction: Redescribing the Descriptions of Modernity*, ed. and introd. William Rasch

Johannes Fabian, *Anthropology with an Attitude: Critical Essays*

Michel Henry, *I Am the Truth: Toward a Philosophy of Christianity*

Gil Anidjar, *"Our Place in Al-Andalus": Kabbalah, Philosophy, Literature in Arab-Jewish Letters*

Hélène Cixous and Jacques Derrida, *Veils*

F. R. Ankersmit, *Historical Representation*

F. R. Ankersmit, *Political Representation*

Elissa Marder, *Dead Time: Temporal Disorders in the Wake of Modernity (Baudelaire and Flaubert)*

Reinhart Koselleck, *The Practice of Conceptual History: Timing History, Spacing Concepts*

Niklas Luhmann, *The Reality of the Mass Media*

Hubert Damisch, *A Childhood Memory by Piero della Francesca*

Hubert Damisch, *A Theory of /Cloud/: Toward a History of Painting*

Jean-Luc Nancy, *The Speculative Remark (One of Hegel's Bons Mots)*

Jean-François Lyotard, *Soundproof Room: Malraux's Anti-Aesthetics*

Jan Patočka, *Plato and Europe*

Hubert Damisch, *Skyline: The Narcissistic City*

Isabel Hoving, *In Praise of New Travelers: Reading Caribbean Migrant Women Writers*

Richard Rand, ed., *Futures: Of Derrida*

William Rasch, *Niklas Luhmann's Modernity: The Paradox of System Differentiation*

Jacques Derrida and Anne Dufourmantelle, *Of Hospitality*

Jean-François Lyotard, *The Confession of Augustine*

Kaja Silverman, *World Spectators*

Samuel Weber, *Institution and Interpretation: Expanded Edition*

Jeffrey S. Librett, *The Rhetoric of Cultural Dialogue: Jews and Germans in the Epoch of Emancipation*

Ulrich Baer, *Remnants of Song: Trauma and the Experience of Modernity in Charles Baudelaire and Paul Celan*

Samuel C. Wheeler III, *Deconstruction as Analytic Philosophy*

David S. Ferris, *Silent Urns: Romanticism, Hellenism, Modernity*

Rodolphe Gasché, *Of Minimal Things: Studies on the Notion of Relation*

Sarah Winter, *Freud and the Institution of Psychoanalytic Knowledge*

Samuel Weber, *The Legend of Freud: Expanded Edition*

Aris Fioretos, ed., *The Solid Letter: Readings of Friedrich Hölderlin*

J. Hillis Miller / Manuel Asensi, *Black Holes / J. Hillis Miller; or, Boustrophedonic Reading*

Miryam Sas, *Fault Lines: Cultural Memory and Japanese Surrealism*

Peter Schwenger, *Fantasm and Fiction: On Textual Envisioning*

Didier Maleuvre, *Museum Memories: History, Technology, Art*

Jacques Derrida, *Monolingualism of the Other; or, The Prosthesis of Origin*

Andrew Baruch Wachtel, *Making a Nation, Breaking a Nation: Literature and Cultural Politics in Yugoslavia*

Niklas Luhmann, *Love as Passion: The Codification of Intimacy*

Mieke Bal, ed., *The Practice of Cultural Analysis: Exposing Interdisciplinary Interpretation*

Jacques Derrida and Gianni Vattimo, eds., *Religion*